# *The* Roosevelts *and the* Royals

# THE ROOSEVELTS

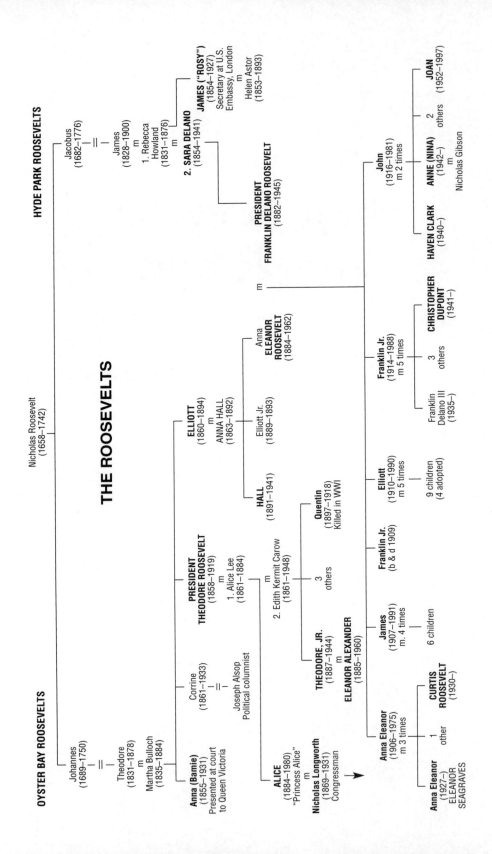

**OYSTER BAY ROOSEVELTS**

**HYDE PARK ROOSEVELTS**

Nicholas Roosevelt
(1658–1742)

Johannes
(1689–1750)
=
Theodore
(1831–1878)
m
Martha Bulloch
(1835–1884)

Jacobus
(1682–1776)
=
James
(1828–1900)
m
1. Rebecca Howland
(1831–1876)
m
2. SARA DELANO
(1854–1941)

JAMES ("ROSY")
(1854–1927)
Secretary at U.S.
Embassy, London
m
Helen Astor
(1853–1893)

**PRESIDENT
FRANKLIN DELANO ROOSEVELT**
(1882–1945)

Anna (Bamie) (1855–1931)
Presented at court
to Queen Victoria

Corrine
(1861–1933)
=
Joseph Alsop
Political columnist

**PRESIDENT
THEODORE ROOSEVELT**
(1858–1919)
m
1. Alice Lee
(1861–1884)
2. Edith Kermit Carow
(1861–1948)

**ELLIOTT**
(1860–1894)
m
ANNA HALL
(1863–1892)

HALL
(1891–1941)

Anna
**ELEANOR
ROOSEVELT**
(1884–1962)

Elliott Jr.
(1889–1893)

m

ALICE
(1884–1980)
"Princess Alice"
m
Nicholas Longworth
(1869–1931)
Congressman

**THEODORE, JR.**
(1887–1944)
m
**ELEANOR ALEXANDER**
(1885–1960)

3 others

Quentin
(1897–1918)
Killed in WWI

Anna Eleanor
(1906–1975)
m. 3 times

James
(1907–1991)
m. 4 times

Franklin Jr.
(b & d 1909)

Elliott
(1910–1990)
m 5 times

Franklin Jr.
(1914–1988)
m 5 times

John
(1916–1981)
m 2 times

1 other

6 children

9 children
(4 adopted)

Franklin
Delano III
(1935–)

3 others

**CHRISTOPHER
DUPONT**
(1941–)

**HAVEN CLARK**
(1940–)

**ANNE (NINA)**
(1942–)
m
Nicholas Gibson

2 others

**JOAN**
(1952–1997)

Anna Eleanor
(1927–)
ELEANOR
SEAGRAVES

**CURTIS
ROOSEVELT**
(1930–)

# THE ROYALS

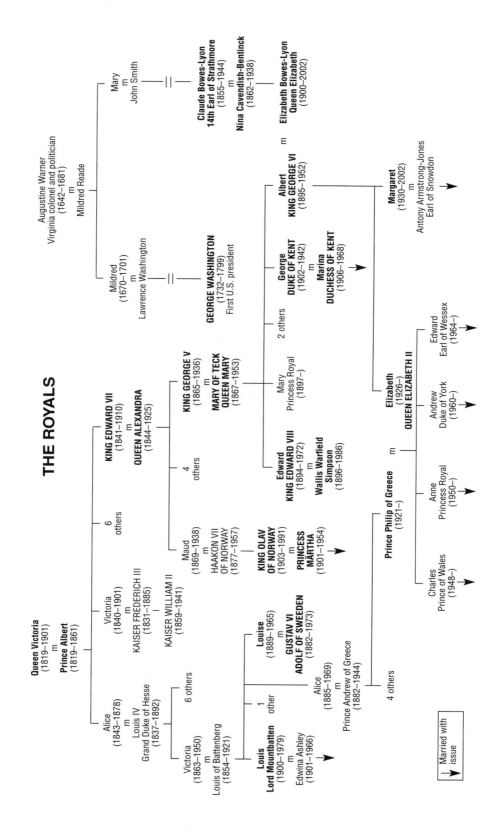

Augustine Warner
Virginia colonel and politician
(1642–1681)
m
Mildred Reade

Mary
m
John Smith

Claude Bowes-Lyon
14th Earl of Strathmore
(1855–1944)
m
Nina Cavendish-Bentinck
(1862–1938)

Elizabeth Bowes-Lyon
Queen Elizabeth
(1900–2002)

Mildred
(1670–1701)
m
Lawrence Washington

GEORGE WASHINGTON
(1732–1799)
First U.S. president

Queen Victoria
(1819–1901)
m
Prince Albert
(1819–1861)

Victoria
(1840–1901)
m
KAISER FREDERICH III
(1831–1885)

KAISER WILLIAM II
(1859–1941)

6 others

KING EDWARD VII
(1841–1910)
m
QUEEN ALEXANDRA
(1844–1925)

4
others

Maud
(1869–1938)
m
HAAKON VII
OF NORWAY
(1877–1957)

KING GEORGE V
(1865–1936)
m
MARY OF TECK
QUEEN MARY
(1867–1953)

Edward
KING EDWARD VIII
(1894–1972)
m
Wallis Warfield
Simpson
(1896–1986)

Mary
Princess Royal
(1897–)

Albert
KING GEORGE VI
(1895–1952)

2 others

George
DUKE OF KENT
(1902–1942)
m
Marina
DUCHESS OF KENT
(1906–1968)

m

Margaret
(1930–2002)
m
Antony Armstrong-Jones
Earl of Snowdon

Alice
(1843–1878)
m
Louis IV
Grand Duke of Hesse
(1837–1892)

Victoria
(1863–1950)
m
Louis of Battenberg
(1854–1921)

6 others

Louis
Lord Mountbatten
(1900–1979)
m
Edwina Ashley
(1901–1966)

Louise
(1889–1965)
m
GUSTAV VI
ADOLF OF SWEDEN
(1882–1973)

1
other

Alice
(1885–1969)
m
Prince Andrew of Greece
(1882–1944)

KING OLAV
OF NORWAY
(1903–1991)
m
PRINCESS
MÅRTHA
(1901–1954)

4 others

Prince Philip of Greece
(1921–)

m

Elizabeth
(1926–)
QUEEN ELIZABETH II

Charles
Prince of Wales
(1948–)

Anne
Princess Royal
(1950–)

Andrew
Duke of York
(1960–)

Edward
Earl of Wessex
(1964–)

Married with
issue

# *The* Roosevelts *and the* Royals

Franklin and Eleanor, the King and
Queen of England, and the Friendship
that Changed History

WILL SWIFT, PH.D.

John Wiley & Sons, Inc.

For Kevin Jacobs and Jim Wilcox.
In memory of my British-American mother, Maud, who would have been so
delighted. She died of Alzheimer's the week the book was completed.
And to my dear friend Theo Aronson, whose vivacious brilliance and love
of the Queen Mother helped inspire this book.

Published by John Wiley & Sons, Inc., Hoboken, New Jersey
Published simultaneously in Canada

Design and production by Navta Associates, Inc.

No part of this publication may be reproduced, stored in a retrieval system, or transmitted in any form or by any means, electronic, mechanical, photocopying, recording, scanning, or otherwise, except as permitted under Section 107 or 108 of the 1976 United States Copyright Act, without either the prior written permission of the Publisher, or authorization through payment of the appropriate per-copy fee to the Copyright Clearance Center, 222 Rosewood Drive, Danvers, MA 01923, (978) 750-8400, fax (978) 646-8600, or on the web at www.copyright.com. Requests to the Publisher for permission should be addressed to the Permissions Department, John Wiley & Sons, Inc., 111 River Street, Hoboken, NJ 07030, (201) 748-6011, fax (201) 748-6008.

Limit of Liability/Disclaimer of Warranty: While the publisher and the author have used their best efforts in preparing this book, they make no representations or warranties with respect to the accuracy or completeness of the contents of this book and specifically disclaim any implied warranties of merchantability or fitness for a particular purpose. No warranty may be created or extended by sales representatives or written sales materials. The advice and strategies contained herein may not be suitable for your situation. You should consult with a professional where appropriate. Neither the publisher nor the author shall be liable for any loss of profit or any other commercial damages, including but not limited to special, incidental, consequential, or other damages.

For general information about our other products and services, please contact our Customer Care Department within the United States at (800) 762-2974, outside the United States at (317) 572-3993 or fax (317) 572-4002.

Wiley also publishes its books in a variety of electronic formats. Some content that appears in print may not be available in electronic books. For more information about Wiley products, visit our web site at www.wiley.com.

*Library of Congress Cataloging-in-Publication Data*

Swift, Will, date.
    The Roosevelts and the royals : Franklin and Eleanor, the king and queen of England, and the friendship that changed history / Will Swift.
        p. cm.
    Includes bibliographical references and index.
    ISBN 0-471-45962-3 (cloth)
    1. Roosevelt, Franklin D. (Franklin Delano), 1882-1945—Friends and associates. 2. Roosevelt, Eleanor, 1884–1962—Friends and associates. 3. George VI, King of Great Britain, 1895–1952—Friends and associates. 4. Elizabeth, Queen, consort of George VI, King of Great Britain, 1900—Friends and associates. 5. Presidents—United States—Biography. 6. Presidents' spouses—United States—Biography. 7. Great Britain—Kings and rulers—Biography. 8. Queens—Great Britain—Biography. 9. Friendship—Case studies. I. Title.
    E807.S95 2004
    941.084'092'2—dc22                                                   2004006063

Printed in the United States of America

10  9  8  7  6  5  4  3  2  1

# Contents

*Photo section begins on page 207.*

# Preface

Although I did not know it at the time, I began working on this book when I was eleven years old. Already a confirmed Anglophile, I had heard that the official biography of King George VI had been published in the United States, and I badgered my British-American mother for a month until she relented and drove me thirty minutes north of our home in Melrose, Massachusetts, to a biography bookstore, where I purchased the book. At the back of the biography was a large fold-out genealogical chart of the descendants of Queen Victoria, showing that the king was a cousin of the monarchs of Europe, Scandinavia, and Russia.

The book and its chart ignited a lifelong passion for studying history and biography. One of my earliest memories is of watching Queen Elizabeth II's coronation on television when I was five years old. As the grandson of a British Protestant minister, and of a New England charities banker who was an avid genealogist and traced the family's roots through the *Mayflower* back to England, I know that my passion makes some sense.

As a boy, I also had what I thought was a completely separate interest in U.S. presidential history and in presidential families. Growing up in Massachusetts and summering at Cape Cod, at times I would cross paths with the Kennedys in Hyannisport. Shortly after reading the king's biography, I became captivated by the presidency of John F. Kennedy. My fascination with the Kennedys led me to their rivals, the Roosevelts. In 1971, when Joseph Lash published his landmark biography of Eleanor and Franklin, I became enthralled with their forty-year relationship. As I completed my doctorate in clinical psychology and began a practice specializing in couples therapy, I became intrigued with how a husband and wife managed the rhythms of closeness and separateness within a marriage, the effect of political and public life on a marriage, and how couples kept a marriage together for higher purposes; and also with the challenges faced by the children of important public figures. I began to see the Roosevelts and the Kennedys (and later the Adamses and the Bushes) as America's democratic versions of the British royal dynasty, possessed of great contradiction and complexity and full of drama that illuminated the nation's experience.

My interest in both the Roosevelts and the royal family has taken various forms over the last twenty-five years. In 1981 I founded the Royalty Bookshop in New York City. The next year I began the Royal Commemorative Association of North America, an international association of passionate royal history buffs and collectors, and edited its journal, *Sceptre*, which offered interviews with prominent royal historians, reviews of royal books, and articles on royal history and collecting. In 1983 I curated the show "Three Hundred Years of British Royal History," mounted at Bloomingdale's as part of the "Britain Salutes New York" celebrations. The show displayed royal commemoratives and memorabilia from the time of the Stuarts up until the first years of the marriage of the Prince and Princess of Wales. In August 2000 I organized British royal historians for a celebration of the Queen Mother's one hundredth birthday. "A Century of Generosity" was mounted at the Asprey and Garrard store on Fifth Avenue in New York City, and included over fifty of the Queen Mother's Christmas cards covering the period from 1928 until the present, along with photographs from her life and written tributes from historians. The Queen Mother sent a message to say how much it meant to her to have a retrospective in the United States. Partly as a result of the exhibition, during the last months of her life the Queen Mother offered to support *The Roosevelts and the Royals* by sharing her thoughts about the Roosevelts and their Hyde Park picnic.

I also wrote for *Majesty* magazine, focusing on the British royal family, beginning in 1984 with an article on Queen Victoria's gifted, hemophiliac son Prince Leopold. The final inspiration for this book came in 2001 when *Majesty* magazine asked me to write an article chronicling the relationship between British monarchs and U.S. presidents. My article, "Resolute Relations," spanned more than a hundred and fifty years, from Queen Victoria and President James Buchanan through Franklin Roosevelt and George VI, to Elizabeth II and eleven U.S. presidents beginning with Harry Truman. I became fascinated with the significance of the alliance between the Roosevelts and the royal family, as evidenced in two decades of correspondence between the two families—most vividly in their wartime letters—and was surprised by the extent and the calculation of the British government's carefully orchestrated campaign to win the United States to England's side in the 1930s and 1940s, when democracy was threatened by totalitarianism.

I began researching this book in the archives of Franklin Roosevelt Library at Hyde Park, New York. Impressed with the wealth of letters and material there about the king and queen's 1939 state visit to Washington and Hyde Park, I continued my research at the Royal Archives in Windsor Castle, where I found further confirmation of the breadth of the connection between the British royal family and the Roosevelts. Also contributing to my understanding of Eleanor and Franklin were several of the Roosevelt grandchildren, most particularly Christopher Roosevelt and Nina Gibson, who were extremely generous with their time and their reminiscences.

As an outgrowth of my research on the Roosevelts' relationship with the royal family, I represented the Roosevelt family in negotiations with the Queen Mother's private secretary to obtain a statement from the Queen Mother for placement on a plaque in Top Cottage, the site of the famous picnic, at the Hyde Park historical site. I met with her private secretary, Sir Alistair Aird, at Clarence House on March 27, 2002, to decide what personal statements would be most appropriate. At that meeting, he said that "it is a very dark day"—the Queen Mother had grown quite ill—and that he would be leaving after our talk to go to Windsor to visit the Queen Mother. It would be their last meeting.

Three days later the Queen Mother died, in her one hundred and second year, the last surviving leader of the generation that saw the Allies through World War II. Elizabeth's death renewed attention to her extraordinary life and her role as a symbol of Britain's pluck during World War II, when—along with her husband, King George VI, and Winston Churchill—she rallied Britons to heroism.

In *The Roosevelts and the Royals*, I tell the story of Queen Elizabeth and King George's crucial bond with Eleanor and Franklin Roosevelt, a connection that began as a vital democratic partnership allied against tyranny and grew into a personal and political friendship that helped shape history.

Franklin Roosevelt initiated the alliance with the most enthusiasm, cannily employing his bond with the British royal family to soften a U.S. citizenry that felt burned by the First World War and was resistant to further entrapment in European countries and conflicts. Eleanor, like her husband an American aristocrat but one whose populist principles made her initially cautious and apprehensive about consorting with royalty, came to value the king and queen as important friends. For his part, George VI not only was passionate about FDR as a friend and ally, but viewed him as a mentor whose assurance as a leader could infuse his own kingship. The support that George VI received from the president and First Lady was psychologically crucial as the king grew from an insecure, self-doubting monarch into a masterful world leader. FDR also had the resources to rescue his kingdom. Like the missives of a young adult importuning his parents for ever more funds, George VI's wartime letters to Roosevelt are full of requests for aid. FDR was able to use his relationship with the royal family to challenge U.S. isolationism, and Eleanor's bond with them— especially during her wartime visit to Britain—helped reinforce her international role as a diplomat. The help that the Roosevelts gave Britain and its royal family—from private encouragement to the institution of the Lend-Lease program, at considerable political cost to the president—helped sustain them during the darkest days of the war.

*The Roosevelts and the Royals* covers the period from Franklin's birth in 1882 until Prince Andrew's visit to Hyde Park in 2002. It details the development into adulthood of all four protagonists, and then focuses on their friendship and chronicles the foursome's challenging wartime coalition. This alliance was fortified by the complex three-way friendship among Winston Churchill, King George, and FDR; and it was threatened at times by the intense rivalries between King George VI and Queen Elizabeth and the Duke and Duchess of Windsor, as well as by the conflicts between Franklin Roosevelt and the unreliable Ambassador Joseph P. Kennedy, who became a vociferous advocate of U.S. isolationism. After FDR's death in 1945 and until her death in 1962, Eleanor Roosevelt deepened her friendship with the royal family. The story concludes with the Queen Mother's last visit with the Roosevelt family in 1967.

.   .   .

*The Roosevelts and the Royals* is the first book-length study of these four complicated characters and their two intriguing and radically different marriages: the Roosevelts' spacious, complex, and quite modern one; the royal couple's tight-knit, traditional, and simple one. During the 1930s and 1940s the happily married king and queen worked diligently to restore the monarchy's family image after the crisis caused by the king's brother Edward VIII, when he abdicated the crown rather than end his relationship with the American divorcée Wallis Simpson. By contrast, the Roosevelts coped with the strains of their marriage by having intense personal and romantic extramarital relationships, and most important, by committing their joint efforts to a higher cause: their vision of national welfare and international democracy. Their marriages focused them and gave them fortitude, as did their personal triumphs over childhood deprivations, illness, family turmoil, and political conflict.

Both Eleanor and Bertie, the man who would reluctantly become King George VI, had been born into prominent and entitled families. Yet they endured troubled childhoods and often experienced life as deficient outsiders. Through enormous effort of will, Eleanor and Bertie each surmounted tremendous insecurities and came to personify a cause. Eleanor would stand for the rights of women and of the poor, and for democratic values worldwide, while the king symbolized the civilization, continuity, and courage of Britain, as well as the essential democracy of its institutions. Neither was gifted with an easy charm. Their sense of duty lifted them beyond their fear and self-criticism into a noble place in twentieth-century history.

In contrast, Franklin and Elizabeth were charming, golden figures, both reared with a sense of utter security and love, which built the foundation for a strong sense of self. Yet both Elizabeth and Franklin demonstrated how even people to the manor born can transcend tragedy and turmoil in ways that vastly increase their contribution to the world. Thrust into the front rank of public life when she became queen amid a constitutional and family crisis, Elizabeth learned to deal with intense attention she had never expected or desired, her inner strength both intensified and communicated under wartime siege. When Franklin contracted polio at thirty-nine, he attained the human sympathy and gravitas he needed to stand for creative and compassion-ate use of government. While Franklin and Elizabeth were two of the most charming and charismatic figures of the twentieth century, they were also bound by a powerful sense of duty.

The relationship between the Roosevelts and the royal couple is most famous for the precedent-shattering picnic that the president and First Lady hosted in 1939 at FDR's estate in Hyde Park, New York, where George and Elizabeth agreeably ate hot dogs for the first time, not only signaling their accessible style and their accommodation to American ways but cementing Anglo-American relations at a danger-ous juncture.

The two couples' accomplishments far exceeded that historic pic-nic. The four of them established a friendship that helped their nations win a war. And their personal bond aided all of them in reaching their full potential as powerful and visionary leaders and exemplars of charm and duty. It would be hard to find a more inspiring pair of couples. The Roosevelts and the king and queen serve to remind us that charismatic leaders can also be admirable individuals. They faced their personal and public challenges with such grace and determination that they became symbols of courage and innovation.

Their efforts laid the psychological foundation for a renewal of what is now known as the "special relationship" between Britain and the United States. Their Majesties' 1939 visit was a final step in the reconciliation of the two great nations that had split during the American Revolution.

# Acknowledgments

During the two years I worked on this book I spent many full days at the FDR Library in Hyde Park. Raymond Teichman, Bob Clark, Robert Parks, and Alycia Vivona were extremely professional and tireless in finding letters and documents, sometimes in the most unexpected places. I owe them a great debt of gratitude for helping me to create a richly detailed book. Karen Anson was particularly gracious and meticulous in finding material and helping me verify source notes. Mark Renovitch worked diligently to help me find the right photographs.

I am most grateful to Professor William Leuchtenburg, who read the book and made corrections at a time when he was extraordinarily busy. Ambassador William vanden Heuvel gave constructive criticism as well. David Woolner, executive director of the Franklin and Eleanor Roosevelt Institute, read parts of the manuscript at several points along the way and kept an eye on the historical accuracy of the book. Chris Breiseth, the president of the Franklin and Eleanor Roosevelt Institute, provided a helpful perspective as well. Cynthia Koch, director of the FDR Library, was generous with her recollections of Prince Andrew's 2002 visit. Alita Black pitched in at key moments in my research, and Maureen Corr provided her memories.

The Roosevelt grandchildren went beyond the call of duty to support and encourage my work. Any biographer would be fortunate to have the staunch support that Christopher Roosevelt, the son of Franklin Jr., gave me. He not only provided his own memories of the 1967 visit to Campobello, but he also made sure that I could talk to other members of the family. Nina Roosevelt Gibson provided a key link with her stories about the Queen Mother's 1954 visit to Hyde Park and her own visit to Buckingham Palace in 1957. Haven Roosevelt, Curtis Roosevelt, Eleanor Seagraves, and Eleanor's cousin Ellie Davis all provided their recollections. Edna Gurewitsch shared memories and photographs. Richard Cain was extremely kind to deliver personally his family photographs of the 1939 picnic.

The letters of the king and queen are published here with the gracious permission of Her Majesty Queen Elizabeth II. At the Royal Archives in Windsor Castle, Mrs. Jill Kelsey assisted me every step of the way; she pointed me to key resources that shaped this book. The staff there made my visit to the archives in the round tower at Windsor Castle a productive and pleasant experience. Frances Diamond assisted me in reviewing photographs.

I wrote much of the book at my country home in Valatie, New York. Jean Pallas of the Valatie Public Library cheerfully responded to many last-minute calls for books. David Smith of the New York Public Library was quick and competent in finding resources for me. Bill Urbin of the National Park Service and Nancy at NancySeans in Chatham were very accomodating. Professor Fred Leventhal of Boston University was extremely helpful. The biographer Phyllis Levin took great care in reading the book and providing feedback.

Hugo Vickers, always a great supporter of royal authors, painstakingly read the entire manuscript, encouraged me, offered key insights on the Queen Mother, and assisted me in contacting other key sources. Sarah Bradford, Kenneth Rose, and Sir Eric Anderson took time to speak to me about King George VI and Queen Elizabeth. Sir Alistair Aird, the Queen Mother's private secretary, enthusiastically supported this book, spoke to the Queen Mother about the Roosevelts on my behalf, and took the time to meet with me during the last days of the Queen Mother's life. The Queen Mother's niece, Margaret Rhodes, was especially kind to me.

I would like to thank Ralph Blair; Marty Sloane; Jeff Young; Charlotte Sheedy; Lisa Drew; Linda Miles; Amy Bunger; Ann Hingst; DeGuerre and Rod Blackburn; Melinda Moreno; Cathy Flanagan; Howard Berman; Steve Hickey; Harold Brown; Billy Talon; Marlene Koenig; Pamela Strousse; Ruth Randall; Ellen Feldman; Leslie and Lucas Maher; Jed, Diane, and Sara Lynn Swift; Michael First; Theo Aronson and Brian Roberts for their wisdom and encouragement; and my son Dylan for keeping me honest.

My wonderful cousin, the novelist Jim Wilcox, taught me to write.

The poet David Groff, who has a gift for finding the perfect word, helped me refine my writing style and offered valuable insights. Gay and Katie Hendricks inspired me to express my creativity fully and insisted I pursue my dream of writing.

Beth Rashbaum and Bobbi Mark assisted me in choosing my agent and my editor. My agent, Judith Riven, who deeply appreciates Eleanor Roosevelt, saw the book's potential from the beginning. Using superb judgment, she provided the perfect blend of faith and practical help. Tom Miller, my editor at Wiley, had genuine enthusiasm for the project and was committed to excellence; he showed me how I could make the book more vibrant, balanced, and readable. Kellam Ayres and Lisa Burstiner at Wiley were thoughtful and extremely competent. Brooke Fitzsimmons, Mark Fortier, and Camille McDuffie were charming and superefficient publicists.

Finally, I am most grateful to my partner, Kevin Jacobs, for his sharp, critical eye; his unwavering belief in the book; and his willingness to help in every possible way.

# Prologue

# A Picnic Savored around the World

It was Sunday, June 11, 1939, supposedly a day of rest at Hyde Park for King George and Queen Elizabeth, who were completing a spectacular and grueling thirty-day, ten-thousand-mile journey through Canada, Washington, D.C., and New York City, where they had brought the Crown closer to the people than ever before. Instead, it would be one of the most pivotal days of their reign as king and queen; it would become a landmark moment in Anglo-American relations, and would solidify the royal couple's fresh friendship with America's leading public couple of their era, Franklin and Eleanor Roosevelt. All because of hot dogs.

On such an intensely paced tour, a "day of rest" meant that the surprisingly shy royal couple had nothing to do but attend a local church service featuring the presiding bishop of the Episcopal Church in the United States, meet a hundred and fifty of the Roosevelts' friends, neighbors, and staff, and endure the ministrations of the president's mother, who fancied herself the American Queen Mary. Sara was scandalized—like much of America—that her daughter-in-law the First Lady intended to serve the royal couple hot dogs during a Sunday afternoon picnic.

After church, FDR drove the king around his Hyde Park property in the car the president had had equipped with hand controls, which allowed him to swiftly negotiate the wooded, winding roads. The two men, one a gregarious if guarded American aristocrat whose paralysis from polio had shattered his life and solidified his character, the other a shy Englishman still settling into the unexpected royal role he had neither desired nor thought he deserved, related easily—two country squires who loved the wooded vistas, the gardens, the crops, and the pleasures of developing their own property. FDR had used his knowledge of husbandry and forestry to develop and profit from his twelve-hundred-acre property, passionately supervising the design of the estate, from the planting of trees to the layout of the roads, all of which he proudly showed off to an easily attentive king.

As they drove, the president and the king spoke of the role the United States would take in the war they knew would inevitably envelop Europe. In their private conversation, FDR went further in his support of England than he ever had in his delicate public pronouncements. If the U.S. Navy spotted a U-boat, he promised, it would "sink her at once" and "wait for the consequences." The president also confided his plan to enter the war if Germany started bombing London. These assurances surprised and pleased the king, a monarch keenly engaged with his country's foreign affairs—far more than Americans or even his fellow Britons ever would have surmised.

There followed the most famous picnic in U.S. history, a powerfully symbolic event that FDR was delighted to host at Top Cottage, the newly erected Dutch-style fieldstone house he had designed himself. FDR happily drove the king, the queen, and his mother through the woods in his blue Ford roadster, up the hill to the back end of his narrow three miles of property that stretched from the Hudson River to Cream Street, the site of his dairy farms. Only in recent years did the British ambassador reveal how frightened the queen had been by the harrowing and fast uphill trek through the woods. The queen had a moment to recover before Their Majesties met all one hundred and fifty guests in a receiving line, including nine Draiss children, whose father worked on the estate, and a neighbor who had crashed the party, despite the declaration by the head of security that without authorization not even an ant could get in. Security was intense at this juncture in time when an Irish Republican assassination plot had been uncovered in Detroit, the Duchess of Kent had been shot at in London, and the Nazis were making plans to kidnap and co-opt the Duke of Windsor as a puppet king.

The king and queen and the most prominent guests were seated at seven tables on the veranda looking west, with breathtaking views of the Catskill and Shawangunk mountains, surrounded by such luminaries as the New York governor and the Treasury secretary and their wives; below them, at tables less protected from the heat, sat a mix of staff, neighbors, and government officials, including the Roosevelts' maids, gardeners, chauffeurs, butlers, cooks, secretaries, and farmers. Along with the hot dogs, guests were also served smoked turkey, potato salad, cured ham, and baked beans. Steaks and other fancier foods on the menu were downplayed for the press. Dessert included Dutchess County strawberries from the estate of Treasury Secretary Henry Morgenthau Jr.

The president broke all protocol when he proposed a toast to the queen. She was so taken aback that she drank to herself. His son Franklin Jr. was given the "honor" of presenting the first hot dog on a silver platter to the queen. She immediately turned to FDR and asked, "How do you eat it?"

"Very simple," FDR answered. "Push it into your mouth and keep pushing it until it is all gone."

Newspaper reports announced that the royal couple had followed the president's lead in eating the hot dogs with the "overhand delivery" to the mouth. The king smothered the hot dog with mustard and "devoured his with gusto." Only when he got mustard on his pants did he lose interest in the hot dogs. After dessert FDR caught the king's eye and asked, "Sir, may we smoke?"

That Sunday night as they huddled over their radios, Americans waited impatiently to hear whether or not the royal couple had actually eaten those hot dogs. By now, they had taken on mythic power as the great symbol of democracy. The royal staff was reluctant at first to admit that the king and queen had, indeed, dined on this democratizing food. It was not until the evening of their departure that the newspapermen were confident enough to report that they had done so. The headlines in the next day's *New York Times* caught the flavor: "King Eats Hot Dog, Asks for More."

More than sixty years after the picnic, in early December 2001—just four months before her death—the Queen Mother, at the age of 101, could still recall what she felt that June Sunday in Hyde Park. Many of her specific memories of that life-changing 1939 trip had faded over an extraordinary lifetime, but to her private secretary, Sir Alistair Aird, she spoke of the "kindness and courtesy" of Franklin and Eleanor Roosevelt, a "wonderful host and hostess." They were, she declared in a typically gracious phrase, "true American gentlefolk."

# I

# Eleanor and Franklin

## 1882–1918

> You could not find two such different people as Mother and Father.
>
> —*Eleanor and Franklin's daughter Anna Boettiger Halsted*

New Yorkers will tell you that no one in his right mind would schedule a formal wedding in a town house off Fifth Avenue during the St. Patrick's Day parade, but that is just what a young bride and groom undertook to do on Friday, March 17, 1905. The couple had made the bargain to accommodate an important guest: the bride's favorite uncle, Ted, the president of the United States, who was to give away his orphaned niece in matrimony. Their personal feelings would be trumped by political duty. That bargain would be a fact of life for the team who would become America's premier version of a royal couple: Eleanor and Franklin Roosevelt.

The venue for the Roosevelt-Roosevelt wedding, the twin homes of Eleanor's cousin Susie Parish and her mother, Elizabeth Livingston Ludlow, at 6-8 East 76th Street, was redolent not only of roses, lilacs, and palms, but of American aristocracy. The houses' two large drawing rooms had been opened onto each other, and were illuminated by candles whose light flickered off the yellow brocade walls and the ancestral portraits that offered an illustrated tour of early U.S. history. Eleanor was descended from Edward Livingston, who had administered the presidential oath of office to George Washington, and from Philip

Livingston, who had signed the Declaration of Independence. Franklin's great-grandfather "Isaac the Patriot" had attended the Constitutional Convention and had been important enough to have his portrait painted by Gilbert Stuart. Franklin's mother, Sara, however, thought that her Delano forebears, who had come over on the *Mayflower*, were far more important than any of the Roosevelts—with the possible exception of Theodore. Sara always claimed that Franklin was "a Delano, not a Roosevelt at all." This opinion, among other of her attitudes, would not endear the dowager "queen" to her daughter-in-law.

Dressing in her long-sleeved satin wedding gown with shirred tulle neck and donning her late mother's lace veil and train stitched with orange blossoms, Eleanor was well aware of how alone she was in the world. The very date of her wedding reminded her that early death had devastated her family: her nuptials would occur on what would have been her mother's forty-second birthday. Her parents and her younger brother Elliott had all been dead more than a decade. Earlier in the day, she had been cheered to receive a cable wishing her *bonheur* from her spiritual mother—her former headmistress in England, Madame Souvestre, who some years before had discerned the sparks of bigheart-edness, intelligence, and moral leadership in her shy, self-conscious fif-teen-year-old student. Yet even the cable stirred palpable sadness; Eleanor knew that Madame Souvestre was dying of cancer. In spite of her bombastically affectionate uncle and her myriad cousins, Eleanor entered marriage like a solitary princess from a faraway dynasty.

Like every bride, she faced the pressure to look beautiful. Her mother, Anna, a woman whose looks had enamored the poet Robert Browning, had called her daughter "Granny." And Teddy's wife Edith Roosevelt once had said of Eleanor, "Her mouth and teeth seem to have no future." After her engagement to Franklin, Eleanor had bro-ken down weeping with her cousin Ethel, declaring, "I shall never be able to hold him. He is too attractive." Edith for her part hoped "the ugly duckling may turn into a swan."

Franklin, according to Teddy's daughter Alice, was indeed "very much in love with Eleanor when he married her." In his diary, Franklin had written, "E is an angel." A genial but intensely guarded young man who had to protect himself from his intrusive mother, and youthfully unfamiliar with his own emotions, Franklin had yet to develop the depth of compassion and breadth of interests that would characterize the mature man. Idealizing his beloved and seeing in her what he did not perceive in himself, Franklin viewed Eleanor as a woman who "had a deep and abiding interest in everything and everyone," possessed of the purpose and depth he lacked.

Downstairs at his bride's relatives' town house, it was Franklin who was acting like the household's heir presumptive, awaiting the arrival of the cousin whose success and vigor he sought to emulate. He was keenly cognizant of the advantages of marrying into Teddy's celebrated Oyster Bay branch of the Dutch-American dynasty, and had taken to sporting the pince-nez Teddy had made famous. Two weeks earlier, Eleanor and Franklin had attended Teddy's inauguration in Washington. As Franklin had listened to the president pledge "a square deal for every man," the future New Dealer had absorbed his cousin's words in ways that would manifest themselves almost two decades later.

President Teddy Roosevelt had a fatherly affection for twenty-one-year-old Eleanor, the daughter of his hapless, alcoholic younger brother. In the intense and indefatigable young woman, he saw himself. Both Teddy and his niece had surmounted childhood vulnerabilities to evolve into fiercely energetic and fearless individuals of high moral purpose. When Franklin and Eleanor had become engaged, Teddy had written to give Franklin some wisdom: "No other success in life—not the Presidency or anything else—begins to compare with the joy and happiness that comes in and from the love of the true man and true woman." Franklin, tragically, would not be able to follow that advice.

Nor did he take the advice of his formidable mother, Sara Delano Roosevelt. She had hoped that Franklin, like his father James, would wait until his thirties to take a bride—and she hadn't even known he was courting Eleanor. Stunned when she learned of their engagement, Sara asked them to keep it secret for a year and to spend time apart to test the bond between them. She tried to get Franklin appointed as secretary to Joseph Choate, a family friend who was ambassador to Great Britain. Sara wanted Franklin to emulate his father, who had served briefly as the secretary to future president James Buchanan when he was the ambassador to the Court of St. James's. Thwarted by Franklin's plan to marry, she wrote her son a guilt-inducing letter: "Darling Franklin, I am feeling pretty blue. You are gone. . . . Oh, how still the house is." By the wedding day, she had hidden her disappointment and was waiting, instead, for an opportunity to reclaim a dominant role in her son's life, guiding him to his proper position of prominence in the extended Roosevelt clan.

The wedding itself was like a political convention in which the Democratic candidate had chosen a Republican running mate. Among the two hundred guests were the many Roosevelt cousins of both family branches and political parties, all competing vigorously to win the approval of a president known for his zealously pursued standards of achievement. At twenty-three, the self-styled crown prince of the Hyde Park Roosevelts already had ambitions to win the presidency himself—in fact, he rather presumed he would. However, even as he presented himself with the genial ease of an aristocrat and natural politician, he was not the family's heir apparent. The president's eldest son Ted was being groomed—against his grain, as it turned out—to be the president's successor. Franklin's incipient aspirations made him a usurper.

Eleanor, too, had a family rival—the cousin who had helped her into her wedding gown. Teddy's imperious and unruly daughter Alice, one of Eleanor's bridesmaids, possessed a childhood bond with Eleanor; both had lost their mothers at a young age. Alice had a habit of saying cruel things behind her cousin's back. Eleanor, she told anyone who would listen, was frumpy and dull. As for F. D. Roosevelt, his initials stood for "Feather Duster"; he was a lightweight, a dandy. Franklin, she declared, was the type "you would invite to the dance, but not the dinner." Eleanor was cordial but not blind to her cousin, but already she knew how to deal with intrigue in the Roosevelt court. The two branches of the Roosevelts may not have been as contentious as the houses of York and Lancaster, but both sides were keenly aware of themselves as American royalty—and how their roles resonated with the British royal family.

Of the Oyster Bay Roosevelts, Teddy's daughter Alice was the most like royalty—or so she thought. When King Edward VII's cousin, Prince Heinrich of Prussia, came to the White House to curry favor with President Roosevelt in February 1902, it was rumored he would marry Alice. The nation dubbed her "Princess Alice," and *Leslie's Weekly* newspaper boasted that America's princess had "all the honors and pleasures of royalty without being in the least hampered by its restrictions." When she wanted to go to King Edward's coronation despite the custom that only children of sovereigns could attend, Teddy worked to arrange it. Faced with American newspapers grumbling about the semiroyal honors bestowed upon her and hinting that Teddy fancied himself a king, the president realized he had underestimated how raw and powerful America's antimonarchist sentiments remained. Alice was not allowed to go.

At Alice's marriage to Congressman Nicholas Longworth in June 1906, the king acknowledged his friendship with the Roosevelts by sending Alice a blue and gold enamel snuffbox featuring a miniature of himself on the lid. In London during their honeymoon, while sitting at dinner between King Edward VII and the Duke of Marlborough, Alice so charmed the king that he offered the newlyweds the honor of lunch in the royal pavilion at Ascot. Yet when Alice and Nick, following in the tradition of the president's sister Bamie, who had been presented to Queen Victoria in 1894, were formally introduced to King Edward and to Queen Alexandra at court, Nick was severely criticized in the U.S. press for undermining American democracy: he had worn black silk knee breeches.

Franklin, too, was smitten by royalty. Years earlier, he had designed his family crest: three feathers over roses. Its plumage so much resembled the insignia of the Prince of Wales that in its report of the wedding, the *New York Times* described the bridesmaids as wearing "tulle veils attached to white Prince of Wales ostrich feathers tipped with silver." Franklin had visited London often as a child and could not have been unaware of the royal associations. In fact, on one of his trips he met the Prince of Wales's sister, Princess Helena (known as Princess Christian). The Prince of Wales's motto associated with the insignia is "Ich Dien"—"I serve"—which fit Franklin's sense of noblesse oblige.

Outside the East 76th Street town house, with the sound of Irish drinking songs in the background, the president, an already wilted shamrock in his lapel, bounded out of the landau and took the steps two at a time. When Teddy Roosevelt escorted the bride down the narrow staircase and down the aisle toward the altar under a bower of pink roses mixed with palm leaves, some guests gasped: with her hair swept high and her blue eyes blazing, Eleanor looked remarkably like her mother. She may have been surprised that the newspaper *Town Topics* reported that she "had more claim to good looks than any of the Roosevelts."

When the Reverend Endicott Peabody asked, "Who giveth this woman in marriage?" the president boomed out, "I do." When the vows were completed, Teddy Roosevelt kissed the bride and said to his new nephew, "Well, Franklin, there's nothing like keeping the name in the family."

The president led the way to the library for refreshments. As Eleanor and Franklin stood alone at the altar, most of the guests followed the charismatic Teddy Roosevelt and his wife rather than stay to offer congratulations. Eleanor was accustomed to stepping into the background, but Franklin bristled. When they cut their wedding cake, Franklin and Eleanor could draw attention to themselves only by offering the president his slice. As Alice said, "Father always wanted to be the bride at every wedding and the corpse at every funeral." Only after the president left at five o'clock did the bride and groom become the focus of their own wedding reception.

Leaving for Hyde Park, as the guests showered them with rice, Eleanor and Franklin were embarking on a forty-year marriage that would be far different from what either imagined—and far more important for the United States than they could ever have expected.

Franklin was born on January 30, 1882, in Hyde Park, New York, at the family home, which was called Springwood. Though not as grand as nearby homes like the Vanderbilt mansion, it was still one of the important houses overlooking the Hudson River. Franklin's godfather was Elliott Roosevelt. Though the boy was an energetic and happy child, Sara monitored her son closely. When he was ten months old, she wrote in her diary, "Baby went to his first party yesterday. He wanted to dance and I could hardly hold him." Once when Franklin was eight, his parents noticed he seemed unhappy and asked why. The boy clasped his hands in front of him and sighed, "Oh, for freedom." His father convinced Sara to give him a day to do whatever he wanted without checking in with his parents. He disappeared the following morning but returned at nightfall tired, hungry, and dirty. The next day he resumed his controlled life with a more accepting attitude. Frighteningly blind to her autocratic ways, Sara would later claim, "We never tried to influence him against his own inclinations or shape his life."

Britain was a favorite destination of James Roosevelt, American country squire and peripatetic traveler, and his son quickly felt himself at ease among his father's aristocratic hunting friends. James Roosevelt's older son "Rosy," Franklin's half brother, had taken on the job of first secretary of the London embassy. In the era when the libertine and portly Bertie, Prince of Wales, ruled over British society, Rosy lived a lavish life, going to the races and attending shooting parties at the country homes of friends. By the time Franklin visited his half brother in 1892, Rosy had even come to look like the Prince of Wales with his beard and his heavyset frame.

After his father's first heart attack when Franklin was eight, Sara grew even more possessive of her son. He did not go away to school until he was fourteen, two years after the rest of his class had matriculated at Groton. While there, Franklin was quarantined in the infirmary with scarlet fever. One day he heard a tapping at the window and was shocked to see his very proper mother peering at him from atop a workman's ladder, having rushed home from Europe to see him. Every day from her spot on the top of the ladder, she talked and read to him until he was well.

Franklin had left for Groton believing that likability and success were his birthright, but his reception at school disabused him of that notion. With his late arrival to the class, his slight frame, refined manners, and failure to shine at team sports, he was not a popular student. He later told a friend, "I always felt entirely out of things," and as he put it, things had gone "sadly wrong" for him at Groton. Franklin's social difficulties continued at Harvard. He was devastated when he did not receive an invitation to join Porcellian, the exclusive social club that counted among its members his father, James, and his idol, President Roosevelt. He later told a relative that the rejection by the Porcellian club had been "the greatest disappointment of my life." Underneath his buoyant sociability and seductive charm, Franklin would always possess a sense of himself as a socially inadequate outsider. He made many friends, but always kept a part of himself reserved from hurt.

Franklin grew up in a golden cocoon and was shocked by the hard winds when he emerged. By contrast, Eleanor's difficulties started very early in life. Her chaotic family was the opposite of the secure, adoring clan surrounding young Franklin. Eleanor's father, Elliott, the president's younger brother, was a man of potential, possessed of the dazzling smile that characterized his godson Franklin. Much was expected of him. He chose as his wife the spectacularly beautiful but sensitive and troubled Anna Hall. As Elliott's alcoholism escalated, his marriage, which at first had seemed so brilliant, began to deteriorate under the pressure of constant fighting, his suicidal moods, and his scandalous behavior, which included impregnating another woman. Anna responded by developing chronic migraine headaches and taking to her bed—where she was attended by her daughter Eleanor.

Eleanor, born on October 11, 1884, had the misfortune of having a character opposite from her mother's. Anna Hall Roosevelt was a society belle who loved parties and the lavish life; her only daughter was a solemn and rather plain little girl. In her memoirs, Eleanor would recall that she lacked "the spontaneous joy or mirth of youth." Her mother once told her, "You have no looks, see to it that you have manners."

Anna's miserable marriage left her too closed and cold to open her heart to her precocious and challenging daughter. Anna, herself extremely sensitive to disapproval, was highly critical of Eleanor. "I was always disgracing my mother," Eleanor would write in her memoirs. Anna was able to summon more warmth and closeness for Eleanor's younger siblings, her sons Elliott Jr. and Hall. The girl's lifelong devotion to the underdog began as a response to being an outsider among her mother and brothers.

Her father was Eleanor's enduring love. The bond was all the more passionate for his intense affection, his unpredictable presence, and his early death. When he was home, he doted on his daughter at the expense of his wife, but he was often away playing polo, hunting, or partying with friends. Even when he spent time with Eleanor, he could abandon her in cruel ways. In the most famous incident, at about the age of seven Eleanor was left standing under the awning of the Knickerbocker Club minding her father's dogs for more than six hours as she waited for her father to emerge. Finally, he was carried out unconscious.

Eleanor would later declare that as a child she was afraid of almost everything. Her desire to please her father, though, equaled her fear. At around age five, in an extraordinary act of will for someone of any age, she experienced a breakthrough. Her father brought a pony from the stable and told her it was time that she learned to ride. The little girl was terrified, but she steeled herself and mounted the pony so that her father would be happy. As she explained, "I learned to stare down each of my fears, conquer it, attain the hard-earned courage to go on to the next." She built her confidence, step by agonizing step. As her uncle Teddy had before her, she forged a powerful personality out of a vulnerable temperament. Eleanor wrote, "I think I must have a good deal of my uncle Theodore Roosevelt in me because I enjoy a good fight."

Anna Roosevelt died of diphtheria when Eleanor was eight. At the time, her father was exiled to Virginia. When he finally returned home to New York, he spun fantasies about the glorious life he and Eleanor would lead. Yet within two years of her mother's death, Elliott Roosevelt himself died, from the effects of his alcoholism.

An orphan, Eleanor was raised by her grandmother and her aunts at the Hall family estate, Seven Oaks, overlooking the Hudson River above Tivoli, New York. While this period of her childhood was not quite Dickensian, it was certainly dour. According to a relative, her grandmother Hall had "the greatest knack for making her surroundings gloomy of all the women in New York." When Eleanor's obstreperous, alcoholic uncles began deteriorating at a young age just as her father had, her prim grandmother sent Eleanor off to an exclusive and progressive preparatory school in England.

At Allenswood Academy, Madame Souvestre recognized Eleanor's remarkable character, writing the girl's grandmother to praise the "perfect quality of her soul," the "nobleness of her thought," and the fact that the teenage girl was "full of sympathy." This depth of appreciation went a long way toward making up for her mother's disapproval. At Allenswood, Eleanor would blossom; and there—in grief after the death of Madame Souvestre—she would return on her honeymoon with Franklin.

Immediately after their wedding, Franklin and Eleanor discovered some fundamental incompatibilities as a couple. Eleanor reacted to her chaotic childhood by becoming quite dependent on her new husband as her source of security and identity. For Franklin, that kind of emotional fusion recalled his mother's control and intrusiveness. He felt smothered. James Roosevelt would say regarding his father, "Of what was inside him, of what really drove him, Father talked to no one." His new wife, in his view, was too needy. Nor did sexual intimacy bring them together. Eleanor would later tell her daughter Anna that sex was "an ordeal to be borne." Perhaps this was her response to having relations with a man who by virtue of his maleness and his self-containment could not meet her needs for romantic closeness. Regardless, when they arrived home from Europe, Eleanor was pregnant.

Within two years, Eleanor had given birth to both Anna and James, each child named for a deceased grandparent. All six of Eleanor's children were born within the first eleven years of their marriage. Like Britain's Queen Mary, who dutifully had borne her husband five sons and a daughter, Eleanor complied with Franklin's desire to please his mother and to have six children just like Uncle Ted, even though, as she later declared, she "never had any interest in dolls or in little children, and I knew absolutely nothing about handling or feeding a baby."

Relishing Eleanor's inadequacy as a mother, Sara Roosevelt dominated the young family's household and the childrearing, which gave the older woman a sense of purpose. She would inform the children, "I was your real mother. Eleanor merely bore you." Sara bought herself and her son twin houses on East 65th Street, complete with doors connecting the two homes on every floor. Eleanor later wrote that she never knew when Sara "would appear, day or night." Slowly she was beginning to realize how much she had allowed her life to be commandeered by her mother-in-law.

Franklin was no happier at his Wall Street law firm than Eleanor was at home. Neither particularly gifted nor interested in business or law, over the years he would indulge in a number of ill-advised business schemes—a proclivity his sons would continue—yet he always managed to emerge from them scandal-free, his sunny and solid reputation intact. In 1910, when the Dutchess Democratic county chairman offered his support for a state senate run, Franklin's first response was, "I'll have to ask my mother." When the county chairman balked, Franklin realized his mistake and accepted quickly. Running on his friendly personality and a vague appeal for clean government, he even removed his Teddy Roosevelt pince-nez so that he would look more accessible. He had found his metier. New York politicians took note when he won an upset victory over the heavily favored and well-connected Republican opponent.

Franklin's astute politicking in Albany brought him to the attention of Woodrow Wilson's new administration; in March 1913, he was appointed assistant secretary of the navy. The very prospect of a Washington job thrilled him—it brought him one step closer to the destiny he wanted to share with Teddy. When President Wilson finally and reluctantly led the nation into war the following year, Franklin was determined to join his Oyster Bay cousins in battle and undertake the European equivalent of charging up San Juan Hill. Wiser counselors convinced him that he could do more by staying in Washington. Still, he did sail off to Europe to see the action—which also led him into his first encounter with royalty.

While Eleanor was in school at Allenswood Academy in London, Queen Victoria died in January 1901 after a reign of sixty years. Eleanor watched as the queen's coffin was borne through the streets of London. "I can still remember how surprised I was when the coffin came into view," Eleanor later told her friend William Turner Levy. "Nothing had prepared me for something so tiny! To think that these were the remains of a woman who would give her name to an age."

During the rest of Eleanor's school years and the time of the young couple's honeymoon, King Edward VII ruled over England, freshly arrived to the throne after a sixty-year apprenticeship as Prince of Wales. His sobersided mother, Queen Victoria, had never trusted him enough to assign him the more serious work of the monarchy. However, when he became king, this genial man surprised everyone by parlaying his personality into diplomatic triumphs, working with the monarchs and politicians of Europe to help keep peace. Theodore Roosevelt, on his way home from a year of big-game hunting in Africa, planned to stop in London to meet his royal pen pal, but Edward died in May 1910, just before Roosevelt was due to arrive. The king was deeply mourned. Nine European monarchs, many of them cousins, attended his funeral, as did the former president, dressed in a black coat, standing out amid the robed and crowned kings, who showed great deference to him. Once again, he stole the show. One onlooker said, "The kings have been fairly scrambling for a share in his conversation."

. . .

Eight years later, at 10:30 A.M. sharp on July 29, 1918, at Buckingham Palace, another Roosevelt was to meet the Peacemaker King's successor, George V, a ruler in a time of war. Thirty-six-year-old Franklin Delano Roosevelt was keen to charm the bluff and sometimes forbidding monarch. As the emerging crown prince of the Roosevelt clan, Franklin felt equal to the task. Sara had raised him to be a supremely confident member of the American aristocracy. Franklin's son Elliott later would write of his father's attitude toward royalty, "He was fascinated by kings and queens, half-amused, half-impressed, by the pomp and pageantry that enveloped royalty."

During their meeting, the king expressed sympathy to Franklin on the death of his cousin Quentin, a lieutenant in the U.S. Air Corps, who had been shot down and killed behind enemy lines a few weeks earlier. The king had great respect for Quentin's father, Theodore Roosevelt, whom he considered a friend of the family. In fact, the king had just received a letter from Franklin's "Uncle Ted" about the loss of his youngest son.

Franklin's official purpose was to discuss the war effort with the king. George V wrote in his diary that Roosevelt, "a charming man, came to see me and told me everything his Navy was doing to help in the war, which is most satisfactory." Franklin found the king to be a "delightfully easy" conversationalist. They became so enthusiastic conversing about their mutual interests—from the navy to their passion for stamp collecting—that at some points they were both talking at the same time, and they chatted half an hour beyond the allotted fifteen minutes. His Majesty felt comfortable enough with Roosevelt to tell him the kind of bawdy story two sailors might exchange.

The king told Franklin that while at a Scottish hospital visiting sailors wounded in the Battle of Jutland, he stopped at the cot of a burly Britisher who had a large tattooed portrait of the king on his bare chest. The king congratulated him on his patriotism, and the sailor proudly pointed out a tattooed portrait of the queen between his shoulder blades, another of the Prince of Wales on his right arm, and one of Princess Mary on his left arm. The king commended his love of country, whereupon the British sailor said, "That ain't the half of it,

Your Majesty. You should see me behind. I 'ave two other portraits—I am sittin' on the Kaiser and Von Hindenberg."

Writing to Sara, Franklin said the king had a "nice smile and a very open, quick and cordial way of greeting one. He is not as short as I expected, and I think his face is stronger than photographs make it appear. This is perhaps because his way of speaking is incisive, and later on, when he was talking about German atrocities in Belgium, his jaw almost snapped." Franklin told the king that he had seen the first preparations for war on a visit to Germany. The king had been educated for a year in Germany, but Franklin reported that he said "with a twinkle in his eye—'You know I have a number of relations in Germany, but I can tell you frankly that in all my life I have never seen a German gentleman.'" George V was forthright with Franklin about his German relatives at a time when the British royal family was embarrassed about their heritage and had endured public mutterings about their strong German blood. Wilhelm II, the bellicose German kaiser who had led Germany into war, was George's first cousin. In a dramatic move the previous year, the king had changed the family name from the German Saxe-Coburg-Gotha to the very British-sounding Windsor.

Franklin was thrilled about his meeting with the king. It marked his emergence into international politics. As ambitious as he was, Franklin could not yet fathom how key a role the Windsors would play in helping him to shape world history in the coming decades. King George V's second son, Prince Albert, would become a crucial ally in Franklin's fight to save democracy.

# 2

# Bertie and Elizabeth

## 1895–1920

✖✖✖

Bertie has more guts than the rest of my sons combined.

—*King George V*

If Roosevelt would become America's most regal president, then George VI would become Britain's most democratic monarch—beginning with the wife he chose. Unlike his relatives who had entered arranged marriages with European royalty, the future king chose his bride in a more American fashion: he wed for love. He was immediately smitten by Lady Elizabeth, but it would take him two and a half years to convince her to marry him. Ultimately he won her over with the remarkable determination and strength of character he would employ to persuade skeptical Americans to ally with England at a pivotal time of world conflict. The effort it took to marry his bride fortified his character; his wife would fortify it further.

It was fortunate that he had such pluck. His early life was an obstacle course. Like Eleanor Roosevelt, Prince Albert Frederick Arthur George had been born into one of the world's most prominent families and grew up believing he was an inadequate outsider. Bertie, as he was known, began with a major disadvantage: his December 14 birth date in 1895 marked the anniversary of the deaths of his great-grandmother Victoria's beloved consort, Albert, and their daughter Alice. December 14 was still an occasion of sorrow for the queen; the royal family called it Mausoleum Day. With good reason, the baby's father, the future

King George V, scrambled to console the distressed queen by suggesting the boy be named Albert and by asking her to be his godmother. Victoria was a kindly matriarch but quite literally an imperious woman, who by the time of Bertie's birth had come to reign over an empire that included one-quarter of the world's population and territory and was the world's premier power. She was known as the "Grandmama of Europe"; her descendants ruled over seven European countries. By the time of her death in 1901, her stellar character was so celebrated that even in the United States, President McKinley ordered American flags to be lowered at half-mast over the White House, and the House of Representatives adjourned.

As a boy, Bertie was extremely shy, slow at school, homely, knock-kneed, and ignored and mistreated by a sadistic nurse who favored his blond and charismatic older brother David. After he developed a stammer at age seven, Bertie had even more difficulty keeping up with his confident brother and his sister Mary, his father's favorite. Family birthdays were a torture; he was expected to read poems aloud to his parents and grandparents, King Edward VII and Queen Alexandra. He found what comfort he could in the company of his younger brothers: the sweet and slow Henry; George, dashing and artistic; and affable John, who suffered from slight mental retardation.

His father, the future George V, was a remote and controlling figure, less an encouraging parent than a sharp-tongued naval commander, committed to maintaining the dignity of the Crown and ensuring that his children adhere to its protocols and traditions. "Now that you are five years old," he wrote his son in a birthday letter, "I hope you will always try to be obedient & do at once what you are told, as you will find it will come much easier to you the sooner you begin. I always tried to do this when I was your age & found it made me much happier." Bertie inherited his father's devotion to duty and, more than his brothers, was all too prone to subjugate himself to his sovereign father's will, despite the cost to his health and his psyche. Fortunately, from his mother he also inherited a disposition toward broad-mindedness that would ultimately serve him well.

At thirteen, Bertie was sent to Osborne, the naval college, and was unprepared for its harsh demands. However, he found a father figure there, Surgeon-Lieutenant Louis Greig, who supported and encouraged him as his own father could not. Greig would continue to provide counsel to Bertie during his service in the navy and air force, and later as the young prince took on greater public responsibility. "My principle contribution was to put steel into him,"[3] Greig would declare.

Following his brother David's path to the Royal Naval College at Dartmouth and still haunted by a miserably inadequate early education, Bertie again placed near the bottom of his class, compounding his feelings of estrangement and inadequacy. It was a relief in September 1913 to begin training as an ordinary midshipman on the battleship HMS *Collingwood*. Known as "Mr. Johnson," for the most part he lived the simple life of a junior officer. But after disembarking in Canada, he got a taste of the celebrity that would later pursue him, in a situation that did not endear him to Americans. A shy man, he would never be truly comfortable with photographers. After touring the U.S. side of Niagara Falls, he wrote in his diary, "I was hunted all the time by photographers and also by the Americans who had no manners at all and tried to take photographs all the time." Not an auspicious first encounter for the man who would become Britain's most Americanized king. He would forgive Americans their manners.

On August 4, 1914, as he was keeping "middle watch" on *Collingwood*, Britain declared war on Germany and World War I began. Before the prince could even contemplate going into battle, he was incapacitated with a recurrence of the severe stomach problems that had plagued him ever since early childhood, and which apparently had arisen from mistreatment by his nurse; she had fed him while rocking him in his pram, which the adult Bertie likened to eating during a "rough channel crossing." Misdiagnosed with appendicitis, he underwent surgery and took painful months to recover—a dispiriting and humiliating ordeal for a young man urgently seeking the chance to test himself in war.

When *Collingwood* put out to sea on May 30, 1916, Bertie was in sick bay. The next day, the German fleet, challenging the British blockade of its harbors, engaged the Royal Navy in what became the war's most important naval engagement, the Battle of Jutland. As the British tangled with the forces of Bertie's German cousin Kaiser Wilhelm, the young prince became the first future king to participate in a naval battle since King William IV in the late 1700s. After months of illness and inactivity, Bertie relished being part of the action. "I was sitting on the top of A turret and had a very good view of the proceedings," he wrote his father. "I was up there during a lull, when a German ship started firing at us. . . . I was distinctly startled and jumped down the hole in the top of the turret like a shot rabbit!! I didn't try the experience again." Through the mist he watched as *Invincible*, on which he had dined several days before, began to sink, with a loss of over one thousand lives. In a letter to David, he described the detachment and determination that overrode fear during the battle: "When I was on top of the turret I never felt fear of shells or anything else. It seems curious but all sense of danger and everything else goes except the one longing of dealing death in every possible way to the enemy." In times of crisis Bertie would be at his best: fearless, thorough, and resolute.

Lady Elizabeth Bowes-Lyon's childhood ended at midnight on her fourteenth birthday, August 4, 1914, when Great Britain declared war on Germany. For a special treat that evening her mother, Lady Strathmore, had taken her to the Coliseum Theatre to see a variety show that included dog comedians, jugglers, and the Russian ballerina Fedorovna. At the end of the evening, as Elizabeth looked on from her box, the audience broke out in patriotic cheers. Very soon, Elizabeth would learn how to tend to wounded soldiers, when Glamis, her family's castle, became a convalescent home.

Elizabeth was born on August 4, 1900, in London, just a few months before Queen Victoria's long reign ended. In later life, when she was asked about rumors that she was born on the side of the road in a taxi, the Queen Mother replied, "In the back of a taxi? How quaint!" In contrast to Bertie, she grew up in idyllic circumstances, surrounded with what she would call "fun, kindness and a marvelous sense of security," as the scion of an ancient but down-to-earth Scottish noble family. When she was four, her parents became the fourteenth Earl and Countess of Strathmore, inheriting fifty thousand acres, an annual income of five million pounds, an ironworks, and a staff of over a hundred at their estates and their London home. In her wide-ranging interests and her vitality, the girl took after her talented and supremely competent mother, who painted, created spectacular Italian gardens, played the piano, and entertained magnificently, all while rearing ten children. Like her mother, Elizabeth had the gift of vivacious attentiveness, making each person feel as if he or she was the only person in the room.

With four of her brothers away fighting the Germans, Elizabeth spent her time "knitting, knitting . . . my chief occupation was crumpling up tissue paper until it was so soft that it no longer crackled, to put in the lining of sleeping bags." She was sensitive to the fact that her mother, having already lost a daughter to diphtheria and a son to a brain tumor, was acutely vulnerable to the bad news that could arrive any time. Every day, Elizabeth kept alert for telegrams and waited anxiously for the mailman, ready to receive any bad news so that she could relay it carefully to her mother. "You would see this tiny dainty figure looking down the drive," recalled one of the soldiers recuperating at the family castle. "She always stood in the same place . . . with her black cocker spaniel Peter at her side."

At the end of September 1915, Elizabeth intercepted the dreaded telegram. Her older brother Fergus had been killed in the battle of Loos. Lady Strathmore never fully recovered from her son's death and spent the remainder of the war trying to find out where her son was buried. Looking after her mother and the wounded soldiers prepared Elizabeth to take on a vulnerable husband and strengthen him.

Two years later, Elizabeth would bring her mother another devastating telegram: her son Michael, Elizabeth's favorite brother, was missing and presumed dead. David, the youngest child, summoned from Eton to join the family in mourning, refused to wear black; the boy, who possessed what the Scottish call the "giftee"—a gift of clairvoyance—had dreamed he saw his older brother "in a big house surrounded by fir trees . . . not dead, but very ill, because his head is tied up in a cloth." Three months later, the family discovered that Michael had cashed a check after he was supposed to have died. Michael was indeed a prisoner of war, in a hospital recovering from a head wound.

Like the prince who would become her husband, Elizabeth excelled in a crisis. On September 16, 1916, a fire broke out in Glamis Castle's ancient central tower, which was almost one hundred feet high. The girl raced to the telephone and summoned the local fire brigade and another from the city of Dundee, and, aided by her mother and the Castle's staff, organized the crowd outside into lines relaying buckets of water from the nearby river to the fire. When a water storage tank at the top of the castle collapsed, hundreds of gallons of water began cascading down the central staircase toward the castle's main rooms, threatening their antique paintings and tapestries. Elizabeth and David rushed to the castle stairs and used brushes to redirect the water down to the stone vaults. Brother David later praised Elizabeth as "a perfect brick." The *Dundee Courier*, in the first of a lifetime of laudatory newspaper articles, proclaimed Lady Elizabeth a "veritable heroine."

Like Franklin Roosevelt, Bertie felt frustrated that he was not able to play a more active role in the war effort. When his health forced him from the navy, he was assigned to train cadets in the new Royal Air Force. Only three weeks later, on November 11, 1918, Germany signed the Armistice.

The U.S. entry into the war in April 1917 had helped turn the tide against the Germans, and the following July, in a gesture of royal gratitude, Bertie and his father attended their first American sporting event, at a football arena in Chelsea: they watched the U.S. Army play the U.S. Navy in baseball. The king pronounced the game "very exciting" and autographed a baseball and sent it to President Woodrow Wilson.

That December of 1918, before peace negotiations began at Versailles, Wilson and his wife paid the first official visit of a U.S. president to Buckingham Palace. In the 1850s a future U.S. president, James Buchanan, had met Queen Victoria and Prince Albert while he was ambassador to the Court of St. James's in London. Buchanan became acquainted with their son Bertie (later Edward VII), and after he became president, hosted Bertie at the White House in 1860. No sitting president had returned the invitation.

Prince Albert and Lady Elizabeth, as yet unacquainted with each other as adults that December, saw the Wilsons during their visit from very different vantages. On a rare sunny winter day, Lady Elizabeth looked on from among the crowds of people jamming the streets as the king and the president drove in a royal coach drawn by four horses and attended by four men dressed in crimson livery. As the procession passed Marlborough House, Queen Alexandra joined the crowds, blowing kisses to President Wilson and waving an American flag. As they entered the courtyard at Buckingham Palace, the Wilsons were greeted by U.S. troops, including soldiers on crutches and in wheel-chairs. The presence of the men had been arranged by the king and queen, which greatly moved the president and his wife. When the Wilsons joined Their Majesties for a balcony appearance before the cheering crowds, the president held up a Union Jack and the king and queen waved small U.S. flags.

Prince Albert had met his first U.S. president, Theodore Roosevelt, at the funeral of the prince's grandfather King Edward VII in May 1910, but he did not have the opportunity to get to know Roosevelt. Now, at a dinner for the Wilsons, he grew acquainted with Theodore Roosevelt's great rival. Bertie listened as his father told the Wilsons stories about the American doughboys he had met during the war. The king was amused by the directness and informality of Americans' reactions to royalty. In France, as the king reviewed some British and U.S. troops, he had heard one American doughboy ask, "Who is that bug?" His friend said, "Why man, that's the King of England." The first man shrugged and said, "Hell! Where is his crown?" The king told Wilson he did not mind being called a bug, but he hated the notion of reviewing his troops wearing a crown. On another occasion, a U.S. private came forward out of a crowd and said to him, "Excuse me, but am I right that this is the King of England?" When the king answered "Yes," the American extended his hand and said, "Put it there!"

The collision between the two cultures is best summarized by Edith Wilson's amusement and alarm at the escort she and the president received at the state dinner in their honor. According to ancient tradition, the Lord Steward and the Lord Chamberlain stood facing the presidential couple, each one holding a slender wooden wand in his hands. Every three feet, the men would bow until their wands almost touched the floor. As was customary when escorting heads of state to dinner, the two men walked backward and bowed up the stairs and through the corridors to the dining room. Years later when Prince Albert was king, this evening must have been very much on his mind when he was the guest of honor at a state dinner in the White House in 1939.

.   .   .

Less than a year later, on the first anniversary of the signing of the Armistice, Bertie observed from London the visit of his brother David, the Prince of Wales, to Washington, D.C. As assistant secretary of the navy, Franklin Roosevelt met the prince for the first time at a naval review. The prince would later remember Roosevelt as his "gay and witty companion" at the Naval Academy at Annapolis. President Wilson, who had conferred with the prince during his time in Paris, invited him to the White House. After feverishly campaigning across the United States to rally support for his proposed League of Nations, Wilson had fallen ill. His vision of an international peacekeeping body had been derailed when ratification of the Treaty of Versailles was narrowly defeated by a Congress unwilling to engage the nation in any other world conflicts.

Wilson received the prince while lying in the bed that had been built for David's grandfather, Edward VII, sixty years before. Initially nervous at meeting the incapacitated leader, David was disarmed by Wilson's stories of his grandfather's mischief. Wilson pointed to a window and told David that his grandfather had climbed out to attend a party. David, already possessed of a reputation as a playboy, could well imagine following his grandfather's example. In fact, when he visited the United States again in 1924, headlines would suggest that he "got in with the milkman."

The Prince of Wales recognized that Americans had begun to embrace their own democratic values, while disdaining the Old World formalities of the monarchs and aristocrats they believed had led them into catastrophic war. The glamour of princes and kings seemed faded and musty. The Prince of Wales sensed that the United States would respond only to a friendly, down-to-earth prince. He gave them exactly what they wanted. What Americans liked best about the Prince of Wales was that he seemed so democratic—in fact, so American. After a ticker tape parade in an open car to welcome him to New York, the *New York Tribune* rhapsodized that the crowds "drowned the sound of brass bands with the din of their voices shouting their welcome . . . they fought the heavy police guards to get to his car, and . . . at City Hall they broke through to cheer him frenziedly."

Bertie, meanwhile, was receiving far fewer cheers and no accolades. While his older brother was conquering the world, Bertie was struggling to overcome his frailties and find a role for himself at home. He admired his brother's phenomenal charm and international successes but felt diminished by them. His father bucked him up by bestowing on him the oldest dukedom in England, the ancient title of Duke of York, Earl of Inverness, and Baron Killarney that traditionally went to the heir apparent's younger brother. The king wrote him saying, "I know that you have behaved very well in a difficult situation for a young man & that you have done what I asked you to do. I feel that this splendid old title will be safe in your hands & that you will never do anything which could in any way tarnish it." George V had realized that as superficially awkward and unpromising as Bertie seemed, he was like his father at his core. They shared a finely honed sense of responsibility and a sturdy integrity. For all David's charisma and quickness, he lacked the judgment and depth of his younger brother. King George V thought his younger son, the Duke of York, would make a superb king.

# 3

# A Radical Partnership

## 1920–1934

He might have been happier with a wife who was completely uncritical. That I was never able to be, and he had to find it in some other people.

*—Eleanor about Franklin*

In August 1921, Franklin Roosevelt sailed a yacht to Campobello, his family's summer home in Maine, for his annual vacation. Age thirty-nine, he was just reaching his prime, physically dynamic and full of blossoming political promise. The year before, he had been chosen as the Democrats' vice presidential candidate, running with Ohio governor James Cox. The two of them were trounced by Republicans Warren G. Harding and Calvin Coolidge—aided and abetted by Franklin's Oyster Bay rivals, Alice and Ted Roosevelt—but with his eloquent and vigorous campaigning, Franklin had further advanced his claim to be the heir apparent to the Roosevelt name and progressive political legacy.

Shortly after his arrival in Maine, while cruising off Campobello, Franklin tripped and fell into the freezing Bay of Fundy. The water was so cold, he said, that it "paralyzed" him. Afterward, he experienced a slight chill, but the next day he was as vigorous as ever. That day, while out boating, he spotted a forest fire on a nearby island. Landing on the island, he and his family spent several brisk hours beating back the flames. With a manic burst of energy, he then swam in a lake, jogged with his children for a mile and a half, and took another dip in the

27

glacial bay. He began to ache all over and later went straight to bed with a chill.

The next morning, when he tried to get out of bed, his leg collapsed and he had a fever. Over the following days he suffered delirium, acute pain all over his body, temporary paralysis of his hands, and lasting paralysis of his legs. Even his eyesight was at risk. The diagnosis was infantile paralysis, commonly known as polio. The man who twelve months earlier had literally leaped into national prominence at the Democratic National Convention, vaulting over four rows of chairs and bounding onto the convention platform in a stunning bid to be heard in a debate, was now paralyzed for life.

Eleanor slept on a couch in his room and nursed him for weeks, doing everything she could to lift his spirits. His vulnerability drew her closer to him; she felt safe in his complete dependence on her. As she once said, "It is probably the sense of being really needed which gives us the greatest satisfaction and creates the greatest bond." Showing enormous reserves of courage, Franklin presented a cheerful facade, maintaining an obstinate optimism that he would recover. When Sara Roosevelt urged her son to retire to Hyde Park to live the quiet life of an invalid country squire, Eleanor, in her first major break with her mother-in-law, resisted. The two women fought openly. Eleanor asserted that Franklin had to return to politics—his psychic survival depended on living a significant life. Aligning himself with his wife, Franklin found new respect for Eleanor's strength.

Politics, which had long divided them, now became a bond between them, providing further adhesion to a marriage that had been enduring four years of profound disruption and strain. When Franklin had entered politics, Eleanor made a deal with her husband; her presence would not be required at the frivolous, alcohol-laced social evenings that so entertained him and that left her bored and exasperated. Yet after their move to Washington, this agreement had led their lives to diverge, resulting in a crisis in their marriage and a turning point in their lives.

In 1914, Eleanor had hired as a part-time social secretary a tall, beautiful, and efficient twenty-two-year-old woman from a prominent and historically important Maryland family. With her throaty voice, irresistible smile, and big blue eyes, Lucy Mercer was sensual, alluring, and feminine in a way that her employer, Eleanor, could not match. By the summer of 1916, Franklin and Lucy had fallen in love—with a big assist from Alice Roosevelt, who could not resist creating difficulties in the marriage of her cousins.

Alice's lifelong insecurity caused her to be such a troublemaker that her father had famously said, "I can either be President of the United States—or—I can attend to Alice." Unhappy in her own marriage, Alice was motivated to act cruelly against Eleanor, whose goodness she admired and felt she could never equal. Alice encouraged Franklin and Lucy's romance and invited them as a couple to dinners. "Franklin deserved a good time," she remarked. "He was married to Eleanor."

In July 1918, Franklin, suffering from double pneumonia and influenza, returned from his tour of Europe and his encounter with King George V. After Eleanor got him safely home, she unpacked his bags and found a packet of love letters from Lucy Mercer. "The bottom dropped out of my own particular world," Eleanor later acknowledged, "& I faced myself, my surroundings and my world, honestly for the first time."

When they had first become engaged in 1903, Eleanor sent Franklin a poem by Elizabeth Barrett Browning that included lines voicing both the intensity of her commitment and her unspoken fear of abandonment: "Unless you can swear, 'For life, for death! Oh, fear to call it loving!'" Then she panicked that she had revealed too much. Franklin wrote to assure her otherwise. She wrote back, "I wondered if it meant 'for life, for death' to you at first but I know it does now."

In proposing, Franklin had told her she could help him truly accomplish something with his life. For all his romantic feelings, he was also aware of her usefulness to him. Eleanor, unable to appreciate her own power, responded, "Why me? I am plain. I have little to bring you." Yet she was deeply infatuated with him. Franklin had the lightness, charm, and physical beauty she thought she lacked. "I lay & wondered this afternoon how life could have seemed worth living before I knew what 'love' and 'happiness' really meant," she wrote her fiancé.

Discovering Franklin's affair with a younger, more beautiful woman whom Eleanor had brought into the family, devastated her. What better proof that she still remained an abandoned, unloved, unlovely, and defective child? Yet for his part, with Lucy, Franklin had discovered in himself a depth of feeling that had been buried by his effort to shield himself from his mother's possessiveness. According to his cousin Corrine Alsop, until Lucy came into his life, Franklin "viewed his family dispassionately and enjoyed them, but he had, in my opinion, a loveless quality as if he were incapable of emotion."

Eleanor confronted Franklin with the letters and offered him a divorce. Having felt so often unwanted, she did not wish to stay where she was not welcome. Sara Roosevelt, however, declared she would not countenance the scandal of a marital split. She made it clear to her son that if he left Eleanor, she would cut him off from all income and not bequeath him the Hyde Park estate. It is not clear how much Sara's threats influenced Franklin. Equally persuasive may have been Louis Howe, Franklin's increasingly influential political adviser, who told Franklin a divorce would ruin his career.

However powerful his passion for Lucy, Franklin could not bring himself to damage his family further or asphyxiate his political hopes. He ended his affair with Lucy and asked to stay married. Eleanor demanded separate bedrooms, and he agreed. Their son James later wrote, "After that father and mother had an armed truce that endured to the day he died, despite several occasions I was to observe in which he, in one way or another, held out his arms to mother and she flatly refused to enter his embrace." Eleanor could never again trust the man she had idolized as a father who would not fail her. She still wrote in her diary at the end of 1919, "All of my self-confidence is gone & I am on edge." From then on, she would have to find her identity independent of her husband.


Now, with Franklin fighting his paralysis, Eleanor developed new respect for her husband. Franklin's protracted suffering, she said, "gave him the strength and courage he had not had before. He had to think out the fundamentals of living and learn the greatest of all lessons— infinite patience and never-ending persistence." For a man to whom almost everything had come easily, his paralysis was life-changing agony. The experience also allowed him to develop the kind of empathy he had previously only admired in Eleanor. Just as Winston Churchill's fight against his "black dog" depressions braced him to stand against the tyranny of Nazism, Franklin's struggle with polio gave him the capacity to lift up America in two of its moments of greatest paralysis: the financial panic of 1933 and the attack on Pearl Harbor in 1941.

With extraordinary determination, Franklin experimented with every possible cure and exercised constantly. He used two-thirds of his personal money to purchase a run-down spa at Warm Springs, Georgia, so that he and others could take its bubbling waters that literally buoyed him into walking movement. Moreover, at Warm Springs, on fishing trips, and on a houseboat in Florida, Franklin had a new companion: his devoted young secretary and playmate, "Missy" LeHand.

Eleanor, grateful for anyone who could lift her husband's spirits and aid his recovery, treated Missy graciously as a member of the family. Missy, for her part, acted like a second, younger wife, studying him so carefully that she could anticipate his needs, and providing him with the uncritical admiration he could not get from Eleanor—as Eleanor herself had grown wise enough to recognize: "He might have been happier with a wife who was completely uncritical. That I was never able to be, and he had to find it in some other people."

Missy also helped facilitate Eleanor's freedom, as the future First Lady began to become a more active Democrat and make her own considerable income from radio shows, lectures, and magazine articles. After Louis Howe coached her through the ordeal of public speaking, there was no stopping her. Advocating better working conditions for women, the abolition of child labor, supporting birth control, and championing adequate housing, Eleanor also spoke passionately in favor of the League of Nations and the World Court as essential components of a secure world order. By the time of Franklin's bid for the governorship of New York in 1928, she herself would be one of the country's best-known Democrats.

Pursuing her own identity through involvement in women's issues, Eleanor became friendly with a number of lesbians who shared her political values. She met Marian Dickerman and Nancy Cook, with whom she founded Val-Kill Industries, which provided jobs for people to make furniture, and the liberal Todhunter School in Manhattan. Franklin endorsed his wife's attachment to what he called Eleanor's "she-men." He could spend time with his own entourage without feeling guilty. Although he worried that her friendships with such avant-garde women might cause him political problems, he was glad to see

her happy with a surrogate family and even designed what he conde-
scendingly called "The Honeymoon Cottage" at Val-Kill, where
Eleanor, Dickerman, and Cook could live apart from Sara Roosevelt,
who must have bit through her lip at the whole venture. The cottage
could be reached by a bridge that made enough noise to announce any
visitors. By 1924, the Roosevelt marriage, with its two separate courts,
had become not only workable but perhaps the era's most radical marital arrangement.


Franklin, meanwhile, was laboring to reinsert himself into the public
realm. Before the 1924 Democratic National Convention in New
York's Madison Square Garden, he spent weeks in his library practicing
for his first major public appearance since he had been struck with
polio. When he arrived in the hall on the arm of his son James, the
crowd erupted in cheers. They watched amazed as Franklin, whom
they had known to be paralyzed for several years, dragged himself
slowly on one crutch the full distance to the podium. With the glare of
the convention lights illuminating his white and gray suit, and sweating from fear (and the ninety-degree heat), Franklin seemed an almost
mythical presence as he began to speak. Then, as if scripted by a
Hollywood director, a shaft of sunlight came through the skylight to
bathe his head. Nominating his friend Al Smith for the presidency, he
ended by holding the podium with only one hand so that he could once
again give the politician's wave. Amid a tumultuous reception, Franklin
had announced that he was back.

FDR continued his physical and political rehabilitation for four
more years, until he narrowly won the governorship of New York in
1928. Two years later, when Franklin won reelection overwhelmingly,
both husband and wife had to ponder the prospect of a run for the
White House. "I did not want my husband to be president," Eleanor
later declared. "It was pure selfishness on my part, and I never mentioned my feelings on the subject to him." She believed that her role as
First Lady would signal "the end of any personal life of my own."
As she often did at times of loss or change, Eleanor became depressed.
She expected to be trapped in the White House as a wifely hostess and
imagined that she would lose the satisfying working partnership she
had struggled to develop with Franklin. After Roosevelt made public

his decision to run, she told reporters that she would b
Roosevelt and not the First Lady.

One of those reporters would in fact provide her v
her personal life, even amid the spectacle of the campaign—and even in
the White House. Lorena Hickok (known as Hick), the nation's foremost female journalist, knew Eleanor from covering New York politics,
but she had never been able to crack Eleanor's standoffishness. In every
way but her sex, Hick was one of the boys; she drank, played poker, told
great stories, and smoked pipes and cigars. At five feet eight inches and
200 pounds, she stood out. When Hick was assigned to cover the candidate's wife, Eleanor hated the idea, but she gradually grew more
comfortable with Hick, who was smart and funny, tough and generous.

Hick in turn was taken with Eleanor's vitality, courage, self-mock-
ing sense of humor, and worldly engagement. On an overnight train
ride to Chicago, the two women shared war stories of their unfortunate
childhoods. (Hick had been raped as a young girl.) By the time the
1932 campaign ended, they had developed a romantic and passionate
friendship. Historians continue to argue vehemently whether their
relationship was ever sexually consummated. Eleanor's passionate written declarations to Hick have fueled the debate: in one letter she
declared, "I remember . . . the feeling of that soft spot just northeast of
the corner of your mouth against my lips." Such utterances may have
been avowals of physical desire or the residual nineteenth-century
womanly rhetoric of friendship. Whatever the extent of their physical
intimacy, the two women were in love, at least for a while.

Unlike his wife, Franklin was never an ideologue, but rather a
highly pragmatic man, primed to compromise now to achieve a greater
goal later. As the Chicago convention deadlocked, FDR recruited
Boston tycoon Joseph P. Kennedy to make a deal with newspaper magnate William Randolph Hearst in which Roosevelt would abandon his
support for the League of Nations and anoint Hearst's candidate, John
Nance Garner of Texas, for the vice presidency. Amid pandemonium,
California switched to Roosevelt, who won on the fourth ballot—
indebted not just to Hearst but to the ambitious Boston businessman.

In the first of his many breaks with tradition, Franklin accepted the
nomination in person, with Eleanor at his side. With words that have
resonated throughout history, he declared: "I pledge you, I pledge
myself a new deal for the American people." He wanted to represent

the Democrats as "prophets of a new order of competence and courage." Yet after the convention, when Franklin gave a speech repudiating the League of Nations and dissociating himself from the World Court, both causes about which Eleanor cared deeply, she shut him out with a cold fury he had not witnessed from her in years.

That Roosevelt would win the presidency was almost a foregone conclusion. Following the traumatic stock market crash in 1929, the country had lapsed into what was being called the "Hoover Depression." FDR's campaign was long on hope and empathy, but short on specifics. He expressed deep concern for "the forgotten man," but craftily stayed away from taking strong positions that would arouse opposition. With Eleanor at his side, Franklin campaigned vigorously to prove that he could be effective and dynamic despite his disability. He carried forty-two of forty-eight states. His destiny achieved after great personal trial, a new scion of America's premier political family had come to lead the country.

In the weeks before the Roosevelts took over the White House, the country was sliding into desperation. One-third of the workforce was unemployed. Eighty-five thousand businesses had failed and five thousand banks had closed their doors, culminating in a financial panic as people began to withdraw and hoard their money. The nation was facing paralysis and a crisis in confidence, just as on more personal terms Franklin and Eleanor had endured their own a decade before.

On a dismal March day that matched the country's spirit, Franklin D. Roosevelt uttered perhaps the most famous passage of any inaugural address: "The only thing we have to fear is fear itself—nameless, unjustified terror which paralyzes needed effort to convert retreat into advance." Having stared down his own terrors, he brought the same steely determination, tempered with ebullience, to soothe and inspire the country. Eleanor said of Franklin, "I've never known a man who gave one a greater sense of security. I never heard him say that there was a problem that he thought it was impossible for human beings to solve." Her high regard for her husband's reliability and resolve suggested how far their own relationship had evolved in the fourteen years since Franklin had betrayed her with Lucy Mercer.

During his first week in office, FDR gave the first of his famous "Fireside Chats," radio addresses in which he spoke hearteningly to the nation. With his love of history and fascination with royalty, he chose to speak from the big oak desk that Queen Victoria had given to the White House in 1880. The desk, called the "Resolute," had been built from the timbers of its namesake ship, which Americans had rescued, restored, and returned to Great Britain some thirty years after the British had burned down the White House during the War of 1812. The Resolute desk augmented the new president's message. In his Fireside Chat, he explained his plans to shore up the banking system—which encouraged millions of Americans to begin making bank deposits again.

In his first hundred days as president, FDR pushed an unprecedented amount of legislation through Congress. The Emergency Banking Relief Act put the banks and their reopening under federal control; the Civilian Conservation Corps hired young men to plant trees and restore areas ruined by forest fires; and the Public Works Administration employed millions to build schools, airports, hospitals, public buildings, and roads, as well as funding the arts and adult education programs. By December 1933 when Prohibition was overturned, Americans had something to celebrate with a legal drink. FDR's campaign song, "Happy Days Are Here Again," seemed to match the country's revived spirits. There were marathon dancing and jitterbug contests. Hollywood films began to show a new vitality.

During the first years of the Roosevelt presidency, the White House functioned as a lively residential community and family compound. Visitors did not even need a pass to go through the gates and walk on the grounds. Eleanor and Franklin established their separate courts on different floors. Franklin's secretary, Missy LeHand, lived on the third floor, while Lorena Hickok had a room near Eleanor's on the second floor. Adviser Louis Howe issued orders from Lincoln's bed, while the president's alter ego, Harry Hopkins, was in the Lincoln suite. Because Franklin could not easily go out, he brought the world to him. Foreign royalty, dignitaries, relatives, friends, and celebrities took turns living in the presidential hotel. Ernest Hemingway's wife Martha Gellhorn summed up the atmosphere: "It was just a great big house . . . full of chums and funny people, and it was one of the most . . . easygoing, amusing places you could possibly be in."

No White House partnership had ever resembled the Roosevelts'. The radical nature of their relationship exploded the conventions of the presidential marriage—as shown by how they managed their extended family in their first days in the White House. Franklin invited Lucy Mercer surreptitiously to his inauguration. The day before, Eleanor took Hick to a Washington park, where they meditated on her new duties in front of her favorite statue of a grieving woman. On Hick's fortieth birthday several days later, Eleanor wrote her that "I ache to hold you close." It would take sixty years before another presidential couple—the Clintons—would come close to redefining their White House roles in as radical a way as the Roosevelts did.

In her first year in the White House, Eleanor was seldom in residence. She traveled over forty thousand miles, from coal mines in Appalachia to the dust bowl in Oklahoma, famously serving as the president's eyes and ears, to monitor the New Deal's emergence. Sara Roosevelt took great pleasure in assuming Eleanor's role as hostess. Imperious and demanding, Sara was dubbed "the queen" by the White House staff. Sara thought of herself more as a queen mother. As the author Bonnie Angelo described her, "With her queenly bearing, her gold lorgnette and her perfectly coiffed white hair," she looked the part.

Sara Delano's fascination with royalty had begun when she was twelve years old in Paris, in 1866, as she watched Empress Eugenie drive past in her royal coach. Years later, Sara's husband bought her the red-velvet-lined sleigh that Czar Alexander II had given to Napoleon III, which she used for her winter rides at Hyde Park. According to a family friend, Sara did not feel that "anyone was her social equal, except maybe the Queen of England and she wasn't sure about that." She soon had a chance to find out.

In June 1934, Sara headed to Europe for a ten-week holiday, her first in four years, at age seventy-nine the first mother of a president to visit England while her son was in office. U.S. ambassador Robert Bingham, an old friend, whisked her off to the U.S. embassy for a week's stay. Arriving at Buckingham Palace for tea with King George and Queen Mary, Sara viewed the visit as a neighborly call and arrived via the garden entrance, which is usually reserved for royalty and heads of state. In a small room hung with watercolors and family portraits on the second floor of the palace, Queen Mary and King George V conversed with her about their four sons and their daughter, their young grandchildren Elizabeth and Margaret, and discussed ships and stamp collecting as well.

The king remembered that FDR had sent him, the year before, some of the stamped envelopes he had received from the king's subjects. FDR had written to the king that he might be "amused by some of the strange ways some of your loyal subjects insist on addressing me." Franklin had joked that "it is bad enough to have my American responsibilities without the addition of Indians, Canadians, Australians, etc. add to my woes at the rate of at least a score of letters a day." The letter was calculated to please the king at a time when relations were tinged with frost due to negotiations over the debt left over from the Great War.

Sara boasted about her son and reminisced with the king about his visit with Franklin sixteen years before. "I gave the King your message & he was pleased," Sara wrote her son. "The Queen . . . was very nice & asked much about you as he did & how you could get about. I even got up & stood behind a chair & put one hand lightly on the back as you do." Reading her words, Franklin must have felt a familiar sinking sensation. He hated to have attention drawn to his disability.

Once when Eleanor visited a grand Long Island mansion, she wrote to Franklin, "I'm afraid I wasn't born to be a high life lady." Just before Sara arrived in England, the First Lady wrote to Hick, "Mama . . . is going to stay with the King and Queen of England. Lord, how I would hate it & and how she will love it." She knew her mother-in-law's grand manner well, but she underestimated herself.

# 4

# The Happy Yorks

## 1920–1933

> She drew him out and made him so strong that she could lean on
> him.
>
> —*A friend's version of Elizabeth's effect on Bertie*

Just at the time when his confidence as a public figure was beginning to
bud, Bertie met one of the most self-assured new members of London
society.

On June 10, 1920, twenty-four-year-old Prince Albert joined his
mother Queen Mary, his sister Princess Mary, and his younger brother
Prince Harry at a dinner dance in Grosvenor Square given by Lady
Farquhar, a friend of the family. According to one observer, Bertie first
noticed Lady Elizabeth Bowes-Lyon when she was talking to his
equerry James Stuart, the handsome, twenty-two-year-old son of the
Earl of Moray. Even though she was short and tended to wear old-
fashioned clothes, Elizabeth stood out. She had a dazzling smile and
striking blue eyes that suggested sweetness and hinted at a devilish
sense of fun. Prince Albert was good-looking and athletic, but he was
also shy, vulnerable, and intimidated by his own stammer.

At the dance, Bertie went directly to Stuart and asked him, "Who
was that lovely girl you were talking to? Introduce me to her." He
would later acknowledge he had fallen in love with Elizabeth that
evening, although it had taken him time to realize it. Bertie did not

remember that he had first met Lady Elizabeth at a children's party when he was ten years old and she was five. Supposedly, Elizabeth had given him the crystallized cherries off the top of her cake.

In contrast to the Roosevelts' spacious yet crowded relationship, the tight-knit marriage of King George VI and Queen Elizabeth would be so traditionally happy as to seem mundane—if the circumstances of their lives were not so dramatic. Yet their union would be hard-won, a marriage between two people who often contradicted the expectations of their roles. The relaxed, vivacious, and charming Lady Elizabeth Bowes-Lyon was a far more natural royal figure than the stammering, uncertain man she would marry—a man who never wanted to be king.

As a debutante after the war, Elizabeth had made her formal debut in society when she was presented to King George and Queen Mary at Holyrood House in Edinburgh. That social season, Elizabeth enjoyed her growing popularity at weekend house parties, charity events, race meetings, and picnics. She was voted best dancer among the aristocratic young women of London. Mabell, Countess of Airlie, a friend and lady-in-waiting to Queen Mary, said that Elizabeth's "radiant vitality and a blending of kindness and sincerity [made] her irresistible." She had many suitors, chief among them James Stuart. On the surface Bertie did not match up well against James, who was as suave as Bertie was awkward. While James was a debonair war hero, Bertie had spent much of the war on a hospital ship. James had an insouciant humor and easy charm that led women to swoon. One friend described him as a heartthrob, but he was also a bright and talented man. Elizabeth, for her part, took marriage quite seriously and was in no hurry to wed.

Although James and Elizabeth had developed feelings for each other, Bertie would not be deterred. That summer Lady Airlie, perhaps nudged by Queen Mary, invited Bertie's sister Princess Mary to stay at her Scottish castle, under the pretense that she could continue her work in the Girl Guide movement—similar to the U.S. Girl Scouts—in nearby Dundee. Not incidentally, she could also socialize with her friend and fellow Girl Guide, Lady Elizabeth. Bertie, happy to leave stultifying Balmoral Castle, joined his sister in visiting Elizabeth at Glamis, her family's ancient, reputedly haunted castle.

Elizabeth's parents, the Earl and Countess of Strathmore, had inherited the castle in 1904. Glamis castle and its twenty-five thousand

acres was originally a fourteenth-century gift from King Robert II of
Scotland to Sir John Lyon when he married the king's daughter Jean.
According to legend, in 1034 King Malcolm of Scotland died there of
battle wounds, and six years later Macbeth murdered Malcolm's grandson King Duncan in the banqueting hall. Shakespeare is supposed to
have written *Macbeth* while visiting the castle. Mary Stuart, Bonnie
Prince Charlie, and Sir Walter Scott were among its visitors. Although
Elizabeth was dubious about the claim, the castle purportedly was filled
with ghosts. The diarist Henry "Chips" Channon described it as
"heavy with atmosphere, sinister, lugubrious." Bertie was enthralled by
the castle, by the informal and fun-loving Strathmore family, which
was such a contrast to his own rigid and demanding clan, and by the
radiant Lady Elizabeth.


By the spring of 1921 he had decided to ask her to marry him, but he
made two mistakes: he told his parents ahead of time, and he followed
the king's advice that he propose through an intermediary. King
George did not want his sons making offers of marriage directly; he
believed that a royal prince should not be in the position to be rejected
in person. The king was already charmed by Elizabeth and told Bertie,
"You will be a lucky fellow if she accepts you." Although there has been
speculation that the Prince of Wales was sent to make the marriage
offer—he later claimed that Elizabeth had been interested in him—
Bertie may have sent his equerry James Stuart as an emissary. It is hard
to imagine a more awkward situation. By this time Elizabeth and James
were emotionally involved. When she turned Bertie down, the young
prince was crushed. His matchmakers were upset as well. Lady
Strathmore said, "I like him so much and he is a man who will be made
or marred by his wife."

Unlike Franklin Roosevelt's mother, Sara, Queen Mary wanted her
son to wed. The queen, disappointed by Elizabeth's refusal, decided to
act. She went to visit Lady Airlie that September and made it plain that
she expected to visit Glamis. Although Lady Strathmore was ill, the
queen, Princess Mary, and a retinue of servants journeyed to Glamis,
where Elizabeth served the queen tea and gave her a tour of the castle.
As Queen Mary was obsessed with royal history, Elizabeth won her over
completely with her thorough account of Glamis's history and legends.

In her memoir *Thatched with Gold,* Lady Airlie gave the official version of Bertie and Elizabeth's courtship. After visiting Glamis, Queen Mary is said to have told Lady Airlie that she was "more than ever convinced that this was the one girl who could make Bertie happy. But I shall say nothing to either of them," she told her friend. "Mothers should never meddle in their children's love affairs." A little meddling seemed in order, however. Elizabeth and Bertie began to drop by Lady Airlie's London flat separately to chat; one would invariably mention the other. Lady Airlie felt that Bertie was "deeply in love, but so humble. . . . Although the romance seemed at an end I continued to plead his cause from time to time" to Elizabeth. Lady Airlie noted that the young woman was "frankly doubtful, uncertain of her feelings and afraid of the public life which would lie ahead of her as the King's daughter-in-law." As a member of a wealthy noble family, she had nothing to gain by marrying into the royal family. In fact, she would lose much of her freedom and would live under constant scrutiny.

At the end of September 1921, Bertie spent a week at Glamis, partridge shooting with Elizabeth's brothers Michael and David. "It is delightful here & Elizabeth is very kind to me," he wrote his mother. "The more I see of her the more I like her." Elizabeth spent the rest of that fall nursing her mother, who had undergone an operation. Bertie consoled Elizabeth and sent her copies of the latest dance tunes to cheer her up.

The Queen Mother's biographer, Ingrid Seward, believes that Queen Mary engineered the marriage—and even conspired to exile James Stuart. Seward writes, "The Queen had let her feelings be known. Lady Strathmore had consulted with Jamie's mother, and together the three women came to a decision" to send Jamie "away for awhile." After a parting New Year's visit with Elizabeth in 1922, Stuart went off to work in the oil fields of Oklahoma as a rigger. Seward describes his time in Oklahoma as akin to "exile to Siberia."

Because Elizabeth was friends with Princess Mary, the next part of the royal plot unfolded with ease. Elizabeth was asked to be a bridesmaid in Princess Mary's wedding in February 1922, to Viscount Lascelles, the older, wealthy mate that the king and queen—in the tradition of the time—had chosen for their daughter. Elizabeth would get to see a royal event from the inside, experiencing both royal traditions and public life firsthand.

As Elizabeth would discover, tradition ruled the court of George V. The king was a creature of habit. He still used his childhood brushes on his hair. Breakfast was held promptly at nine every morning; as soon as he finished, he would light a cigarette in a holder and walk outside to scan the weather. Dinner began exactly when the clock stuck the hour. The king dined alone with his family and wore a white tie and his Garter Star. As he left the dining room, Queen Mary would remain standing. Their sons would go up to her and bow in order of age before withdrawing from the room. Such a man would vehemently disapprove of the free-spirited "Roaring Twenties" generation then coming of age. As late as August 1922 he wrote to his wife on his feelings about having daughters-in-law, saying, "I must say I dread the idea and always have"; he feared they would dress like flappers and spend their evenings sipping cocktails and dancing at the latest clubs.

The king was lucky that Elizabeth was the first serious candidate to marry one of his sons. Once he sensed that she was centered and responsible as well as charming, he took to her with alacrity. He was so smitten that when she apologized for arriving several minutes late for dinner, he told her an uncharacteristic lie: "You are not late, my dear, I think we must have sat down two minutes too early." After she and his son married, the king would write to Bertie from Balmoral, "The better I know & the more I see of your dear little wife, the more charming I think she is & everyone fell in love with her here." Windsors possessed either charm or a sense of duty. Elizabeth was singular in possessing both.

That September Bertie paid Elizabeth another visit at Glamis. Lady Strathmore noticed that her daughter began to appear "really worried" and "torn" after that visit. In early January 1923 the *Daily News* reported that David, the Prince of Wales—not his brother Bertie—was going to marry the daughter of a well-known Scottish aristocrat. The article made it clear that the intended bride was Lady Elizabeth Bowes-Lyon. This false information increased the pressure on the young woman, who remained uncertain as to whether she should accept Bertie's impending proposal.

Bertie decided to give one last try. "It's the third time and it's going to be the last," he told the Duchess of Devonshire. On Saturday morning, January 13, at the Strathmores' home at St. Paul's Walden Bury, he asked the earl for permission to marry his daughter. While the family went off to church, he took Elizabeth for a walk in the woods, having deliberately chosen the scene of some of her happiest childhood hours. She once described the place to a friend: "At the bottom of the garden is The Wood—the haunt of fairies, with its anemones and ponds and moss-grown statues and a big oak." Bertie asked for her hand while they were standing in a grove of trees. She thought about his offer for a full, agonizing minute. Finally she gave him the answer he had been seeking for two years. The press reported that she laughed easily and said, "If you are going to keep it up forever I might as well say yes now." Despite her subtle lack of enthusiasm, Bertie was ecstatic. "My dream has at last been realized," he wrote his mother. "Chips" Channon spoke for London society: "There is not a man in England today who doesn't envy him. The clubs are in gloom."

Shortly after her engagement was announced, Elizabeth gave her first and last press interview. When Harry Cozens-Hardy of the *Star* newspaper showed up at the Strathmore home on Bruton Street, Elizabeth appeared just as the butler was shooing him out. Assuming that he wanted to offer congratulations, she ushered him into her study, whereupon he asked if it was true that the Duke of York had to ask three times for her to marry him. "Now look at me," she said coyly. "Do you think I am the sort of person that Bertie would have to ask twice?" When King George saw the interview in print, he was furious. He ordered her not to speak to the press again. She honored his wishes for seventy-nine years.

As their future friends Eleanor and Franklin were beginning to live more independent lives, Elizabeth and Bertie embarked on their own marriage. When Elizabeth left her London home at the royally precise time of 11:12 A.M. on April 26, 1923, it was raining. As she entered Westminster Abbey's great west door, the sun came out. Bertie wore the uniform of the Royal Air Force; Elizabeth was dressed in an ivory-colored chiffon moiré dress for the ceremony. She was the first commoner to marry an heir to the throne since Lady Anne Hyde had wed the future King James II in 1660.

As the service came to an end, the new Duchess of York placed her bouquet of white York roses and Scottish heather at the tomb of the Unknown Warrior in remembrance of her brother Fergus, killed in

France. Almost seventy-nine years later, at the Queen Mother's funeral, her daughter Queen Elizabeth II had her bouquet of lilies, roses, and Scottish heather, which sat on top of the casket, placed on that same tomb in remembrance of the gesture her mother made on her wedding day.

The Archbishop of Canterbury told the newly married couple, "You have received from Him at this Altar a new life wherein your separate lives are now, till death, made one. But you cannot resolve that it will be happy. You can and will resolve that it will be noble." Their marriage was definitely noble, but it would also prove to be extremely happy.

Once the duke had the consistent love, understanding, and support that he had craved all his life, he blossomed. A natural underlying gaiety emerged to replace his frequent depressed moods and bouts of self-pity. His awkwardness and self-consciousness softened into greater spontaneity. He still had trouble with his Hanoverian temper, which he had inherited from his father and grandfather. When he did have his "gnashes," as he called them, his wife knew how to lightly shift his mood. Over time as he felt more secure, his natural common sense ripened into wisdom and sound judgment. Speaking of Bertie's marriage, a friend paid Elizabeth the ultimate compliment: "she drew him out and made him so strong that she could lean on him."

By contrast, the marriage did not, at first, appear to offer Elizabeth rewards commensurate with her sacrifices. She knew that not only was she giving up superficially more attractive suitors and her autonomy as a member of the aristocracy, but she was also committing herself to the British people and a vulnerable man, embarking on a life of scrutiny and obligation. In her decision to marry him, Bertie had detected a sense of duty. According to the biographer Anthony Holden, Elizabeth later told a friend: "It was my duty to marry Bertie and I fell in love with him afterwards." Her deepening feelings for him would testify to his determination and decency.

The nineteenth-century political journalist Walter Bagehot famously said that "a princely marriage is the brilliant edition of a universal fact and as such it rivets mankind." Bertie was well aware of the importance of marriage to the monarchy. In 1919 the king had sent Bertie to Cambridge, where he studied Bagehot's *The English Constitution*, accepted as the best depiction of the British form of government. The function of the monarch, Bagehot wrote, is to advise, consult, and to warn. Bertie took particular note of Bagehot's observation that "we have come to regard the Crown as the head of morality." He knew well his father's obsession with keeping the monarchy above reproach.

Not only above reproach but above ridicule. In October 1925 Bertie faced one of the most daunting and humiliating ordeals of his public career. He had succeeded his brother David as the president of the British Empire Exhibition, which showcased the artistic and industrial progress of the empire. The exhibition was of crucial importance to the king, who sought every opportunity to advance the cause of the British Empire. Bertie would have to deliver the exhibition's closing speech before a crowd of thousands at Wimbledon, in the largest stadium in England. Even more daunting, his words would be broadcast by microphone to ten million people around the empire. Most intimidating of all, the king would be listening to his son speak in public for the first time.

King George VI's official biographer, John Wheeler-Bennett, himself a stammerer, wrote eloquently of the torture Bertie must have endured around his speech impediment: "Only those who have themselves suffered the tragedies of the stammerer can appreciate to the full their depth and poignancy—the infuriating inhibitions and frustrations, the bitter humiliation and anguish of the spirit; the orgies of self-pity; and the utter exhaustion, mental and physical; perhaps above all, the sense of being different from others." Franklin Roosevelt would understand Bertie's anguish, having struggled for years to learn to walk again after he contracted polio. The duke matched FDR in his determination to surmount setbacks, exhaustion, and shame.

Bertie wrote a painfully open letter to his father begging for his understanding: "I do hope I shall do it well. But I shall be very frightened as you have never heard me speak & the loud speakers are apt to put one off as well. So I hope that you will understand that I am bound to be more nervous than I usually am." In his speech to the thousands gathered before him, the millions on the radio, and his own father, Bertie struggled to get the words out. The king wrote a kind appraisal of the speech to Bertie's younger brother George: "Bertie got through his speech all right, but there were some rather long pauses."

The torment of the speech promised to be the first in a lifetime of such tortures for a young man beginning his public role. When the king selected the Duke and Duchess of York to open the Commonwealth Parliament building in the new capital city of

Canberra, Australian premier Stanley Bruce was demonstratively unhappy; he had heard the duke speak in public and was appalled. The duke, everyone agreed, needed help. The nine speech experts brought in to advise on Bertie's case over the past decade had all told him his stammer was the result of a psychological problem, reinforcing his sense of being defective. As John Wheeler-Bennett put it, "The disillusionment caused by the failures of previous specialists to effect a cure had begun to breed within him the inconsolable despair of the chronic stammerer and the secret dread that the hidden root of the affliction lay in the mind rather than in the body." Wary of having his hopes dashed once more, the duke was reluctant to consult more experts. The duchess, realizing the crucial importance of the upcoming tour, prevailed upon him to make one last effort.

Australian speech therapist Lionel Logue's often quoted first impression was of "a slim, quiet man with tired eyes and all the outward symptoms of a man upon whom habitual speech defect had begun to set the sign." The duke could not call his parents the "King" and "Queen" because he had difficulty pronouncing the letters $K$ and $Q$ along with $G$ and $N$. Logue had two great gifts, which he used to good effect on Bertie: he transmitted a remarkable sense of confidence that he could help, and he convinced the duke he could cure himself—if he made a total commitment. Bertie responded well to that kind of challenge. Logue also intuited the duke's fear that he was fundamentally different from other people. In Logue's view, Bertie was a normal person with some breathing problems, which careful practice would correct. In the ten weeks before the tour, Bertie saw Logue almost daily. At home he practiced for one to two hours daily. By the time they left, the duke and duchess were amazed at the progress he had made. Although the duke would never look forward to public speaking, he would never again be humiliated by his failures.


In January 1927 the duke and duchess began their seven-month world tour, leaving behind their daughter, Elizabeth, born in April 1926. They had to circle Grosvenor Square several times in their car so that the duchess could compose herself for the departure ceremonies. As they left she said, "The baby was so sweet playing with the buttons on Bertie's uniform that it quite broke me up."

The duke and duchess embarked on their trip with the vigor and tenacity of a U.S. presidential candidate and his wife campaigning in their opponent's home state. Dogging them was the expectation that they live up to the extraordinary popularity of Bertie's brother the Prince of Wales, who had a genius for publicity. The royal couple knew that the Australians were disappointed that they were representing the king rather than David, who had made several extended and celebrated visits there. Showing the first signs of the natural charm that would later captivate North America, Bertie and Elizabeth worked hard to fulfill their royal duties while exhibiting increasing comfort with their public roles. By the end of the trip, one colonial governor reported to the king that despite the Prince of Wales's popularity, "almost every-where people liked the Duke of York better." People thought he was "trying to do his job better."

After an exhausting round of dinners, balls, receptions, and speeches on New Zealand's North Island, the duchess suddenly developed tonsil-litis. The duke was inclined to cancel a tour of the South Island. He was convinced that people turned out to see his vivacious wife, not him, and he worried that he would not perform adequately without her presence and support. After Elizabeth persuaded him to carry on alone, he was amazed to find that crowds were eager to see him on his own. He delivered a fluent public speech without her coaching, which represented a major step forward in his ease as a public figure. This solo part of the journey was a key component in building the confidence he would need for his spectacular visit to North America twelve years later.

When the duchess was well enough to rejoin the tour, she received enormous ovations. For the first time, she showed her galvanizing effect on crowds and her remarkable ability to give each person the impression she was focused on him or her alone. One young Scotsman wrote that "she shines and warms like sunlight." In the most famous example of her social magnetism, a well-known communist agitator in Auckland gave up communism after the duchess waved back at one of his children and smiled into his face from two yards away. As he put it, "I've done with it for good and all." By the end of the tour, the gover-nor of South Australia wrote to the king that the "whole continent" was "in love with her."

As they sailed home on the battleship *Renown*, the duchess exhib-ited the sangfroid that would make her famous during the war when a fire broke out in the ship's boiler room. As the duchess explained, "Every hour someone said that there was nothing to worry about, so I knew there was real trouble." The fire was difficult to control and was barely tamed before it almost ignited the oil tanks and blew up the ship. The *Renown's* captain was amazed at Elizabeth's cool. Her exposure to so much death and suffering during the First World War had steeled her. It would not be her last encounter with personal danger.

Bertie and Elizabeth returned to a happy home life and had a second daughter, Margaret Rose, in 1930. With the Prince of Wales often touring the empire, the duke and duchess maintained a vigorous schedule domestically, representing the Crown at hospital, school, and museum openings as well as charitable events. The duke was particularly devoted to programs aiding underprivileged boys. Like Eleanor Roosevelt, Bertie turned his childhood deprivation and alienation into lifelong empathy for the plight of the underdog; both worked diligently to improve living conditions for the underprivileged. The duke's work on behalf of youth—notably his Duke of York camps—made him a popular public figure; he was head of the Boy's Welfare Association and trained youngsters through the Industrial Welfare Association.

The royal historian Theo Aronson has pointed out that as the Prince of Wales was bringing the monarchy closer to the empire by his trips throughout the dominions, the Duke of York drew the royal family closer to the working classes at home. As the first royal family member to focus on industrial relations, he became known as the "Industrial Prince," though his brothers joked, perhaps envious of his successes, that he should be known as "the Foreman." He helped the monarchy begin to shift from charitable and social activities to an emphasis on social and economic development.

As the 1930s began and Franklin Roosevelt tackled the depression that had followed the stock market crash in the United States, the royal family felt the economic constriction as well. The king cut fifty thousand pounds from his annual Civil List of monies, and the duke's income was reduced by twenty-five thousand pounds. Bertie found it painful to sell off his hunting dogs and horses to reduce expenses, but both he and the king curtailed their hunting. The Prince of Wales was furious to learn that he had to pare his outlays as well.

Despite these economies, the early thirties were a rewarding and domestic time for "us four," as the Yorks called themselves. The duke and duchess enjoyed a period of tranquillity at their new pink-washed home at Royal Lodge in Great Windsor Park. Elizabeth inherited her mother's passion for gardening, and the duke had a talent for designing gardens; together they expanded the Royal Lodge gardens from fifteen to ninety acres. The whole family rolled up their sleeves, carried dirt in wheelbarrows, and cleared shrubbery. Guests and staff were put to work as well.

Like the Roosevelt clans at Hyde Park and Oyster Bay, the Windsors had two rival courts existing in close proximity. Near Bertie's family-centered circle at Royal Lodge was the country home of the Prince of Wales, where David entertained a series of slender, maternal, and safely married mistresses and his high-living and fashionable international friends. His dalliances with unavailable women did not augur well for his future role as a king, but they were harmless until he met an American divorcée named Wallis Warfield Simpson.

# 5

# Rocking the World

## 1934–1938

That boy will ruin himself within twelve months.

—*King George V, of David*

## The United States

In the middle of the night of July 12, 1934, a California state trooper pulled up to the Hotel Senator in Sacramento, picked up a set of car keys from the desk clerk, and drove a small gray Plymouth convertible to a hiding place where a Secret Service agent exchanged its Washington, D.C., license plates for a California set. The two men then returned the car to its getaway location at the back of the hotel.

The next morning, Lorena Hickok met with her press buddies in the hotel lobby and asked sweetly if they would give their prey, Eleanor Roosevelt, time to freshen up before she submitted to interviews. Hick had just collected the exhausted First Lady at the airport after an overnight flight. Sensing a good story, the Sacramento newspaper reporters agreed to be patient, but they were not stupid. They staked out every entrance to the hotel. Eleanor and her friend sneaked out the back entrance and—just as a famous princess would do more than sixty years later—slipped into Hick's waiting car and sped off. Their driver reported the same bad news that Diana would hear—that a carful of reporters was in hot pursuit—but Eleanor had better judgment than the ill-fated princess. The First Lady lost her freedom that day, but not her life.

Their driver, a state trooper, accelerated to seventy-five miles an hour with a state police car escorting them with flashing lights, but they could not elude the press. Eleanor had the trooper pull over. The reporters encircled the car and demanded that Eleanor reveal her destination. The First Lady offered them an interview instead. When the press badgered her about her "secret" vacation, Eleanor said if they persisted, she would cancel it. They agreed to leave her alone after a breakfast interview at a coffee shop. The next day, William Randolph Hearst made sure that his *San Francisco Examiner* called Eleanor and Hick "intimate friends." After a relaxed week of picnicking, the pair joined Eleanor's daughter Anna and her children at a Nevada ranch for a week of swimming and horseback riding.

With her youngest son, John, ready for college, Eleanor was free of maternal responsibilities for the first time in almost thirty years. After dutifully assisting Franklin into the presidency and helping to give a public face to the New Deal, she now sought to put herself first. As FDR was happily spending the month of July cruising on the USS *Houston* from the Caribbean to Hawaii, Eleanor surprised Hick with four days of camping at Yosemite National Park. While the heavy-smoking Hick panted her way through the high altitude, Eleanor exercised as if preparing for a decathlon, with dawn swims in an icy lake, strenuous hikes in the mountains, and horseback riding over hazardous trails. After one climb to thirteen thousand feet, according to Hick, Eleanor's ranger guide looked like he was "going to have a stroke. His face was all purple." Theodore Roosevelt would have been proud of his inexhaustible niece.

An increasingly public woman who had recently begun to do a weekly radio broadcast and write regularly for newspapers, Eleanor was realizing how difficult it would be to maintain her privacy. In Yosemite, while she and Hick were bending over to feed chipmunks, tourists took unflattering photographs of Lorena's broad behind. Having already endured four grimy, strenuous days, Hick exploded with vulgar language. Hick had given up her great passion—newspaper reporting—for Eleanor. Now she was miserably unhappy. Eleanor tried desperately to calm her. Raised to have perfect manners, Eleanor was humiliated by Hick's outburst.

In San Francisco, Hick discovered that souvenir-seeking tourists had stripped her car of maps, sunglasses, chocolate bars, a cigarette lighter, and the St. Christopher's medal Eleanor had given her. After facing a barrage of press and tourists in Portland, it was Eleanor's turn to explode. "Franklin said I would never get away with it . . . and I can't," she declared. "From now on I shall travel as I'm supposed to travel, as the President's wife and do what is expected of me." Precocious as always, Eleanor was trying to have it all: she wanted to be a crusader for peace and human rights as well as a wife, mother, and free spirit, all the while maintaining her privacy. Even with her prodigious energy and commitment, such a combination was impossible. The most intense phase of her relationship with Hick ended that night in Portland. Afterward, Eleanor would rejoin her official life, and her husband.

Franklin Roosevelt had begun 1935 with a fresh, two-thirds legislative majority, but Congress stalemated over his crucial anti-lynching bill, resisted his Social Security bill, and thwarted his campaign for ratification of the World Court, which had constituted a reversal of his 1932 convention pledge to William Randolph Hearst. He was exasperated. On March 26, FDR happily retreated to Vincent Astor's yacht *Nourmahal* for a ten-day cruise in the Bahamas.

The next day he invited the Duke and Duchess of Kent, honeymooning nearby, to dine on the yacht. After reading about their wedding the previous fall, FDR had become intrigued by Prince George, Queen Mary's favorite son, a handsome man with dark blue eyes who shared his mother's interest in theater, antiques, and family history, but also frequented racy nightclubs. Known for his affairs with aristocratic women, the dashing prince was also rumored to have been involved with playwright Noël Coward, an Italian aristocrat, and an Argentinean diplomat. Winston Churchill's son Randolph once told diplomat Sir Robert Bruce Lockhart that a large sum had had to be paid to retrieve a compromising letter Prince George had written to a young man in Paris. He was also briefly addicted to morphine and cocaine, but after a "cure" in the country had resumed his royal role. He redeemed himself with his father by marrying Princess Marina of Greece and Denmark, who was descended from both the king of Greece and the brother of the czar of Russia, and was one of Europe's most chic and beautiful women; Cecil Beaton loved to photograph her. A charming and cosmopolitan couple, George and Marina enjoyed a good cocktail and were the kind of fun-loving friends FDR craved. The president took to them immediately and invited them to visit him in Washington.

While FDR could tolerate incremental social progress and easily restore himself after setbacks, Eleanor would get depressed when her righteous causes were thwarted. Not only had the isolationist Hearst and Detroit's rabble-rousing radio priest Charles Coughlin rallied the Senate to defeat U.S. entry into the World Court—which she believed encouraged Hitler to declare he intended to "achieve territorial revision" and abrogate Germany's treaties—but Congress had failed to pass anti-lynching legislation. Lorena Hickok had begun to worry that Eleanor was so despondent and fed up with Franklin that she would seek a divorce, which would be disastrous for the couple's progressive agenda. But late in April Franklin placated Eleanor, delivering a Fireside Chat promoting two of her beloved projects: Social Security legislation and the Public Works Administration, which promised to provide millions of jobs. Eleanor's depression lifted. "My calm has returned and my goat has ceased bleating. Why do I let myself go on in that way?" she asked Hick. "I know I've got to stick. I know I'll never make an open break and I never tell FDR how I feel."

## London

When Eleanor tested the limits of her freedom during her travels with Hick on the West Coast, she had sought for herself the kind of license that the Prince of Wales had employed all his life. During most of the 1920s, David had been involved with a leader of the café society he frequented, Mrs. Freda Dudley-Ward. In 1929 he jettisoned her for the easygoing and dimwitted American socialite Thelma Morgan Furness, aunt of the famous "Poor Little Rich Girl," Gloria Vanderbilt.

David grew closer to Bertie after his brother married Elizabeth, whom David considered a "lively, refreshing spirit." David enjoyed romping in the gardens and reading stories with his nieces Elizabeth and Margaret, and he told the duchess, "You make family life such fun," but he made no effort to settle down and start his own family. Although the Yorks "tended to be withdrawn from the hurly-burly of the life I relished," as David put it, they did show up at pool parties at the prince's weekend home, Fort Belvedere. Also in attendance were Wallis and Ernest Simpson.

By the spring of 1934, Wallis Warfield Simpson had replaced Thelma as David's mistress. Although with her mannish jaw, large hands, and harsh voice she was no traditional beauty, she was stylish, witty, and coolly elegant in a way that typified the 1930s. David's younger brother George, who lived with him before he married Princess Marina, told the rest of the family that David appeared to enjoy the way Wallis dominated him. When she interrupted him or kicked him under the table for committing some infraction, he did not seem to mind. The servants deeply resented her bossiness.

That November, David caused an uproar at a prewedding reception for his brother George, newly named the Duke of Kent, when he introduced Wallis to his parents. Wallis curtsied to the king and queen, who suppressed their rage and treated her with impeccable manners. For the royal family, Wallis was not only a still-married American woman but a self-centered status-seeker with little charm and less sense of public duty. They believed she had cast an evil spell over a man who had been the charismatic hope of the Commonwealth. Some observers said that the prince's disregard for the dignity of the monarchy contributed to the sharp decline in his father's health.

Just before the Jubilee festivals that spring celebrating his twenty-five years on the throne—a quarter century in which George V had provided a fatherly sense of security and continuity to an empire beset by war and economic disasters—the king demanded to know if David was having an affair with Mrs. Simpson. The prince boldly lied to his father: Wallis, he said, was just a good friend who made him happy. Naively believing his son, the king allowed David to invite Wallis to the Silver Jubilee Ball. The prince met their worst expectations that night. He began the evening as the dutiful son, dancing with Queen Mary, but what he did next shocked his family: he danced with Wallis, in a gesture that placed her second in importance to the queen.

By the summer of 1935 as the king's health declined, David seemed to veer out of control. Bertie watched with growing unease as David took Wallis yachting on the Riviera and dined with her and the French prime minister. Still dazzled by his flashy older brother, Bertie was hurt by David's obstinacy, his unwillingness to listen, and his increasing withdrawal from his family. His father declared, "I pray to God that my eldest son will never marry and have children, and that nothing will come between Bertie and Lilibet"—Princess Elizabeth—"and the throne."

On January 20, 1936, seventy-one-year-old King George V died in his sleep. Bertie was distraught, and Elizabeth was too sick with pneumonia to comfort him. Later she wrote the king's physician, Lord Dawson of Penn, "Unlike his own children . . . I was never afraid of him. He was so 'dependable.' And when he was in the mood, he could be deliciously funny too!" Responding to the British Empire's shock about the king's death, Eleanor Roosevelt declared in her newspaper column, "No, one can't be sorry for people who are dead unless one believes in a hell after death which I do not, but it is bad for those who live on here and don't know what the future holds beyond the barrier."

There was chaos and controversy from the start. The new king wept hysterically and kept embracing his mother, who had knelt to kiss his hand in homage. While some have suggested David was weeping over the death of his father and his new responsibilities, the biographer Sarah Bradford marshals convincing evidence that he was distraught because his elopement with Wallis had been foiled.

In the first days of King Edward's reign, the Yorks were chilled to see photographs of Wallis sitting in a window with him as heralds proclaimed him king. In what seemed a bad omen, as George V's children walked behind their father's coffin in the procession to Westminster Hall, the Maltese cross fell off the imperial crown atop the royal coffin and clattered into a gutter. The new king muttered, "Christ! What's going to happen next?" A member of Parliament declared, "That will be the motto of the new reign."

During what would become the year of the three kings, the nation divided into two camps. Edward VIII, initially popular with both London society and his subjects because of his informal and modern manner, would contend with the Duke of York, the church, the older members of the royal household, and the court, all of whom were concerned with the continuing stability of the monarchy.

The eleven months of Edward VIII's reign were like a slow-motion train wreck. The Duke of York watched helplessly as the gleaming engine car jumped the track, knocking down familiar landmarks, and headed in his direction. The Yorks and Queen Mary watched the king's behavior with mounting horror. The new king infuriated leaders of the church and state by showing little interest in the routine of monarchical duties, such as attending Sunday services or reading the government papers in their famous red boxes; the papers, which often lay about where Wallis and their guests could peruse them, were sometimes returned to the king's ministers with cocktail rings on them. Because

Wallis was rumored to be a paid informant for American newspapers or a Nazi spy, the government screened papers before delivering them to the king. The king's pro-German leanings were reported in the U.S. press, which was unfettered by the British newspapers' gentleman's agreement to refrain from commenting on the king's personal life, when the king held up a reception line to speak in German to Hitler's foreign minister and then withdrew for a private meeting with him. He shocked government officials by hosting Mrs. Simpson at his first official dinner for the prime minister. During a summer cruise, King Edward was photographed shirtless, walking hand in hand with Wallis. That fall, claiming he was still in mourning for his father, he sent the Yorks to represent him at the opening of the Aberdeen Infirmary—only to be seen across town, thinly disguised in sunglasses, picking up Wallis at the train station to take her to Balmoral. The next day, the outraged Scottish papers carried headlines about his deception. His disregard for appearances was beginning to erode the dignity of the Crown and seriously undermine his popularity.

When the king motored over to Royal Lodge to show his brother and Elizabeth his brand-new American station wagon, Mrs. Simpson was sitting in the front seat. Elizabeth was pleasant but cool. Mrs. Simpson later quipped, "I left with the distinct impression that, while the Duke of York was sold on the American station wagon, the Duchess was not sold on David's other American interest." The relationship between the two brothers and their powerful consorts had begun its downward spiral into bitter rivalry and mistrust. The king and his paramour sensed the Yorks' disapproval; they soon cut them off their social list.

Wallis had made her reputation as a hostess, but lacking knowledge of royal rules and conventions, she violated most of them. She ordered the king to get her champagne and announced to guests touring the castle that "these tartans must go." Already infuriated by reports of Wallis's arrogant behavior, Elizabeth attended a dinner party that fall. When Wallis broke protocol by greeting the guests as if she were the official hostess, the duchess expressed her outrage by marching right past Wallis, announcing, "I came to dine with the King." The two women would not meet again privately.

On October 27, Wallis received her divorce decree. After a five-month waiting period, she would be free to marry the king—just before the May 12 coronation. However, given the king's role as head of the Church, Prime Minister Stanley Baldwin gathered evidence that the dominion prime ministers, the rest of the British government, and the subjects of the British Empire would not countenance a marriage with a twice-divorced American woman. Baldwin made it clear to the king that he could give up Wallis, marry against his ministers' advice and have the government resign, or marry and abdicate.

The king summoned his courage and told his mother that he was going to marry the twice-divorced American commoner whether the government approved or not. Even if she could not be his queen consort, he hoped to rule with his wife Wallis at his side, but if he had to abdicate, so be it. In the conflict between marrying for love and fulfilling one's duty, the new king and the dowager queen could not agree. "For me the question is not whether she is acceptable but whether I am worthy of her," he declared, to his mother's horror. He insisted that she meet Wallis. When the queen adamantly refused, he pressed her for a reason. In a rage, Queen Mary cried, "Because she is an adventuress!"

## Philadelphia and Washington, D.C.

With his party energized and united behind FDR, the Philadelphia Democratic Convention was as close to a coronation as a U.S. president could ever expect. On a misty night just before he was to speak, however, FDR was jostled by the crowd; his right brace buckled and FDR keeled over, with the startled Secret Service agents catching him before he hit the ground. His speech fell in the mud. Unnerved, he calmed himself, gathered his crumpled sheets of notes, and was assisted onto the platform to accept renomination before a crowd of a hundred thousand thronging Franklin Field stadium. Although he was a confirmed royalist, FDR played upon Americans' anti-aristocratic sentiments. He struck out at "economic royalists" and "privileged princes of these new economic dynasties, thirsting for power, [who] reached out for control over Government itself. They created a new despotism and wrapped it in the robes of legal sanction." Speaking of the darkening world situation, he famously declared, "There is a mysterious cycle in human events. To some generations much is given. Of other generations, much is expected. This generation of Americans has a rendezvous with destiny." FDR was prescient; by the end of his second term in office, he would be the leader of what we now call the "greatest generation."

Earlier that day Eleanor had written to a childhood friend that "for the good of the country I believe that it is devoutly to be hoped that he will be reelected, but from a personal point of view I am quite overcome when I think of four years more of the life I have been leading." She was exhausted for good reason: she got up at 7 A.M. and regularly went to bed at 3 or 4 A.M. She not only wrote her column six times a week and worked on her autobiography but that year entertained 9,211 tea guests, 4,729 dinner guests, and 323 houseguests. During the campaign, because she was such an easy target due to her insistent support for the rights of black Americans and other liberal causes, her unorthodox role as First Lady, and the money she made from her radio broadcasts and column, FDR's campaign advisers shoved her into the background. Accusing her of lusting for power, Republicans wore buttons saying, "We don't want Eleanor either." GOP nominee Alf Landon proudly announced that as First Lady, his wife would be caring for her family rather than trying to reform the nation.

Though she would tell other women that they had to develop "a skin as tough as a rhinoceros hide" to succeed in public life, Eleanor grew depressed and detached, as she had learned to do as a child in painful situations. "Gee! I wish I could even be excited about all this," she complained to Hick. "I can't and I hate myself." By September she had fallen seriously ill with a high fever. Frightened, FDR missed his mother's eighty-third birthday party at Hyde Park, rushing to Washington to attend to Eleanor. Her physical collapse brought them closer. Realizing how much he had been taking her for granted, he planned a special birthday party for her—something she usually did for him, but which he rarely reciprocated.

Alice Longworth, full of her usual intrigues, inadvertently helped rouse Eleanor out of her depression. Eleanor had learned how to deal with her long before. Once the First Lady had approached her cousin at a White House party and asked to see Alice's infamous imitation of her. "Alice is good at that sort of thing," she had remarked with sly mildness. Alice, now seeking to boost the uninspired Alf Landon and still angry at FDR's usurpation of the Roosevelt legacy, struck out at Eleanor. "We didn't elect her, what is she horning in for?" she wrote. In another article entitled "His Mollycoddle Philosophy Is Called Typical of Roosevelt," she claimed her father, Theodore, had taught the nation toughness while Franklin's New Deal was cosseting

Depression-ridden America. Eleanor fired back: "No man who has brought himself back from what might have been an entire life of invalidism to physical, mental, spiritual strength and activity can ever be accused of preaching or exemplifying a mollycoddle philosophy."

"Never before in all our history have . . . forces been so united against one candidate as they stand today. They are unanimous in their hate of me—and I welcome their hatred," Franklin proclaimed in a pugnacious speech at Madison Square Garden, challenging the nation's wealthy elite just as Theodore Roosevelt had. In his first administration, "the forces of selfishness and lust for power have met their match," FDR declared; in the second term, "they have met their master." The election was the closest the United States has yet come to a class war, and Roosevelt won it, in a huge electoral vote landslide.

After the election, the Roosevelts again went their separate ways. Eleanor started a monthlong speaking tour while FDR cruised to South America for an official visit. "Loads and loads of love," he wrote Eleanor. "Another year let's cut out and take a trip to Somoa and Hawaii instead. Devotedly F."

The day after the inauguration, Eleanor wrote Hick that she had hosted 710 for lunch and 2,700 for tea: "I confess that the arrangements & people bothered me but even more my sense of 4 more years beginning bothered me. Why can't someone have this job who'd like it & do something worth while with it? I've always been content hiding behind someone else's willingness to take responsibility & work behind them & I would rather be doing that now, instead I've got to use my opportunities & I am weary just thinking about it! Well we'll live thro' it."

After the election landslide, Eleanor wrote to her daughter Anna, "Darling, if he wanted to be King . . . they [would] fight for him." Emboldened by his victory, FDR grew imperious. He had long been furious at the "nine old men" of the Supreme Court who kept declaring New Deal programs unconstitutional and, in his view, thwarted the popular will in favor of big business. In the winter of 1937, consulting neither Eleanor nor his advisers, he demanded that Congress allow him to appoint an additional justice (up to a total of fifteen) for every sitting justice over seventy. Opponents dubbed his plan "packing the court," and Congress defeated it. Though the loss damaged both his power and prestige, the courts did rule more often in favor of his programs. Eleanor was appalled by his misjudgment.

# London

The Duke of York did not fully realize his predicament until Prime Minister Baldwin briefed him in late October after his return from Scotland. On November 16, 1936, after speaking to the prime minister, the king told his mother that he could not reign without Wallis as his wife. Queen Mary was stunned and furious. On November 17, King Edward told his brother he was prepared to abdicate and marry Wallis Simpson. The Duke of Windsor reported in his memoirs, "Bertie was so taken aback by the news that in his shy way he was unable to express his innermost feelings." But he had an immediate visceral reaction to the idea of being king: "Oh, he said, that's a dreadful thing to hear. None of us wants that, I least of all." The duke's stammer, which he had controlled, returned as he awaited his fate. He told his private secretary he felt "like the proverbial sheep being led to the slaughter." At the end of November as he returned to London's Euston Station after a brief trip to Scotland, he was "surprised and horrified" to see the *Daily Express* headline "The King's Marriage" blazoned on placards in bold letters. The duke's distaste for Wallis can be seen in his diaries for the dramatic week that followed; he could only refer to her as "Mrs. ———."

Meanwhile, Wallis, who had fled the country for France, offered the king advice. Impressed by the effectiveness of FDR's Fireside Chats, she suggested the king appeal directly to the nation. The British government adamantly opposed the king's plan for a broadcast—it was unconstitutional for the king to appeal above the head of the government to his people—so Edward dropped the idea. To his credit, the king acted with integrity; he would not be crowned with the intention of making a marriage that would subvert the Crown's connection with the Church of England and cause the government to resign.

Over the next four days, Bertie tried repeatedly to see the king, but David rebuffed him. He likely was buying time to review all of his options and mollify Wallis before making his decision absolute. Finally on December 7, the king telephoned Bertie and told him to visit him at his personal residence, Fort Belvedere, after dinner. In a burst of assertiveness, the duke said, "No, I will come and see you at once." Bertie later wrote in his diary, "The awful and ghastly suspense of waiting was over. I found him pacing up and down the room, and he told me his decision that he would go." Yet Bertie was still filled with admiration for his brother's dynamic personality. "Isn't he wonderful," he declared repeatedly the next night to a fellow dinner guest at the fort. Edward was still, to him, the "life and soul of the party." The duke went to Marlborough House, and in his mother's drawing room he "broke down and sobbed like a child." For her part, Elizabeth was deeply resentful of reports about her brother-in-law's relieved, even happy demeanor. David, who had caused everyone around him such agony, was, she said, "the one person it did not touch."

In what he called a "dreadful" and "never-to-be-forgotten" moment, the duke and his younger brothers watched as David signed the Instrument of Abdication at the fort. The next day in his abdication speech, King Edward VIII spoke of his brother's particular fitness to be king: "He has one matchless blessing, enjoyed by so many of you and not bestowed on me—a happy home with his wife and children." After the speech, the two brothers kissed, and David bowed to the new king, who would reign as George VI.

In the aftermath of the abdication the queen wrote to Cosmo Gordon Lang, the Archbishop of Canterbury, that: "We were so very unhappy over the loss of a dear brother—because one can only feel that exile from this country is death indeed. We were miserable, as you know, over his change of heart and character during the last few years and it is alarming how little in touch he was with ordinary human feeling—Alas! He had lost the common touch."

His family would never understand the choice David made. "You did not seem to be able to take in any other point of view but your own," his mother would write to him. "I do not think you ever realized the shock . . . you caused your family and the whole nation. It seemed inconceivable to those who had made such sacrifices during the war that you, as their King, refused a lesser sacrifice."

The two brothers hoped to find a way to coexist, but the rivalry between the two couples grew increasingly bitter as the year progressed. Partly in an attempt to preserve at least a thin thread of fraternal affection, David and Bertie would each blame the other's wife for much of the conflict between them. Goaded by Wallis, who thought that "the King's wife runs the King and the King's mother runs his wife," David believed that his younger brother never would have treated him so badly had it not been for Elizabeth's machinations. For his part, Bertie saw the evil wife behind his brother's every move. In truth, Wallis was continually prodding David with letters entreating him: "Don't be weak, don't be rude, be firm and make him ashamed of himself, if possible." She referred to the new king as "the puppet they"—the government—"have placed on the throne."

The former monarch resisted surrendering his psychological kingship. From his temporary exile in Austria, he barraged his brother with phone calls offering advice, which often contradicted the government's recommendations. David's meddling painfully undermined the confidence of the new king, who still considered his older brother to be smarter and more experienced than he. In late February, Bertie deputized their mutual confidant, attorney Walter Monckton, to order David to stop calling. Thereafter, they communicated through letters or through their various representatives. The king judiciously decided to give his brother the title Duke of Windsor. As a peer, David could not return to Britain and run for the House of Commons.

The two brothers soon were fighting over finances. Even as he lavished Wallis with gifts of antiques and extraordinary, glamorous jewels, the duke cried poverty. A few weeks before the coronation, by threatening to go public with family finances and with claims that the king had not given him a fair financial settlement, the duke tried to extract more money from his brother. David's intrigues came at a critical time for the king, who worried that the monarchy itself might "crumble under the shock and strain of the Abdication." The last thing the royal family needed was a financial scandal or undue attention paid to the former monarch. The king would have to negotiate shrewdly.

Franklin D. Roosevelt was returning from a cruise to South America when he heard that King Edward VIII had abdicated. FDR was stunned and dismayed. The king's departure would do nothing to stabilize European-American relations at a time of increasing danger. Germany and Japan, both countries now led by bellicose nationalist governments, had formally allied with one another at the end of November 1936. Communists were battling fascist forces backed by Hitler and Mussolini for control of Spain. Eleanor was so incensed about the destruction caused by Spain's civil war that she reconsidered her own pacifism. A year before, she had given a speech claiming that war was obsolete; now, in the face of fascist aggressions abroad and growing racial provocation at home, she declared there were times a country had to use force.

Roosevelt had been sure that Edward VIII would find a way to keep his throne. He said he was "disgusted" by the king's lack of guile and resourcefulness in resolving the conflict over his paramour. FDR knew how to keep government, respectability, and romance in their separate corners. Why hadn't the king forced the issue, FDR wondered, by going through with his coronation and later making Mrs. Simpson the "Duchess of Cornwall"? Kings had always kept mistresses. Scheduled to dine with British officials in Trinidad, FDR wrote to Eleanor on December 10, "Do I or do I not propose the 'health of the King'? Awful dilemma. It is however to be solved by good manners and not by State Dept. diplomatic protocol."

Eleanor was appalled. Like Queen Mary, Eleanor could not imagine giving up a sacred duty for the pursuit of personal happiness. Several years before, she had written Hick that of paramount value to her was "never any one person's happiness, it is that of the greatest number of people." It was important to remember that you are "damned unimportant." If happiness came of its own accord, you were fortunate, but you should not seek it for its own sake. Eleanor had undergone her own abdication crisis of sorts, giving up her romantic attachment to Hick in favor of her role as a wife and social advocate. When the king abdicated, she wrote Hick, "Well, and so—all is lost for love. Too bad he couldn't have served his people and had his love too!"

Hick, having given up her career for the woman she loved—who now had trouble fitting her into her schedule—thought the former king would suffer the same kind of anger and frustration she endured. "Poor little King!" she told Eleanor, presciently. "I wonder what he will do. . . . I'm sorry for Mrs. Simpson. She will have an awful job on her hands. . . . They can't go sailing around on yachts forever. I wonder if he won't be very bored and restless and unhappy. . . . I'm afraid he is in for some very bad times."

"I can hardly now believe that we have been called to this tremendous task," the new queen wrote the Archbishop of Canterbury. "And the curious thing is that we are not afraid. I feel that God has enabled us to face the situation calmly and although I at least feel most inadequate, we have been sustained during these last terrible days by many, many good friends."

"Dickie, this is absolutely terrible," the king wrote his cousin and friend Louis Mountbatten. "I'm quite unprepared for it. David has been trained for this all his life. I'm only a Naval officer—it is the only thing I know about." Mountbatten, a fellow naval officer, told him that "there is no finer training for a King," and predicted that Bertie would win the same kind of esteem and affection his father enjoyed. The new king called himself George VI to stress the continuity with his father's values, a first step in a long campaign to restore respect for the monarchy. He wrote Prime Minister Baldwin that he hoped that "time will be allowed me to make amends for what has happened." Bertie knew that his consort's charisma and character would be essential to the success of his reign. Addressing his privy council, the king emphasized that his reign would be a full partnership: "With my wife and helpmeet by my side, I take up the heavy burden which lies before me."

In the weeks before his coronation the king faced another hurdle: the reemergence of his stammer. In a speech to prelates at Buckingham Palace the king stammered badly, and he faltered wincingly during a luncheon speech to eight hundred Commonwealth dignitaries. "For a few terrible seconds there was dead silence as he could not get the words out," Chips Channon said. The Archbishop of Canterbury, Cosmo Lang, fueled anxieties about the king by declaring, "When his people listen to him they will note an occasional and momentary hesitation in his speech. But he has brought it under full control, and to those who hear it need cause no sort of embarrassment, for it causes none to him who speaks." The king was humiliated; his speech therapist, Lionel Logue, was exasperated. In the months before the coronation, rumors ran wild in London, particularly so in society and in the financial markets, that the king could not handle the stress of the coronation, that it would be shortened or canceled, that the new monarch would be a recluse, a puppet king unable to perform his duties. For Bertie and Elizabeth, the ceremony loomed as an enormous ordeal.

The new king was to be crowned on the same day—May 12—that his brother had chosen to be anointed King Edward VIII. That aborted coronation haunted him. It was an event his well-spoken, much-admired brother would have performed with ease. With the specter of his brother peering over his shoulder, the king practiced the speaking parts of the coronation and his talk to the nation with fanatical concentration. For all the participants, and for the country at large, the anxiety about the state of the monarchy—and the new monarch—created additional pressure to get everything right as a positive augury for the new reign. The king's biographer Sarah Bradford says of the coronation, "The actual ceremony was something of a case of the King keeping his head when all about him were losing theirs." The coronation would prove an extraordinary blend of sacred moments and farce.

The king recorded his own bemused account of the challenging day in his diary. Their Majesties were awakened at 3 A.M. by the testing of loudspeakers. Bands and troops arrived on the street outside at 5 A.M. The king could not even eat breakfast; he had a "sinking feeling inside." Exhausted and nerve-wracked, he found the long wait before the procession began excruciating. He left for Westminster Abbey in driving rain, but when he arrived, a ray of sunlight dashed through the dark clouds.

The queen's procession was held up when a chaplain fainted. During the ceremony, the Duke of Portland and the Marquess of Salisbury managed to get their Garter collars tangled in the fringe of the cushions on which they presented the crowns to the archbishop at the altar. At one point in the service, the Lord Chamberlain's hands shook so badly when he was dressing the king that he "nearly put the hilt of my sword under my chin trying to attach it to my belt," as the king explained. When the new monarch knelt at the altar to take the coronation oath, he was supported by two bishops, who were to hold the Order of Service before him so that he could read the oath. "When this great moment came neither Bishop could find the words, so the Archbishop held his book down for me to read, but horror of horrors his thumb covered the words of the Oath," the king remembered.

The most significant moments of the ceremony were almost disastrous. The king nearly fell down and the crown was almost put on the wrong way around. During the preparations for the coronation, he had been concerned that the seven-pound crown be placed correctly on his head. A small piece of red thread was put under the key jewels to guide the archbishop in placing the crown the right way forward. An "officious person" removed it, as the king would recall. The archbishop barely got it right. The final indignity occurred when the king rose from the ancient coronation chair to proceed to his throne. "I was brought up all standing, owing to one of the Bishops treading on my robe. I had to tell him to get off it pretty sharply as I nearly fell down."

Despite the tension and errors, the king felt spiritually transported during the ceremony. At the moment of his crowning, the peers shouted out "God Save the King" as they placed their coronets on their heads, trumpets sounded, and the guns of the Tower of London were fired. The Archbishop of Canterbury knelt in homage, followed by the princes of the royal blood and representatives of the orders of the peerage. Overcome with fatigue and with the religious fervor the event inspired, the king felt, as he later told the archbishop, that throughout "Some One Else was with him."

The queen, too, would say that the ceremony was transformational. Within a week of the event, Alan Campbell Don, chaplain and secretary to the Archbishop of Canterbury, would note that Their Majesties had "gained greatly in presence and dignity," and observed how easily the king met challenges placed before him: "It is as though the charisma of the Coronation had effected a deepening and enlightening of the inner man."

By the end of the day, the strain showed on the queen—she lost her voice—while the king prepared to address his people with steadying confidence. Speaking over the radio without any noticeable stammer, he said, "I cannot find words with which to thank you for your love and loyalty to the Queen and myself. I will only say this. If in the coming years I can show my gratitude in service to you, that is the way above all others that I should choose."

David and Wallis, staying at a borrowed chateau in Touraine, France, listened to the broadcast of what was supposed to have been his coronation. The Roosevelts, however, would be represented on coronation day by FDR's oldest son James and his wife Betsey, in spite of the fact it had been decided that no foreigners, other than members of official delegations, were to be seated in Westminster Abbey. Their presence attested to America's special relationship with Britain and to the Roosevelts' status as America's First Family, closely allied with the House of Windsor.

The following day, the new king and queen rode among the cheering crowds through the place that would become their reign's emotional and spiritual home: the East End of London. Later, during state visits to Scotland and Northern Ireland, they encountered greater enthusiasm than they expected—evidence of their growing popularity, and an enormous boost to the confidence of a man who had never wanted to be king.

Along with Franklin Roosevelt, Winston Churchill was among the very few who managed to maintain good relationships with both the king and the Duke of Windsor. Others felt they had to choose between kings new and old. Among them was the astute, socially ambitious Joseph Kennedy, the movie and real estate magnate, who was aiming to be named ambassador to England. Kennedy ordered his wife Rose not to accept an invitation by William Bullitt, the U.S. ambassador to Paris, to dinner with the Windsors. He did not want to be caught on the wrong side of the social divide.

Blindingly resentful of the cold shoulder he received from the British establishment, the Duke of Windsor could not fathom the depth of humiliation and anguish he had inflicted on his family, particularly on his mother. Her daughter-in-law Queen Elizabeth wrote to the politician Victor Cazalet that the abdication "very nearly killed poor Queen Mary . . . there is indeed such a thing as a broken heart and hers very nearly collapsed." Having endured the abdication with a stiff upper lip a few weeks before, the dowager queen retreated to her room for the entire period between Christmas and New Year's. On June 3 the following year, the duke added a final indignity to his treatment of his mother, choosing the late king's birthday to marry the woman his mother abhorred. For years Queen Mary could not bring herself to mention the duchess in letters to her eldest son.

David could not grasp that his relatives saw him as a toxic force that had almost extinguished the monarchy. The day before the wedding ceremony at the Chateau de Cande in France, the duke received from his brother King George VI one of history's most incendiary wedding presents: the Letters Patent stating that the king "was pleased to declare that the Duke of Windsor shall . . . be entitled to hold and enjoy for himself only the style and attribute of Royal Highness, so . . . that his wife and descendants, if any, shall not hold the . . . title." If the king had given Wallis the honorific "Royal Highness," she would possess it for life, even if she divorced his brother. The last thing the king and queen needed was a renegade Royal Highness. For the duke, this "damnable" wedding present was like a thrust below the belt in the duel between them. Wallis wrote, "Now we must protect WE"—their expression for Wallis and Edward as a couple. The Letters Patent incited a long-lasting and nerve-wracking war between the court in exile and the palace.

As close as the two brothers had been, there had always been tensions between them. Back in 1928, when George V had almost died of a severe bronchial infection while the Prince of Wales was in Africa, David overcame his initial reluctance to cut short his trip and hurried back to London. Later Bertie wrote to his brother, "There is a lovely story going about . . . that the reason for your rushing home is that in the event of anything happening to Papa I am going to bag the throne in your absence. Just like the Middle Ages!" Now that his formidable sibling, egged on by his scheming wife, was forming his own court in France, the new king did not feel secure. Ronald Lindsay, the British ambassador to Washington, observed that George VI was "like the medieval monarch who has a hated rival claimant living in exile . . . the situation operates on the King just as it must have done on his medieval ancestors—uneasiness about what is coming next—sensitiveness—suspicion." As late as the middle of 1939, the king talked constantly of his brother, according to the novelist Marie Belloc Lowndes. "It is as if he can't think of anything else; he seems haunted by him," she said.

In the fall of 1937, the duke began a campaign to reposition himself as a world figure and reclaim his former popularity. He announced plans to visit Canada and the United States to study international housing and labor problems. But first, without consulting the king, he undertook a tour in Germany. The king and queen watched in disbelief as the naive former king had tea with Hitler, dined with Rudolf Hess and Joachim von Ribbentrop in Berlin, and inspected the National Socialist Party headquarters at Nuremberg.

While he was in Berlin, the Duke of Windsor wrote to Ambassador Ronald Lindsay asking him to arrange a meeting with the Roosevelts. The thought of the Windsors in Washington on any kind of official visit filled Lindsay with "unmitigated horror." Lindsay, the king, and Foreign Secretary Anthony Eden wanted the duke neither to appear as a martyr snubbed by the United States on Britain's orders nor to gain credibility as an important representative of Britain. They decided that Lindsay would invite the Windsors to stay at the British embassy, host a small dinner party for them there, and ask the president to receive them. For his part, the president was eager to avoid doing anything that would embarrass the king or his government. FDR was also sensitive about the political implications of the Duke of Windsor's visit: he did not want to reject the former king, nor did he want to seem to endorse the Windsors after they had encouraged the increasingly menacing Nazi regime.

Fascinated with the Duke of Windsor's decision to give up his throne for love, FDR was interested in meeting the Windsors, but would have to wait because of the duke's association with Charles Bedaux, a French-American industrialist and supporter of fascism. Bedaux was willing to bankroll the duke's visit to promote the German cause, creating publicity that would position the duke to be a "Savior of the Monarchy" after a fascist takeover or a political upheaval. Reports circulated that the former king had also talked with representatives of the Labour Party and was positioning himself to become president of a future English republic.

Convinced by Bedaux that the American press would treat the duchess like royalty and thus enhance her status, and recalling his previous successes in the United States, the duke was keen to go. However, the couple's visit to Germany had tarnished their reputation; the Baltimore Federation of Labor protested the proposed visit so strongly that Bedaux backed out. The duke and duchess considered going on their own, but realized they had compromised themselves by their association with the Third Reich. The Duke of Windsor decided to lie back and wait for his opportunity. The king and queen monitored every move he made.

# 6

# Joining Forces

## JANUARY 1938–APRIL 1939

> We may not like pomp and ceremony . . . but there is a glamour
> for us about royalty.
>
> —*Eleanor Roosevelt in her "My Day" column*

## The United States

Given the seamless Anglo-American alliance of the twenty-first century,
it is hard to fathom how frayed British-American relations were in the
1930s. Americans, particularly in the heartland, felt hostile and suspicious
toward Britain. Many ethnic groups, including Irish Americans and Jews,
perceiving their place in the United States as tentative and uncertain, saw
the British as part of an elitist and class-conscious Europe they had come
to the United States to escape. Americans were offended by the British
reaction to the American-born Wallis Simpson; for them, Edward VIII's
abdication was the result of anti-American prejudice and snobbery. Even
traditional liberals were wary of British imperialism, resistant to the influence of an empire on which the sun never set. Americans viewed the
monarchy of King George V and Queen Mary as old-fashioned, rigid,
and arrogant—and not without reason. In fact, King George V was anti-
American; he had bragged that, during his naval service, he had actively
avoided entering the United States when he visited Niagara Falls: "The
nearest I ever got to the United States was when I half-walked across
Niagara, took off my hat and walked back again."

Americans were suspicious of foreign allegiances and entanglements of any kind, bitter about the costs and results of the last world war, and resentful about Britain's failure to pay war debts. The resulting isolationism was deeply entrenched in the United States of the 1930s, especially in the Midwest, where many mainland European immigrants had settled after fleeing monarchies and dictatorships. As late as March 1939, 77 percent of respondents in a Gallup poll said the United States should not send its army or navy to fight in a European war. In an April 1939 poll, 66 percent said that, in the advent of a war, the United States should not lend money to Britain or France to buy airplanes or war materials. The Munich Pact, the fall 1938 effort of Britain's prime minister Neville Chamberlain to appease Hitler by granting him the right to annex the German part of Czechoslovakia, would add to the American distaste for England. At a time when totalitarian governments were on the rise around the world, isolationists had a stranglehold on Congress. The influential *Chicago Tribune* was a bastion of isolationism and anti-British sentiment. The West Coast was less friendly to the British than were the Anglophiles of the East Coast.

In the mid-1930s the British Foreign Office, in concert with Sir Ronald Lindsay, the longtime British ambassador to Washington, began a determined but subtle campaign to win over American opinion and strengthen the alliance. For the European war they believed was likely, U.S. aid would be essential. Lindsay was an astute observer of the American political scene. He had served in Washington off and on since 1905, beginning as the embassy's second secretary and then serving for several periods as first secretary before his appointment as ambassador in 1930. His first wife was the daughter of a U.S. senator, and his second, Elizabeth Hoyt Lindsay, was a longtime friend of Eleanor Roosevelt.

Lindsay recognized that the United States was not ready for any formal political alliances that would bind them to Britain in case of war. He believed that economic agreements and public relations were the best route to solidifying Anglo-American relations. He told British foreign secretary Anthony Eden, "I hold that East and West and even the middle can be worked on through their emotions. The late King George broadcasting to his Empire, Mr. Baldwin's speech in the House on the abdication crisis, the Stratford Shakespeare Company, *Goodbye Mr. Chips* by Hilton, Noel Coward's film *Cavalcade*, the successes of

Great Britain, the calmness and dignity of her people, these are the things that move America." Lindsay cautioned against any direct attempts to promote positive perceptions of Britain in the United States. It was in this thorny context that negotiations would proceed very carefully about the possibility of a royal visit to the United States.

When Franklin Roosevelt first contacted King George VI to invite him to make a historic visit to the United States—the first visit ever by a reigning British monarch—he presented his appeal in personal terms: "I have had, as you know the great privilege of knowing your splendid father, and I have also known two of your brothers. Therefore I am greatly looking forward to the possibility of meeting you and the Queen." By invoking the Roosevelt connection with the Windsor family, FDR hoped to persuade the king that a meeting of the heads of what he considered to be two of the world's most prominent dynasties (the Roosevelts and the British royal family) was not only long overdue, but a natural culmination of their family histories.

The king's "splendid father" George V had never had any interest in visiting the United States, although he had spent time in Canada in the 1880s and in 1890 when he was posted to the North American and West Indies station on several occasions during his naval service. As king, George V was further annoyed with press reports during the visit of his eldest son David, Prince of Wales, in 1924 to the United States. The king worried about the effect of the brash and mercenary Americans on his son's already mercurial character. He was outraged at American headlines broadcasting David's late hours: "The Prince Gets In With the Milkman."

## Canada

The former Prince of Wales, now the Duke of Windsor, who had purchased a ranch in Alberta after his 1919 tour of Canada, remained widely popular there. Still distressed about what they saw as Edward VIII's forced abdication, the Canadian people felt a loyalty to the former king. His brother, King George VI, who was the first British monarch to have taken an oath at his coronation making him king of Canada, was largely unknown there. As signs of war were appearing in Europe, Canadians were increasingly feeling their own version of the isolationist sentiments rampant among their southern neighbors. In order to reaffirm the country's feelings for the monarchy and its ties to Britain, it made good sense for the mother country to introduce the new monarchs in person.

It was in the spring of 1937, as the coronation approached, that the Canadian governor-general Lord Tweedsmuir, also known as the writer John Buchan, first had suggested the idea of a royal tour of North America. When Canadian prime minister Mackenzie King attended the coronation ceremonies, he had presented the king and queen with an official invitation to visit his country. Bertie had happy memories of his tenure in Canada as a naval midshipman, and was eager to tour the country now that he was king, but only after his private secretary and the government ascertained an opportune time for the visit. The king was unsure when conditions in Europe would be stable enough to allow him to leave England. That spring, civil war was raging in Spain, and the German air force helped Spain's Generalissimo Francisco Franco bomb Guernica in Spain, much to the world's anxiety.

## Washington, D.C.

Prime Minister King had alerted his friend President Roosevelt about his offer of a royal tour, so that the president could also extend an invitation at the coronation through his representative, former diplomat James Gerard. At the end of 1937, Robert Bingham, a former newspaper editor who had been the U.S. ambassador to the Court of St. James's for four years, became so ill with Hodgkin's disease that he submitted his resignation. And there was one American who ached to be his successor and bring the United States and England closer—but on his own terms and to advance his own power.

The controversial Boston Irish tycoon Joseph Patrick Kennedy had angled for the job ever since FDR had thwarted his bid to become secretary of the Treasury. Kennedy was desperate to become the ambassador to Britain so that all of London's social doors—often closed to the Irish—would open for him, salving a lifetime of feeling like an outsider. The tall, redheaded, and dynamic Kennedy had made most of his money, sometimes in questionable ways, in the stock market, real estate, the movie business, and, allegedly, in bootlegging. A big contributor to the Democratic Party and a man who had his own presidential aspirations, Kennedy had become FDR's first chairman of the Securities and Exchange Commission, the board that regulated Wall Street—an appointment that has been likened to putting the wolf to work policing other wolves. Sending Kennedy to Europe would give FDR the opportunity to reward him for his support during the 1936 election and keep him from making trouble as the 1940 election approached. Roosevelt knew that Kennedy was wealthy enough to entertain the British in grand style, and was a shrewd bargainer who could facilitate the Anglo-American trade agreement currently in negotiation. As Michael Beschloss reports in his book *Kennedy & Roosevelt*, sending an Irishman to the Court of St. James's also "appealed to Roosevelt's weakness for the droll gesture and his Revolutionary War–vintage indignation over the imperiousness of British officials toward their American counterparts."

In their negotiations over this plum diplomatic post, the confident and manipulative president and the brash, socially ambitious, and fundamentally insecure Irishman continued the game of one-upmanship they had been playing ever since they had first tangled with each other in 1917, when FDR was assistant secretary of the navy, managing America's ship production during World War I, and Kennedy was the assistant manager of Bethlehem Steel's Fore River shipyard in Quincy, Massachusetts. FDR had unnerved Kennedy by sending in marines to forcibly tow away two battleships, ordered by the Argentine government, which Kennedy refused to release before Argentina paid for them. Now, when Kennedy came to the Oval Office to lobby for the job, Roosevelt submitted him to a humiliating interview in front of FDR's son James, which may have been revenge for Kennedy's mistreatment of James several years before, when Kennedy had used the president's son as bait in his bid for a liquor distributorship—an incident that would come to beleaguer them both. FDR promptly ambushed Kennedy by telling him to stand by the fireplace so he could get a better look at him. When Kennedy obliged, FDR said, "Would you mind taking your pants down?" Kennedy was shocked but, eager to please Roosevelt, he removed his suspenders, dropped his pants, and stood in his underwear before the president.

Roosevelt broke the awkward silence when he said, "Someone who saw you in a bathing suit once told me something I now know to be true. Joe, just look at your legs. You are about the most bowlegged man I have ever seen." The new ambassador would have to wear knee britches and silk stockings during the presentation of his credentials to the king at Buckingham Palace, Roosevelt explained. Then he threw his grenade: "When photos of our new Ambassador appear all over the world, we'll be a laughingstock. You're just not right for the job, Joe."

After Kennedy left, FDR had a good laugh with his son. The president thought that the appointment of the Irish Catholic Kennedy to the British court was "a great joke, the greatest joke in the world."

Kennedy was not to be outmatched by the president. He asked FDR to give him two weeks to convince the British government to allow him to wear a cutaway coat and striped pants to the ceremony. Kennedy did get an exemption, but only after FDR did what he had planned to do all along—appoint the man he had ridiculed to be ambassador to the Court of St. James's.

Because Kennedy bore a healthy skepticism toward the British, and was known to be blunt in offering his opinions, Roosevelt thought he could count on him to provide objective assessments of the situation in England. Yet while Roosevelt and Kennedy may have shared an initial desire to keep the United States out of involvement in Europe, FDR's position evolved, while Kennedy's did not. The new ambassador would become a staunch isolationist in the very position where Roosevelt needed someone to be realistic about the danger Hitler posed to the United States—and he would skew his reports to Roosevelt accordingly.

## London

Kennedy arrived in London in March 1938 and quickly set his public relations team to the task of promoting his handsome family and thus advancing his dynastic ambitions. The tabloid press raved about "America's nine-child envoy." Within days of his arrival, the aggressive and vigorous new ambassador made international headlines by shooting a hole in one on the second hole of the Stokes Poge golf course in Buckinghamshire. Then almost immediately afterward, Hitler invaded Austria and declared the Anschluss, the uniting of Austria with Germany. Kennedy's fear of losing both his sons and his fortune in a war, and his pessimism about England's capacity to defend itself against Germany, led him to proclaim himself against war at all costs. "Peace above all," as he put it, self-protectively.

The ambassador and his wife, Rose, spent the weekend of April 9 at Windsor Castle with the royal family, Prime Minister Chamberlain, the foreign secretary Lord Halifax, and their wives. Mrs. Kennedy called it "one of the most fabulous, fascinating events" of her life, and her husband told her, "Well, Rose, it's a hell of a long way from East Boston." After being greeted by the king and queen in the castle's magnificent Grand Reception Room, hung with Gobelin tapestries and furnished in the style of Louis XV, they proceeded to dinner in the Garter Throne Room, with its spectacular chandeliers and tables with centerpieces so tall that the king could barely see the queen across the flowers. Elizabeth was flanked by the ambassador on her right and the prime minister on her left. Rose Kennedy shared the king with Mrs. Chamberlain.

Conversing with the queen during dinner, Kennedy propounded the U.S. isolationist position about involvement in Europe's affairs. "What the American people fear more than anything else is being involved in another war," he told Elizabeth. "When they remember 1917 and how they went in to make the world safe for democracy and then they look now at the crop of dictatorships, quarrels, and miseries arising out of that war they say to themselves, 'Never again!' And I can't say I blame them. I feel the same way myself."

According to Kennedy's unpublished *Diplomatic Memoirs*, although the queen understood that American reluctance, she did not hesitate to declare Britain's position and challenge Kennedy: "But if we had the United States actively on our side, working with us, think how that would strengthen our position with the dictators."

Joe Kennedy did not let the queen's resistance to his anti-interventionist argument interfere with his plans for her. Kennedy reported that he saw in the queen a charm that never showed in photographs: "Fired by an idea, speaking rapidly, her face acquired a charming animation that never shows in photographs." Dazzled by her extraordinary charisma, Kennedy told Elizabeth that a visit by the king and queen would greatly improve Anglo-American relations. Not incidentally, knowing that Americans considered him one of the top candidates for the presidency in the 1940 elections, he knew a royal tour would advance his own prospects. As he put it to the queen that night, "You could charm them as you are charming me." He broached the same idea privately with the king. Their Majesties, who had long wanted to come to the United States, renewed their enthusiasm about the idea. The queen later told Kennedy, "I only know three Americans—you, Fred Astaire, and J. P. Morgan—and I would like to know more."

The next afternoon, on Palm Sunday, while out for a walk with the aristocratic Lord Halifax, Prime Minister Chamberlain and Ambassador Kennedy began to develop the intense bond between them that would lead both men into trouble. The dour Chamberlain and the ebullient Kennedy seemed an unlikely pair, yet they shared a loathing for war, having witnessed the devastation wreaked by World War I. Both were pessimistic about England's ability to win a war against the powerful German army and believed fervently in a policy of appeasement that minimized the evil intentions of the Nazis. As self-made businessmen who had risen above backgrounds about which they were extremely sensitive, they shared a common sensibility and became genuinely fond of each other. Neville Chamberlain and Winston Churchill were the two great forces in British politics in that era. Kennedy's affinity with Chamberlain rather than Churchill, who became aligned with Roosevelt, would ultimately cast Kennedy into the tragic role of outsider, the status he had spent his life trying to surmount.

## Canada

Meanwhile, Canada's governor-general Lord Tweedsmuir was working with Prime Minister King and President Roosevelt to avert the threat of war. Lord Tweedsmuir, a Scot and a devout monarchist, had a close affinity with the British aristocracy. His wife, the former Susan Grosvenor, was a cousin of the Duke of Westminster, whose substantial property portfolio included a large amount of London. Together they served as a very literary vice-regal couple in Canada. Susan wrote plays and novels; Tweedsmuir's classic suspense novel The Thirty Nine Steps (written under the pseudonym John Buchan) was turned into a film thriller by Alfred Hitchcock.

In his effort to shore up alliances, Lord Tweedsmuir vigorously argued the case for a royal Canadian tour. As he told his sister, "I pressed it with the persistence of a horse-leech." He lobbied Chamberlain to agree that the official visit could occur unless war became imminent. War indeed seemed a near-immediate possibility. After Germany invaded Austria in the spring of 1938, England began preparing for war; gas masks were issued to children and Parliament funded the building of air-raid shelters. When the summer brought no further escalations of tensions, Chamberlain made the royal tour a priority once more. By the time President Roosevelt visited Canada in August 1938 for the dedication of the International Bridge at the Thousand Islands, connecting the United States and Canada on the eastern shores of Lake Ontario, Prime Minister King was able to assure his old friend that the king and queen would most likely visit Canada the next year.

## Washington, D.C.

Roosevelt, ever the master of persuasion, added his own voice to those urging a North American royal visit. Right after he returned to Washington, FDR sent a personal letter to the king. This friendly, informal missive was in fact historic; it initiated the first ongoing correspondence between a U.S. president and a British monarch: "I need not assure you that it would give my wife and I the greatest pleasure to see you," Roosevelt told George, "and, frankly, I think it would be an excellent thing for Anglo-American relations if you could visit the United States."

Roosevelt's most immediate personal goal for the trip was to entertain the king and queen in Hyde Park, where they could talk without the political pressures and intense scrutiny of Washington. As a closet royalist and a comfortable longtime member of the American aristocracy—for all his populist policies—Roosevelt felt entitled to host the king and enjoy the patrician validation a visit would confer. In addition to the public relations benefits a private visit would offer him, he hoped that entertaining Their Majesties at Hyde Park would dispel public fears about a formal Anglo-American alliance. Wanting enough private time with the king to deploy his charm and forge a close bond, he played up the personal benefits to the royal family of a visit to his Hudson River estate: "It occurs to me that a Canadian trip would be crowded with formalities and that you might like three or four days of very simple country life at Hyde Park—with no formal entertainments and an opportunity to get a bit of rest and relaxation." However, he underestimated Bertie's sense of duty and appetite for new experiences in attempting to influence the king's opinion by putting Washington in the worst light. Roosevelt focused on the summer heat, the necessity of being received by and addressing Congress, and the formalities the king would encounter, but he shrewdly left it to the king to decide whether he wanted to tackle a visit to the capital city.

The importance of the royal visit to Roosevelt is evident in the U.S. president's willingness to honor the king's preferences. Displaying a determinedly casual, American-style hospitality, FDR wrote: "There would probably be great pressure for you to be received by the Congress. You and I are fully aware of the demands of the Protocol people, but, having had much experience with them I am inclined to think that you and Her Majesty should do very much as you personally want to do—and I will see to it over here that your decision becomes the right decision." The most historic aspect of this letter is that a U.S. president was offering to accommodate himself to the will of the king. This kind of ingratiation was possible only for a president who felt very secure in his sense of equality with a monarch. As a postscript to the letter, Roosevelt emphasized the connection between the two families: "I forgot to mention that if you bring either or both of your children with you, they will also be very welcome, and I shall try to have one or two Roosevelts of approximately the same age to play with them!"

In her memoirs Eleanor clarified the president's political and diplomatic motivations: "Believing that we all might soon be engaged in a life and death struggle, in which Great Britain would be our first line of defense, he hoped that the visit would create a bond of friendship between our two countries. He knew that, although there is always in this country a certain amount of criticism and superficial ill-feeling toward the British, in time of danger something deeper comes to the surface, and the British and we stand firmly together, with confidence in our common heritage and ideas. The visit of the king and queen, he hoped, would be a reminder of this deep bond." Although Eleanor, more the true populist than her husband ever was, had never been comfortable with the concept of royalty, she held great affection for Great Britain. Her commitment to building relationships, which would bolster the prospects for world peace, far outweighed her personal prejudices and discomforts.

## London

Ambassador Kennedy called on the king bearing the sealed letter of invitation from the president. The king read it aloud to Kennedy, who did not know the contents beforehand. Having already presented himself to the British as the mastermind of the royal visit to the United States, the ambassador was annoyed and embarrassed that he had not been privy to the proposal before the king saw it. As usual, Kennedy regrouped quickly and made a plan to get back into the center of the action. The ambassador petitioned the State Department for the right to accompany the king and queen as their personal guide on the trip to the United States. He realized that the visit would be a public relations gold mine and hoped to bask in the spectacular publicity and popular enthusiasm such a visit would engender. He was turned down.

The king had received FDR's extraordinary letter just as the crisis over Czechoslovakia peaked. On September 12, 1938, at a mass rally in Nuremberg, Adolf Hitler demanded immediate justice for the German-speaking people in Czechoslovakia's Sudetenland. Hitler claimed the province had been unjustly cut off from the German Reich by the Treaty of Versailles after World War I. By the end of the month, British prime minister Neville Chamberlain, famously dressed in black and carrying a black umbrella, met with Hitler in Munich for thirteen exhausting hours. He gave in to all of Hitler's demands and returned home saying that he had brought "peace with honor," "peace in our time." Winston Churchill, long exiled from the British cabinet by both Chamberlain and his predecessors for his confrontational and imperialist attitudes, stood up in the House of Commons the next day to decry the Munich Pact: "We have sustained a total, unmitigated defeat."

The king did not have time to answer the president's letter until October 8, after the crisis had passed. After conferring with his ministers about the U.S. offer, he wrote the president that his invitation "came as a pleasant relief at a time of great anxiety," and assured him "that the pleasure, which it would . . . give us personally, would be greatly enhanced by the thought that it was contributing in any way to the cordiality of relations between our two countries." He wanted to wait until the plans for his Canadian tour were more evolved before setting a definite agenda for the visit to the United States. He added, "I am afraid that we shall not be taking the children with us if we go to Canada, as they are much too young for so strenuous a tour." In ending the letter, he thanked Roosevelt for his interventions with Hitler and the Czech president in the recent crisis: "I have little doubt that they contributed largely to the preservation of peace."

Ambassador Joseph Kennedy wrote Secretary of State Cordell Hull that the king was "deeply touched" by the president's invitation. Because the president was handling all of the arrangements on his own, Kennedy complained to Hull that he was made to look like "a dummy." Protesting to the president that his talents were being wasted, he wrote that he felt like a "glorified errand boy." He feared that his prestige and influence would suffer. Throughout his life, Kennedy would polarize people. In London he was admitted to all the fashionable clubs and social gatherings, but he also damaged his reputation among some of the British aristocracy with his brash, self-aggrandizing behavior. Lord Francis Williams claimed that Kennedy had "all the disagreeable traits of rich men without any of their virtues."

Interior Secretary Harold Ickes, after conferring with the outspoken M.P. Sir Josiah Wedgwood, of the Wedgwood china family, about Kennedy, wrote in his diary, "At a time when we should be sending the best we have to Great Britain, we have not done so. We have sent a rich man, untrained in diplomacy, unlearned in history and politics, who is a great publicity-seeker and who is apparently ambitious to become the first Catholic President of the United States." In fairness to Kennedy, the musty British establishment wasn't about to be generous to a self-made Irish Catholic American even if he did look good in breeches. Lacking diplomatic skill and a depth of historical understanding, Kennedy was unprepared for the job. At that extraordinary moment in history, the role of ambassador required a talent for diplomatic nuance and a generous vision, qualities that were not in Kennedy's character.

Time and again, Kennedy misjudged crucial situations. Just before Hitler invaded Austria, Kennedy cabled Roosevelt that he was only bluffing. Roosevelt was increasingly irritated by Kennedy's bad judgment about the Nazis and his staunch support for Chamberlain's appeasement policies. As a consequence Joe Kennedy was soon thoroughly marginalized during the negotiations over the royal visit. Kennedy professed his loyalty to the president while denouncing him in London's drawing rooms. The president, in his genially duplicitous way, mollified Kennedy by writing him that he himself was conducting the negotiations personally, since they were in the "preliminary stage." In fact, the sensitive international implications of the trip led to an unprecedented degree of planning that involved almost everyone but Kennedy. Suggesting the enormous importance of the event, top officials at the State Department and the British Foreign Ministry worked for a whole year with the Canadian prime minister, the British ambassador to the United States, the king's private secretary, the president, and the king, to plan a four-day trip to the United States that would include a stay at the White House, a meeting with all the members of Congress, and visits to the World's Fair in New York City and the president's home in Hyde Park.

## Washington, D.C.

With the distance of more than six decades, it is difficult now to imagine the crucial importance the 1939 royal visit assumed in the public and political imagination. From the perspective of the twenty-first century, a royal visit to the United States almost seems ordinary. Queen Elizabeth II has made state visits in almost every decade since the 1950s. Her participation in the 1976 bicentennial events in New York, Virginia, and Washington was a significant part of the celebrations. In the 1990s, the late Princess of Wales seemed to turn up in the United States every couple of months, whether she was touring Disney World, rafting in Colorado, auctioning dresses, accepting awards in New York, or visiting powerful friends in Washington, D.C. Prince Charles plays polo in Florida, stays in private homes in Charleston, South Carolina, and other places, and visits presidents at the White House. But sixty years ago, a visit by the reigning monarchs was a spectacular event possessed of enormous international ramifications—suggesting that the stable, constitutional monarchies could implicitly fortify democracies against totalitarian governments, which were emerging around the world. When Americans were asked, in a Gallup poll in December 1939, which news events of that year most interested them, the visit of the king and queen placed fifth after the declaration of war in Europe, the conquest of Poland, the repeal of the arms embargo, and the attempt on Hitler's life, but ahead of Germany's seizure of all Czechoslovakia.

The historian Arthur Schlesinger Jr. has described the way that in the late 1930s democracy was on the defensive: "The democratic hope had been in retreat ever since the Great War of 1914–1918 shattered old structures of security and unleashed angry energies of revolution . . . against democracy: Bolshevism in Russia, Fascism in Italy, Nazism in Germany." Twelve year later, the Depression further strained democratic nations. "Democracy . . . could secure neither international order nor domestic prosperity. . . . The impotence of the democratic regimes before mass unemployment seemed to verify the fascist claim that parliamentary methods were bankrupt. Meanwhile the millennial creeds of Fascism, Nazism, Communism promised a new heaven and earth. The totalitarian gospel appealed to the fears of the rich, to the frustrations of the lower middle class, to the yearnings of the workers, to the illusions of the intellectuals."

President Roosevelt had long been concerned about both the lack of confidence in democracy and the inevitability of war in Europe. From the time Hitler took power in Germany, FDR had considered him a direct threat to the United States. Most Americans did not share his prescience: they believed fascism could overtake Europe without threatening the United States. With the aim of building alliances that could further combat totalitarian governments, Roosevelt encouraged any royal head of state he could to visit and get to know him. As Eleanor pointed out in her memoirs, "He wanted to make contacts with those he hoped would preserve and adhere to democracy and prove to be allies against fascism when the conflict came."

## Hyde Park

The Roosevelts' preparations for the British royal visit began in the summer of 1938, when they entertained Scandinavian royalty who were relatives of the British king and queen. Crown Princess Louise of Sweden was a great-granddaughter of Queen Victoria; her nephew Philip would later marry George VI's daughter Princess Elizabeth. The cultured crown princess and her progressive and scholarly husband Crown Prince Gustav Adolf arrived in Hyde Park for a weekend visit on July 1, 1938. Gustav Adolf, fascinated by politics, history, and gardening, had much to talk about with Roosevelt. His passionate interest in Chinese antiquities gave him a bond with Sara Roosevelt, who prized her family's collection of Chinese porcelains.

Writing to her friend Hick, Eleanor suggested the whirlwind character of a royal weekend visit: "We drove them around then a dinner & movie & the picnic, hot dogs & all was a success yesterday & then they left." The pattern was now set for royal visits: dinner at the Big House and a picnic at a cottage on the estate. Eleanor liked the Swedish couple, whom she found to be "nice & simple," but she did not envy them. "Lord it must be awful to be royalty. They gave everyone presents & how do you suppose one manages to travel with so many?"

## London

In his speech opening Parliament in early November 1938, the king announced that Their Majesties would visit the United States. Writing to accept the president's invitation, he committed to a four-day visit. The king's letter crossed in the mail with the president's second personal letter. Roosevelt wrote to the king that "to the American people the essential democracy of yourself and the Queen makes the greatest appeal of all." He pressed his case for the stay at Hyde Park by saying that "the simplicity and naturalness of such a visit would produce a most excellent effect." However, the British Foreign Office received criticism about a visit to Hyde Park, including a letter from the wife of the previous British ambassador, Lady Reading, warning the British foreign secretary about the Big House: "I am one of the few English people who have stayed at Hyde Park. . . . It is a dismal small house, extremely badly run and most uncomfortable. I shiver to think of what would happen if the King and Queen went to stay there."

Thus ensued a complex tug-of-war between the British ambassador, the British Foreign Office, and the president over the appropriateness and diplomatic usefulness of a stay at Roosevelt's "dismal small house." Ambassador Lindsay was concerned that the president was pushing Hyde Park at the expense of Washington and New York City. He feared politicians and regional groups would be incensed by Roosevelt's co-opting of the king. In his view, "New York ought to be made secondary to Washington; but Hyde Park . . . secondary or even incidental to New York."

In planning the visit, the president met with Ambassador Lindsay to discuss possibilities for the king's U.S. schedule. The ambassador convinced the president that Washington should be an integral part of

the plan, but Roosevelt was annoyed that Lindsay's subsequent memorandum to the British Foreign Office did not mention Hyde Park. "I
think that Lindsay should not call the visit to Washington the princi-
pal part of the plan," Roosevelt wrote directly to the king. "I say this to
you quite frankly because he does not even refer to your coming to stay
with me at Hyde Park."

Both British and American diplomats carefully weighed every
aspect of the visit for its potential political perils and benefits. Lindsay
pushed Chicago as a stop because the king could allay the intense anti-
British and isolationist sentiment in that city and in the Midwest, while
Roosevelt was "not in the least bit insistent on it." With some reluctance it was later dropped from the schedule because it would interfere
with the royal couple's Canadian plans.

The palace initially feared that a visit to the World's Fair in New
York City would give the tinge of commercial endorsement to the trip.
Lindsay recommended a brief visit despite concern that the fair was
being "rather vulgarized by over-advertisement." New York City's traditional ticker tape parade for visiting dignitaries was thought by
Lindsay to be "too much cheapened to be suitable for reigning monarchs." Concerned about security, Roosevelt agreed; he did not want
the king to ride through New York's "narrow, crowded streets." FDR
did suggest, however, a visit to a cultural institution in the city.

The king requested a visit to Columbia University, which had been
founded in colonial times as King's College. Because Bertie detested
the idea of an honorary degree, the chief of the State Department's
Division of Protocol wrote to the president of Columbia University to
suggest that the king be presented a book or "whatever you wish
except an honorary degree." He also made clear that the king should
not be asked to speak. He added that "if any talking pictures are taken,
the President suggests that you and the king move your lips but that
the king should not speak." The king asked to be excused from the
ordeal of addressing Congress, giving the official reason that he did not
wish to set a precedent of having to address foreign governmental bodies while on tours. Personally, the king did not want to face stammering before such an august body.

It was important for the king to reciprocate the White House state
dinner by hosting the president at the British embassy. Roosevelt was
reluctant to dine at the embassy because he would then have to wear his

painful leg braces, standing to greet guests, for two days in a row. However, when he sensed how important this was to the king, he gave in and decided that, to preserve his own energy, he would not accompany Their Majesties to New York City and instead take a day of rest before meeting them at Hyde Park.

## Washington, D.C.

Both sides took great care to assure the American people that the royal trip was not motivated by an attempt to achieve political advantage. In their public pronouncements, President Roosevelt and Ambassador Lindsay pretended there would be no substantive political agenda, despite their private intention to shore up the Anglo-American alliance in the face of the European and Asian challenges to democracy. As they concealed the true political nature of the trip, they questioned whether to include the British foreign secretary, Lord Halifax, on the visit to the United States. Lord Halifax was eager to have discussions with the president and Secretary of State Hull, but he was aware that his presence might be interpreted by isolationists as evidence that Britain and the United States were forging a formal alliance. Both Tweedsmuir and Lindsay argued successfully that the foreign secretary should not be included.

Roosevelt suggested Canadian prime minister Mackenzie King travel with the royal party to the United States as the monarch's minister in attendance. As a friend of the president, the prime minister had made frequent visits to Washington; he was a less threatening alternative to Lord Halifax, whom the king at first had wanted at his side. After campaigning tirelessly by letter to all the key players to ensure that the king should not "cast him aside at the frontier like an old boot," the Canadian prime minister won his invitation to Washington. George VI wanted the American people to see his visit as a friendly, historic reconciliation, without stirring suspicions that a secret deal was brewing.

For the most part, the American press responded favorably to the announcement of the visit. Not surprisingly, the *Chicago Tribune* was hostile and the Hearst newspapers were not enthusiastic. Putting aside her own reservations about royalty and hoping to encourage Americans to welcome Their Majesties' visit, Eleanor declared in her "My Day" column: "We may not like pomp and ceremony and we may approve of democracy in our government and in our everyday lives, but there is a glamour for us about royalty in other nations." She explained how our "English cousins" savored America's "pride with which a small boy feels in showing off his older brother." Even though many European nations still looked upon the United States as a juvenile nation, she thought that the country had "outgrown our elders," just as a "younger brother frequently outdistances the elder whom he has admired and looked up to." Eleanor emphasized the United States' ascendance because she was well aware that Americans were still afraid that Britain—their strong mother country—might have power over them.

## London

On March 31, 1939, Britain announced plans to go to war if Germany invaded Poland. This long-deferred stand against totalitarian Germany exacerbated the high tensions in London. It was not clear, by any means, that the king and queen would be able to make the trip, now set for late spring. Nonetheless, that April, James Roosevelt, who had recently taken a job in the movie business under Samuel Goldwyn and Louis B. Mayer, went to England in conjunction with the overseas promotion of the movie *Wuthering Heights.* His father had asked him to help arrange details for the upcoming visit of the king and queen.

James, tall, slender, and prematurely balding, was the most self-effacing of the Roosevelt sons. Eager to please and easily upset by emotional conflict, he did not handle well the role of crown prince assigned him by the media. His lack of political instincts repeatedly led him into trouble, both in his business affairs and his political associations. He had been manipulated by Boston's powerful mayor, James Michael Curley, and Joe Kennedy. Kennedy had paid for James and his wife Betsey to go to England with him several years earlier. Parading James in front of Haig & Haig distillers in London, Kennedy had suggested he had the president's endorsement for his efforts to get a liquor distribution for the United States. Once he had the contracts, he did not make James a partner, although James later denied there was an agreement, and Kennedy kept most of the money for himself. On another occasion James made such large commissions in the insurance business that FDR grew alarmed about the political consequences and squashed his son's career. After a period of exile during which he managed the farms at Hyde Park, James came to Washington to serve as a presidential assistant in 1937. However, he soon developed such painful stomach ulcers that it took him two hours to get up every morning. He lasted in the job for less than two years before going off to Hollywood.

When James arrived in England as his father's emissary, Ambassador Kennedy arranged for him to spend a weekend with the king and queen at Windsor Castle. In the careless spirit of the Roosevelt children, James managed to violate protocol repeatedly. He had been carefully coached to bow when he met the king and queen. He forgot and extended his hand. Naturally, Their Majesties overlooked his gaffe and shook hands. At dinner he forgot he was supposed to finish everything on his plate before the next course was served. He was so busy talking to the queen, on whose right he was seated, that he only had a few spoonfuls of soup. Everyone else had already been served their fish dish. The queen rescued him by signaling her butlers to bring him the next course.

After dinner, James went to Ambassador Kennedy's suite for further talks with the older man. At two-thirty in the morning he got lost on the way back to his room. As he wrote in his memoirs, "I hadn't the faintest idea where *my* suite was located! I almost panicked—what if I should open the wrong door and walk in on the sleeping King or Queen?" Fortunately, he found a guard, who looked like a "fugitive from a Gilbert and Sullivan operetta." James was shown to his room, where he took a piece of stationery bearing the royal crest, and wrote a letter to his father: "Dear Pa: It's a little larger than the White House but the beds are no longer." James claimed that FDR laughed "uproariously" when he recounted his breaches of protocol. His bumbling would have appealed to FDR's ambivalent attitude toward royalty.

## Washington, D.C.

As the U.S. and British governments negotiated the terms of the royal visit, the American people—who had gotten better acquainted with the king and queen during the abdication crisis—were presented with contradictory pictures of the royal couple. Echoing America's competing desires to embrace and rebuff the king and queen, some newspaper and magazine articles humanized them and made them seem, if not regular Joes, then approachable royalty, while other articles still seemed to be angry over George III's behavior toward his American colonies.

In a story about Their Majesties in the *Saturday Evening Post*, American readers learned that "Bert" and "Betty" liked to eat "beef and mashed potatoes" and have London water for their brewing tea. The queen, they were told, loved biographies and novels, while the king read detective stories and mysteries. This profile was benign compared to a widely publicized *Scribner's* magazine article, which horrified the palace. The February 1939 feature, entitled "Selling George VI to the U.S.," portrayed the king and queen in the worst possible light. The article focused on the king's speech impediment and passed on the rumor that he suffered from epilepsy (the king's youngest brother Prince John, who died as a teenager, did have epilepsy). While the author warned that the success of the state visit "will be the difference between the success and failure of British-American relations during the next critical international period," he suggested that the king and queen were not up to the job: "If a public relations counsel had the power to choose from scratch which British personalities he would drop into the American scene for the greatest British profit, they would not have been King George and Queen Elizabeth. The important fact about the United States is that a large part of the country still believes that Edward, Duke of Windsor, is the rightful owner of the British throne, and that King George VI is a colorless, weak personality largely on probation in the public mind of Great Britain, as well as for the United States."

The author attacked the queen in the cruelest way possible. He zeroed in on her weight, her most vulnerable spot, and contrasted her negatively with the Duchess of Windsor: "As for Queen Elizabeth, by Park Avenue standards, she appears to be far too plump of figure, too dowdy in dress to meet American specifications of a reigning Queen. The living contrasts of Queen Mary (as regal a woman as can be) and the Duchess of Windsor (chic and charmingly American) certainly does not help Elizabeth."

Those were fighting words. Josef Israels II, the author of this derisive article, did the royal couple a favor. By throwing down the gauntlet, he helped to stiffen the will of the "weak" king and the "dowdy" queen. They committed themselves fully to making a brilliant success of their trip to the United States. The queen had watched what she ate for six weeks before her state visit to Paris, but she would diet for six full months before coming to North America. "Bertie" and "Betty" were determined to astound their critics—and win America to Britain's side.

# 7

# A Genius for Publicity

MAY 1–JUNE 7, 1939

There must be no more high-hat business . . . the feeling that certain things could not be done.

—*King George VI to an adviser*

## The United States

As May began, the Roosevelts accelerated their preparations for the king and queen's visit. FDR pressed Congress for legislation allowing him to ship arms to Britain, and the Roosevelts were hosts for two other royal visits to the Big House in Hyde Park. Eleanor, with her populist values and her lifelong insecurities, found royal entertaining stressful. Before her guests arrived, she wrote Hick that she would soon have the "Norwegians and Danes on our hands." After the Norwegians left she sighed, "One is over."

Crown Prince Olav and Crown Princess Märtha of Norway spent the first weekend of May 1939 at Springwood. Their visit served as a dress rehearsal for the king and queen's upcoming stay. Princess Märtha was tall and lively with an attractive face and high cheekbones. The president was instantly drawn in by her flirtatious manner, and when she asked him his opinion about a speech Hitler had given that morning, even though he had avoided commenting to the press all day, he told her that Hitler "had left the door open an inch." Their interchange made the next day's headlines.

Of the Norwegian royal couple, Eleanor commented, "They are nice young people but how bored they must be" with all their public duties. Later Eleanor would learn what mischief could be born of boredom. After it became too dangerous to remain in hiding in Norway under Nazi rule, Princess Märtha came to live at the White House with her children. She became so close to FDR, and played up to him in such an adoring, flirtatious way, that both Eleanor and his mistress Missy LeHand became jealous.

In what would become Eleanor and Franklin's protocol for entertaining royalty, Crown Prince Olav and Crown Princess Märtha were served Saturday dinner at the Big House and a picnic on Sunday afternoon at Top Cottage that was followed by entertainment, in this case featuring the Roosevelts' Norwegian neighbors singing and dancing on a stage erected in front of the cottage. Eleanor "worked like a dog over the picnic." The Roosevelts' Norwegian neighbor Nellie Johannesen, who would later cook for the world-famous hot dog picnic for King George and Queen Elizabeth, made Norwegian dishes. Afterward, the two couples went to the Astors' estate up the road for tea.

Right after the Norwegians left, Crown Prince Frederick and Crown Princess Ingrid of Denmark arrived at Hyde Park, as part of a visit to the Danish exhibit at the World's Fair. The elegant Ingrid, another great-granddaughter of Queen Victoria, was practical and sports-loving, but she also appreciated opera, books, furniture, and fashion. Her handsome, easygoing husband was a man of simple tastes, with interests in music, mechanics, and the navy. The Roosevelts were disappointed that he was more interested in talking about his vacation than in discussing the dangers of Nazism. Eleanor declared the first evening of their stay pleasant enough, but she wrote Hick she was already looking forward to the visit's end: "a day tomorrow & [the] 2 visits are over!" Her final verdict on both royal couples was that they "are all nice, simple young people & one can't help liking them."

## London and at Sea

While the Roosevelts were entertaining royalty in the United States, the Kennedys held their first dinner party for the king and queen at the ambassador's residence in London. Two days before their departure, Their Majesties were treated to a full American evening as a warm-up for their visit to North America. Rose Kennedy went overboard to win over the king and queen. She served an all-American menu including both Virginia ham and shad roe, which she imported. The flowers and strawberries were flown in from Paris. To make an impression on Their Majesties, Rose seated her six youngest children at a small table in the dining room in full view of the royal couple. There was much talk about the upcoming trip, and the king and queen spoke privately with select American guests for further briefing. The entertainment included a couple of Walt Disney films, and the queen had "a little weep" during *Goodbye, Mr. Chips.*

With Hitler making it increasingly clear that his territorial ambitions went beyond the German part of Czechoslovakia, the king was reluctant to depart the country. "I hate leaving here with the situation as it is," he wrote his mother. His advisers convinced him that war was not imminent and the trip was vital; he could best serve the British cause by strengthening ties with North America. During his absence, a Council of State—whose members included not only the queen, but the king's brothers the Duke of Gloucester and the Duke of Kent, and his sister Princess Mary, who served as regents—could act, if necessary, on his behalf.

Queen Mary and the two princesses traveled with the king and queen to Portsmouth on May 6, 1939, to see them board the old German-built liner *Empress of Australia,* which had been handed over to Britain by Germany as part of the defeated nation's reparations after the First World War. Thirteen-year-old Princess Elizabeth looked after her nine-year-old sister Princess Margaret, who began to cry as the ship departed. As Queen Mary waved her handkerchief, Princess Margaret searched for hers. Princess Elizabeth told her "to wave, not to cry."

Their Majesties had similar mixed emotions. Unhappy at leaving their children behind, they knew they were facing a series of formidable obstacles and risks. Crossing the ocean, they might encounter icebergs or be intercepted by Nazis, who were rumored to want to hold the royal couple hostage. They were uneasy about visiting countries with isolationist and antimonarchist sentiments. The task of winning support for Britain would be delicate and difficult. Yet the king and queen embraced both the political and historic significance of their visit and were motivated not only by duty but by personal curiosity.

Bertie was eager to introduce Elizabeth to Canada, and both of them had long been fascinated by the United States. As one hundred thousand people looked on, two cruisers escorted the *Empress of Australia* out to sea.

During the trip, the king and queen and their entourage of thirty received an unexpected respite. The voyage to Quebec was supposed to take seven days, but soon the ship encountered treacherous conditions, lengthening the journey by two days. The northern ice fields extended farther south into the Atlantic than usual, and the ship had to maneuver through them in dense fog. Writing to Queen Mary, Queen Elizabeth captured the drama of the crossing: "For three & a half days we only moved a few miles. The fog was so thick, that it was like a white cloud round the ship, and the fog horn blew incessantly. Its melancholy blasts were echoed by the icebergs like the twang of a piece of wire. Incredibly eery, and really very alarming. . . . We very nearly hit a berg the day before yesterday, and the poor Captain was nearly demented because some kind cheerful people kept on reminding him that it was about here that the Titanic was struck, & *just* about the same date!" The presence on board of a survivor of the April 1912 *Titanic* disaster did nothing to reassure the voyagers.

On their fourth day at sea, they faced a more familiar obstacle. The Duke of Windsor chose the time when the king was virtually incommunicado to seek attention for himself. Broadcasting to America from Verdun on the anniversary of the World War I battle fought there, he appealed for world peace, but appeared to favor appeasement of dictators. The duke justified his speech by claiming that only U.S. intervention could avert Europe's plunge toward a disastrous war. This speech, made without warning to his brother, was the kind of one-upmanship that the king and queen feared. Yet the duke's effort at international relations and Machiavellian manipulation failed badly. He was widely perceived as irresponsible, an embarrassment to himself. The king must have been furious, but he made no comments for the public record.

The Americans were well aware that the former Edward VIII was an international loose cannon. While Bertie and Elizabeth were en route to Quebec, the U.S. ambassador to Paris, William Bullitt, wrote a secret memorandum to Washington cautioning the president not to bring up the duke and duchess, as "brotherly love . . . was not at fever heat." For his part, the Duke of Windsor had written to Queen Mary that he could have no further relationship with the king because "Bertie had behaved toward him in such an ungentlemanly way because of 'the influence of that common little woman.'" His sister-in-law lacked the elegance required of a queen, the duke implied, in contrast to his chic duchess, who deserved royal treatment. The Duke of Windsor's slur against Elizabeth was motivated by his fury over her role in denying the Duchess of Windsor the title of Her Royal Highness, and for her steadfast efforts to keep the couple out of Britain. Moreover, David believed that the king had acted on orders from the queen in refusing to support his efforts to play a significant role in Britain's international relations.

Preoccupied with the wrongs and slights he felt he had endured, the duke ignored his own contribution to his enforced exile. Both the duke and duchess had showed bad judgment in visiting Germany and appearing to support Hitler, and also in constantly haranguing his younger brother with demands. The queen was determined that the Duke of Windsor would not have the opportunity to outshine his brother, as he had during his years as Prince of Wales, and thus further undermine the monarchy. As King George struggled to gain the confidence to lead the British Empire, he did not need a charismatic rival. Although he was friendly with the Duke and Duchess of Windsor, FDR knew better than even to mention them to Their Majesties, lest he undo his singular diplomatic feat of keeping active friendships with both.

When the king finally disembarked in Quebec, he wrote to his mother to assure her that he had arrived safely and rested: "Last Sunday when the fog cleared we spent the whole day in loose clumps of ice, & in the afternoon we had to push our way through a quarter of a mile of quite thick and solid ice." He told her that the extra respite was good for him but "I should not however have chosen an ice field surrounded by dense fog in which to have a holiday, but it does seem the only place for me to rest nowadays!"

With extended coverage in British, Canadian, and American papers, the drama of the ship's dangerous journey increased public anticipation of the tour. From May 14 to May 20, the *New York Times* gave daily front-page headlines to the ship's progress: "Reception to King Postponed A Day As Fog Holds Ship"; "King Is Now Due To Arrive in Quebec Tomorrow Night"; "King's Ship Enters Canadian Waters"; "King's Ship Reaches Quebec"; "King Welcomed in Colorful Quebec

Rites." Americans would attentively follow every event on Their Majesties' Canadian tour and learn a great deal about the hitherto largely unknown couple who had recently taken possession of the British throne.

## Canada

As the king and queen made their thirty-day, ten-thousand-mile journey through North America, they followed in the footsteps of four previous kings who had tested their mettle and broadened their perspective in what had become a royal coming-of-age ritual. The future King William IV was the first to arrive in Canada in 1787, two years before he was declared Duke of Clarence. In the early 1800s, his brother, the Duke of Kent, would enter into an officially unrecognized marriage with an actress and adopt children in Canada, before he settled down, married, and fathered Queen Victoria. The nineteen-year-old Prince of Wales, later Edward VII, represented his mother, Queen Victoria, in knighting two leaders of the Canadian Parliament in Quebec in 1860. His son George V and his grandson Edward VIII both visited Canada before they ascended the throne.

Facing the scrutiny of Canadian and U.S. citizens and hundreds of members of the press, King George and Queen Elizabeth began an arduous continental journey that one sympathetic Canadian paper called "royal torture." For a month they would endure constant pressure and receive little rest. Their historic trip began on a hesitant and reserved note in the French-identified cities of Quebec and Montreal when at 10:32 A.M. on May 17 the king, dressed in the uniform of the Admiral of the British Fleet, and the queen, behind him wearing dove gray and chinchilla, stepped onto Canadian soil at Wolfe's Cove, Quebec. The restrained curiosity of Quebec's French-speaking citizens led John MacCormac of the *New York Times* to observe that "Canadian crowds are given to taking their pleasures silently, if not sadly."

After greeting Canadian prime minister William Lyon Mackenzie King at dockside, the royal couple traveled in a big maroon convertible sedan with bulletproof windows up to the Provincial House of Parliament in the old city. In the Parliament Red Room, the king and queen sat on two thrones under a large wooden crucifix and listened to the provincial premier welcome them in English and French. During the official presentations, Their Majesties received the blessing of one of the most influential men in Quebec. The Catholic cardinal Villeneuve, the spiritual head of 90 percent of Quebec's inhabitants, gave the king's hand a "lingering, fatherly patting."

Afterward at an official lunch at the Chateau Frontenac, both Bertie and Elizabeth were nervous before the king's first formal speech. They barely picked at their lobster tails and grilled chicken, and the king could hardly wait for the chance to calm himself with a cigarette. Protocol demanded that he could not smoke until after the prime minister toasted him (with Veuve Clicquot '28). After the toast, the king lit up so quickly that a startled waiter did not have time to offer him a match. As he spoke about their "anticipation too great for expression," the king stammered slightly. Yet when he shifted to French, he was able to speak without hesitation: "It is here today that two great races dwell happily side by side," he declared.

The next day the king and queen boarded the royal train, an elegant silver, blue, and gold mini-palace on wheels, a twelve-car streamliner with gold-plated telephones, a barbershop, and a post office. The queen's bedroom and dressing room were painted in blue-gray with dusk-pink curtains, and the king's suite was done in blue and white glazed chintz. They shared a mauve-tiled bathroom. The king conducted official business from an oak-paneled office, while the royal couple took their meals in a dining room painted a rich Nile green. When they wanted to know where they were, the king and queen could pull down specially designed wall maps, which hung like blinds, and determine the exact distance the train had traveled by consulting a "mileometer" installed in one of the sitting rooms.

As they headed to Montreal, they had a foretaste of the extraordinary attention they would receive in the rest of North America. People waved energetically along the tracks. Along their way, cars and carts were decorated in their honor and their initials were inscribed on stones along the train bed. In Montreal, the king and queen had their first triumph, winning over the Italophile fascist mayor Camillian Houde along with many of the city's two million residents, who greeted them on their twenty-mile drive through the city's streets. One member of the royal staff thought the crowds were as impressive as the coronation throngs in London two years before.

That evening as they dined at a parliamentary banquet at the

Windsor Hotel, one hundred thousand people gathered outside. The royal couple made one balcony appearance, but the crowd wanted more, all through dinner chanting, "The King, *Le Roi*, The Queen, *La Reine*." After dinner, the king and queen made a second balcony appearance, picked out by brilliant floodlights as the crowd in the dark below serenaded them with the national anthem.

In Ottawa the next day, they were greeted by the governor-general Lord Tweedsmuir and his wife, driving through the streets in a landau drawn by six horses, with an escort of the Princess Louise Dragoon Guards, named after Queen Victoria's daughter Princess Louise, whose husband had been governor-general of Canada sixty years before. Queen Victoria's son Prince Arthur, Duke of Connaught, also served as governor-general of Canada during World War I. With the queen at his side, the king became the first British monarch to preside over the Canadian Parliament. He exercised his seldom-used royal prerogative to give his assent to a series of bills—in this case on trade and economic issues.

The real news of the week, however, occurred on May 20 during a celebration of the king's official birthday with a Trooping of the Color in Ottawa's Parliament Square. During the mundane ceremonial laying of a foundation stone, the queen realized that many of the masons working on the building were Scots. While seventy thousand people and the international press watched in amazement, she spontaneously led the king down to stand among the workmen. As the royal couple laughed, joked, and shared stories about Scotland with ordinary people, they conveyed an easy democratic attitude, one that would forever change the perception of the monarchy and Great Britain as well.

This was the first royal walkabout, which would become a fixture in royal visits and celebrations. Describing the queen's gift for engaging the public, Tweedsmuir wrote that "she has a perfect genius for the right kind of publicity, the unrehearsed episodes here were marvelous." Over fifty years later, the Queen Mother would be modest about her role in changing the relationship between the public and the monarchy. Interviewed by the historian Theo Aronson, she said, "It is just that life was getting more informal. We never consciously set out to change things. We never said 'Let's change this or introduce that.' Things just evolved." As the king and queen became more approachable, the entire institution of the monarchy would grow more popular and would seem more relevant.

On the fifth day of the trip, while American newspapermen looked on in astonishment, Their Majesties made another dramatic plunge into the crowds. Even if President Roosevelt could have walked unencumbered by braces, the Secret Service never would have allowed him to risk such crowds. The second royal walkabout occurred after the unveiling of a memorial to soldiers of the "Great War" of 1914–1918 in Ottawa's Connaught Square. After the conclusion of the king's speech, military veterans surged forward toward the royal couple and chanted, "We want the king!" The king and queen waved away the guards and milled about with seven thousand ex-soldiers, who slapped the king on the back and grabbed the queen's hand and wept. One old man shouted, "You don't need any bullet-proof glass here, Your Majesty," while another added, "Ay, man, if Hitler could see this." Indeed, Hitler and all of Europe paid close attention.

The king embraced his new way of engaging with his subjects. "There must be no more high-hat business," he told an adviser, "the sort of thing that my father and those of his day regarded as essential to the correct attitude—the feeling that certain things could not be done." The normally hard-boiled American newsmen covering the royal tour were pleasantly surprised when they saw his informal and democratic philosophy in action. They began telling U.S. readers how extraordinarily charming, popular, and democratic the royal couple were. Americans began to realize that the monarchy was not as remote or as elitist as they had imagined.

In Toronto, Their Majesties continued their spontaneous charm offensive when they met the only Canadians who were more famous than they were themselves: the Dionne quintuplets. Just short of their fifth birthday, the five sisters, wearing white organdy frocks and flowers in their hair, curtsied incorrectly and called out their names: Yvonne, Marie, Cecile, Emilie, and Annette. Instead of presenting her posies to the queen as her sisters had been told to do, Marie gave hers to the king, which pleased him. Then, as *Time* magazine told American readers, "Cecile departed from protocol. She rushed over and kissed the Queen. In a trice Elizabeth, lonesome despite the previous day's telephone call from her own two daughters, was on her knees in a flurry of kissing Quintuplets. Forgotten man for the moment was the King, in his naval uniform, but Yvonne fixed that, running to him and taking his hand. Soon they were in brisk conversation in French over the King's Navy buttons."

## Washington, D.C.

Back in Washington, Franklin D. Roosevelt was hoping to welcome the king and queen to the United States with congressional passage of legislation providing more active support for Britain if war broke out. Roosevelt challenged the House of Representatives to repeal the arms embargo provision of the Neutrality Act, which currently forced him to deny armaments to all nations, whether aggressors or victims, in the event of war.

All of FDR's internationalist efforts met with furious opposition from congressional isolationists, who had broad support among the American public. The Atlantic Ocean created a barrier that dissuaded any country from invading the United States, isolationists believed—so why should America expend blood and power in conflicts that didn't concern them? Most Americans had been embittered by the Great War, remembering the devastation in Europe and the great social costs of the conflict at home—a price that was not justified by postwar democratic progress in an unstable Europe they saw as dominated by dictators. In a January 1937 poll, 70 percent of Americans said it was a mistake to have entered the Great War. By one estimate, a third of the U.S. population was involved in some type of antiwar movement during the time between the two world wars.

In August 1935 the spirit of isolationism had been codified into law. Determined to keep the United States from ever entering a European war, Congress had overwhelmingly passed the Neutrality Act, which prohibited the shipment of arms to nations at war and indicated that Americans traveling on belligerent ships would not be protected. The law was later amended to prohibit extension of American credits and loans to warring nations, forbid loans to third parties, and ban aid to combatants in civil wars. Roosevelt had fought to amend the bill to limit the arms embargo only to aggressors, but he was defeated. With a full domestic agenda to get through Congress and an upcoming election in 1936, Roosevelt banked on altering the provisions to his advantage when the arms embargo section would be reviewed six months after the original bill was passed. He lost his gamble to the increasingly powerful isolationists, whose numbers transcended party lines. While Hitler and Mussolini watched for signs that the United States might thwart their expansionist agendas, Congress eviscerated the president's attempt at the kind of saber rattling that might have dissuaded them. In retrospect, this American policy of neutrality encouraged worldwide tragedy.

From 1934 to 1936, the stern and outspoken Republican senator Gerald Nye of North Dakota headed a committee investigating the war loans made by private citizens and corporations to the Allies during the Great War. The committee's findings, which received a great deal of public attention, suggested that American businessmen—whom newspapers dubbed "Merchants of Death"—had brought the United States into the war for their own profit. Nye's committee discovered evidence that arms makers bribed politicians and made enormous profits while helping to foment war. A key group of Midwestern isolationist senators, including William Borah of Idaho and Bob La Follette of Wisconsin, joined Nye in a campaign to strengthen Americans' antipathy to interventionism.

By the first part of 1939, in the face of Hitler's aggressive takeovers of Austria, Czechoslovakia, and the Rhineland, and Mussolini's grab of Albania, U.S. public opinion had finally begun to shift. Americans, increasingly convinced war was coming in Europe, had grown to abhor Hitler and feel more protective of their European allies. An April 1939 Gallup poll showed that 57 percent of the American people thought that the Neutrality Act should be changed to allow the sale of munitions to Britain and France.

Since January, the president had allowed Nevada senator Key Pittman—an ineffectual alcoholic who was more concerned about the price of silver for his Nevada constituents than he was about Hitler's threat to the rest of Europe—to lead the Senate fight for repeal of the Neutrality Act. FDR assumed that Pittman, as head of the Senate Foreign Relations committee, could muscle the bill onto the Senate floor. At the beginning of May, Pittman let the president and Secretary of State Cordell Hull know that he could not get the repeal past the strong and stubborn isolationist senators on his committee. On May 19, with the king and queen in Ottawa, the president turned from the Senate to the House of Representatives in an effort to get the bill unstuck, meeting with House leaders to formulate a new strategy. Despite warnings that the bill would be difficult to pass in the House, the president insisted that Speaker William Bankhead; Representative Sol Bloom, who was acting chairman of the House Foreign Affairs Committee; and Majority Leader Sam Rayburn try to push it through.

If the House passed a new bill before the royal visit, FDR thought, the Senate would be more likely to pass it after Their Majesties left.

Lobbying Congress, Secretary Hull emphasized that the inflexible provisions of the arms embargo might drag the country into conflict instead of keeping war at bay; it would weaken America's allies, who served as the nation's bulwark against the dictators of Europe and Asia. The president reiterated his public position that he had no intention of sending U.S. troops into a European war. (In private, his sentiments were more complex; he believed the United States eventually would have to intervene in the impending conflict.) On May 29, Representative Bloom would introduce a bill repealing the Neutrality Act. But no final action would be taken before the king and queen were to arrive on June 8. Roosevelt was frustrated. He and his internationalist supporters could not be sure that the royal visit would sway public opinion or change any votes in Congress.

## Western Canada and Back

As they journeyed west across Canada, Their Majesties monitored the president's critical battle, but could help only by making the best impression possible in Canada. Heading through the economically depressed wheat country and into the mountains, the king and queen frequently interrupted their sleep and appeared at the back of the train so that people in small towns and hamlets could see them late at night or early in the morning. As the train stopped to service its locomotive at White River, "the coldest spot in Ontario," the king and queen emerged from the train to greet the overjoyed Indians, schoolchildren, and townspeople on a train platform still snowy in late May. In Ottawa the king had been slapped on the back for the first time, but in Brandon, Manitoba, Canadians pushed aside conventional protocol in a new way, hugging and kissing the king and queen as they stepped into the crowd after watching ten thousand children sing to them in a flood-lit amphitheater. As they passed through Calgary, near where the Duke of Windsor still maintained a ranch, the king was given the title of "Great Chief Albino" by a council of Indian chiefs.

At the Banff Springs Hotel, in Banff, Alberta, where Bertie and Elizabeth had a well-earned rest, American reporters were impressed by their first encounter with the king's sense of humor. When the king asked a reporter where he lived, John Barry of the *Boston Globe* volunteered, "I'm from Boston. You remember we'd trouble with another George there once." The king smiled and replied, "Oh yes. I think I've heard about it. Something about tea, wasn't it?" Lord Tweedsmuir, witnessing the emergence of the king's true character, wrote, "What a wonderful mixture he is of shrewdness, kindliness, and humor."

Reporters noted that the response to the king and queen seemed to grow more enthusiastic daily, and expressions of isolationism and anti-war sentiment appeared to recede from newspapers and public discourse as they headed toward the western gate of the British Empire at Victoria. When half a million people greeted them in Vancouver, Prime Minister Mackenzie King wrote Tweedsmuir, "Words cannot begin to describe the triumphal nature of the royal tour to date. It has surpassed all expectations in every particular."

As the royal train began the weeklong journey back east, the royal party passed through the lonely night darkness of the Rockies, with watchmen lighting lanterns every quarter mile of the track. When the train stopped at one desolate depot to take on water, Their Majesties stood on the platform of the observation car in the moonlight. One man in the small crowd began singing Kate Smith's famous ballad, "When the Moon Comes over the Mountain," until everyone joined in. Enchanted, the king asked about the song. When he got to Washington, he requested that Kate Smith sing it to him after dinner at the White House.

The king and queen had one final night of relaxation in a rather splendid log cabin (with five bathrooms) at Jasper National Park, before facing the daunting, seven-day procession to Niagara Falls and entry into the United States. As they passed through Canadian towns with more familiar names like London and Windsor, the number of public receptions increased dramatically and the press coverage of the tour escalated once again. The queen got her first view of the United States at Windsor—the king had seen it on a previous visit—when she looked across the border to the Detroit skyline. An electric sign flashed the greeting, "Detroit Welcomes Their Majesties the King and Queen."

At Detroit in September 1860, the king's grandfather Bertie, as Prince of Wales, had first entered the United States for a private tour under the protective name "Baron Renfrew." Queen Victoria had ordered that her callow nineteen-year-old son, arriving during

Abraham Lincoln's campaign for the presidency, should visit "in the character of a student" and stay informally in hotels. Nonetheless, the first future British king to visit the United States was greeted by passionate crowds. In St. Louis, one hundred thousand people had gathered to see him when he visited the town's autumn fair. Over the course of his extensive tour of Midwestern and East Coast cities, the prince matured noticeably from an undistinguished and undeveloped young man into a charismatic and respected world figure, whose visit would help bind England to the United States of America during the Civil War, when both the Union and the Confederacy would vie for British support. In one crowd a man shouted to the prince, "Come back in four years and run for President."

King George VI had toured Niagara Falls in 1913 as a naval cadet on a visit to Canada, traveling under the pseudonym "Corporal Johnson." On this 1939 trip, he and his wife had stayed at the Brock Hotel and dined overlooking the falls—which the king's grandfather had visited quite dramatically in 1860. The young prince had almost entered the United States in a wheelbarrow. The prince had watched the French acrobat Charles Blondin wheel a man in a barrow across the falls on a tiny tightrope suspended one hundred and sixty feet above the rushing waters. Blondin crossed back on stilts. When the prince visited Blondin's enclosure to give him a purse of gold coins as a thank-you for providing such a spectacle, the acrobat, described in newspapers as "a short, sallow-complexioned man with sunken cheeks and rippling muscles," offered to wheel the prince to the U.S. side. The adventurous prince was inclined to accept the offer, but his aides interceded. King George and Queen Elizabeth would enter the United States in the safest manner possible—and be the first sitting monarchs to do so.

## Washington, D.C.

Americans read about the upcoming visit with escalating interest, as journalists offered them a combination of fact, myth, and speculation about the royal couple. The *Washington Post* reported that the king, who had served on a gun turret at the Battle of Jutland in World War I, was at his happiest around war veterans as well as children. The king was portrayed as fascinated by war medals, to the point where he often delayed his schedule talking to other veterans about them; he was also said to be an avid amateur photographer who used movie and still cameras. The *Post* reporter noted that the king had gained considerable confidence and ease during his visit to Canada. Americans, who had been so captivated by the romance of the Duke and Duchess of Windsor, were told that the king was very much in love with Queen Elizabeth.

For her part, the queen, slender with rich coloring and vivid blue eyes, was described as being much more attractive than her photographs showed. Readers were told the queen had brought along a fortune in royal jewels and that she never made up her mind until the last moment about which jewels to wear with any of her fifty different gowns or ensembles. Americans heard about the queen's talent for looking directly at people and making each person feel as if he or she were the only one in the crowd. The reporter emphasized her thoughtfulness in giving gifts to people who had crossed her path in Canada.

Happy to focus on the democratic aspects of the royal couple's personalities and thus stir greater interest among newspaper readers and radio listeners, the press downplayed the ritualized and elaborate nature of the king and queen's traveling party. The king had brought along two valets and a page, five footmen, his private secretary, a lord-in-waiting and two ladies-in-waiting, their servants, two police officers, a physician, and other assistants. The queen had two dressers, a hairdresser, and her lord chamberlain. Only nine of the large group would be able to be housed at the White House; the rest would stay at the British embassy or on the royal train.

As the U.S. segment of the royal visit drew near, the Roosevelts and the State Department were bombarded with requests, offers, and concerns from private individuals, businesses, and public organizations. There were many appeals for photographs, autographs, special viewing opportunities, delivery of personal messages, and individual audiences with Their Majesties. A Mrs. Spiller, who claimed to be a third cousin of the queen, requested a meeting. Doctors and quacks offered the king speech therapy, and fortune-tellers and clairvoyants proposed to give both of them spiritualist readings. J. H. Perskie of Atlantic City wanted to do an etching of the king and queen while they were guests at the White House. A mother suggested that her son's high school band perform at Hyde Park, while twelve-year-old Poughkeepsie resident

Frances Wilbur, who claimed, "I may someday be one of the finest woman trumpet soloists in the world," wanted to play for Their Majesties.

Public and private institutions also chimed in with invitations for the royal couple. The mayor and board of supervisors of Los Angeles sent a special proclamation inviting Their Majesties to visit during the trip. So did the North Dakota legislature. William and Mary College wrote to Joe Kennedy to request that he help arrange a royal visit to Williamsburg, Virginia. St. Thomas Church in Washington, D.C., known as "the president's church," wanted the king and queen to attend Sunday services. The Warrior's Shrine in Hoboken, the International Poultry Conference, and the Brooklyn Sunday School Union all hoped for a visit. Once the king and queen's actual schedule was announced, many local spectators wrote to request a change of route or a slow drive through their community so that as many people as possible could glimpse the royal couple.

Already there was interest and even controversy in what the king and queen would eat. Many Americans offered to cater the royal dinners and receptions; others sent food directly. Mrs. Roosevelt's secretary wrote to one lady who sent figs that "unfortunately they arrived too late" to be served to Their Majesties. American grape growers and vintners, one hundred thousand strong, were outraged about a report that American wines would not be served at the White House dinner, because "failure to do so infers that American wines are inferior." An indignant man wrote a simple telegram telling the president that "We don't want the King or Queen in the United States."

Eleanor wrote to U.S. ambassador William Bullitt in Paris requesting that he share what he had learned about entertaining the royal couple during their spectacular 1938 visit to France. She got more than she bargained for. Bullitt sent a secret memorandum full of excruciatingly detailed information, listing what furniture should be put in the king and queen's rooms, the way the comforters on the beds had to be folded, and exactly what toilet items should be placed in their bathroom. Amused by the memorandum, the First Lady refrained from asking him whether he had not discovered the soap, water glasses, and towels in the White House bathrooms when he had visited there. She would regale guests with stories about the ambassador's directives. The most hilarious instruction was to put a hot-water bottle in each bed, including those for staff. This struck everyone who heard it as bizarre, since the king and queen would visit in the heat of the Washington summer.

As Their Majesties were crossing the Atlantic, Ambassador Bullitt had sent another memorandum to FDR, this one a patronizing report on Their Majesties: "The little Queen is now on her way to you together with the little King. She is a nice girl . . . and you will like her, in spite of the fact that her sister-in-law, the Princess Royal, goes about England talking about her 'cheap public smile.' She resembles so much the female caddies who used to carry my clubs at Pitlochry in Scotland many years ago that I find her pleasant." Bullitt's comments about the king were even more condescending: "The little King is beginning to feel his oats, but still remains a rather frightened boy." The Roosevelts had little reason to disbelieve Bullitt's assessment of their characters, and so began the visit with low expectations of the king and queen. They would be pleasantly surprised.

On the day before the royal couple were to cross Niagara Falls, Eleanor invited her old friend Lady Lindsay, the American wife of the British ambassador, to tea so that they could make final preparations. The two ladies shared a wicked sense of humor and a similar point of view about protocol and pretentiousness. Eleanor showed her William Bullitt's list of furniture, toiletries, and hot-water bottles and had a good laugh. Lady Lindsay recounted the king's private secretary Sir Alan Lascelles's injunction that the king was not to be offered suet pudding or capers and that he should be served thirty seconds before the queen. As it was customary for the president to be served first at the White House, FDR was asked to make a protocol decision. FDR decreed that the king and president would be served first, followed by the queen and the First Lady.

The weekend before her ordeal began, Eleanor went to Hyde Park to organize the house for the royal guests: "I've been housekeeping hard ever since I got up here [Hyde Park], inside & out," she said to Lorena Hickok. "The cottage will need a good check up before the house is filled with my children over the King and Queen's visit." It is not surprising that while she was preparing for the visit, Eleanor wrote Hick, "Gee I will be glad when the K&Q have been here and gone!"

# 8

# Conquering Washington

The British sovereigns . . . have left a better impression than even their most optimistic advisors could have expected.

—*Arthur Krock*, New York Times

At around ten o'clock on the evening of June 7, 1939, a British monarch entered the United States of America for the first time. In a dingy, small, brick and sandstone station at Niagara Falls, Sir Ronald Lindsay and his wife introduced the royal couple to the U.S. secretary of state Cordell Hull and his wife, who gave the queen a corsage of orchids. Being shy, the king and queen were nervous, but eager to see the United States.

For weeks, Washington society and the entire nation had been heatedly debating protocol for greeting the royal couple. Would "bending the knee," the traditional attitude of introduction to royalty, be kowtowing to America's former rulers? Would an informal, all-American handshake be too rude? Diplomatically, the Hulls took care to do both. A twenty-one-gun salute rang out as the royal train—embossed with a crown and according to the *Washington Post* "the most opulent royal caravan" ever to travel to the U.S. capital—began its overnight journey to Union Station in Washington. In Buffalo, the roads were clogged with cars as people drove into the city hoping for a nighttime glimpse of George and Elizabeth as the train passed by.

The level of security for the royal visit was unprecedented—and for good reason. In London two days earlier, a mentally ill Australian man had fired a sawed-off shotgun at the king's sister-in-law, the Duchess of Kent, as she was leaving her Belgrave Square home to attend a showing of the film *Wuthering Heights*. She was unaware of the assassination attempt until police told her after the film ended. At about the same time at the home of the king's sister, Princess Mary, the same Australian man had shattered a panel of glass. The outlawed Irish Republican Army had been waging a terror campaign of bombing that year in England, and these incidents incited further anxiety in the royal party and the U.S. and British forces protecting them. A couple days before, while Their Majesties were approaching Windsor, Ontario, the FBI had detained Sean Russell, the IRA's chief of staff, in Detroit, right across the Canadian border. Suspicious that Russell was plotting to assassinate the royal couple, they held him on a deportation warrant, charging he had overstayed a visitor's permit. Now, as the royal train progressed from Buffalo to Washington, a line of one hundred sixty thousand local police and Secret Service agents were positioned twenty feet apart at rights of way; government agents checked all crossings and bridges for safety. In case the IRA or another terrorist group attempted to blow up the train, a pilot train preceded the royal caravan along the tracks.

Despite Ambassador Kennedy's prediction that the visit itself would be "simply thrilling," the queen's senior lady-in-waiting, Lady Nunburnholme, had revealed to reporters, as the train approached the United States, the king and queen's severe apprehension. They viewed the visit as the most important experience of their lives, she said, as fraught with risk and significance as the coronation ceremony itself. However, when they were crowned, they had been sustained by a thousand years of tradition; in the United States, they would be breaking new ground.

Along with their worries over security and the kind of reception they would receive, the specter of the king's brother David haunted both Elizabeth and Bertie. In the United States, they would be judged against the still-vivid memories of the frenzy of his first U.S. tour in 1919, and the slavish press attention devoted to his breezy charm and democratic manner on his 1924 visit. *Scribner's* magazine reminded Their Majesties that much of the United States felt loyal to the Duke of Windsor and believed that the British had mistreated his American paramour. In June 1937, after the duke's abdication, a Gallup poll showed that a majority of Americans wanted the former king and his wife to come live in the United States. Protective of her husband, the queen was determined to banish David's shadow. Stepping off the train on a brief stop at Baltimore, Wallis Simpson's hometown, she almost fainted when she saw her nemesis, the Duchess of Windsor, approaching her bearing a bouquet of flowers. When Elizabeth finally realized that the lady was just a dead ringer for the duchess, she still thought the woman might be the duchess's sister. The queen did not easily calm down after the incident.

At the same time that the king and queen were embarking on the most challenging and delicate diplomatic mission of their new reign, the Duke of Windsor was in Paris working on his golf handicap at the St. Germain Club. Having had his fill of shaking hands on his Commonwealth visits as Prince of Wales, David told the press that he preferred playing the forest course at St. Germain to being on a royal tour. He expressed his official delight at the warm reception his brother had received so far, but as the U.S. visit progressed, he undoubtedly had mixed feelings watching his royal rivals celebrated in a country from which the U.S. and British governments had banned him, following the outcry over his meeting with Hitler.

Washington anticipated the king and queen with awe, anxiety, and suspicion. In her book *There's No Place Like Washington*, Vera Bloom, the daughter of Representative Sol Bloom, described the social storm that raged in the capital for the month preceding their arrival. The party stoked Washington's social insecurities and caused a furor in the press. The garden party had "caused more heartburns, more adverse press comment, [and] more of a tempest in a teapot than any social event . . . in this country," one diplomat declared. Government officials and society figures agonized over who among them would receive invitations to the British embassy's royal garden party, and if they did get an invitation, how to dress and whether to curtsy. Ambassador Lindsay aggravated the situation by declaring that the garden party was like heaven—"some are taken and some are not." When Ambassador Lindsay's wife declined to invite the minority leader of the Senate and fifty of the ninety-six senators who would soon be voting on the Neutrality Act, a massive protest forced to her expand the guest list to include most legislators and their spouses.

Three weeks before the royal arrival, press interest compelled Lindsay to conduct his first news conference as ambassador, during which Lady Lindsay stoked further controversy when she insisted that during the garden party the king and queen must not be spoken to unless they spoke first. Reporters were particularly interested in how she had chosen the thirteen hundred and fifty "representative Americans" who would receive invitations. And, the press inquired, had Lady Lindsay invited any of the relatives of the Duchess of Windsor? The ambassador's wife claimed not to remember. In fact, Mrs. George Barnett, the Duchess of Windsor's cousin, was pointedly excluded from the guest list.

Eleanor had been tense for days before the visit. She was not confident she would be up to the demands of such a crucial meeting and worried about how the king and queen would fare. Addressing the frenzy over who should meet the king and queen and how those lucky Americans should behave, Eleanor Roosevelt mused in print whether "royal visitors ever have the same kind of qualms about the people with whom they are going to stay that we ordinary mortals have. I always wonder whether I will have the right clothes and whether my hosts will find having people attached to the President's family more of a burden than a joy." This was an unusually candid revelation for a First Lady of that era. Having heard about the queen's sartorial triumph during a recent state visit to Paris, when she, in honor of her father who had recently died, wore all-white mourning dresses to spectacular effect, Eleanor was privately concerned about the suitability of her own wardrobe. Her letters to Hick reveal the pressure she felt during the entire visit. Franklin, however, with his love of pageantry and his outgoing nature, could not wait for the visit to begin.

As anxious as they were, the king and queen were well prepared for the byzantine ways of Washington and the serious issues of Anglo-American relations they would confront, thanks to a thirty-four-page research document, meticulously prepared for them by F. R. Hoyer Millar of the Foreign Office, which detailed the career and personality of every government official with whom they would have a significant meeting. The report gave President Roosevelt mostly good reviews, chronicling the triumphs of the president's first term and the mistakes of his second, from his socially heartening New Deal programs to his disastrous attempt to pack the Supreme Court. For all their grievances against their nation's mother country, Millar wrote, most educated Americans were committed to seeing Britain win any war against the Nazis. Millar believed that resentment over Chamberlain's capitulation at Munich was fading; the Americans would eventually enter a war. The king paid close attention to the report's thorough review of the pending revision of the Neutrality Act.

As Their Majesties' train approached Washington, newspaper editorials reminded readers they were not just making a social call. Implying that the United States would have to give up its isolationism, the *Washington Post* predicted the visit would "subtly strengthen" the United States' commitment to exercise leadership and responsibility in handling the current crisis. The *New York Times* declared the British throne a "safeguard against tyranny" and warned that the "liberties of England could not be destroyed without danger to our own." According to the *Washington Star*, the royal visit "is notice to all concerned that on the fundamental question now dividing the world, democracy vs. dictatorship, the peoples which share in common the principles, that gave birth to the Magna Carta and the Bill of Rights, see eye to eye."

King George and Queen Elizabeth were the fourth pair of reigning monarchs to visit Washington, D.C., but the first to stay at the White House. Emperor Pedro II and Empress Teresa of Brazil had come to the U.S. capital in 1876 and joined President Ulysses Grant in Philadelphia for the centenary of the signing of the Declaration of Independence. In 1919, King Albert and Queen Elisabeth of Belgium visited President Wilson, incapacitated with a stroke, in his sick room at the White House. The king and queen of Siam had also visited.

Ironically, Queen Elizabeth, who was particularly excited to visit Washington, D.C., was one of the closest living descendants of George Washington, her second cousin six times removed. The queen, Washington, and Confederate general Robert E. Lee were all descended from the Virginia colonel and politician Augustine Warner, who had left England with his parents in 1650 to escape the Puritan repression of the Cromwell era. Colonel Warner's daughter Mildred married Lawrence Washington; his grandson would be chosen America's first president. The queen was descended from Colonel Warner's other daughter, Mary, whose grandson, Robert Porteus Jr., moved back to England in 1720 and became a minister.

. . .

Disembarking from their train in Union Station promptly at 11 A.M. on Thursday, June 8, the king, in the dark uniform of Admiral of the Fleet and wearing a cocked hat, and the queen, in a pearl gray ensemble, walked down a royal blue carpet flanked by marines presenting arms. A crowd roared greeting. Reporters, who saw a "young, fit and earnest" king, dwarfed by tall Ambassador Lindsay, and a "perfect Queen: eyes a snapping blue, chin tilted confidently, two fingers raised in greeting as girlish as it was regal," carefully monitored the introductions made among the two heads of state and their wives: Eleanor and FDR shook hands with both the king and the queen. Joseph Kennedy, in London and far from the action, described the greeting as "perhaps the most important handclasp of modern times." It was a gesture guaranteed to encourage American affection for Britain.

Franklin was excited to meet Their Majesties and proud of his role in convincing them to come to the United States. He had no doubt that he could make the visit a triumph. "Well, at last I greet you," the president began, his choice of words indicating the two years of delicate, intense planning and persuasion this moment had required. "I am glad to see you," he added. After Secretary of State Hull had formally introduced the royal couple as "Their Britannic Majesties," the king replied, in the kind of locution that protocol required, "It is, indeed, a pleasure for Her Majesty and myself to be here."

The American and royal parties proceeded through the station amid a guard of honor, two national anthems, and a twenty-one-gun salute. Entering his car, Roosevelt almost sat on his top hat. The king smiled. The two leaders rode in an open car, their wives following in a separate vehicle, through Washington's ninety-four humid degrees. Waves of heat rose from the streets. In the first car "Roosevelt was almost suffocating in his cutaway, striped pants, and high hat," according to FDR's secretary, Grace Tully, while the king, in his heavy uniform, "came near to fainting from the heat." The king "could not have been more wretched had he been encased in a suit of armor," Tully said. However, the king was surprised at how quickly he felt at ease with the president.

The president doffed his silk hat and the king saluted as tanks and cavalry escorted them past the Capitol and down Pennsylvania Avenue through the largest crowd ever assembled in Washington—estimated at between six hundred thousand and seven hundred fifty thousand, almost twice the capital's population. Much of Washington was shut down for a half day in honor of the royal visitors. "In the course of a long life I have seen many important events in Washington, but never have I seen a crowd such as lined the whole route between Union Station and the White House," Eleanor wrote in her diary. Over six thousand American soldiers, sailors, and marines stood and saluted at ten-foot intervals along the route. Army planes flew overhead. The only mishap occurred when a tank at the end of the procession caught fire. Fortunately, no one was injured. Over the course of the day, five hundred people fainted from the heat.

As they inched down Pennsylvania Avenue, Eleanor tried to point out significant buildings to the queen, but the roar of the crowds often made conversation impossible, and the two women spent most of their energy responding to the onlookers. Eleanor immediately noticed the queen's talent for engaging with the public. "She had the most gracious manner and bowed right and left with interest, actually looking at the people in the crowd so that I am sure many of them felt that her bow was for them personally," she noted in her diary. One veteran reporter commented, "That's the Queen. Give her a crowd, and she mows 'em down." The crowd yelled to the king, "Hiya, King," and "You are a great queen picker." Eleanor, perplexed at why the queen wore a light cover over her knees on such a hot day—and how she was able to bow so often and so effortlessly—discovered that the Queen's seat had a special spring installed within it, to facilitate bowing.

At the White House, after greeting the heads of all of Washington's diplomatic missions and their wives, the king and queen went to their rooms for their first quick change of clothes. George stayed in the royal suite, named in honor of his grandfather Edward VII, its four-poster bed the one the late king had slept in. Elizabeth stayed in a bedroom that had been Abraham Lincoln's study, later named the Queen's Room; it was painted in rose tones and furnished with antiques, including a four-poster bed, from the New England Federal period. At the last minute, someone had the diplomatic savvy to remove from the queen's room a print, on loan to the White House, depicting British general Burgoyne's surrender at Saratoga.

Bertie and Elizabeth lunched informally with Franklin and Eleanor, the Canadian prime minister, the three eldest Roosevelt sons—James, Elliott, and Franklin Jr.—their wives, and several members of the royal party. To his father's great dismay, James was separating from his wife Betsey, whom FDR adored. Flirtatious and witty, Betsey had often presided over FDR's fittingly named cocktail time, "The Children's Hour," earning Eleanor's resentment. The charming and complicated second son, Elliott, named for Eleanor's alcoholic father, had been dropped from the social register for divorcing his first wife, and denounced twice on the floor of Congress for questionable business dealings. He had become the mouthpiece for conservative Texas oilmen and power brokers, attacking New Deal policies in a weekly radio broadcast. Just before the royal visit, the third son, Frank, who was in law school at the University of Virginia, had to deny rumors of an impending divorce from his wife Ethel, of the Republican and anti–New Deal DuPont family. Neither the Roosevelts' eldest child, Anna, nor her youngest brother, John, attended the lunch. Anna Boettiger, married for a second time, had just given birth; she remained in Seattle where she and her husband ran William Hearst's *Seattle Post-Intelligencer*, while John and his wife, Anne, who were mourning the stillbirth of their first child the previous week, stayed in Boston. Often, family meals featuring the three oldest Roosevelt boys were raucous and argumentative affairs, and their parents must have wondered how their rebellious sons would comport themselves among royalty. The queen liked the Roosevelt boys, and was particularly drawn to James Roosevelt's wife, Betsey. Elizabeth wrote to Queen Mary that "they are such a charming and united family."

After lunch, during a sightseeing tour of Washington, Eleanor started to relax. The queen won her over by revealing that she and the First Lady shared common values, and that she keenly appreciated Eleanor's controversial public role. "I saw in the paper that you were being attacked for having gone to a meeting of the WPA workers," she said, as Eleanor recounted in her memoirs: "It surprises me that there should be any criticism, for it is much better to allow people with grievances to air them; and it is particularly valuable if they can do so to someone in whom they feel a sense of sympathy and who may be able to reach the head of the government with their grievances." Both women were committed to serving as their husband's eyes and ears, and actively advised their mates. While Elizabeth handled Bertie with a light touch, Eleanor barraged FDR with so many memos demanding action on one issue or another that he had set a limit of three memos a day.

After another rapid change of clothes, the king and queen went to the much-ballyhooed British embassy garden party to mingle with fourteen hundred leaders of society, finance, and government, entering to the strains of "God Save the King" with their entourage of ladies-in-waiting, equerries, and detectives. Before the party, a rainstorm had passed through the city, leaving it hotter than ever. Greeting the queen, Representative Sol Bloom said, "You see, Your Majesty, I stopped the rain for you!" "Indeed you did," the queen agreed. "But," she added with a chuckle, "didn't you forget to turn off the heat?" Rich and prominent private citizens like Admiral Byrd, the explorer of the North and South Poles, the Rockefellers, and the Lodges merited personal introductions and conversations with the king and queen, who extended their hands in greeting rather than wait for a bow or curtsy, though half the women did eventually bend the knee. Mrs. Cornelius Vanderbilt gave a low curtsy to the queen, and waved her gold fan while talking to the chain-smoking king. Mrs. Woodrow Wilson, who had dined with the king's parents at Buckingham Palace twenty years before, stood apart from the crowd in the shade of a portico and fanned herself.

The king and queen devoted much attention to the members of the House and Senate, who sported Stetson hats, Irish green carnations, lounge suits, elaborate formal attire, and even a straw hat. One senator sought attention by carrying a white ten-gallon hat. The wife of Vice President "Cactus Jack" Garner commandeered the queen with her notorious "whimsical, homespun" stories, and Garner himself broke all rules of protocol when he gave the king a big slap on the back—which, according to Interior Secretary Harold Ickes, indicated not only bad breeding but a faulty notion of democracy. For his part, the king had defied protocol to cry out "Finder's Keepers" when a nervous guest dropped a coin in the receiving line.

Ickes, the royal visit's acerbic diarist, had turned down his invitation to the gala. He was not interested in mingling with "a lot of uninteresting, climbing and supercilious people." Instead, he went to a stag cocktail party hosted by an ambitious congressman named Lyndon B. Johnson. Isolationist legislators, including their leader Senator Nye, bristled when the king spent almost half an hour conversing with financier J. P. Morgan, whom Nye had blamed in Senate hearings for engineering America's entry into the First World War. Nye and others thought that Morgan's tête-à-tête with the king could serve as evidence of collusion with Britain in the impending Senate battle over the Neutrality Act. In fact, J. P. Morgan was an old personal friend of the king, who had often hosted him for grouse shooting at his estate in Scotland. However, even such an innocuous conversation held political import in a tense and contentious Washington.

While the social climbers and the social arbiters mingled with the king and queen at the garden party, tensions between the royal and presidential staffs backstairs at the White House—exacerbated by the elaborate protocol and the heat—boiled over into cultural clashes. The president's butler, Alonzo Fields, carped that the king's servants required more service than the king and queen did. When a White House usher asked the queen's maid to tell the lady-in-waiting that the queen wanted to see her in her room, the woman retorted, "I am the queen's maid," and marched off down the hall in a huff. The exasperated usher yelled out to her, "Oh, you're a big shot, hey?"

One of the White House messengers, fancying himself an artist, made an "almost life-sized, black-and-white portrait of the queen, which was not very good," according to Eleanor's diary, and convinced one of the maids to put it on the queen's dressing table with a note requesting her autograph and comments about the drawing. When the queen discovered it, she had her lady-in-waiting remove the offensive artwork and give it to one of the White House ushers. He recognized the artist, reported the affront to his boss, and was heard to say, "If that man ever again utters the word autograph, it will curdle in his throat."

In her book *White House Diary*, the executive mansion's housekeeper, Henrietta Nesbitt, complained about the royal staff's irksome directives, which had begun arriving months before the visit. Now as the visit began, she was appalled that the queen's staff requested heavy woolen blankets, hot milk, and hot-water bottles be ready for Her Majesty despite Washington's heat wave. Mrs. Nesbitt was infuriated at the king's valet for his constant criticism about the White House cuisine, offerings that she thought should be "plain foods plainly prepared." The valet was in good company, however: author Ernest Hemingway once had called the White House food "the worst I have ever eaten," and the president himself said "the food around here would do justice to the automat." As budget-conscious as Mrs.

Roosevelt herself, Mrs. Nesbitt served him broccoli even though she knew that he hated it. FDR's fear of confrontation was so great that, despite his unhappiness, he never summoned the nerve to fire her.

Returning from the sweltering garden party, the king joined FDR, Eleanor, their son Elliott, and his wife Ruth for a swim in the White House pool. The queen had never been in a hotter place than the White House, she later told Joe Kennedy. Exhausted after the garden party and on edge about the formal evening ahead, she lay on the floor in her room, in which portable air conditioners had been installed. Then she made her fourth change of clothes that day to be ready for the state dinner and the musicale.

At the dinner, guests were presented to the royal couple in the East Room, after which the president led the queen, who looked the role in her semi-Victorian white tulle dress, to the State Dining Room. The king followed with the First Lady, whose natural lace gown was accented with family heirloom diamonds. Protocol experts had worried for days about the picture the First Lady and the British monarch would make at this conspicuous moment, with Eleanor towering over the king. She paid no mind. Only Harold Ickes would note that Their Majesties "looked like pigmies" next to the Roosevelts.

The main table in the State Dining Room was almost hidden with thousands of white orchids, a gift from the country's orchid growers. The six-course menu of uniquely American food, served on the ivory-tinted, gold-edged Roosevelt china, included boned capon and terrapin, which was a gift to the king and queen from Maryland. The queen found it unappealing and could not eat it. They were also served calf's head soup, clam cocktail, sweet potato cones, corn sticks, and ice cream and cake. At one side of the horseshoe-shaped table, the queen sat between the president and Vice President Garner, who played the role of court jester. During dinner he told a little joke on his "boss," as he called the president. The king reportedly laughed when Garner declared, "Why I believe that you have a more democratic system of government over there than we have . . . when you have a vote of confidence in your legislative body, if it goes against the prime minister, he resigns and has to have a general election. But over here he hangs on."

Later, Cactus Jack grabbed the king and placed his arm behind His

Majesty's back "as if in a semi-embrace," complained Harold Ickes to his diary; Garner had "no breeding or natural dignity," treating the king as if he were a "poker chrony," or a "visiting Elk," showing no more restraint at the state dinner than he would have at a church supper in some small Texas town. Their Majesties did not complain about Garner, but FDR was appalled at his vulgar behavior. In 1940, he would remove him from the presidential ticket. The queen grew irritated with House Speaker John Bankhead, who leaned all over her during dinner, but she would have some measure of revenge at the British embassy event the next night, when the crinoline of her gown covered his chair, forcing him to wait to be seated.

Toasting the king, FDR called the royal visit a special moment in the history of the United States. "I am persuaded that the greatest single contribution our two countries have been enabled to make to civilization, and to the welfare of peoples throughout the world, is the example we have jointly set by our manner of conducting relations between our two nations," he said. "It is because neither of us fears aggression on the part of the other that we have entered into no race of armaments, the one against the other." To illustrate his point, he described the amicable resolution of a recent conflict over two small, uninhabited Pacific islands, which both Britain and the United States wanted to use as stepping stones for commercial air flights between the United States and Australia.

The king, speaking about the great anticipation around this visit, declared, "If we have had our moments of anxiety, they have served to make us realize how intensely we have been looking forward to the present occasion." He concluded with an entreaty that "our great nations may ever in the future walk together along the path of friendship in a world of peace."

After a long day, the dinner guests were fatigued and hot. Vera Bloom noted that recently installed White House air conditioners contributed "nothing, but 'nerve-wracking noises'" to the august event. Jane Ickes, the pregnant young wife of the interior secretary, wrote to FDR's daughter that she "nearly swooned away at the State Dinner." She added that "men's shirts buckled in the middle and collars wilted. Women, including the unfortunate Queen, turned beetlike." The queen suffered, her arms and face "flushed and slightly swollen with sunburn," but she never stopped smiling. Following dinner, the receiving line was held up because the queen was feeling faint. The Roosevelt boys took the king and queen outside to cool off.

After greeting the king and queen in a receiving line, the guests gathered in the East Room for an "American Musicale," which Eleanor had planned in defiance of the long-standing White House tradition of having Steinway and Company arrange after-dinner concerts with internationally known classical music concert artists. Braving an uproar from traditionalists, Eleanor hosted a celebration of American folk arts for Their Majesties. The First Lady introduced radio's "Songbird of the South," Kate Smith, "one of our greatest singers," who sang her signature song, "When the Moon Comes over the Mountain," at the request of the king, who had heard it the week before in Canada. Harold Ickes sniffed that Smith was "a type one would expect to hear in a cheap music hall" and was "awful, both in appearance and performance."

Garner quipped that the queen might have "dozed off" during the musicale if she had not been kept awake by the North Carolina Soco Gap Square Dancers, who "raised the roof" with their stomping and clapping. The Coon Creek Girls from Pinchem-Tight Hollow, Kentucky, provided a special dose of regional flavor when they strummed several folk songs, including "How Many Biscuits Can You Eat?" Folk singer Alan Lomax was barely able to sing after a frightening encounter earlier in the evening. Because his aunt had told the FBI he was a dangerous Bolshevik, the Secret Service and Scotland Yard took turns frisking and interrogating him. The crowd whispered that he looked like a troublemaker, sockless, his hair unshorn.

The highlight of the evening was the performance of Marian Anderson, the great black contralto whose gentle and powerful voice was often described as soul stirring. Conductor Arturo Toscanini once told her that "a voice like yours is heard once in a hundred years." By including Marian Anderson on the program, the president and First Lady used the high-profile evening to make a powerful statement against racial prejudice. Enlisting the king and queen in a singular moment in U.S. civil rights history, they hosted the first African-American person ever to perform at the White House.

Earlier that spring, Marian Anderson had applied to sing a concert in Constitution Hall, which was the largest and most appropriate indoor location in Washington, D.C., for such an event. The Daughters of the American Revolution, which owned the hall, refused because all their contracts stipulated "concerts by white artists only." In protest, the First Lady resigned from the DAR. With Eleanor's encouragement, Harold Ickes had arranged for Anderson to sing at the steps of the Lincoln Memorial on Easter Sunday, in what became a legendary concert before the seventy-five thousand people who crowded the Mall, and millions listening on the radio.

Standing by her invitation to Marian Anderson, the First Lady ignored a letter from the president of the Miami Acacia Club calling it "an insult to the British king and queen to present a Negro singer for their entertainment," and many similar missives, some verging on illiterate, describing the black singer in vitriolic terms. Eleanor convinced Anderson that the British monarchs wanted to hear the "Negro spirituals" that the opera singer loathed to perform. Anderson belted out "My Soul's Been Anchored in the Lord," "Tramping," and "Ave Maria." Eleanor found Marian Anderson "divine" and was relieved at the fervent response her singing inspired.

Afterward, the king and the president talked late into the night. The overwrought king began to unwind; he loved nothing better than a political discussion. Having expected a bland and inexperienced man, FDR was surprised by George VI's breadth of knowledge and his shrewdness. He was delighted with their immediate rapport. He and the king had much in common, sharing interests in gardening, forestry, and the navy, as well as a history of overcoming physical handicaps. Roosevelt also relished talking with a leader who foresaw the coming war in Europe and the need for U.S. intervention. In a comment that suggested how much word of the king's stammering had influenced the Roosevelts' image of him, Eleanor wrote Hick, "He is very nice & doesn't stutter *badly* when speaking aloud & not at all in quiet conversation."

At a press conference the next day, FDR gave his official verdict on the royal couple: "they are very, very delightful people." In her "My Day" column, Eleanor wrote, "These sovereigns are young, and though the weight of responsibilities matures people early, still one does not always find in sovereigns such ability or even desire to comprehend the problems which confront so many people in every country today, and which must be solved before we can feel that the average man and woman can have security and liberty."

Referring to Elizabeth's dignity and her regal bearing, not her looks, Eleanor told Hick that "the Queen reminds me of Queen Victoria!" In her memoirs, she elaborated: "I was fascinated by the queen, who never had a crease in her dress or a hair out of place. I do not see how it is possible to remain so perfectly in character all the time." The burden of being a consummate public hostess wore Eleanor out. "The heat is oppressive and I am weary," she wrote Hick after the dinner. "Four hours of sleep last night! Swam tonight & hanker for a regular regime of exercise, little food & work, with a good bit of reading wedged in."

The king and queen's final day in Washington was even more grueling than the first. They had ten engagements in eleven hours. That morning, the king became the only man ever to participate in one of Eleanor's press conferences. Since it was a conference for female reporters, Eleanor brought the queen in with her. In another sly demonstration of royal approachability, the king slipped in unannounced and stood in affable silence in the background as the eighty-four reporters present demanded details from Eleanor of the royal visit's first day. The queen, who was much shyer than her public persona suggested, did not feel comfortable talking to reporters. They were disappointed that the queen, who did not hold press conferences in Britain, would not answer questions. The queen had "a keen sense of the difficulties under which a great many people live and labor today," Eleanor said, and "it is interesting to find one so young with as compassionate an understanding of the conditions which push people to desperation." Looking slightly reticent, the king joined the queen in greeting the long line of newswomen after the conference ended.

Heading to the Capitol, Bertie and Elizabeth worried about their reception. For them, it was one of the most stressful moments of their whole trip. The day before, they had been greeted at the White House with a telegram from Democratic representative Martin Sweeney of Ohio requesting that Britain repay its billions of dollars in war debts to the United States and immediately announce a payment schedule. Adding to the tensions, Their Majesties had arrived in Washington the very day the proposal to revise the U.S. neutrality policy had come out of congressional committee. It would be debated in the House of Representatives the following week. One Republican congressman decried the bill as a "present for King George." Isolationist legislators were wary about seeming to pander to Britain's wishes, and most congressmen were personally anxious about encountering royalty. A week earlier, Representative Albert Austin of Connecticut had announced he would bow low to the king only if the king bowed low to him, too. If the king looked down at him haughtily, then Austin would reciprocate.

There had been concern about whether Their Majesties would have time to meet all of the 531 members of Congress within the scheduled forty-five minutes, but ultimately one hundred of the legislators found all kinds of appropriate and inappropriate reasons for not showing up. Some were out of town, while others peeked at the royal couple in front of the Capitol but refused to be presented formally. Representative Sweeney stayed away because his telegram had not been answered, while Washington senator Homer Bone claimed he could not "get used to these fancy affairs." New York Democratic representative William Barry announced that he would refuse to participate in "British propaganda to entangle us with them."

As the congressional members awaited the royal couple in the Capitol rotunda, Vice President Garner told inappropriate jokes and stories in an attempt to ease the tension. Spotting the king and queen, he yelled, "The British are coming!" Leading isolationist senator William Borah of Idaho was first in line to meet Their Majesties as they stood awkwardly beneath a painting of British general Cornwallis's surrender at Yorktown, which no one would even have considered removing for this event. The queen acknowledged congressional compliments on her appearance, while the king winningly greeted Senator Ellison Smith of South Carolina by his nickname "Cotton Ed."

Sol Bloom, acting chairman of the Foreign Affairs Committee, fumbled with his hat and mispronounced names as he introduced the members of the House. Nat Patton of Crockett, Texas, shouted at the king, "Cousin George, I bring you greetin's from the far-flung regions of the Empire State of Texas." Turning to a colleague, he said with Texas gallantry, "If America can keep Queen Elizabeth, Congress will regard Britain's war debt as cancelled." Robert Moulton, from a Creole district in Louisiana, outdid his Texas colleague by calling the royal couple *"Vôtre Majesties"* and kissing the queen's hand.

· · ·

Back at the White House, FDR was changing clothes and Eleanor was going through her mail when the head usher announced that Their Majesties were ahead of schedule. Rattled, the president and First Lady rushed to their car and headed toward the presidential yacht, the USS *Potomac*. Their chauffeur drove so fast, they had to hold onto their hats and could barely wave to the crowds. The king and queen delayed their arrival until loud cheers from bystanders indicated their hosts had boarded the yacht. The Roosevelts and the royal couple lunched on the deck during a stop on the fifteen-mile trip to Mount Vernon to pay homage to George Washington. In 1860 the king's grandfather, Bertie, then the future King Edward VII, had planted a chestnut tree beside Washington's tomb during a visit with President Buchanan, who had taken a fatherly interest in the prince after meeting him during his time as U.S. minister in London. It was a gesture of reconciliation fewer than fifty years after the British had burned Washington. In 1919 Bertie's grandson David had laid a wreath at George Washington's grave, but George VI would be the first reigning monarch to honor the man who had wrested America from his ancestors.

On Mount Vernon's green slope, Washington's tomb is housed in a small redbrick structure surrounded by cedar and pine trees. While the president, the First Lady, and the queen waited outside the iron gates, and with James Roosevelt filming the ceremony, the king walked silently inside and placed on the grave a wreath of white lilies, red carnations, and blue irises, with a card inscribed "George R.I. and Elizabeth R." Then he took two steps backward, emerged, and stood with a bowed head.

The Scottish-born gardener at Mount Vernon, almost fainting from nerves, then presented a bouquet to the queen. He told the press, "It is just that her loveliness takes the breath and the memory oot of a mun." After greeting well-wishers, the royal couple had time only for a brief visit to the house and gardens. The queen told Eleanor that Washington's colonial white mansion was "one of the loveliest places she had ever seen."

Next, the Roosevelts and the king and queen drove to the Fort Hunt Civilian Conservation Corps for Unemployed Youths, a New Deal public works project that the king and queen had asked to visit. Disappointed that he could not be present for every moment, FDR waited in the car while Eleanor, Bertie, and Elizabeth walked down a long reception line of teenagers in the blistering sun. Between the two of them, the king and queen spoke to every boy present, asking each one what he was learning, how he was treated at the camp, and what his work prospects were. The king and queen could have skipped a sweltering walk across a field and an inspection of the barracks and mess hall, but the king told his aides, "If they expect me to go, of course, I will go."

They made one of the most thorough inspections of a public project that Eleanor had ever witnessed. The king felt mattresses, examined shoes and clothes, looked into pots and pans, and turned over tables that the boys had made to see how they were put together. After hiking back across that broiling field, Elizabeth whispered to Eleanor that she was feeling rather peculiar, and returned to the car. The king persevered on his own, reviewing bulletin boards that showcased pictures of boys working in camps nationwide. With plans to set up similar camps in Britain funded by the government, the king studied all aspects of this one. Eleanor was deeply impressed with Their Majesties' level of commitment; she realized they had social consciences as acute as her own.

As Their Majesties entered Arlington National Cemetery, a twenty-one-gun salute boomed from the hillsides nearby. Cabinet officials and their wives joined members of the royal entourage and thousands of spectators gathered on the slopes and in the amphitheater, and witnessed the playing of the two national anthems and a guard of honor's presentation of arms. After the king laid a wreath of white lilies and white carnations, bearing another card inscribed "George R.I. and Elizabeth R." on the Tomb of the Unknown Soldier and another of calla lilies on the Canadian Cross, honoring U.S. soldiers who had served with the Canadian army from 1914 to 1918, he took four paces backward and bowed his head. The guard of honor presented arms again, four ruffles were played on drums, and a marine bugler played taps before the group left the cemetery amid another twenty-one-gun salute. Eleanor found the ceremony very moving.

At the White House, while FDR husbanded his energies, after a brief rest the king and queen joined Eleanor for tea, where they would meet cabinet officials and government agency heads administering the New Deal's social and economic programs. Eleanor worried how she could follow the president's elaborate instructions on presenting each official: she had to bring each official to the king, who was seated beneath a tree on the White House lawn, give a concise description of his or her job, leave the official alone for exactly three minutes of royal questioning, and then direct each one to the queen. Remembering how her husband tarried when talking to government officials, she was relieved to discover that the king, who had been thoroughly briefed by the Foreign Office report, easily recognized the officials and maintained the time limit himself. Initially, Eleanor thought the king was better trained and more disciplined than her husband, but she later decided the king might simply have been exhausted.

Eleanor had long taken a proprietary interest in Commerce Secretary Harry Hopkins's eight-year-old daughter Diana, who had lived in the White House with her father after her mother died of cancer. Diana appreciated Eleanor's interest in her, she would later say, but she never found Mrs. Roosevelt particularly warm. The girl did confide in Eleanor how excited she would be to see Queen Elizabeth, whom Diana had decided must be the fairy queen she had heard so much about. When Eleanor told the queen about her young admirer, Elizabeth offered to meet the girl before she left for the British embassy dinner that evening. Eleanor and Diana waited in the upstairs hall while the royal couple dressed for dinner. When they appeared, Diana was transfixed: the queen was dazzling in her white, spangled dress, embroidered all over with Queen Alexandra roses and touches of aquamarine stones that matched her eyes; a diamond tiara with its straight rows of diamonds like icicles in her hair; and two diamond necklaces. Eleanor presented Diana to the king and queen; the girl curtsied shyly to them, and they spoke with her briefly. When she saw her father later, she uttered her oft-quoted exclamation, "Oh, Daddy, I have seen the Fairy Queen."

Many Americans felt the same way about Elizabeth. One besotted Washington newspaperman saluted the royal couple, saying, "Three cheers for the King—and four for the Queen." Washington bestowed on Elizabeth the title "Queen of Hearts" and was warmed by the king's unselfish pleasure in his wife's triumphs, not the least of which—to the queen's delight—would be a sudden shift in American fashions in the coming months. Duchess of Windsor–like "brittle sophistication" gave way to the queen's style of "soft femininity," according to Vera Bloom. That night, as Their Majesties left the British embassy, where they had hosted the Roosevelts at an informal dinner for sixteen couples, Bloom noted that "group after group of good Americans, standing under the lamplit green arches of Washington's trees, spontaneously began singing 'God Save the King,'" concluding their visit to Washington with what she called the "climax of climaxes."

Eleanor wrote Hick that night: "This day is also over & has gone well . . . even FDR is content and I am glad for him. The young royalties are most intelligent. At the tea they asked everyone questions & left them with the feeling that their subject was of interest & well understood. At dinner the King told me he felt that he had learned a great deal. She seems equally interested. I begin to think there is something in training."

Privately, Eleanor thought that the king had better manners than her own husband.

# 9

# Hot Dog Diplomacy

## JUNE 10–11, 1939

> Oh, dear, oh, dear, so many people are worried that "the dignity of
> our country will be imperiled."
>
> —*Eleanor Roosevelt in her newspaper column, about the upcoming picnic*

As the king and queen slept, their train traveled from Washington,
D.C., to Red Bank, New Jersey, passing by the battlefield at
Monmouth where George Washington's Continental Army defeated
George III's redcoats. Exhausted after the relentless events of the previous two days and tense over the schedule of meetings, greetings,
receptions, and tours to come, the king did not sleep well. He awakened at 6 A.M. when the train was put on a freight siding in Red Bank
to await the morning's programs.

The visit to New Jersey and New York City would have given even
a well-rested man a severe headache, and this high-strung and now
sleep-deprived king certainly felt the stress, as he and his more resilient
queen faced enormous demands on their energy and attention on
another ninety-degree day. Under the best of circumstances, the naturally reserved king did not like public appearances. He once exclaimed,
just before reviewing his troops, "Oh my God! How I hate being King!
Sometimes at ceremonies I want to stand up and scream and scream
and scream."

Having waited all night to greet them, thousands of people at Red
Bank were disappointed when they could barely glimpse the king and

queen during a brief welcoming ceremony with the governor of New Jersey and the mayor of Red Bank. In Sandy Hook, the royal couple boarded the U.S. destroyer *Warrington* to be ferried across New York Bay to Manhattan. On board, they were greeted by a twenty-one-gun salute while army planes roared overhead and a guard of honor presented arms. For the first time in history, the royal standard flew alongside the Stars and Stripes on a U.S. warship.

Haze obscured their vista of the city, but as the destroyer passed the Statue of Liberty, it lifted enough for the king and queen to get a full view of the famed symbol of democracy. The king saluted stiffly. Another twenty-one-gun salute met them as they passed Governors Island amid a flotilla of festively decorated small boats, cabin cruisers, speedboats, and steamers. Entering the inner harbor of New York, they were greeted with the sounds of bells, sirens, whistles, blimps, and airplanes; fireboats shot plumes of water in the sky. By the time the ship tied up at the New York Battery, to the sound of yet another twenty-one-gun salute, the king was probably ready for a rest. Instead, they stood through another formal welcoming ceremony with Mayor Fiorello La Guardia and Governor Herbert Lehman. Newspaper coverage of their arrival would point out that the royal party landed close to the place where Sir Guy Carleton, the last British commander in New York, had given up the keys to the city and sailed back to England one hundred and fifty-six years before.

As in Washington, the security was extraordinary. Three and a half million people greeted Their Majesties in New York. Only Charles Lindbergh, greeted by four million in 1927 after his transatlantic flight, ever had drawn a larger crowd. Planted among the cheering crowd could be members of the violent Irish Republican Army or Nazi sympathizers, all elements of New York's polyglot community. For Scotland Yard, this New York visit was more daunting than protecting the king and queen on their coronation day in 1937, when two million people had watched Their Majesties along a six-mile route. This royal journey through Manhattan and into Queens covered fifty-one miles, and more than thirteen thousand New York police (out of a whole force of eighteen thousand) guarded them along their route.

Making their way up the West Side Highway in an open, bulletproof limousine amid a caravan of fifty cars, the king ordered the motorcade to slow down so that he and Elizabeth could see more of the city skyline and spectators could observe them. Viewing the Empire State Building, the Chrysler Building, and parts of Rockefeller Center from the West Side Highway, they were disappointed that time did not allow them to see more of Broadway and Fifth Avenue. Traveling from the West Side Highway to Riverside Drive, they crossed the Upper West Side on 72nd Street on their way into Central Park. The king impressed the mayor, sitting beside him, by asking about the levels of unemployment in the city and whether the newly erected Triborough Bridge was financially self-supporting.

Cheering New Yorkers showered the king and queen with ticker tape from rooftops, windows, fire escapes, and streets along the route up Riverside Drive and into Central Park. As bands played, Manhattan's Central Park was filled with one million schoolchildren, waving flags and screaming greetings. The queen requested that they again slow down so as not to disappoint the children, who were much louder than the adults. By the time they arrived at the World's Fair in Queens, they were forty minutes behind schedule, highly unusual for a king who prized punctuality.

The centerpiece of the royal trip to New York was this visit to "The World of Tomorrow" as the World's Fair was called. The 1939 fair, held amid the anxiety of the escalating world conflict between democracy and totalitarianism, had been designed to showcase democratic ideals, international cooperation, and technological progress as a route to economic prosperity and personal freedom. When they arrived at Perylon Hall, the fair's main reception area, Grover Whalen, the bombastic president of the Fair Corporation, and his wife commandeered the royal couple for the official welcome to the fair. Grinning widely, he hovered over them and presented them with souvenirs of the fair as they sat on the dais in two chairs made for Louis XVI, on a carpet once owned by Louis XIV, and signed the World's Fair guest book under a seventeenth-century tapestry of the life of Don Quixote. There followed a reception where everyone waited in silence for the king's first words. "When do we eat?" the king asked. Whalen ignored his question, hustling him to another reception of dignitaries. When the king and queen greeted an Italian commissioner, he gave a fascist salute. They were appalled.

Exhausted and impatient, the king showed a glimmer of his famed temper. After greeting half of the guests, the king strode away. Grover

Whalen protested, but the king had to use the bathroom. The king then walked outside and on to the next event with Whalen forlornly following behind. Eleanor, pleased that a pompous man got what he deserved, wrote to her friend Hick that "the King and Queen did not fall for Grover."

Heralds in blue and gold played trumpets from the rooftops as Their Majesties left the Federal Building, where they finally had a quick chance to lunch. They visited the Irish pavilion, where the king paid homage to a country that after centuries of struggle against England had recently become a republic and, while still recognizing him as head of state, now managed its own affairs. Then they entered one of the fair's blue and orange trains, this one bearing the royal coat of arms. Preceded by a mounted guard of Haskell Indians dressed in scarlet uniforms while a band played "The Sidewalks of New York," they made a whirlwind tour of the South Rhodesian, Australian, New Zealand, and Canadian pavilions, each one featuring exhibits of their cultural heritage and the latest developments in technology and consumer products. Back home, as it were, at the British pavilion, bands played "Land of Hope and Glory" while rockets exploded.

At the British pavilion garden party, after touring exhibits on public welfare and education, they paid particular attention to a copy of the Magna Carta, which had been loaned to the fair as part of the British public relations campaign to enhance Britain's image in the United States. The Magna Carta, the first document of democracy, recognized that the king was not above the law. Placing this document in the British pavilion next to a wall panel showing the pedigree of George Washington, with his descent from some of the signers of the Magna Carta, reinforced common notions of U.S. and British democratic traditions in contrast to Revolutionary times, when the then king and his government had tried to trample American rights.

While their guests were slogging through the World's Fair, Eleanor and Franklin were making final preparations for the royal couple's weekend visit. Eleanor took reporters on a tour of the lower floors of the Hyde Park house. "My responsibility in Hyde Park is only for one picnic," Eleanor told her "My Day" readers, "and even if everything should go wrong, the only result would be to make our neighbors across the water realize that we are still a young country and don't do some things here as well as they do." Privately, Eleanor struggled with her usual lack of confidence. In reassuring the country about the picnic, she appeared to expect that she would, indeed, make the kind of mistakes that would reveal her lack of sophistication.

Eleanor likened her situation to that of a hostess who pretends to be a mediocre housekeeper so that her "guests are so pleased to feel how very much better they are" at the household arts. It will be the differences between North American and British ways, she claimed, that the king and queen "will remember and laugh over when they return to their own fireside." Eleanor was challenging America's neurotic obsession with looking good enough to the "superior" British royal family, and was rebelling, at the same time, against her own feelings of inadequacy. The president had disingenuously promised that the royal couple is "coming away for a quiet weekend with me. I'll put the King into an old pair of flannels and just drive him about in my old Ford." He was excited about entertaining the king and queen at his family home.

After they left the World's Fair, the king and queen made a final stop in Manhattan at Columbia University, which had been given its original charter as King's College by the king's great-great-great-great-grandfather George II in 1754. When they arrived, the president of the university and the chairman of the board of trustees escorted the king and queen into the much-needed cool of the air-conditioned Low Memorial Library while a string orchestra played Elgar's "Pomp and Circumstance." An audience of five hundred trustees, faculty members, and guests watched as the royal couple examined the original charter and signed the distinguished visitors' book. George VI had not wanted an honorary degree, and his wish was granted.

It was an eighty-mile drive from Columbia University to the Roosevelts' home, called Springwood, in Hyde Park, population eight hundred. The hamlet had not changed greatly since George III had last reigned over the colony of New York. The king and queen were headed to "The Big House," the Roosevelts' handsome tan stucco colonial with pale green shutters and white cornices, situated on the steep bank of the Hudson River. The Roosevelt family had lived there for one hundred years. The king's official biographer Sir John Wheeler-Bennett wrote of the Roosevelts' pedigree that "they came of that proud, solid Knickerbocker stock which even Ward McAllister,

New York's social arbiter of the 'eighties, had found 'unsnubbable,' and which formed the backbone of that curious organism of New York society depicted in the novels of Henry James and Edith Wharton."

The king and queen's party, by now several hours late, stopped at several points to call and update their hosts on their progress. Their sleek limousine made its way along roads closed to other traffic, packed with bystanders and strewn with flowers. As they passed through each small town, church bells blended with honking horns of automobiles. James and Betsey Roosevelt gave officials a scare when their battered 1935 car suddenly took off onto the closed parkway ahead of the royal caravan; state troopers flagged down the car only to discover the identity of its occupants. By the time Franklin Jr. and his wife followed in their car, they were allowed easy passage.

While the Roosevelts waited for their guests, they played out another scene of their drawing room drama. Eleanor and Sara shared rare common ground in their moral distaste for Franklin's fondness for alcohol. Eleanor viewed drinking as dangerous and was temperamentally unsuited for the joys of cocktail hour. Never good at small talk, she found it difficult to relax, and could not be playful and silly over cocktails like most of Franklin's cronies and female admirers.

Unable to dispel the tensions of running the country with athletic pastimes like golf or tennis, FDR cherished the pleasures of drinking, socializing, and flirting with women. At Hyde Park, to counter his exuberance, Sara and Eleanor monitored his drinking. Sara even outdid Eleanor in suggesting FDR should curb his intake. Elliott Roosevelt reports that his grandmother would lift his father's martini to her lips, sniffing disdainfully at the alcohol, and say, "Now Franklin, haven't you had enough of your *cocktails*?"

Now, while they waited in the library, FDR set up a shaker of martinis on a card table by his chair. He sat defiantly on his side of the fireplace while Sara sat in her chair on the other side, scowling at her son, telling him she was sure the king would prefer tea. "My husband, who could be just as obstinate as his mother, kept his tray in readiness," Eleanor wrote in her memoirs. Having sized up the king in Washington, FDR believed he knew what would revitalize him after a daunting day. Sara held firm in her view of royal protocol.

"Granny, naturally, found nothing at all amusing in a manner of such gravity. To her, reigning monarchs were among the few people in the world ranking in dignity with herself. Hyde Park became a sort of petit palais when royalty visited," wrote James Roosevelt. For Sara, this visit was a royal validation of her lifelong quest to put herself at the apex of American nobility. Sara fancied herself an American counter-part to the upright Queen Mary, who had so graciously hosted her at Buckingham Palace in 1934. She had much at stake in her role as host-ess to the king and queen and only twenty-eight hours to impress her visitors and repay Queen Mary's hospitality. The cocktail war was to be the first of several embarrassments for the Roosevelt matriarch during the visit.

Finally, one and a half hours late, the sound of church bells and car horns signaled the arrival of the royal guests in Hyde Park. When the limousine came up the flower-lined drive to the handsome Georgian Colonial mansion with its white portico, Their Majesties were greeted by four flags flying in welcome: the royal standard, the president's flag, the American Stars and Stripes, and the British Union Jack. When the royal car pulled up to the house, FDR, Eleanor, and Sara greeted them. When the king started to apologize for being late, the president told him, "Kings are never late . . . there is plenty of time."

When Their Majesties entered the mahogany-paneled front hall-way, they could see into the music room, otherwise known as the Dresden Room for its German-imported chandelier; Sara had spruced up the space with new chintz curtains and slipcovers. It was here she kept her prized Chinese porcelains, and atop the piano, her collection of royal presentation photographs of her royal friends and visitors, including her most recent guests, Crown Princess Märtha and Crown Prince Olav of Norway, and the Crown Prince and Crown Princess of Denmark.

Across from the entrance to the hall were a series of framed Currier and Ives prints depicting U.S. naval victories over the British in the War of 1812. The first print a visitor was likely to see was the colorful caricature "British Valor and Yankee Boasting." It shows British sailors on the deck of a British warship holding American seamen across their knees and spanking them. While the Americans howl in pain, the British laugh at their embarrassment. For three days before the visit, Sara Roosevelt insisted to her son that they be removed lest they upset the king. Sensing that Bertie would enjoy them, FDR overruled her. He was right.

Eleanor showed the royal guests to their rooms so that they could freshen up before dinner. The tired travelers did not linger long upstairs. The king would sleep in the Pink Room with its rose trellis wallpaper. His rosewood bed and bureau were among the few family pieces salvaged from the 1865 fire that had destroyed the Roosevelts' original house at Mt. Hope. The queen stayed in the floral-patterned Chintz Room, which was separated from the king's room by a common bathroom. She had a choice of two simple beds made by Eleanor Roosevelt's Val-Kill Industries, which employed local people to make furniture.

Downstairs before dinner, as the king approached him in the library, FDR offered him a choice that would be famously reported. "My mother does not approve of cocktails and thinks you should have a cup of tea."

"My mother would have said the same thing," the king answered, "but I would prefer a cocktail."

Both men took their martinis, raised them up in a silent conspiratorial toast to each other, and drank. FDR had his revenge on his mother. Eleanor believed his exasperation with Sara contributed to the sinus infection that had laid him low just before the royal visit.

After surviving the cocktail hour, Sara had her grand moment when the king escorted her into dinner ahead of the other guests. At dinner, FDR reciprocated the king's gesture by raising a toast to the health of the king's mother. Soon enough, however, Sara must have wondered if she was participating not in royal dining but in British farce. The servants may well have played out the underlying British-American tensions that simmered beneath this carefully planned event. Sara Roosevelt's English butler had departed Hyde Park in a snit when he discovered that the president's service staff—which included African Americans—was being imported from the White House. He could not abide seeing the king and queen served by African Americans: "I cannot be a party to the degradation of the British Monarchy," he exclaimed. His departure was a blow for Sara, who could not exert control over the service provided to the king and queen.

During the middle of dinner, a serving table loaded with extra dishes suddenly collapsed. Part of the Limoges china dinner service broke as it hit the floor. Sara, who must have been mortified, tried to pretend nothing had happened, while the servants stood by in petrified silence. Mrs. Helen Astor Roosevelt, wife of FDR's stepbrother James, took pity on the server who had overloaded the table. Helen said to Sara, "I hope none of my dishes were among the broken." Most everyone laughed loudly, and the tension dissipated. The king and queen took the event in stride, while Eleanor was secretly amused at the flaw in Sara's perfect party. FDR ended the meal by catching the king's eye and calling out, "Sir, may we smoke?"

When FDR, Eleanor, and the king and queen retired to the library, the evening's misadventures continued. The foursome heard a terrible crash as the butler tripped down the steps to the library and sent a tray of glasses, decanters, liquor, and ice crashing to the floor. The tray "hurtled into space," and the butler "bounced after it like a ballplayer sliding into second base," leaving a large puddle of water and ice at the bottom of the steps. According to Daisy Suckley, the king remarked: "That's number 2, what will be the next?" Eleanor got her final revenge on her mother-in-law when she wrote up both incidents in her "My Day" column. FDR initially balked at her wish to write about the mishaps, but Eleanor convinced him that it was good for people to know that accidents happen even at the president's house. Sara, however, was furious that the evening's failures were not kept a family secret. For the rest of her life, she would declare, "If *my* butler had been used instead of those White House people, none of these things would have happened."

There were two more mishaps. On Sunday morning, a butler who was serving the ladies-in-waiting and aides breakfast bumped into a mantelpiece and dropped a whole tray of eggs and toast on the floor. During the picnic that afternoon FDR, who was sitting on the grass, pushed himself backward on his hands so that he could get out of the sun. He landed right on a tray of glasses and bottles.

Sara would endure another humiliation after the royal visit. She had purchased a new lavatory seat in the town of Hyde Park and had it installed as part of a refurbishment of the royal couple's bathroom. As rich as she was, Sara Roosevelt was notorious for her tardiness in paying bills and her penny-pinching ways. When the bill for the lavatory seat arrived, she decided that it was too expensive and refused to pay. The shopkeeper sent a plumber to Springwood to retrieve the seat, and then hung it in the window of his shop in downtown Hyde Park. Underneath the seat was the sign: "The King and Queen sat here." The bill was paid rapidly thereafter.

After drinks it was late, so the queen and Eleanor retired upstairs—perhaps feeling sympathy for the king, who had to stay up even later to talk politics with FDR and Canadian prime minister Mackenzie King, who had accompanied the king to the United States. The king, however, could not have had a better time. As he said of Roosevelt, "He is so easy to get to know and never makes one feel shy. As good a listener as a talker." They spoke of the deterioration of events in Europe and of Roosevelt's interest in easing the restrictions of the Neutrality Act. FDR was also gravely concerned about the defense of the Western Hemisphere and particularly focused on the need to develop Caribbean bases so that islands like Bermuda and Jamaica, among others, would not be taken over by enemies and used as staging areas to attack the United States and Canada.

Around one-thirty in the morning, FDR, playing his fatherly role to the hilt, patted the king on the knee and said, "Young man, it's time for you to go to bed." With his potent mixture of charm, respect, and paternal guidance, the president had boosted the king's self-confidence. The king was so thrilled with their talks, he invited Mackenzie King to his room to share his excitement before he could go to sleep. "Why don't my Ministers talk to me as the President did tonight?" Bertie asked the Canadian premier. "I feel exactly as though a father were giving me his most careful and wise advice." Given how intimidating and impatient the king's own father, George V, had often been with his son, FDR had given the king a new perspective.

Profoundly moved and encouraged by his conversations with Roosevelt, the king would carry his notes from those talks with him in a briefcase wherever he went during the war, like a talisman. These notes reveal what the two heads of state discussed on this purportedly apolitical royal visit:

> We talked of the firm & trusted friendship between Canada & U.S.A. F.D.R. mentioned that he thought it was a waste of money to build a Canadian fleet as he had already laid his plans for the defense of the Pacific Coast of Canada, especially Vancouver Island. . . . On mentioning the Neutrality Act the president gave us hopes that something could be done to make it less difficult for the U.S.A. to help us. Cordell Hull & others

as well as himself were doing their best to lead public opinion on to the right tack.

FDR told the king his plan to convince Midwestern farmers of the need for U.S. participation in a war by asking them how they would like to lose Britain as a customer after the British and French were defeated by Germany and Italy. "Then again Hitler could say to our great neighbors to the south the Argentine & Brazil You cannot sell your wheat or your beef or your coffee in Europe except through me & Germany. I am the Master of Europe & in return I will send you the articles I *think* you will require in return at my price."

The king noted: "He showed me his naval patrols in greater detail about which he is terribly keen. If he saw a U boat he would sink her at once & wait for the consequences. . . . If London was bombed U.S.A. would come in. Offensive air warfare was better than defensive & he hoped we should do the same on Berlin." On the question of debts they agreed they had "better not reopen the question" because "Congress wants repayment in full, which is impossible, & a small bit is of no use, as they will want more later."

These notes show history that the worst fears of isolationist congressmen were true: FDR was actively planning with the king and the Canadian prime minister to swing public opinion toward intervention in Europe and, if necessary, to rescue Great Britain.

On Saturday night, the king and queen sorely needed a good night's sleep. According to the Duke of Kent, who told the story to Rose Kennedy, in the middle of the night the queen and king were awakened by a terrific noise from downstairs. One of the king's equerries went to investigate, and found that the four Roosevelt boys were dancing around their mother, Eleanor, saying, "At last we have heard you tell a funny story!" The tale is lost to history, but under the circumstances, might well have recounted Sara's obsessive preparations for the royal visit. Fortunately, they could all sleep in before church on Sunday morning.

After breakfast, the two couples left Springwood for the three-quarter-mile trip to the village of Hyde Park for the morning prayer service at the tiny, 125-year-old, vine-covered, stucco St. James Episcopal Church, where FDR was the senior warden. With security provided by the National Guard and both state and city police, as well as by American Legionnaires and Boy Scouts, the heads of state and their wives were met by enormous crowds. Eleanor worried that the clamor of the onlookers would be draining for the king and queen on what was supposed to be their one day of rest while in the United States, but they told her that they were moved by the extraordinary friendliness of the throngs.

FDR had stage-managed the visit to the church, exercising the same attention to detail he had applied to the entire five-day royal visit. In May he had written to Reverend Frank Wilson, who had been his rector for ten years, to direct who would get tickets to attend, when they were to arrive, and where they would sit. He even indicated to Wilson where the royal guests, the clergy, the parishioners, and the security people were to stand after the service, so that the maximum number of people could glimpse the king and queen as they were being photographed. On May 16, FDR had sent a memo to Eleanor requesting information about the royal entourage and the attendant U.S. officials and their family members; he needed the information by the next day, he told her, so he could arrange the seating in the sanctuary. FDR's careful planning was almost derailed by his leg braces. When he entered the church during the service, "he walked with great difficulty [because] only one side of his right brace was fastened & if it had broken he would have collapsed in the aisle," he later told Daisy.

Roosevelt had paid particular attention to the royal visit to St. James because he was bringing the king and queen to his family church, where three generations of Roosevelts had worshiped. He wanted this intimate spiritual gesture to bond the two couples further. FDR had instructed Wilson that the service, with its two lessons, four hymns, and prayers for the welfare of Their British Majesties, be designed to be identical to that offered in any village church in England. His intricate spiritual choreography succeeded: Queen Elizabeth later wrote to Queen Mary that "the service is *exactly* the same as ours down to every word, & they even had the prayers for the King & the Royal Family. I could not help thinking how curious it sounded & yet how natural?" The only real difference was that the service ended with a traditional prayer for the president.

The king later sent the church a special Bible to commemorate the event, which, to Wilson's delight, FDR delivered personally that October. At the Bible's consecration service, FDR read a prayer from the Church of England prayer book that included a phrase asking God to ensure victory over the king's enemies. Newspapermen attending the service seized on his reading, suggesting it revealed the president lacked genuine neutrality in the war between Britain and Germany. Opposition forces in Congress tried to use the controversy to help defeat the Neutrality Bill, which would allow the president to provide arms to Britain.

At the June service, the presiding bishop of the Episcopal Church of America, the Right Reverend Henry St. George Tucker, delivered a sermon about Britain's and America's responsibilities in the face of a deteriorating world situation: "The nations represented at this service . . . must assume a large share of the responsibility for saving the world of our time from the ills that threaten its well-being," he declared. Wilson struck a lighter note when he coupled a blessing for the royal pair with an appeal: "One sees what happens when the parishioners bring their guests to church . . . if everyone would do this we would fill the church every Sunday." In the days before the service, there had been a frenzy for seats. Wilson had shut off his telephone during meals so that he would be able to eat.

When they returned from church, the king and queen telephoned their two daughters in England, who plied them with questions about the trip and were fascinated that their parents were headed to lunch just as Margaret was about to go to bed. Then the president drove the king around his Hyde Park property in his manually operated car, wildly negotiating the winding roads and heavily wooded areas. There must have been moments when the king felt as if he were at home in the woods on his family estate at Sandringham or his summer home at Balmoral. The two men further discussed FDR's eagerness to defend Britain. The president also discussed his dislike of Russia's totalitarian system, his mistrust of its territorial ambitions, and his fears that Stalin could ally himself with his fellow dictator, Hitler, in an attempt to avert a German invasion of Russia. The king offered his opinion that Britain and the United States would have to make an agreement with Russia to avert a Russo-German pact.

FDR then took the royal couple on their famous wild ride up to the hot dog picnic. Years later, the Queen Mother would tell the author Conrad Black that this ride was more frightening than anything she experienced during the war. She told him that "President Roosevelt drove us in his car that was adapted to his use, requiring great dexterity with his hands. Motorcycle police cleared the road ahead of us but the president pointed out sights, waved his cigarette holder about, turned the wheel, and operated the accelerator and the brake all with his hands. He was conversing more than watching the road and drove at great speed. There were several times when I thought we could go right off the road and tumble down the hills. It was frightening, but quite exhilarating. It was a relief to get to the picnic."

The picnic took place at Top Cottage, the Dutch-style fieldstone cottage situated on Dutchess Hill three miles from his mother's home, Springwood. The president was delighted to host this powerfully symbolic event at his new cottage, which the architect Henry Toombs had just recently completed. In the cottage a large fieldstone fireplace stood at the back wall of a large living/dining area looking out onto a veranda, which faced west toward the Shawangunk and Catskill mountains.

Top Cottage had its own "first lady," FDR's sixth cousin, Margaret "Daisy" Suckley, who was nine years younger than Franklin and was also Eleanor's fourth cousin. In 1922, Sara Roosevelt had asked thirty-one-year-old Daisy to serve as Franklin's companion and help him recuperate from his polio. Daisy was the kind of subservient and adoring woman with whom FDR felt most comfortable; she loved him unquestioningly and considered it an honor to minister to him. It was Daisy who gave FDR the black Scottie dog he named Fala, who became a great comfort in the last years of his life and would famously help him win his fourth presidential term. Early in his struggle with polio, he and Daisy began taking long drives in the woods around Hyde Park, where Franklin had ridden horseback as a child. In March 1935, FDR wrote Daisy, "There is a hill—in the back country—perhaps this spring we can go to it." They both developed an attachment to the area around Dutchess Hill. In her letters to FDR and in her diary, Daisy began to call it "our hill." That fall when they returned to the hill, something happened between them that FDR called the "start of a voyage." Geoffrey Ward, who edited Daisy's letters in *Closest Companion*, believed the incident was a passionate kiss, but it could have been some form of commitment between them. From then on in their letters, there were hints of a more romantic relationship. When Daisy sent him an article about a police crackdown on driving a car with just one hand, she underlined the admonition "both hands must be on the wheel." Franklin, for his part, wrote her that he was in need of the services of a young Dutchess County woman "experienced in gardening, trees & hilltops," while adding suggestively that "I have other qualifications in mind."

In 1935 they began to make plans to build themselves a retreat on Dutchess Hill. As the official town historian of Hyde Park, FDR had been drawn to the area's Dutch Colonial architecture; he wanted to design a small fieldstone cottage in that style. Two years later, after purchasing the land, FDR drew sketches and sent them to his architect, Henry Toombs, who had supervised the building of Eleanor's retreat, the Val-Kill Cottage, some ten years before. FDR made detailed comments on each stage of the design process. Toombs ultimately listed Franklin as the project's primary architect—outraging licensed architects, who found the arrangement not only unethical but a bad precedent to set for untrained dabblers who might claim to be architects based on an interest in drafting.

Now Top Cottage would be the site of what was arguably the nation's most politically and socially controversial dining event of the twentieth century. The picnic, and particularly the hot dogs, were the Roosevelts' deliberate symbol of the convergence of two cultures, where the values of the reuniting countries would be melded. The prospective event had made many Americans indignant, for different reasons. Over the previous weeks, the country had become obsessed with the hot dogs. People had reacted as if serving hot dogs to a king and queen was a crucial matter of foreign policy.

The FDR Library has huge files stuffed with anxious and angry letters sent to Mrs. Roosevelt in the month before the picnic. A letter from Bradley Stafford expressed disgust over "this begging trip of the King and Queen." In a telegram from New York City's Hotel Pennsylvania to Mrs. Roosevelt, A. M. Newell wrote, "Must you feed the Queen Hot Dogs? It is not exactly fare. I think we all agree that the Queen is a lady." A Pittsburgh woman wrote to express her Christian indignation and "great sorrow and regret at the report . . . of your Hotdog-Beer Sunday picnic . . . that does not in any way show to the Honored King and Queen even the average way . . . citizens from the Atlantic to the Pacific observe God's Most Holy Day. Some do spend it in dissipation, but why show that to our Royal Visitors . . . Your actions were beneath the leader of a Christian nation."

The uproar was so strong that Eleanor Roosevelt was compelled to write about the controversy in her column: "Oh, dear, oh, dear, so many people are worried that 'the dignity of our country will be imperiled,'" by inviting royalty to a picnic, particularly a hot dog picnic. She told the country how Sara Roosevelt had forwarded a letter begging the president's mother to control the First Lady in some way. "To spare my feelings," Eleanor wrote—knowing full well that her mother-in-law had never done anything to spare her feelings—"she has only written on the back: 'Only one of many such.' But she did not know, poor darling, that I have received 'many such' right here in Washington. Let me assure you, dear readers, that if it is hot, there will be no hot-dogs, and even if it is cool, there will be plenty of other food, and the elder members of the family and the more important guests will be served with due formality. It might be possible," she continued, "to meet the desire of these interested correspondents if there were not quite so many who berate me for too much formality and too much courtesy. I am afraid it is a case of not being able to please everybody and so we will try to please our guests."

Those who didn't object to the picnic on moral, patriotic, or culinary grounds wanted to profit from it. Nedick's Stores, New York's self-styled "outstanding distributors," with 120 outlets offering the "lowly, American 'hot-dog,'" sought to furnish the grills and prepare the hot dogs and buns. They wrote to the president's secretary that they were "anxious . . . to perform this service without any thought of using this incident for our own publicity, unless it be that we may be allowed to post a small dignified sign in our shops to the effect that Nedick's 'hot-dogs' were served to Their Majesties." Their offer, like so many others with mixed motives, was declined.

The controversial hot dogs were actually purchased by Harry Johannesen, who was a friend of Frank and John Roosevelt, and the twenty-five-year-old son of the Roosevelts' Springwood cook, Nellie Johannesen. Harry went to Poughkeepsie to buy the entrees from Swift and Company, because, as he told the author, "they are the best." Nellie did all the cooking, and all the food was brought up from the kitchen at the tearoom at Val-Kill. Other entrees included cured hams, smoked turkey, steak, potato salad, and baked beans—all staples of the American table, if lacking the symbolism of the all-American hot dog. Steaks and other fancier foods on the menu were downplayed for the press. Dessert included Dutchess County strawberries from the estate of Treasury Secretary Henry Morgenthau Jr.

Before the picnic started, Eleanor told all the estate's workers they could take pictures of the event for about fifteen minutes on the condition that they would not allow any photographs to be published. Harry Johannesen, proud of the expensive thirty-five-millimeter Argus camera his wife had given him for Christmas, took some of the few photographs of the picnic that survive. Almost sixty years later, he allowed the *Hyde Park Sportsman* to publish them. Many of the Roosevelt staff's photographs did not come out; they were using cheap box cameras. At a reunion picnic fifty years later, seventy-one-year-old Fred Draiss, one of ten children whose father had worked for the Roosevelts, revealed that his family had taken a picture of the most symbolic and controversial moment of the whole tour: the king eating his first hot dog. Unfortunately, the photograph did not come out.

Daisy Suckley, the president's distant cousin, and Angier Biddle Duke, whose wife was a relative of FDR's mother, were official guests at both the original picnic and a fiftieth anniversary picnic in 1989. They agreed that too much attention was paid on both occasions, fifty years apart, to those hot dogs. At the anniversary picnic, ninety-eight-year-old Daisy, who had witnessed the original hot dogs delivered on a silver dish to the king, declared, "It's all so silly." Duke recalled the king "standing around with a cup in his hand, eating and drinking. It was all very natural, no big deal in the act, but made into one in the press."

But in 1939, it was as if consuming hot dogs would mark a moment of equality between the two countries, finally balancing the relationship between the superior British culture and the American upstarts. Even more than the placing of a wreath at the tomb of George Washington, who had rebelled against their ancestors, the king and queen's willingness to eat a cardinal American food would signal their final acceptance of Americans as equals.


After the picnic lunch, Princess Te-Ata, a half-breed Choctaw-Chickasaw Indian from Oklahoma who lived in luxury on Park Avenue in New York City, and the singer Ish-Ti-Opi, both dressed in beaded buckskin costumes, entertained the one hundred and fifty guests with Native American folk tales and songs. They received tepid reviews from the guests ("boring," said one; "not very good," according to another), but the king and queen appeared to enjoy their introduction to American indigenous culture.

The king seemed relaxed and pleased with the informality of the picnic, drinking several beers and taking home movies of the performers and the guests. (The king's movies survive, but are in storage somewhere in one of the present queen's homes—and not available to the public at this time.) As guests were photographing him, he turned his movie camera on them. Eleanor was annoyed that some of the guests, including her friend Nancy Cook, the co-owner of Val-Kill, snapped photographs of everyone around them: "She felt that even the *maids* 'would know better,'" according to Daisy Suckley. Eleanor dashed "about in a little brown gingham dress, seeing that lunch was properly served and that everybody was comfortable, just as though it was a family party," recalled one of her sons. Angier Biddle Duke remembered that as soon as the picnic was over, there was a mad dash through the heat and dust to get into cars to drive the short distance to the Val-Kill Cottage for swimming and tea.

After the picnic, the king changed into a one-piece dark blue swimming suit, which James Roosevelt called "a thing with vestigial remnants of legs and arms that appeared to me to be a genuine relic from the era of his grandfather King Edward VII." Also wearing his bathing suit, FDR drove James and the king down to the Val-Kill Cottage, where they could swim. Motoring past a line of National Guardsmen, who saluted them, the king seemed mortified at having to review the troops in his bathing suit. FDR found the informality amusing. When they reached the gate, the president noticed a group of news cameramen. He stopped the car and deputized James to tell the press that no photographs would be allowed of the two heads of state in their bathing suits. If they refused to comply, they would be denying the king and the president a chance to relax. The press was thus deprived of a classic photograph; "the wails of anguish and protest were heart-rending," according to James.

The queen had been invited to swim as well, but she chose to sit with Eleanor and her lady-in-waiting under the shady trees by the side of the green-tiled pool at Val-Kill. Eleanor understood by then that "if you are a Queen, you cannot run the risk of looking disheveled," as she said in her memoirs. As the women sipped iced and hot tea, they could look over the lawn, which ran down to a pond fringed with willow trees and a meadow lit up with blue irises, daisies, and buttercups.

When tea and the swim were over, the president drove the king and queen and his favorite daughter-in-law, Betsey, to the banks of the Hudson River, where he showed them the first-growth timber on his estate, which he believed to be part of the primeval forest of America, existing before the arrival of European settlers. The queen was particularly impressed with the prospect; fifty years later she remembered Hyde Park for "the beauty of its woods and fields leading down to the banks of the Hudson River."

That night the royal train would leave for Canada. Early in the evening, the king and queen joined the rest of their traveling party for a low-key dinner of fish chowder and oyster crackers. During dinner there was a thunderstorm. The queen told everyone that the storm completed the cycle of weather they had experienced during their tour: ice and snow at White River, rain in Winnipeg and Moose Jaw, great heat in Washington, and thunder and lightning with high winds at Hyde Park. Playfully, the king ended the meal by calling out to FDR from the other end of the table: "Mr. President, it's my turn now, *may* we smoke?"

After dinner they exchanged gifts. The royal couple presented Sara Roosevelt, the president, and the First Lady with signed presentation photographs; Sara's set went onto the piano, where it sits today. The king gave FDR a gold inkwell decorated with the royal coat of arms, while the Canadian prime minister presented him with a silver bowl. FDR sent the king home with two books of his speeches and gave a volume of his memoirs to the queen. Roosevelt later sent them aerial photos of their visit to Washington and a scrapbook from the Civilian Conservation Corps. The king and queen asked the Roosevelts to spend an informal week with them at Windsor or Balmoral Castle.

On the first anniversary of the picnic, the queen would be sufficiently moved by her memories of Hyde Park to write Roosevelt an extraordinary thirteen-page letter not only updating him on how war had since transformed their lives but recalling the "lovely" and "sustaining" time they had spent at Hyde Park. "The picnic was *great* fun," she wrote, "and our children were so thrilled with the description of the Indian singing and the marvelous clothes—not to mention the Hot-Dogs!"

At the station in the evening, James, John, and Franklin Jr. joined their parents and watched the king, still dressed in a dinner jacket, and the queen, in a rose dinner dress with a white fur piece at the neck, as they boarded the blue and white train. The king and queen shook hands with the New York state troopers who had protected them, and the queen sought out their chauffeur to thank him for driving so carefully. Eleanor was impressed by the gesture and the training it took to be so thoughtful.

In her memoirs, Eleanor recalled the final moments of the visit as the royal couple stood on the rear platform of the train and "the people who were gathered everywhere on the banks of the Hudson and up on the rocks began to sing 'Auld Lang Syne.' There was something incredibly moving about the scene—the river in the evening light, the voices of the many people singing this old song, and the train slowly pulling out with the young couple waving goodbye. One thought of the clouds that hung over them and the worries they were going to face, and turned away and left the scene with a heavy heart." As the train departed, FDR yelled out in his "vibrant tenor voice," "Good luck to you. All the luck in the world."

Sara Roosevelt had firmly reminded her son and daughter-in-law about an old superstition that you must not watch departing friends until they are out of sight, lest you risk their safety. So the presidential couple stood and waved as the train departed, but headed to their cars before the train went around a bend and moved out of view.

Eleanor went right to bed, too exhausted to write letters. The following morning she wrote Hick: "FDR was satisfied & all went well. I liked them both but what a life! They are happy together however & that must make a difference in the life they have to lead. . . . They undoubtedly made friends." In fact, Eleanor had noted earlier on that the royal couple had "a gift for friendship."

While Eleanor liked both Their Majesties, she was particularly drawn to Bertie. She felt more at home with the king's authentic and down-to-earth manner than she initially did with the queen's bubbly charm. Eleanor and the king shared a powerful commitment to duty, a quality sometimes overshadowed by the incandescence of their spouses. Having struggled to overcome handicaps and shyness, they were modest and self-sacrificing, and identified more with society's underdogs than with high achievers. "They themselves were nice & I wish you could have *talked* to him especially," Eleanor wrote to Hick.

"She is a bit self-conscious, but who wouldn't be? Turning on graciousness like water is bound to affect one in time!"

Daisy Suckley recorded FDR's reactions to the king in her diary:
"He says the king is '*grand*' with an almost American sense of humor—
He never seemed to miss the funny side of anything. . . . He was completely natural and put all the 'royalness' aside when in private . . . F
said he tested out the king's sense of humor with two of his oldest jokes
which he can't laugh at himself! The king rocked back & forward with
laughter, repeating over & over, 'It can't be true—It *can't* be true.'"
Suckley shared Eleanor's initial slight reservation about the queen,
who, "on the other hand, could *never* quite forget she was a queen, &
is a little lacking in humor, though a fine person."

For their part, the king and queen felt at home in Hyde Park,
almost literally. Sara Roosevelt and her son had modeled their country
life on that of the English aristocracy. With some care, they had created the illusion that the royal couple was visiting friends at a country
estate in England. The queen wrote Queen Mary that the Roosevelts
were "living so like English people when they come to their country
house." Fifty years later, the Queen Mother would recall that "our time
in America was an idyllic experience." Very late in her life, in response
to questions posed for this book through her private secretary, she
would still be impressed by the American couple she called "true
American gentlefolk."

In a message sent by the Queen Mother in 1989, on the anniversary
of the picnic, she recalled that the memory of the Hyde Park stay was
"a source of strength and comfort to the king and me through the dark
days of the Second World War, which followed so soon after our visit."
The king would be even more personally and profoundly affected by his
encounters with FDR. Bertie told Mackenzie King a number of times
about the impression Roosevelt had made on him, that "he had never
met a person with whom he felt freer in talking and whom he enjoyed
more." In fact, Franklin Roosevelt would change his life. Through their
conversations and by virtue of the example he set, like a master giving a
talented student tutelage and blessing, the president encouraged the
king to step fully into his power as leader of the Commonwealth.
Unlike the king's own father, Roosevelt helped the young monarch
appreciate his own strengths and realize his full potential as a leader;
like Roosevelt himself, the king could transcend his insecurities and his

disability. FDR, who excelled at giving the illusion of intimacy, created a friendship in which the still untested and tentative monarch felt fully accepted as an equal. The confidence the king gained would help sustain him during the most dispiriting days of the war.

A week after Their Majesties left, FDR was still warmed by the congenial promise the royal visit afforded. He sent a telegram that reached them aboard the SS *Empress of Britain:* "I cannot allow you and the Queen to sail home without expressing once more the extreme pleasure which your all too brief visit to the United States gave us. . . . Americans were deeply touched by the tact, the graciousness, and the understanding hearts of our guests. I shall always think that you felt the sincerity of this manifestation of the friendship of the American people." The king responded with "heartfelt thanks" for the hospitality, and noted that the brief visit "has given us memories of kindly feeling and goodwill that we shall always treasure."

Rose Kennedy had returned to the United States in case Their Majesties needed her assistance, but she had come alone: her husband Joe's request for leave had been denied by the State Department. Refusing an invitation to the state dinner at the White House, and staying in New York, Rose claimed to be tired, but more to the point, she did not want to highlight her husband's obvious exclusion from the event. In spite of the indignities she and Joe had suffered thanks to his reputation as an unreliable, self-aggrandizing opportunist, she had an astute perspective on the royal visit. She wrote in her diary on the Sunday of the Hyde Park picnic: "Everyone unanimous in their praise of the King and Queen, especially of the Queen. Her charm, her kindness, her understanding, her constant smile, which puts everyone at ease. Then, too, the unexpected incidents, the fact that they mingled with the crowd on different occasions, the fact that they spoke to the newspaper reporters on the train and saw the press at the White House, their willingness to fulfill the social engagements under sweltering heat and overcrowded programs. Then, too, the king's slim, straight, almost boyish face and figure, his simplicity, unaffected charm, his readiness and even eagerness to cooperate."

The British screenwriter and broadcaster Eric Knight, who would effectively promote the British cause to Americans during the war, wrote to the filmmaker Paul Rotha about the royal visit and said that the queen, single-handedly, had transformed U.S. public opinion:

"The American people, very suddenly and unreasoningly, merely went mad and riotously crazy over the Queen, and as a result in England today—almost overnight—now stands in popular estimation in the position she did several years ago. In admiration of this one woman, America has somehow blinded herself to Chamberlain, has forgotten Munich, and now sees only the strong British nation again."

In the immediate aftermath of the royal visit, and in the years following, politicians and professors have debated its historical importance. Fred Leventhal, a Boston University history professor who is an expert on Anglo-American cultural relations, concluded that the great achievement of the royal visit "was to overcome Yankee republican ambivalence by stripping the monarchy of the visible trappings of majesty." Writing in his book *Singular Continuities: Tradition, Nostalgia, and Identity in Modern British Culture*, he said, "While Americans were certainly fascinated by immemorial traditions and pageantry, so alien to their own national culture, they could openly countenance a monarch who represented kindred political institutions, thereby reinforcing mutual Anglo-American values . . . the royal visit did let in daylight upon magic, exhibiting the king and queen not as Olympian figures, but—within limits—as approachable, even ordinary, mortals with familiar concerns and domestic responsibilities." In the United States, King George became a fully democratic, people's king. The United States and Britain showed they were ready to merge for a greater purpose, without losing their separate identities.

Two years later, during Christmas dinner at the White House in 1941, FDR told his guests, including Winston Churchill, that the king and queen's visit had been "a beginning of the coming together of the two English-speaking races, which would go on after the war."

Right after the visit Mackenzie King, who was capable of hyperbole, wrote FDR that "nothing fraught with so great significance or good has happened since 'the great scism [*sic*] of the Anglo-Saxon race.'" Yet while the visit went a long way toward a final healing of the separation of Great Britain and the United States, it did not have the immediate tangible benefits that many had hoped for. British ambassador Ronald Lindsay made a more balanced assessment than that of the Canadian prime minister. In a cable to the Foreign Office, Lindsay wrote that "Americans today feel closer to the Empire than they did a fortnight ago, and this cannot fail to be of immense importance. . . .

While we cannot at present feel certain of having received an immediate dividend we can be assured that our hidden reserves have been immensely strengthened."

One of the king and queen's many triumphs in America was to win over the crusty Harold Ickes, who admitted in his diary that the royal couple had made an excellent impression—"although I doubt that there will be any relaxation of the wariness with respect to possible entanglements in foreign affairs." Ickes was right to doubt. Even though Eleanor had written Hick about her hope that the visit "might give Hitler and Mussolini food for thought," by the end of June 1939, the House of Representatives had failed to revise the Neutrality Act and eliminate the arms embargo provision. Despite the president's hopes, he was not going to be able to deliver on some of his promises to the king. The administration's devastating failure to reverse the arms embargo meant that FDR would not be able to come to the aid of his new friends when London was bombed by the Luftwaffe in the spring of 1940. The triumph of the king and queen's visit could not make up for the failure of Europe and the United States to thwart the territorial ambitions of the world's dictators. It would take war, not just the power of majesty, to transform two increasingly friendly nations into absolute allies.

# 10

# "Our Hearts Are Near Breaking"

## JUNE 1939–NOVEMBER 1940

> When we think of our gallant young men being sacrificed to the terrible machine that Germany has created, I think that anger perhaps dominates, but when we think of their valor, their determination & their grand spirit, their pride and joy are uppermost.
>
> —*Queen Elizabeth in a letter to Eleanor Roosevelt*

## London

At Guildhall on June 23, 1939, following a tumultuous welcome home the day before, George VI went on the radio with an emotional declaration that the monarchy could be "a potent force for promoting peace and goodwill among mankind." The queen was proud of his fresh confidence and that he sought to renew the tarnished value of the Crown; Winston Churchill, still in political exile, was stirred by his oratory. To a nation growing ever more anxious about war, and to the world beyond Britain, the king reported that his North American visit showed British institutions flourishing everywhere. They "mean more to us even than the splendor of our history or the glories of the English tongue," he said, "because they are grounded root and branch on British faith in liberty and justice."

A week later, the king would be disappointed in his new friend

Roosevelt. It would be the first of many disappointments and conflicts between the royal family and the Roosevelts, and between the United States and Britain, in the months and years to come. There were dark times ahead when all of Roosevelt's heady promises at Hyde Park would seem empty. FDR, caught between his desire to help Britain and his need to respond to American public opinion, at first dangled before Ambassador Lindsay and then withdrew an offer to establish a U.S. naval patrol in the western Atlantic—to stop belligerents from engaging in warlike actions against ships of any nation—in exchange for use of British naval bases in the Caribbean and Canada. Then isolationist congressmen won a stunning victory over the president, sending world dictators a signal that the Unites States' foreign policy was gutless, by voting not to drop the arms embargo provision of the Neutrality Act. The hopes engendered in Hyde Park were temporarily but seriously set back.

As Germany came closer to daring Europe into war, the royal family got a brief respite: they took a summer cruise, stopping at the Royal Naval College at Dartmouth, where thirteen-year-old Princess Elizabeth became enamored of her future husband, Prince Philip of Greece, eighteen, who in turn focused on teasing Princess Margaret. In August near Balmoral, the king held what would be his final Duke of York boy's camp—the war would soon halt the yearly event—where he joined the boys' campfires for songs like "Under the Spreading Chestnut Tree." At the visit's final bonfire, pipers circled the royal family as they played; the evening ended with a passionate singing of the British national anthem.

On August 22 came the deathblow to any hope of peace. Germany and the Soviet Union announced a nonaggression pact, freeing Germany's eastern border from attack and allowing Hitler to attack Poland. The king and queen returned to London early, while FDR cut short his rest cruise on the USS *Tuscaloosa*. By the end of the month, the British fleet was mobilized and civilians began to evacuate London.

## Hyde Park and Washington, D.C.

At 5 A.M. on September 1 at Hyde Park, Eleanor "received a spiritual shock," according to her friend Harry Hooker, when FDR called her from Washington to say that Germany had invaded Poland. She was distraught. Her decades-long fight for peace lost, she wrote Hick: "It is all so senseless, he [Hitler] must have all [the territory] he wants & so Europe will be a battlefield." FDR was "restrained and wise," she thought, when he addressed the nation that night, declaring, "When peace has been broken anywhere, the peace of all countries everywhere is in danger." Within days, the British Royal Air Force would be attacking the German navy. As the war began, the king broadcast to the Commonwealth: "We are called to meet the challenge of . . . the primitive doctrine that Might is Right . . . with God's help we shall prevail." Inconsolable, Ambassador Kennedy called the president from London to say repeatedly in a choked voice, "It is the end of the world . . . the end of everything."

## France and England

At this daunting moment, skirmishes broke out again between the Duke and Duchess of Windsor and his brother and the government. The duke, summoned home to consider a job as a major-general providing liaison with the French army or as a civilian working under the Civil Defence commissioner in Wales, refused to return unless his wife was welcomed at Windsor Castle. Highly stressed, Their Majesties were in no mood to make concessions to the Windsors, who were consorting with a so-called Peace Movement, which was actually a Nazi front working against the Allied cause. After Churchill intervened, the brothers met on September 14 for what the king told Lord Mountbatten was a "friendly" but "not very pleasant interview." The duke, oblivious to the unresolved trauma of the abdication for the rest of the royal family and the British government, sought front-line administrative war jobs for himself and his wife.

The duke, in his current role as a liaison to Britain's military mission in Paris, soon usurped his brother's military role by accepting the salute of British troops already in France. When the king banned him from further contact with the armed services, the duke struck back. In January 1940, he made a secret trip to England. While there, he engaged in discussions with the troublemaking press baron Lord Beaverbrook, planning a campaign for accommodation with Germany. Such discussions were treasonous. When the duke realized that living in Britain meant paying income taxes, he jettisoned his grand schemes to form an opposition government, preferring to stay in France, where he could better finance the duchess's taste for high royal style.

The king, who had discontinued George V's tradition of making Christmas Day radio addresses for fear he could not match his father's legendary performances, bowed to government pressure to deliver his first Christmas Day broadcast. He practiced and reworked his speech for weeks, to project a reassuring confidence to Britain, and to demonstrate British resolve to the Nazis. He drew on a little-known poem to encourage his anxious subjects: "I said to the man who stood at the Gate of the Year, 'Give me a light that I may tread safely into the unknown.' And he replied, 'Go out into the darkness, and put your hand in the Hand of God. That shall be to you better than light, and safer than a known way.'"

In a wintry period that U.S. newspapers dubbed the "Phony War," the Nazis would wait for six nerve-wracking months before striking again once the weather was favorable. Meanwhile, the queen crisscrossed Britain in the royal train, visiting wartime facilities, hospitals, factories, and even children whose parents had sent them to safety in the countryside. When Lord Woolton, the food minister, set up a meal delivery service, he publicly asked Her Majesty if he could call it the Queen's Messengers, explaining that "the vast majority of the people think of you as a person who would speak the kindly word, and, if it fell within your power, would take the cup of hot soup to the needy person." Visibly moved, the queen replied: "Oh, my lord," as her hands flew up to her face. "Do you think I mean that? It is what I have tried so hard to be."

When Hitler invaded Norway and Denmark on April 9, 1940, the king visited the Admiralty War Room, but had "a bad day," as he wrote in his diary: "everyone working at fever heat except me." As commander in chief of the armed forces of Great Britain and the empire, George VI possessed one real power, which was the right to advise and encourage the prime minister and the members of Parliament. As badly as he wanted to be involved in war planning, he had no more authority to direct the war effort than he had had as a midshipman in 1914. However, as the war evolved, he found a way to have a genuine effect, far more than symbolic power, through his great influence on Winston Churchill and his ability as emblem and emissary of the state to receive and exchange information with soldiers, government officials, and civilians involved in the war effort.

geared up to fight a war that had not really begun, the
ing ahead to the postwar period, pondering ways to
ring the war would inflict. He wanted the U.S. diplo-
Sumner Wells to bring the president a letter proposing an Anglo-
American relief organization. When Wells told him that carrying
home a letter would be tantamount to U.S. collaboration with Britain,
the king was furious. He wrote in his diary: "The U.S. is not coming in
to help us, & nothing yet will make them." On April 2, he wrote
directly to the president about the possibilities of "a serious dearth of
the necessities" and "widespread distress and misery," and suggested
prompt stockpiling of goods and food.

With letters like this, the Roosevelts and the royal family began a
wartime correspondence in which they would constantly remind each
other of their happy memories of the Hyde Park visit and thus reaffirm
their friendship amid the strains of the war and their nations' differing
agendas. "Last June seems years distant," FDR wrote on May 1; he
referred to their late-night talks at Hyde Park and of how, after Congress
refused to engage the European conflict in even the most monitory way,
he had to tolerate the "charge of being a 'calamity-howler,'" exaggerat-
ing a small conflict into a big crisis. FDR reassured the king he was satisfied the European war would "bring home the seriousness of the world
situation to the type of American who has hitherto believed, in much too
large numbers, that no matter what happens there will be little effect on
this country." The king felt desperate about the British military's need
for arms, and was hopeful Roosevelt would come through, but was also
dubious whether FDR would or could deliver on the promises he so fervently had made at Hyde Park the year before.

Eleanor wrote with "warm sympathy" to the queen: "I have wanted
to write and tell you how constantly you and the king are in my
thoughts. Since meeting you, I think I can understand a little better
what a weight of sorrow and anxiety must be yours."

Exactly a year after the Hyde Park picnic, the queen sent a heartfelt thirteen-page letter to Mrs. Roosevelt in which she expressed her
sorrow, her gratitude to the United States, and her hopes for spiritual
renewal:

> Sometimes one's heart seems near breaking under the stress of
> so much sorrow and anxiety—where we think of our gallant

young men . . . we think of their values, their determination, & their grand spirit, their pride and joy uppermost. . . . We are all prepared to sacrifice everything in the fight to save freedom . . . our hearts have been lightened by the knowledge that friends in America understand what we are fighting for. . . . It is so terrible to think that all the things we have worked for, these last twenty years are being lost or destroyed in the madness of such a cruel war . . . but . . . I do believe that there is a gradual awakening to the needs of the spirit, and that, combined with adversity and sorrow overcome, may lay the seeds of a far better world.

Aware how ill prepared Britain was for war, Their Majesties had fervently supported Prime Minister Chamberlain's appeasement of Germany, but now—tainted by his capitulation at Munich— Chamberlain resigned. The king suggested Lord Halifax to Chamberlain as his successor, but Halifax was not interested. When all of Parliament agreed that Churchill should be the new leader, the king and queen were strongly opposed; they perceived him as an egotistical risk-taker, and a staunch supporter of the Duke and Duchess of Windsor. The king wrote in his diary, though, that "there is only one person whom I can send for who had the confidence of the country & that was Winston." The queen was also appalled by his tactlessness and his dismissive attitude toward women. A day after receiving Churchill, the king wrote in his diary: "I cannot yet think of Winston as P.M." Nevertheless, the king dutifully accepted Churchill—and so began a remarkable wartime partnership in which all three leaders would come to symbolize British pluck and stamina in the face of great risk and hardship. They would need all the pluck, and luck, they could muster: just as Churchill took office, the Nazis invaded France, Belgium, Luxembourg, and the Netherlands.

On May 13, Winston Churchill addressed the House of Commons, memorably offering the nation nothing "but blood, toil, tears and sweat" with the aim of "victory at all costs . . . victory, how-ever long and hard the road may be." A month later he would proclaim, "Let us . . . so bear ourselves that, if the British Empire and its Commonwealth last for a thousand years, men will say, 'This was their finest hour.'" Their finest hour was darkening every moment. By the end of May, Holland and Belgium had surrendered to Germany, and

British and French troops were surrounded at Dunkirk; many were killed. The tiny British expeditionary force destroyed its weapons, then retreated on a flotilla of small boats to England. Over 335,000 British and French troops were rescued from the Nazis in the most significant military evacuation in history, one that heartened the harried Allies. After the terrible losses at Dunkirk, Churchill appealed to Roosevelt, who authorized the sale of rifles, field guns, and machine guns to Britain. Courageously using his full authority and going against the unanimous advice of his secretary of war, his military advisers, and the leaders of Congress, Roosevelt ordered the War Department to search until they found a statute allowing "surplus" arms to be put up for sale to a private corporation. The arms were then sold to Britain. On June 10 Roosevelt gave a commencement speech at the University of Virginia in Charlottesville (his son FDR Jr. was getting his law degree that day), saying, "We will extend to the opponents of force the material resources of this nation. . . . We will not slow down or detour . . . full speed ahead."

June brought no relief. Italy teamed up with Germany. France fell. At this gloomy hour, Churchill and the king, recognizing how much they had in common as former soldiers with a passionate interest in geopolitics and combat strategy, began to meet for private weekly Tuesday lunches, often served, for reasons of privacy, by the queen from a sideboard. Churchill grew to trust the king's judgment, decisiveness, and thorough preparation; he discussed every aspect of the war with him, and the two men came to support and hearten each other. They were jointly committed to campaigning for America's life-saving support.

In this mortal crisis, the duke and duchess yet again made pests of themselves. When France had been on the verge of falling to the Nazis, the duke had been summoned home to ensure his own safety. As a condition of his return, he insisted on guarantees of what he termed "proper" treatment (that is, status as Her Royal Highness) for the duchess. Churchill sent him a stern telegram ordering him back on threat of military subordination. Churchill and Their Majesties, uncomfortable with the duke's profascist sentiments and determined to keep the duke and duchess away from the Nazis, who saw them as potential puppet monarchs once England fell to Germany, banished them to the Caribbean. Far away from his homeland and unable to

cause trouble, the duke would become the governor and con
chief of the Bahamas. Wallis called the posting "the
of 1940."

The British monarch endured not only difficulties with his family
but also frustrations with his friends, namely the U.S. president. He
wrote FDR again on June 22, reminding him how he and the queen
savored "the delightful days" with the Roosevelts the previous year, and
imploring him to make good on his Hyde Park promises. Beyond selling Britain weapons it could not afford, Roosevelt had to meet what the
king called his country's "urgent need of some of your older destroyers
to tide us over the next few months. I well understand your difficulties,
and am certain that you will do your best to procure them for us before
it is too late . . . the need is becoming greater every day if we are to
carry on our solitary fight for freedom to a successful conclusion."

The king waited impatiently while Roosevelt shepherded the
request for destroyers through the balky but increasingly sympathetic
Congress. In early September, Congress approved sending eight wob-
bly old destroyers to Britain; forty-six more would follow.

Amid these conflicts, which challenged the king but also helped
him develop a role that gave his monarchy fresh meaning, Bertie
trusted his wife's judgment and sought her out for solace. "The King
was told everything," the queen later said, "so, of course, I knew about
everything as well." While Elizabeth appeared more comfortable in
public, often stepping forward while the king held back, in private each
leaned on the other for strength. But as the king and queen drew even
closer in their effort to elevate Britain's spirits, the Roosevelts would
drift farther apart.

## Washington, D.C.

Eleanor and Franklin had worked closely to humanize government and
to renew national prosperity during the previous decade, but in the
1940s the overwhelming demands of managing a world war on two
fronts divided them from each other. FDR did not include Eleanor in
any of the major wartime conferences he traveled to. He needed desperately to relax in his spare moments, while Eleanor wanted to push social
agendas he could not muster the energy to face. He avoided her because
she was not relaxing; she could not relax because she was shut out.

They both turned to other people to find the support and intimacy they needed. During the summer of 1940, Eleanor formed an intensely sustaining and intellectual mother-son relationship with Joseph Lash, a young socialist who would become her Pulitzer Prize–winning biographer. She also became emotionally attached to her secretary and aide, Tommy Thompson, who lived and traveled with her. Lorena Hickok worked for the Democratic National Committee and lived secretly in the White House during the war. Hick accepted the small amount of time that Eleanor's schedule allowed for her, and the two met for occasional breakfasts and late-night chats.

When Eleanor was away, FDR's secretary, Missy LeHand, acted as social hostess and surrogate wife. Even as Missy wrapped her world around Franklin, she was careful to stay close to Eleanor and treat her with deference. Missy hoped that she would be able to retire with Franklin at Hyde Park, but in June 1941, she suffered several strokes that deprived her of speech. For all his public sympathy toward those who suffered sickness or privation, Franklin had little private tolerance for pain and illness among those close to him. He visited Missy infrequently in the hospital—a great cruelty—although he did look after her in his will, at some cost to his children's inheritance. Missy despaired; on several occasions, she tried to take her life.

Other women, including Daisy Suckley, would assume Missy's place. In August 1940, after defying the Nazis for as long as she could, Crown Princess Märtha left Norway and moved into the White House with her three children. His aides teasingly called her "the president's girlfriend," and Franklin's son James thought they might have been lovers. The president lit up in her presence, especially at cocktail hour. After Märtha moved to an estate in Maryland, FDR visited frequently. "There was always a Martha for relaxation and for the nonending pleasure of having an admiring audience for every breath," Eleanor complained to a friend.

## Canada and Hyde Park

After Lord Tweedsmuir died in February 1940, the king, advised by the Canadian government, offered the job of governor-general to his sixty-five-year-old uncle, Lord Athlone, the dutiful younger brother of Queen Mary. Lord Athlone, affable and confident, arrived in Canada with his wife Princess Alice, a first cousin of the king's father. The vivacious and highly intelligent princess had the strong personality and the wit of the American "Princess" Alice, but without the bitterness that made Teddy Roosevelt's daughter so caustic. Establishing themselves at Rideau Hall, the governor-general's home, they were tireless in supporting Canada's war effort.

When the Athlones visited Hyde Park in June 1940, the princess described the Big House as an "old fashioned muddle," but found FDR to possess "real greatness of character." Despite a wild car ride through the woods at the president's estate, they both "fell completely under his spell," according to Alice. When Eleanor arrived home "like a whirlwind" from a trip to Seattle, Alice was drawn to the equally bossy and energetic First Lady, but Lord Athlone felt nearly deafened by Eleanor's loud conversation at lunch. FDR's eighty-four-year-old mother, Sara, was "a great dear, but such a matriarch," Alice decided.

## London

In London that summer, the queen took revolver lessons on a firing range set up in the palace gardens. "I shall not go down like the others," she told the diplomat Harold Nicolson, meaning that she did not intend to leave her country like her exiled royal relatives. Nicholson lunched with the royal couple and was surprised that, amid the unrelentingly dire war news, the king seemed as lighthearted as his older brother had once been. "He was so gay and she was so calm," Nicolson wrote his wife, Vita Sackville-West. "They did me all the good in the world." He left the luncheon confident, against all immediate evidence, that the British would triumph.

Bertie and Elizabeth's two daughters stayed at Windsor Castle for safety during the war. In a famous statement that put the royal family squarely on the same footing as the British public, the queen displayed her personal grit in explaining why she would not send her daughters out of England during the war: "They will not leave me. I will not leave the king—and the king will never leave." At times, Their Majesties were actually careless about their own safety; for a long time, even after the Nazis began bombing England, there was not even a proper air-raid shelter at Buckingham Palace. Queen Wilhelmina of the Netherlands, living in exile at the palace, asked one day what would happen if "German paratroopers started landing in that garden right now." The king pressed a special alarm bell. Nothing happened. Furious, the king tightened security and ordered an air-raid shelter to be built.

In the later part of August 1940, Nazi bombs destroyed parts of Bath, Coventry, Plymouth, Manchester, and Birmingham. To bring comfort and boost national morale, the king and queen began a series of visits to affected areas; during the course of the war, they would travel over forty thousand miles, making three hundred separate trips on the royal train. Only once, hours after the town of Coventry had almost been destroyed, did the king spare the queen an inspection. Normally they journeyed together. In two September weeks during the 1940 bombing raids known as the Blitz, eight thousand Londoners were killed or injured. During one air raid, the royal couple shared tea in a public shelter with London East Enders. Dressed in designer Norman Hartnell's dusty pastel concoctions, their style and colors chosen to convey solace and comfort, the queen said, "If the poor people had come to see me, *they* would have put on their best clothes." Famously, a Cockney woman watching the queen help a disabled woman dress her baby cried out, "Oh, ain't she lovely. Ain't she just *bloody* lovely."

"We all feel a warmth radiating from you," an official told the queen. "I can't describe it, something intangible. Do you feel that you are giving something out?" The queen's response was startlingly frank. "I must admit that at times I feel something flow out of me. It is difficult to describe what I mean. It makes me feel very tired for a moment. Then I seem to get something back from the people—sympathy, goodwill—I don't know what exactly—and I feel strengthened again, in fact, recharged." Churchill said of her, "Many an aching heart found solace in her gracious smile."

On Monday, September 9, 1940, a bomb dropped on the palace and lay ominously beneath the king's study before exploding during the night. Ambassador Kennedy joined the king for tea the next day in a makeshift office. The king, shaken, was infuriated when Kennedy, who tended to view events in economic rather than political terms, suggested that Britain let Hitler have the resource-poor Balkan countries. With his abhorrence of war, Kennedy did not think these countries were worth fighting for. The king was appalled that Kennedy did not seem to understand the importance of England's role as the defender of the rights of small nations. He wrote Kennedy a sharp letter saying that there were important principles at stake, namely the survival of democracy and the right of any nation to exist. Kennedy, rattled, and realizing he had alienated the king, sent an ingratiating letter back.

On the rainy morning of September 13, 1940, the king and queen returned to London from Windsor during an air raid. They were in a small sitting room overlooking the palace quadrangle when an aircraft headed down the Mall toward the palace. "We heard an aircraft make a zooming noise above us, saw 2 bombs falling past the opposite side of the Palace, & then heard two resounding crashes as the bombs fell in the quadrangle about 30 yards away," the king wrote in his diary. "We were out into the passage as fast as we could get there. . . . We all wondered why we weren't dead. . . . It was a ghastly experience . . . but one must be careful not to become 'dugout minded.'"

Six bombs had fallen on the palace. The chapel and a plumber's workshop were destroyed. If the windows of the sitting room had not been open, the king and queen would most likely have been splintered with broken glass and seriously injured. Afterward, the palace windows were boarded up, leaving it a cold and depressing fortress for the rest of the war. Their Majesties downplayed the incident. The king, initially exhilarated by sharing the danger his subjects faced, succumbed to shock and was unable to concentrate for days afterward. The queen's reaction became famous: "I am glad we have been bombed. We can now look the East End in the face."

The bombing of Buckingham Palace marked a turning point: the British people, who had respected the royal couple, now loved them and were inspired by their courageous defiance and their willingness to share so personally in their suffering. From the summer of 1940 until the fall of 1942, as the British endured one military disaster after another, Their Majesties visited one bombed-out city after another to express their sympathy and their admiration for their people's fortitude. The king and queen took seriously their role to encourage not only the king's government and his people, but the empire, and most particularly, the American people.

Writing to thank her friend Ava, Lady Waverly, for a gift of poetry books, Her Majesty would reflect on Britain's redemptive spirit during this time:

I think it is odd that *our* poets were dumb at that glorious moment when the British Isles stood alone against the oppressor, it is disappointing that they do not seem to see the significance of our crusade against slavery and lies—do you not agree? I know that the cruelty & the ugliness & the bestiality of the bombing in 1940 must have been difficult to write about, but through all the horror shone such courage & hope & trust—perhaps our poets will rise to the occasion soon.

## Washington, D.C., and Chicago

As the 1940 election approached, FDR was caught in a dangerous political bind. He believed the United States needed him to run the war that he now saw as inevitable. But seeking a third term as president would challenge a tradition begun by George Washington, that no chief executive serve more than eight years. Announcing that he wanted another term would leave him vulnerable to charges, already in his enemies' arsenal, that he was a power-hungry dictator trampling American political mores, and could derail his campaign before it started. He would have to be crafty, appearing to be a leader reluctantly accepting the torch thrust upon him by a grateful and anxious electorate. He would keep everyone in suspense about his intentions—most of all Eleanor, who wanted him to retire to Hyde Park and exercise his influence from the sidelines. When his cousin Laura Delano asked FDR in Eleanor's presence whether he would run again, he told her, "I am a tired and weary man," which was true, but he was not too tired and weary to want to remain president.

The suspense climaxed at the Chicago Democratic Convention. As FDR had orchestrated, the delegates begged Roosevelt to run again, but after the president made a show of reluctantly acceding to their wishes, they rebelled over his insistence that they nominate the liberal secretary of agriculture, Henry Wallace, as his running mate. FDR pressed a reluctant Eleanor into leaving the quiet of Hyde Park to go to Chicago to rally the delegates. "This is no ordinary time, not time for weighing anything except what we can best do for the country as a whole," she told the convention, convincing the delegates to do FDR's bidding.

The sacrifice was at least as much hers as his. At the rainy 1937 inaugural, Eleanor had consoled herself with the belief that she was embarking on the second and final half of her husband's presidency. When she was once asked to summarize her thirty years as a politician's wife, she called it hell. She listed the claims on the political spouse: "Always be on time. Never try to make any personal engagements. Do as little talking as humanly possible. Never be disturbed by anything. Always do what you are told to do as quickly as possible. . . . Don't get too fat to ride three in a seat [in a parade]. Get out of the way as quickly as you're not needed."

The campaign would not be a cakewalk. The polls that fall showed Roosevelt running evenly against the surprise Republican candidate, the refreshing and folksy newcomer Wendell Willkie. At this tense time, FDR received word from Ambassador Halifax that Joseph Kennedy planned to publish an article condemning Roosevelt's administration a couple days before the election. Kennedy was losing faith that Roosevelt would keep U.S. soldiers out of the war and was determined to do all he could to make sure that his sons would not have to risk their lives. Whereas FDR thought of himself first as the father of the nation, Kennedy's first priority was his children's future. Kennedy questioned, in any case, whether FDR could win election to a third term. The president ordered Kennedy to come directly home from London through Bermuda without speaking to the press. On October 27, the ambassador called FDR from Bermuda just before he was to return to Washington. FDR said, "Ah, Joe. It is good to hear your voice." With House Majority Leader Sam Rayburn and his protégé Lyndon Johnson watching, he told Kennedy, "Please come to the White House tonight for a little family dinner." Smiling, FDR added, "I'm dying to talk to you," as he drew his finger across his throat. He would charm Kennedy into submission and then freeze him out for good.

When Kennedy arrived in New York, he felt pressure from *Time* magazine founder Henry Luce and his wife, Clare Booth Luce, to declare himself for Willkie. At the airport, maritime commissioner Max Truitt handed him a personal letter from the president inviting him to spend the night at the White House. Like a scheming child caught in a tug-of-war between divorcing parents, Joe refused to commit himself until Rose convinced him to see the president. At dinner that night at the White House, Roosevelt deftly defused Kennedy's complaints about being frozen out of the diplomatic process that had planned the king and queen's visit and transacted important war business—such as the deal to provide Britain with destroyers. FDR pretended not to know that the State Department had excluded Kennedy and claimed to be offended by their callousness toward an old friend. Playing on Kennedy's ambitions to run for president in 1944, FDR maneuvered the ambassador into endorsing him in a radio address. Kennedy publicly declared that Roosevelt wanted to keep the United States out of war and would safeguard the nation's children. "After all, I have a great stake in this country," he said. "My wife and I have given nine hostages to fortune."

Nine days later, FDR won a third term with 449 electoral votes over 82 for Willkie. Kennedy promptly outraged the British by telling the *Boston Globe* and the *St. Louis Post-Dispatch*, "Democracy is all finished in England. It may be here." Kennedy believed that severe economic problems, stemming from the war, and the loss of foreign trade would be the downfall of the British system and perhaps the United States as well. Newspaper editorials and columnists said that Kennedy lacked any insight into the British character. The comments marked the disastrous end of his disintegrating ambassadorship.

## Hyde Park

Two days after Thanksgiving, Kennedy arrived at Hyde Park to submit his formal resignation. FDR spent only ten minutes with Kennedy before he summoned Eleanor, and, out of Kennedy's earshot, told her, "I never want to see that son of a bitch again as long as I live. Take his resignation and get him out of here." When Eleanor reminded FDR that Kennedy had been invited for the weekend, he told her, "Then you drive him around Hyde Park, give him a sandwich and put him on the next train." Eleanor had lunch with the now-former ambassador and said later that listening to Kennedy's defeatist views about the war, and his expressions of resentment over his treatment at the hands of the press, the British, and the Roosevelt administration, were "the most dreadful four hours of my life." Worse was to follow.

# 11

# The Propaganda
# Campaign

Despite the constant & murderous bombing our people are full of
courage and determination to win through.

*—King George VI to FDR*

## London

The king and queen knew that Roosevelt's reelection triumph was also a
victory over isolationism, and they tentatively sought to capitalize on it,
advocating on behalf of a Britain battered by the Blitz. "In these grave &
anxious days it is a great relief to feel that your wise and helpful policy
will continue without interruption," the king wrote to FDR in a letter
that he asked British ambassador Lord Lothian to bring to Washington.
"It must have been a great sacrifice to you personally to have stood for
re-election, & I hope that when you lay down your burden, we shall have
victory & peace . . . our two countries will be more closely linked in both
sympathy & fellowship." He ended the letter by continuing his full-
throttle campaign to boost Britain's reputation and ensure the United
States' and the president's full cooperation in the war."

Roosevelt also hoped that his election victory would benefit
Britain. He wrote the king to promise his utmost "in the way of acceleration and in the way of additional release of literally everything we

can spare." FDR also reminded Their Majesties of America's deepening affections for them personally. In fact, the previous year, the queen had been voted Woman of the Year by the readers of syndicated U.S. newspaper columns.

The carefully orchestrated British propaganda campaign to win over the United States was spearheaded by the BBC, the Department of Overseas Trade, and the Ministry of Information. The campaign steamed ahead, with such efforts as the 1939 royal visit, the extremely popular British pavilion at the World's Fair—with its movies of the coronation and its focus on America's and Britain's shared democratic heritage—Churchill's stirring wartime radio speeches, the British war art exhibit, traveling around the United States, the BBC's and U.S. correspondents' direct coverage of the London Blitz, and speeches by the British ambassador Lord Lothian highlighting German treachery and Anglo-American common democratic ideals. Pro-British films (including *London Can Take It*, *The Forty-Ninth Parallel*, and the anti-Nazi documentary *The March of Time*) aided the cause. Churchill, the Foreign Office, and Their Majesties feared the vengeful Duke and Duchess of Windsor could torpedo the British propaganda efforts. It could be hard to tell whose side the duke and his wife were rooting for. When Clare Booth Luce expressed horror about the bombing of Britain's cities, the duchess told her, "After what they did to me, I can't say I feel sorry for them—a whole nation against a lone woman!"

## United States

In August 1940, when the Windsors arrived in Nassau to begin the duke's posting as governor of the Bahamas, the duke and duchess were told by the British government that they would not be able to visit the United States before the November elections. "I think we are fated never to go to America," the duchess wrote to her aunt. "Great Britain hates the idea of us going, because the Duke is an independent thinker and they don't want him to open his mouth." Indeed, the royal family and the government feared he would inadvertently encourage U.S. isolationists and campaign to increase his own popularity.

In early December, the duchess had severe dental problems. Her Nassau dentists advised her that she would need to go to Miami for surgery. The duke was surprised when his request to join his wife in the

United States was quickly granted. He did not know that the British government wanted to keep him away from the president, who was planning a West Indian cruise to inspect U.S. bases. Courting public sympathy, the duke and duchess gave an interview in the Bahamas to an American journalist, who wrote a romanticizing article that was published to coincide with their visit.

In Miami the duke and duchess acquitted themselves better than expected. The British consul-general in Florida, James Marjoribanks, later wrote that, despite the British government's fears, "He never missed a chance to perform some act of public relations in aid of the British war effort. On one occasion I remember him addressing in Spanish a group of fifty South American businessmen whom he ran into by chance. . . . A holiday atmosphere prevailed; Britain's stock soared with the advent to Miami of our former monarch."

On December 12, while the duchess was still in the hospital recovering from her operation, Roosevelt, to the horror of the British government, invited the duke to fly back to the Bahamas for an informal meeting with him the next day aboard the USS *Tuscaloosa*. After lunching, ironically, on kingfish, they spoke for several more hours about their families, politics, and the strategic importance of proposed Bahamian naval bases for defending the United States. Roosevelt inquired about George V's stamp collection, and the duke explained that it had been placed at the disposal of the empire. The president amused the duke by telling him: "Your father was a sailor king with a sailor's heart and a sailor's vocabulary, and when he got on the subject of the Germans, he used some good old Anglo-Saxon monosyllables with deep conviction." The duke, shrewdly, spoke favorably of his brother to the president, but alienated him anyway by expressing insufficient loyalty to the British war effort. A few months later, with the president's lend-lease legislation pending in Congress—an effort that would be vital to Britain's hopes of victory—the duke gave an interview advocating a negotiated peace with Germany. When Churchill reprimanded him for his interview, the duke protested that his recent visit to Miami had been "most dignified and no harm was done to British interests that I am aware."

Back in Washington, with nearly three-quarters of the nation supporting his presidency, a jubilant Roosevelt took the oath of office for an unprecedented third term on January 20, 1941. Eleanor, however, was exhausted and overwhelmed. "At times like these, I try to be a machine or I would burst into tears or run away. I am always thankful for the hours between 1 and 3 A.M.," Eleanor wrote to Hick.

That spring of 1941, the British government thwarted the Duke of Windsor's plans for an official visit to the United States, but he did return on an informal trip in the fall, once again meeting with the president. Michael Bloch in his book *The Secret File of the Duke of Windsor* claims that the president and the duke became friends. Certainly, FDR would have been drawn to the duke's charming and fun-loving manner, but the former monarch's political views—at times similar to those of the president's archrival Joseph Kennedy—troubled the president. FDR's biographer, Conrad Black, reports that Roosevelt once wrote to the journalist Fulton Oursler that he "had more respect for the opinions of Oursler's eight year old daughter than those of 'little Windsor.'" According to his grandson Curtis Roosevelt, FDR excelled at hiding his real feelings and often would charm people he disliked. On this visit, Roosevelt found the duke "very robust on war and victory and his attitude generally showed a great improvement on the impression the president had formed when he met him a year ago in the Bahamas," according to Viscount Halifax, who had succeeded Lothian as British ambassador to Washington in 1941. The duke seemed to realize that he needed to appear more supportive of the Allied cause if he wanted to keep his political options open and the United States on his side.

## London

Having long distrusted Joseph Kennedy's gloomy assessments, Roosevelt sent Harry Hopkins, his alter ego, to scout Britain for him. Winston Churchill saw the sickly Hopkins as a "crumbling lighthouse from which there shone the beams that led great fleets to harbor," and loved how he glowed with purpose while discussing ways to defeat Hitler. As Hopkins sat down to lunch with Their Majesties at the palace, an air-raid alarm went off. The royal couple paid no mind until a bell signaled them to retreat to an air-raid shelter, where they continued their meeting. The queen forcefully sought to communicate to Hopkins her nation's resilience amid war: "The one thing that counted was the morale and determination of the great mass of the British people," she told Hopkins. For his part, Hopkins noticed how much the king admired the president, and concluded of the king and queen, "If ever two people realized that Britain is fighting for its life, it is these two."

Churchill, responding to Hopkins's request for British help in passing lend-lease legislation, delivered a worldwide radio address in which he told Americans, "Put your confidence in us. We shall not fail or falter. . . . Give us the tools and we will finish the job."

## Washington, D.C.

Back in December, in the middle of a crisis over how to help Britain, FDR suddenly disappeared for a ten-day Caribbean cruise on the USS *Tuscaloosa*. He needed quiet time to think through a knotty problem: Britain was near bankruptcy and could not afford to pay for the war materiel necessary to compete with the Nazis' superior war production, which had been further enhanced by the resources of the countries they had conquered. However, Congress remained in no mood to lend money to a country that had defaulted on substantial debts to the United States from World War I. Sailing the ocean he loved, FDR had an inspiration—the United States would send Britain all the weaponry and supplies they needed and Britain would repay later, with the same materials they had purchased. He called it lend-lease.

Once in Washington, the president presented the idea to the country in a Fireside Chat. "No man can tame a tiger into a kitten by stroking it. There can be no appeasement with ruthlessness," he said. With Gallup polls indicating Americans were ready to support Britain, he exhorted Americans to become a great "arsenal of democracy" producing weapons so Britain could keep the United States out of the war.

After the Lend-Lease Bill was signed on March 11, 1941, the king wrote to FDR to express his gratitude and relief. "After so many years of anxiety" it was "wonderful to feel that our two great countries are getting together for the future betterment of the world." He recognized that his friendship with the president and his campaign to win over the United States was beginning to pay dividends. Slowly but inexorably, American public opinion was shifting toward providing more arms to the British, but more intense campaigning would still be needed to convince Americans to give all the help Britain needed.

That spring, FDR came under extreme pressure, caught between

Germany's intimidating and provocative successes and the still-strong resistance of Americans who saw further U.S. involvement as a guarantee of national disaster. Germany conquered Yugoslavia and Greece, and Nazi submarines were sinking British ships at an alarming rate and appeared to be winning the Battle of the Atlantic. Britain was choked of the imports required to feed its people and keep factories functioning. FDR wanted to send U.S. convoys to protect British ships, but he dared not because of American fears that such action would spark war. His stress and anxiety led to anemia and stomach problems. He was bedridden for two weeks for transfusions and rest.

His energy restored, FDR declared a state of "unlimited natural emergency" on May 26 and invoked special powers so that, if necessary, he could respond to any threat against the Western Hemisphere. He would add more ships and planes to U.S. patrols and increase defense orders to plants and factories. In a Fireside Chat the next night, he explained to the American people that Hitler planned world domination and might soon find ways to launch attacks against the Western Hemisphere. On June 22 Germany invaded Russia. Miscalculating badly, thinking he could finish off Russia quickly, Hitler would soon become bogged down in the East instead of finishing off England.

## London

In spite of increasing U.S. assistance, the friendship between the Roosevelt and Windsor dynasties hit a low point in the summer of 1941. Encouraged by Roosevelt's May 27 speech, the king wrote a personal appeal to the president on June 3. The king wanted nothing less than for Roosevelt to provide all the support he had offered at Hyde Park—including America's willingness to attack Germany, as he had promised, for bombing England. Flattering FDR for the way he "led public opinion by letting it . . . get ahead of you," he reiterated deep affection for the American people and trumpeted once again Britain's human resources: "the truly remarkable . . . spirit of the people under the strain of terrible & indiscriminate bombing" and the "indefatigable," and "great" prime minister. The king then made a plea for personal contact between the two leaders. "I would like to feel that I can write to you direct. So many communications between Heads of State have to go through 'official channels' and I hope that you will be able to write back to me in a personal way." Because the king no longer trusted Joe Kennedy, he wanted to press his public relations campaign directly with the president. In response he received nothing but a formal telegram on his official birthday.

Both the king and queen were hurt the Roosevelts did not respond to their letters, their need for encouragement, and provide as much military support as FDR had promised them at Hyde Park. When a friend told the king how much the president had enjoyed getting his letter, the king said bitterly, "Oh, so he's got it, has he?" The king had consoled himself by thinking that his letter, like a previous one to the president, had been lost in transit. When the friend reiterated how much the president appreciated the letter, the king said, "Oh, it is about five weeks since I wrote it and I never had any acknowledgement yet." The queen chimed in that Mrs. Roosevelt had not responded to her letter, either. The king felt FDR had slighted him as a fellow head of state and as a friend. He did not realize that Roosevelt felt he could not help Britain further, and moreover, feared confrontation and the needs of his intimates; he had difficulty facing the personal pain of friends, and was unwilling to deliver bad news directly. He could not bring himself to write without offering hope.

Loyal, direct, and affectionate, the king and queen could not fathom the remoteness at the core of FDR's character. Missy LeHand knew FDR well; she once told a friend that her boss and paramour "was really incapable of personal friendship with anyone." The life-or-death diplomacy of wartime, which so often required secret missives sent over back channels, exacerbated his tendency to compartmentalize his life and keep his deepest feelings to himself. Eleanor knew how her husband functioned. "Each imagines he is indispensable to the President," she declared to Joe Lash. "All would be surprised at their dispensability. The president uses those who suit his purposes. He makes up his own mind and discards people when they no longer fulfill a purpose of his."

## Newfoundland

Like a schoolboy who casts aside his best friend for the charming new boy in the class, FDR had become fascinated with Winston Churchill at the expense of the king, who had introduced them. On August 9, 1941, Churchill sailed into Placentia Bay, Newfoundland, on a British battleship for his first meeting with the president, who waited for him on the USS *Augusta*. Churchill presented Roosevelt with a letter from the king saying "how glad I am that you have an opportunity at last of getting to know my Prime Minister. I am sure that you will agree that he is a very remarkable man and I have no doubt that your meeting will prove of great benefit to our two countries in pursuit of our common goal."

Roosevelt and Churchill's discussions resulted in the Atlantic Charter—a joint declaration of the principles and aims of the two allied nations. FDR sent Churchill back with a conciliatory letter to the king: "I wish you could have been with us at Divine Service yesterday on the quarterdeck of your latest battleship. I shall never forget it. Your officers and men were mingled with about three hundred of ours, spread over the turrets and superstructure—I hope you will see a movie of it." His personal note did little to dispel the impression that he had relegated the king to a secondary position, now that he had allied with Churchill.

## London

On August 10, the queen continued her own charm campaign with a radio broadcast to the women of the United States thanking them for sending so many "Bundles for Britain," including clothing, bandages, other necessities, and toys. Speaking with informality and passion, she highlighted the heroism and industry of British women: "Here in Britain our women are working in factory and field, turning the lathe and gathering the harvest. . . . Their courage is magnificent, their endurance amazing . . . they are driving heavy lorries . . . ciphering . . . air raid wardens or ambulance drivers, thousands of undaunted women who quietly and calmly face the terrors of the night bombing." In the hope that touting Britain's fortitude and heroism would further soften U.S. isolationism, she said, "wherever I go I see bright eyes and smiling faces, for though our road is stony and hard, it is straight, and we know we fight in a great cause." FDR gave her speech the highest accolade: it was "really perfect in every way."

In late August the royal family enlisted the king's younger brother to continue their personal appeal to the Roosevelts and their public relations crusade with the American people. Their ultimate goal was to end U.S. neutrality and enlist American manpower and resources in the fight against fascism. The Duke of Kent, chief welfare officer of the Royal Air Force, sandwiched a three-day U.S. visit into the middle of an official Canadian war inspection tour. The duke wanted to spend more time touring the United States, but the British government feared a longer visit would seem too provocative to the strong anti-British lobby in the U.S. Congress, which monitored British propaganda carefully.

## Hyde Park and Washington, D.C.

On August 23, the duke stopped at Hyde Park for thirty-six hours. The president was "charming," during their "endless conversations," and Eleanor "pleasant," the duke wrote his brother. "He drove me in his car at great speed & I thought of you & what you had told me."

The duke accompanied the president by train to Washington for the official part of the visit. Enduring great heat, he visited Washington's sights and attended a cocktail party given by the National Press Club, calling it a "most unnerving performance," facing reporters. Mentioning a small White House dinner in his honor, he told his brother, "I can't write what the president discussed, but will tell you when I see you," suggesting the president had entrusted him with classified war reports. The duke requested the king's permission to make an inspection in Iceland after FDR had asked him to review the war situation there.

In Norfolk, Virginia, he had "an endless day . . . seeing the shipyards . . . I went to Langley Air Port where they have operational squadrons—& wind tunnels etc. . . . Few have aircraft as we have them all! The shipyards were working hard—& doing good work," he reported to the king. "I went to Baltimore (city of renown!) & the mayor etc. kept on making allusions to our Wallie etc." In Baltimore he inspected the Glenn Martin aircraft factory and addressed the thirteen thousand employees. "They couldn't feel they were working for anything tangible & I explained to them what it was all about." Back in Quebec with the Athlones, the duke wrote to FDR:

> The gratitude of the British people for what you have done for us is immeasurable—& their admiration is unbounded—but I

feel I must add my own word of admiration for all that you are doing. . . . I was so glad to see something of your forces & also of the naval & air force plants. . . . I am only sorry my stay was so short. . . . I . . . shall take back to the king not only many messages from you but also many heartening words of all I have seen in your country.

After the duke left, Eleanor reflected in her "My Day" column: "I think what impresses me most of all in meeting English people today is the great strain under which they have been and their sense of obligation in fulfilling whatever they consider is their duty. In coming to Canada and the United States, they represent the British people and they try in every way to express to us the appreciation they feel for the constant flow of aid from this country." The royal propagation of British pluck and gratitude had scored another victory.

## Campobello and Hyde Park

That June at Campobello, Sara Delano Roosevelt suffered a stroke. She spent the summer sequestered in her bedroom. Franklin was frightened. Sara refused Eleanor's suggestion of a nurse's help until Franklin, her "one and only," appealed to her to accept, for his "peace of mind." At breakfast the morning after her mother-in-law returned with her to Hyde Park on September 5, Eleanor became alarmed that Sara was very pale and labored to breathe. Remembering how painful it had been for her to miss her father's death forty-seven years before, she urgently summoned FDR from Washington.

Sara announced she would greet her son on the front porch, but she was too weak to venture out of her room. Instead, she insisted on being dressed in an elegant bed jacket and having her hair wound into a braid. When Franklin rolled in, Sara was waiting for him, propped up in a chaise longue. He entertained her all day with stories about Winston Churchill, reports on Washington politics, and family reminiscences. That evening, she developed a clot in her lung and became unconscious. The president was at her side the next day, September 7, 1941, as she died, just before noon. Less than five minutes after her death, the biggest oak tree on the property collapsed to the ground. The president went to look at it and contemplate the symbolism. He was distraught.

According to the *New York Times*, after his mother's death FDR "shut himself off from the world more completely than at any time since he assumed his present post." Eleanor made all the arrangements for the simple Episcopal funeral service and for a funeral procession that would bear Sara's body to St. James Church for burial. "I think Franklin will forget all the irritations & remember only pleasant things," Eleanor said of Sara in a letter to her aunt, Maude Gray. In "My Day," Eleanor gave her own careful but forthright testament to her mother-in-law: "a very vital person" whose "strongest trait was loyalty to her family. . . . She was not just sweetness and light, for there was a streak of jealousy and possessiveness in her where her own were concerned." Writing to a friend, she was more revealing: "It is dreadful to have lived so close to someone for 36 years & feel no deep affection or sense of loss."

One afternoon while he was going through his mother's belongings with his secretary Grace Tully, FDR discovered an unfamiliar box. Opening it, he found mementos of his early childhood: a lock of his hair, his first pair of shoes, his christening dress, and small gifts he had made for his mother. When the president started to cry, Grace quickly left the room. Neither she nor the president expected such deep sorrow. Eleanor canceled a long-awaited trip to the West Coast to be at her husband's side. "Mother went to father and consoled him," according to James. "She stayed with him . . . through the difficult days immediately afterward. She showed him more affection during those days than at any other time I can recall. She was the kind that you could count on in a crisis, and father knew that."

FDR was also heartened to receive support from all his British royal friends. The Duke of Kent cabled his "most sincere sympathy in your great sorrow," while his new friends the Athlones sent a telegram with "heartfelt sympathy in your sad bereavement. We share your grief in the loss of your charming and remarkable mother." The king and queen cabled their condolences as well.

## Washington, D.C.

During the week Sara died, Eleanor's only surviving brother, Hall, a chronic alcoholic, was hospitalized. As self-indulgent as Eleanor was dutiful, Hall begged his sister to bring him a bottle of gin in the hospital. She did so reluctantly when she realized he was dying. Brilliant, charming, and feckless, Hall brought out his sister's playful side as no one else could. Distraught, she stayed by his bedside until he died on the morning of September 25.

After the two deaths, James Roosevelt was amazed by his parents' reunion at the White House:

> Father struggled to her side and put his arms around her. "Sit down," he said, so tenderly I can still hear it. And he sank down beside her and hugged her and kissed her and held her head on his chest. I do not think that she cried. I think Mother had forgotten how to cry. She spent her hurt in Father's embrace. . . . For all they were apart both physically and spiritually much of their married life, there remained between them a bond that others could not break.

"If I feel depressed, I go to work. Work is always an antidote for depression," Eleanor told the *Ladies' Home Journal*. Only days after Hall's death, Eleanor became an assistant director in the Office of Civilian Defense. Working with colorful New York mayor Fiorello La Guardia, she planned for civilian protection and needs during wartime. Her OCD work, marrying social programs and wartime preparedness, would later be seen as misguided and would fail. Social programs were not a public priority in wartime. Eleanor resigned herself to the fact that the nation did not yet seem ready to allow a First Lady to have an official role.

In September 1941 a German submarine fired a few torpedoes at the USS *Greer*. FDR made the murky incident, in which no one was harmed, sound like an attack on the United States. He used it as a pretext for changing policy: the U.S. Navy would "shoot on sight" any enemy vessels that entered its defensive zones: "When you see a rattlesnake poised to strike, you do not wait until he has struck you before you crush him. The Nazi submarines and raiders are the rattlesnakes of the Atlantic," he told the public. U.S. isolationism was finally beginning to wane. The Nazis' invasion of Russia had converted the American Communist Party into interventionists overnight, while conservative isolationists believed that Americans could stand on the sidelines and take comfort as two dictatorships wore each other down.

FDR gave the king the good news in an October 15 letter: "Public opinion is distinctly better than six months ago. In fact, it is more strongly with us than is the Congress."

Watching German submarines torpedo other U.S. ships near Iceland and Greenland that fall, FDR hoped the painful loss of life and supplies would finally melt isolationist sentiments in Congress, as it was softening public opinion about arming U.S. ships. FDR knew his lend-lease policy would fail unless Congress amended the Neutrality Act legislation so that merchant ships could be armed. On November 8, Congressmen finally permitted U.S. seamen to sail into war zones. Congress was not ready to allow him to declare war on Germany. It would take far more direct provocation for that.

In the Pacific, Japan's bellicose language and intrusions into Indochina accelerated. In July, after the Japanese had invaded Indochina, FDR had imposed sanctions including a high-octane oil embargo on them. "I am a bit worried over the Japanese situation at this moment," FDR wrote the king. "The Emperor is for peace, I think, but the Jingoes are trying to force his hand." The United States was negotiating with Japan to stop their territorial expansion, which was threatening U.S. interests in the Pacific, including the Philippines. On December 6, FDR addressed a personal plea for peace to the Japanese emperor, Hirohito. At one-thirty the following afternoon, Franklin was sitting with Harry Hopkins when the secretary of the navy called to tell him it appeared that the Japanese had attacked Pearl Harbor. Hopkins thought the secretary was mistaken, but FDR did not doubt it. At seven-thirty that morning in Honolulu, 189 Japanese planes had scored direct hits on all eight of the U.S. battleships, lined up in the harbor like sitting ducks, along with cruisers, destroyers, and half of the U.S. planes exposed on the airfields. In all, 2,403 servicemen and civilians were killed, and 1,178 were wounded.

Eleanor saw the torrent of activity in the president's office and watched senior military aides gather, and understood that war had begun. She went directly to her room to write Anna, who lived on the West Coast, suggesting she send her children east. It seemed possible the Japanese would make a direct attack on the continental United States. The president's butler overheard FDR discussing how to cut enemy supply lines if an invasion reached as far as Chicago.

With that day's outbreak of war, Eleanor found her husband "more serene than he had appeared in a long time." Underneath, he felt a cold fury at the Japanese for attacking while negotiations between the two countries continued. That his beloved navy had been caught unaware and decimated was, for him, an agony. Eleanor found it "steadying to know that the die was cast" for war. In a radio broadcast that evening, she told the nation, "We know what we have to face & we know we are ready to face it."

The king and queen were at Windsor when "a bomb shell arrived in the 9 o'clock news (B.B.C.)" that evening, as the king wrote in his diary. Winston Churchill was meeting with U.S. ambassador John Winant and the railroad magnate and diplomat Averell Harriman at the moment the news came over the wireless. The prime minister rushed to call the president, who told him the awful news he had been waiting to hear for over a year—the dire news that might provide the salvation of Britain: "We are all in the same boat now."

Seeking a declaration of war before a joint session of Congress, FDR called December 7 a day that would "live in infamy." The king telegraphed the president to express solidarity: "My thoughts and prayers go out to you and to the great people of the United States at this solemn moment in your history when you have been treacherously attacked by Japan. We are proud indeed to be fighting at your side against the common enemy."

Eleanor and Mayor La Guardia, the head of the Office of Civil Defense, soon headed west to Los Angeles to calm Californians, who feared a Japanese invasion. En route, they received false reports that the Japanese were bombing San Francisco, and diverted their plane there. During her trip, Eleanor was excoriated in the press when she defended the civil liberties of Japanese Americans, who had already come under suspicion as enemy sympathizers. On December 22, FDR told her that Churchill would be arriving a day early for a three-week stay at the White House. Feeling ambushed by the news, Eleanor had a rare lapse of judgment and vented her anger at Franklin before the whole country—in her column: "It had not occurred to him that this might require certain moving of furniture to adapt rooms to the purposes for which the Prime Minister wished to use them. Before all orders were finally given, it was 10 AM and I was half an hour late for my press conference."

The tensions and fresh uncertainties of wartime were already exacting their price on everyone. For Eleanor, this Christmas—her first without any of her children present—was depressing. She missed her sons, who had all enlisted in the military. Because of security risks, the Secret Service almost succeeded in vetoing the lighting of the national Christmas tree. Her brother had died, not to mention her mother-in-law. After one phone conversation, Joe Lash was so concerned about her that he rushed to the White House and found her in tears. Her husband was preoccupied with Churchill's visit; the prime minister would keep him up until the early hours of the morning talking, smoking, and drinking brandy. "Mother would just fume," Elliott wrote later, "and go in and out of the room making hints about bed, and still Churchill would sit there."

Ever playing the wily diplomat, Roosevelt courted the Duke and Duchess of Windsor, who were visiting Washington, by giving them tickets to hear Prime Minister Churchill—their staunch defender at the time of the abdication—speak to a joint session of Congress the day after Christmas. Churchill electrified the legislators and the listening allied nations. "I cannot help reflecting that if my father had been American and my mother British, instead of the other way around, I might have got here on my own," he remarked. Then, more seriously, he said, "The task which has been set is not above our strength, its pangs and trials are not beyond our endurance." Shouting in a convincing show of rage, he challenged the enemy dictators: "Is it possible they do not realize that we shall never cease to persevere against them until they have been taught a lesson which they and the world will never forget?" When Churchill finished his oration, there was silence and then a spine-tingling roar from a Congress converted to his cause. Britain and the United States had become absolute allies at last.

# 12

# Hitting Close to Home

## January–October 1942

> From Berlin, Rome and Tokyo we have been described as a nation
> of weakling-playboys. . . . Let them tell that to the boys in the fly-
> ing fortresses. Let them tell that to the Marines.
>
> —*FDR to the American people during a February 23, 1942, Fireside Chat*

In 1942 the Allies were losing the war. The Japanese seemed unstoppable; they had conquered Thailand, Burma, Hong Kong, the
Philippines, Malaya, and the Dutch East Indies. The low point came
when Singapore, the bastion of Western power in the East, fell to
Japan. On the European front, by spring the Nazis were on the outskirts of Moscow and Leningrad, and the German U-boats seemed
close to winning the Battle of the Atlantic. Merchant ships were being
sunk at such an alarming rate—in January alone, forty-three ships were
lost—that new ships could not make up the difference.

The war hit close to home in every way. In early 1942 a Japanese
submarine bombarded from the ocean an oil field near Santa Barbara,
California. German agents came ashore in Florida and in Amagansett
on Long Island and made it to New York City before being appre-
hended by the FBI. FDR ordered a swift and secret military tribunal to
try and execute them, but Americans were frightened and disheart-
ened. Eleanor spoke to their desperation in her February 16 column:
"Perhaps it is good for us to have to face disaster, because we have been
so optimistic and almost arrogant in our expectation of constant suc-

cess. Now we shall have to find within us the courage to meet defeat and fight right on to victory. That means a steadiness of purpose and of will, which is not one of our strong points. But somehow, I think we shall harden physically and mentally as the days go by."

To galvanize the American people, in his State of the Union message the president set seemingly impossible war production goals. The U.S. Maritime, which had built 100 ships in 1941, was expected to build 2,900 more vessels as soon as possible. The president ordered 60,000 new planes, and 45,000 factories that had been underproducing in the Depression years were ratcheted up to full capacity, while new factories were sprouting up everywhere. The nation would still suffer enormous losses before its superior production capacities could provide it with a powerful military arsenal. On the evening of February 23, sixty-one million Americans, looking at world maps they had purchased at the president's request, listened as he exhorted them: "From Berlin, Rome and Tokyo we have been described as a nation of weakling-playboys. . . . Let them tell that to the boys in the flying fortresses. Let them tell that to the Marines."

The queen's brother, David Bowes-Lyon, came to Washington and worked with White House and State Department officials to set up an organization that would coordinate the Anglo-American propaganda effort. On March 11, he presented FDR with a long letter from the king thanking him for his plans to aid Britain. "Shipping is our one great obstacle in retarding our immediate aims," the king wrote, "but although it will take time & great effort on all our parts to prepare, the final issue, i.e. Victory is without any doubt to be with us."

Eleanor was deeply disturbed when FDR caved in to military and political pressure and—in probably the most debatable decision of his presidency—incarcerated Japanese Americans in camps. She tried to tell her husband that such an action violated the Bill of Rights; Roosevelt froze her out, widening the gap between them. She then had to attend to a personal crisis, one partly of her own making, when her involvement with the Office of Civilian Defense came under vicious attack. Showing a rare lapse in judgment, Eleanor had allowed some friends to take high-paying jobs at the OCD. After a congressman pointed out that her friend Mayris Chaney was paid more than double the salary of an air force pilot to teach ballet at the OCD, the House of Representatives voted to deny funds for any activity that included dance instruction. *Time* magazine snidely called Eleanor the "OCDiva." She resigned from the office.

Spring did not bring relief. Joe Lash, Eleanor's primary emotional support, left to join the military. "A little of my heart seems to be with you always Joe," she told him. When he contacted her from a training camp in Miami, she responded, "I could have kissed the telegram. I was so glad to have word from you." Adding to her isolation, Hick began a relationship with another woman, a tax court judge. After her humiliating experience at the OCD, Eleanor was functioning without structure, purpose, or an outlet for her prodigious energies. In New York City that spring, she emptied out Sara Roosevelt's East 65th Street house while she figured out what to do next.

In June, the president and Mrs. Roosevelt entertained Winston Churchill at Hyde Park, where FDR agreed to Churchill's request that the United States begin serious work on developing an atom bomb, initiating what would become the Manhattan Project. Not long after they had returned to the White House, the president received a telegram announcing that a British garrison of twenty-five thousand solders in Libya had surrendered to the Nazis after eight months of siege. Responding to this blow to Churchill and the Allied cause, FDR committed the United States to an invasion of North Africa, rather than the direct assault on Europe that his military advisers were demanding. FDR was unwilling to launch a cross-channel invasion because Churchill feared another disaster like the one in Libya. The invasion of North Africa would help pull German troops away from the eastern front, strengthen the British hold on the Middle East, and by making the first direct Allied attack on the Germans, provide the American people and the Allied troops a badly needed boost in morale.

That June, the president invited the Duke of Windsor for lunch at the White House. After the meal, FDR asked the duke to revise his schedule and stay for several extra hours of conversation—newspapers called it the president's longest lunch since the attack on Pearl Harbor. The duke later wrote that the president "talked and talked" about his "experiences integrating negroes in the armed forces . . . and the military reasoning behind the American decision to mass and train troops for the invasion of the Continent." The duke was puzzled by their conversation: "I haven't a clue what he wanted of me"—but surmised that the president was "a man who had achieved on his own the highest summit of political power within a man's reach, was curious about the motives and reasoning of a man who could give up an inherited position of comparable renown."

## England

On July 4, 1942, the Duchess of Kent gave birth to her third child and second son. The duke cabled to ask FDR to be the baby's godfather. "We should be especially pleased, as he was born on Independence Day," the duke said in his formal invitation. A week later FDR cabled back: "I am much thrilled and very proud to be Godfather to the youngster and I send him my affectionate greetings. Tell the Duchess that I count on seeing him as soon as the going is good." Over the next month he cabled several times to check on his young godson. He loved the idea of having a prince named after him, and hoped to take up the king and queen's invitation to visit England as soon as the war eased. On August 4 at Windsor Castle, the duke stood proxy for the president as the boy was christened Michael George Charles Franklin, becoming the only member of the royal family named after a U.S. president. That day FDR cabled the duke: "Tell the king that I will hold him to strict accountability until I am able to take over the responsibility of a godfather myself."

After a massive wartime buildup, the Allies were planning to take their first main offensive in the fall of 1942, with a landing in North Africa, code-named Operation Torch—disappointing Stalin, who pressed for a European invasion to divert the Nazis from their siege of Russia. Churchill flew to Moscow to deliver the bad news in person to Stalin. Meanwhile, General Dwight David Eisenhower, the Supreme Allied Commander of the Expeditionary Force, came to England to begin invasion planning. On July 12, Eisenhower had the first of many private wartime conversations with the king, finding him to be "most personable and very much 'in the know' as to current and prospective plans for the Allied operations."

The king entertained Eisenhower with a story about Americans visiting Windsor Castle. On a lovely spring Sunday, the king had led his family out into the garden for tea. He had forgotten a promise to Clive Wigram, the deputy constable of Windsor Castle, to stay inside while Wigram gave a tour of the castle to several high-level American officers. Suddenly hearing Wigram's unmistakable voice pointing out flowers to the visitors, the king exclaimed, "This is terrible, we must not be seen." Knowing the tour would be canceled if the visitors encountered them—Wigram would not have continued lest he bother Their Majesties—the royal family crawled on their hands and knees to the garden wall and hurried through a door into the castle just before the American visitors spotted them. When the king finished his story, General Eisenhower revealed that he had been one of the mystery visitors the king had fled.

On August 25, the Duke and Duchess of Gloucester were dining with the king and queen when the king was asked to leave the room and take an important call. As the Duchess of Gloucester recalled, "We were all left in silence at the table . . . suspecting something awful had happened. The King came back and sat in silence. I could feel he was in deep distress and soon the Queen caught my eye, signaling me to rise with her and lead the ladies from the room. . . . Then the Queen left us and came back with the King who told us that it was the Duke of Kent who had been killed."

The king and the Duke of Gloucester had spent that day picnicking with a shooting party on the misty moors near Balmoral, as part of the first family vacation since the war began. The Duke of Kent had been traveling across England in a Sutherland flying boat aircraft, on his way to tour Royal Air Force installations in Iceland, when his plane flew too low through the thick mist and hit the top of a hill on the estate of the Duke of Portland in Scotland. The king's brother was killed when the plane tumbled down the far side of the hill and burst into flames. It took rescuers a long time to locate the wreckage.

The Duchess of Kent had gone to bed early that night. When she heard the approaching footsteps of her son's nanny, who had taken the phone call, she "immediately sensed catastrophe." As soon as Miss Fox opened her door, Princess Marina gasped, "It's George, isn't it?" Marina had been deeply committed to her marriage and distant from the rest of the royal family; she was shattered. Once again she would become a foreigner in the palace. As a Greek princess, related to many of the royal houses of Europe, she had looked down on her husband's British relatives, and they, in turn, had not accepted her.

When Queen Mary's lady-in-waiting approached her saying she had bad news, the queen asked immediately if the king had been killed.

Told it was her son George, the queen "was so stunned by the shock I could not believe it." Covering her grief with her sense of duty, she visited the Duchess of Kent and commanded her to avoid self-pity and set a national example as a war widow.

As so often occurs when a public figure dies in confusing circumstances, rumors and conspiracy theories sprang up around the duke's death. One theory suggested the crash was caused by sabotage, perhaps by Nazi agents, while another posited wildly that British intelligence had killed him to avert his plans to help the Duke of Windsor reclaim the throne. The most likely cause of the crash was the pilot's disorientation in poor visibility or a defect in the gyromagnetic compass guiding the plane.

The king wrote to Edwina Mountbatten, "It really is a tragedy, of all people, just when he was coming into his own, should have been taken from us. I will miss him terribly." The funeral in St. George's Chapel in Windsor Castle was particularly difficult for the king. "I have attended very many family funerals in the Chapel, but none . . . have moved me in the same way," he wrote in his diary. "Everybody there I knew well but I did not dare look at any of them for fear of breaking down." No British king had ever cried in public, and he was not going to be the first. At a memorial service in the Nassau Cathedral in the Bahamas, the Duke of Windsor sobbed uncontrollably. Returning from the funeral service in a dramatic thunderstorm, Queen Mary encountered two soldiers walking in the road and ordered her driver to stop and offer them a ride. They were Americans, a parachutist and a sergeant observer, whom she found charming. They had no idea they were chatting pleasantly with a queen who had just buried her favorite son.

The king's only solace was that his brother died on "Active Service" in the military. The tragedy drew the king and queen closer to their subjects, who had lost so many family members, and FDR wrote remembering the duke, saying, "We had such a good time together at Hyde Park. I had great affection for him."

The war would hit home for the royal family in another eerie and unnerving episode. One evening at Windsor Castle as the king walked the dogs outside, the queen was in her bedroom dressing for dinner when from behind the curtains, a hand grabbed her leg. A man emerged and sat down on the carpet before her. Summoning all her royal nerve, the queen said quietly, "Tell me about it." He relaxed his grip; and then she went across the room to ring a bell summoning a page from the next room. Together the queen and the page listened to the man's story: he was a deserter from the services and his whole family had been killed in air raids. Using a false name, he had obtained work with a firm doing repairs at the castle and gained access to her room by pretending he had been sent to change a light bulb. The man was harmless but despondent; and the chilling incident reminded the king and queen how vulnerable they were, and how traumatic war was for everyone in England.

## The United States

FDR grew increasingly lonely as 1942 wore on. The year before, his mother had died and Missy had suffered her stroke. Harry Hopkins, now married, was no longer available for regular evening companionship. FDR convinced Eleanor, who hated the slow pace of trains, to accompany him for part of a September trip making wartime inspections in the South, a region where so many people saw her as the most dangerous woman in America. Southern newspapers decried her attitude toward African Americans; many people believed the preposterous myth that female black domestics had formed so-called Eleanor's Clubs, secret efforts to sabotage white home life throughout the South.

Upon his return to Washington on October 1, Franklin was excited about the progress of the U.S. war effort. Holding a press conference, he reported to the nation on his two-week inspection tour of army camps, wartime factories, and navy yards throughout the Midwest, California, and the South. Sitting casually at his desk and smoking a cigarette in a long holder, he praised the morale of the American people. A week later, in a radio address, he told Americans that they were "united as never before in their determination to do a job and do it well." However, he criticized some employers for failing to hire women or blacks. "We can no longer afford to indulge such prejudices or practices," he declared.

During the trip, Franklin had suggested to Eleanor that they yet again reinvent their marriage. She would stay put in the White House and be his hostess at cocktail hour and for dinners. They would spend weekends together. Their son James said, "I think he was really asking her to be his wife again in all aspects." But FDR was asking her to do

the impossible, to turn back the clock twenty-five
her hard-won independence, again centering
request was bred of desperation, and Eleanor's ℩℩
lent. She had long hoped that Franklin would recommι ℩.
But now she was wedded to her professional life, however inι
had become in wartime. And understandably, she mistrusted her hu.
band; Crown Princess Märtha and cousins Laura Delano and Daisy
Suckley were all currently competing for her husband's affections.
Now, sensing his vulnerability, she offered to think about his suggestion during her trip west to see Anna. When they both returned to
Washington, they would talk again.

Eleanor never responded directly to FDR's request. Instead, she
answered him by asking for a new wartime assignment: she was keen to
visit the troops in England as soon as possible. Understanding the
implications of her answer, Franklin offered to arrange the trip on her
behalf. The visit had been long rumored in the British press.
Thousands of U.S. service members were already stationed in England,
their presence transforming the lives of the British people in small vil-
lages all over England. Eleanor hoped she could shore up Allied morale
and ease racial and economic tensions among the U.S. and British
forces. The Americans had better food and higher pay, which rankled
British troops, and white Southern soldiers were upset that the British
women seemed to take kindly to the black GIs among them.

Queen Elizabeth sent Eleanor a formal invitation. Hoping Eleanor
could counter lingering U.S. perceptions of the British as spoiled aristocrats, she and her husband wanted the First Lady to witness the
range of sacrifice made by the British people. Eleanor wrote back to the
queen offering to spend two nights at the palace before devoting "my
entire time to seeing all that I can of the British women's war effort,
and our own groups over there." FDR was amused when the Secret
Service code-named Eleanor "Rover" for her trip. Just before Eleanor
left, FDR wrote to Prime Minister Churchill: "I confide my Missus to
the care of you and Mrs. Churchill" and added, "I know our better
halves will hit it off beautifully."

# 13

# Eleanor in England

## 1942

> Mrs. Roosevelt has done more to bring a real understanding of the spirit of the United States to the people of Britain than any single American who has ever visited these islands.
>
> —*London reporter Chalmers Roberts*

## England

The *New York Times* headlined an article about her arrival in England "Mrs. Roosevelt Breaks Still More Traditions." Eleanor was the first president's wife to fly across the Atlantic, to expose herself directly to the dangers of war, and to visit Europe on her own. She and her secretary, Tommy Thompson, traveled in great secrecy, making a supposedly clandestine stopover in Ireland, where security people—on the lookout for Nazi agents—were rattled when someone recognized the First Lady. Because Their Majesties never met any visitor arriving at the airport, Eleanor and Thompson were greeted in Bristol by U.S. ambassador John Winant, who accompanied them to London on the prime minister's special train. Eleanor would develop a close friendship with Winant, whom she found to be an extremely sensitive man with great intellectual integrity—quite the contrast to Joe Kennedy.

When the ambassador briefed her on the red carpet treatment she would receive, Eleanor recoiled. "I can never get used to being treated as an important person," she told Winant. "What makes all the fuss harder is that, thanks to the regulations about luggage on a plane, I can't even dress the part." En route, Eleanor remembered how intimidating she had found London during her school years there, and her old insecurities surfaced. "I quaked over this visit," she wrote Anna. Eleanor did not think of herself as a "high-life lady," and wondered whether she could master royal protocol or impress a citizenry used to regal presence. "I had been worried by the thought of having to visit Buckingham Palace, but I was determined to live each moment, aware of its special interest. Though certain situations might be unfamiliar and give me a feeling of inadequacy and of not knowing the proper way to behave, still I would do my best and not worry," she later wrote.

At 4:30 P.M. on Friday, October 23, a cold, foggy day, Eleanor's train pulled into Paddington Station. Eleanor was intimidated by the grandly dressed stationmaster, who presented her to Their Majesties and accompanying military officials. As she stepped off the train in the surprisingly cold autumn weather, carrying a large handbag and wearing a long black coat and a striking beret-style hat of red and kingfisher-green feathers, she hid her trepidation with her trademark toothy smile.

The king's face twitched in discomfort as photographers turned on electric lights. "I hope you left the President in good health," he said awkwardly. Eleanor had brought with her a letter for the king, in which Franklin had written, "I wish much that I could accompany her, for there are a thousand things I want to tell you and talk with you about. I want you and the queen to tell Eleanor everything in regard to the problems of our troops in England which she might not get from the Government or the military authorities. You and I know that it is the little things which count but which are not always set forth in official reports."

Ever socially adept, the queen, who had recently recovered from the flu and was dressed in a black velvet coat and three strands of pearls, told Eleanor, "We welcome you with all our hearts. We have been looking forward to your visit with the greatest pleasure." Eleanor's welcoming committee included her official hostess, her friend Stella, Marchioness of Reading, the widow of the former British ambassador to the United States and a social worker who had set up the Women's Voluntary Service for Air Raid Precautions; Foreign Secretary Anthony Eden; and General Eisenhower. Her train's conductor marveled at the

First Lady. "I have never seen such energy," he said. She "never stopped talking and writing for one moment."

London newspapers did not announce her arrival, lest Nazi agents have time to prepare an attack on her, but her previous statements about her imminent visit to Britain, earlier rumors in the British press, and the American flags positioned at the station gave away her presence at the station that afternoon. Loud cheers burst forth from the large crowds who had joined U.S. soldiers at the station. Their Majesties whisked Eleanor to the palace in the royal Daimler. Joining her there would be her son Elliott, who had been released, by request of the king, from his duties in the photo reconnaissance unit of the Army Air Corps, currently training for the North African invasion.

At Buckingham Palace, Eleanor stayed in the queen's large suite, its windows blown out by Nazi bombs, and fully absorbed the paradox of being royal in wartime. She could have only a small fire in her sitting room, the queen explained apologetically. Pointing to shell holes in the courtyard, she asked Eleanor to draw the curtains when the lights were on. All the windowpanes had been shattered in a bombing; they were replaced with wood and isinglass. In her elegant bathroom, her bathtub could only be filled to a black line at the five-inch mark. "Buckingham Palace is an enormous place, and without heat," she wrote in her diary. "I do not see how they keep the dampness out. . . . In every room there was a little electric heater."

For her twenty-four-day trip, Eleanor made do with one evening dress, two day dresses, one suit, a few blouses, and two pairs of shoes— one for touring and one for fancier evenings. She fretted that the palace maids, hanging her meager collection of clothes in the huge wardrobes, would find her garments pathetic. Eleanor had to dress up immediately as the queen had invited Cecil Beaton to take a formal photograph of Mrs. Roosevelt with the royal family in Buckingham Palace.

That afternoon as she met the two princesses for tea, she felt "as though I had dropped off after a number of years to visit with some friends of my school days in a very homelike environment," she told readers of her column. Her conversation with Princess Elizabeth initi-ated a twenty-year friendship that lasted until Eleanor's death. She found the sixteen-year-old princess to be much like herself, "quite seri-ous and a child with a great deal of character and personality. She asked me a number of questions about life in the United States and they were serious questions." However, in her letter to Anna, Eleanor compared Elizabeth unfavorably to Anna's daughter Sisty: "She is about the same age tho' neither so tall nor so pretty."

In her autobiography, Eleanor praised the king and queen for "doing an extraordinarily outstanding job for their people in the most trying times . . . and you admire their character and their devotion to duty." She did not always agree with the king on international affairs, especially colonial matters—the king's inbred belief in empire clashed with the colonies' rising demand for independence, which Eleanor had espoused—but that did not tarnish her appreciation of him.

That night dinner at the palace with the Churchills and the Mountbattens was a historic event in itself—never before had a First Lady dined at Buckingham Palace without the president—but also because General Bernard Montgomery had begun his campaign that day to drive the Axis forces out of Egypt. Eleanor sat between the king, whose company she always enjoyed, and Churchill, with whom she often was at odds. In Washington she had resented the way Churchill had turned the White House upside down and his bellicose influence on the president, "like two boys playing soldier." Churchill was an ardent imperialist, a firm believer in England's destiny as the ruler of an empire, while Eleanor was already envisioning a new postwar order of equal and independent nations policing the world. "Churchill wasn't very fond of Mother," Elliott Roosevelt recalled. "They were always very polite to each other but they were totally different personalities. She believed in the future and the expansion of democracy everywhere, while he was basically a monarchist at heart."

Churchill also chafed at Eleanor's ability to challenge male authority and her role as the defender of equal rights for women. Detecting the whiff of alcoholism in him, she was uncomfortable in his presence. "Sometimes I think by the end of the day there has been a little too much champagne because he repeated the same thing to me two or three times," she once remarked. They tolerated each other for the sake of the greater goals they had in common, but at times tensions flared.

Eleanor and her hosts dined on meager portions of fish cakes, cold ham and chicken, Brussels sprouts, jellied pâté, pudding, and fruit, all served on gold and silver plates. A twitchy Churchill finally left in the middle of dinner to get a report from the front. He came back singing joyfully, "Roll out the barrel!"

Recognizing the opportunity the evening presented, Their Majesties chose entertainment that would reflect the best of Britain and further enhance the royal family's reputation in the United States. They screened Noël Coward's new film *In Which We Serve*, which told a fictionalized version of the story of their cousin Lord Mountbatten's ship *Kelly*, sunk off Crete in May 1941. Mountbatten had served as a consultant to the film, and Their Majesties had intervened to overrule the Ministry of Information, which thought showing a film depicting the sinking of a British ship would be bad for the country's image abroad. In the movie, British sailors and officers from all classes come together on the HMS *Torrin*, enduring intense suffering for a great cause, and putting personal happiness second to devotion to duty. The film appealed to Eleanor's values. She noted in her column how extraordinary it was to see a movie surrounded by people who had lived through the story. She and Elliott stayed up until 2 A.M. talking, with her son expressing admiration for Britain's handling of the war, which, she was pleased to see, had dissolved his prejudices about the British people. "He looks well but is in for a long, hard pull I fear," she noted to Anna.

The next morning Eleanor was visibly startled by the large turnout at her U.S. embassy press conference. Hiding her nervousness, Eleanor was a commanding presence, explaining she had come to see how women could help in the war effort because she was working to convince the federal government and private industry to hire married women and mothers back home. When asked about the possibility that American women would be conscripted, she said, "You come to everything as you need it. It is very difficult to make people realize the importance of work until it is badly needed." As the United States got more involved in the war and sent more men overseas, additional workers would be needed on the home front to produce supplies to support the war. Stella Reading would show her how the Women's Voluntary Services were organized to provide food and other basic human services to bombed-out towns and to reorient workers who had transferred factories.

The king and queen then led Eleanor through what she called the "wanton destruction" of London's old City and East End. Their first stop was St. Paul's Cathedral, its nave open to the sky. They met the cathedral's dean, Walter Matthews, who slept with other church leaders in the crypt during some of the worst air raids, in case they needed to extinguish new fires in the cathedral. The dean pointed out where a bomb had entered through the cathedral roof and damaged the high altar. A statue of George Washington had been removed for safety. She inspected a plaque dedicated to the first American-born pilot to die for England, inscribed, "He died that England might live." Standing on the steps of the cathedral, Eleanor could witness the extensive destruction of London's financial center and the loss of London's Guildhall and many beautiful old churches.

As they toured the devastated East End, the queen told Eleanor she took solace in knowing that new housing would replace the slums the bombs had leveled. With characteristic empathy, Eleanor noted that however poor the houses were, people would still suffer over losing them. The destruction of many homes in Stepney, where the population had lived over small shops in rows of two-story houses, was even more poignant. Since the Nazi bombing raids began, two-thirds of the district's population had been killed. In the big shelters where twelve hundred had been sleeping through the night, only three hundred were left. Eleanor was impressed by the good cheer with which people handled being herded together underground in the shelters.

When Eleanor took leave of Their Majesties to continue her tour, newspapers remarked that they parted more like friends than formal political allies. The king immediately wrote the president, saying how pleased he was by her visit: "That she should have made the long journey in these dangerous war days has touched and delighted our people. . . . We had some good talks and are looking forward to hearing her impressions of our women's war activities after she has completed the strenuous programme arranged for her."

Visiting an American Red Cross club to talk to U.S. service members, Eleanor took on the role of surrogate mother. She was mobbed by hundreds of sailors and soldiers, who cried out, "Hi, Eleanor," and "Heyah there Mrs. Roosevelt." Listening to all the inevitable complaints about military life, she was told of their main hardship: the soldiers had been issued thin cotton socks, which were difficult to march in. The next day, she brought up the problem with General Eisenhower, who ordered that two-and-a-half million wool socks be distributed to the troops. Eleanor made her first report to FDR on the conditions of the servicemen she'd interviewed:

Saw a lot of boys at the Red + Washington Club this a.m. The woman in the dispensary even said they came in with terrible blisters because their socks are too tight. All coming here should be issued *wool* socks. No heat is allowed till Nov. & most of them have colds. The boys are very upset over the mail situation, some have been here two months & not a line from home. Also their pay in many cases is very late—& they buy bonds & don't get them. . . . The spirits seems good but of course I've only seen a few. The spirit of the British people is something to bow down to . . . Tommy bears up well & now finds staying with Kings quite ordinary! Love, ER

Starting a practice she would continue on other inspections, with her typical thoroughness, she collected a daunting group of names and addresses of the families of boys to whom she spoke. When she returned to the States, she wrote to every family. At a time when she was worried about the safety of her four enlisted sons, her new maternal role of surrogate mother suited her well.

On the night of October 27, the underlying tensions between Eleanor and the prime minister flared up during a small dinner party hosted by the Churchills at 10 Downing Street. While discussing the Spanish civil war, Churchill said that he had been a proponent of the Franco government until the Axis powers went in to help them; but Eleanor, whose natural sympathies went toward working-class leftists, jumped in to express her frustration that the United States, and her husband, had not done more to help the Loyalists during the war. Churchill retorted that he and Eleanor would have been among the first to lose their heads if the Loyalists had won. Eleanor claimed she did not care whether she lost her head, but Churchill growled, "I don't want you to lose your head and neither do I want to lose mine." Mrs. Churchill quickly intervened, declaring, "I think Mrs. Roosevelt is right." Churchill, who held a deep-seated antipathy for communism, became even more agitated. "I have held certain beliefs for sixty years and I'm not going to change now," he huffed.

Eleanor and Elliott spent a weekend with Winston and Clementine Churchill at Chequers, the country estate of British prime ministers. Watching Winston playing a game on the floor with his baby grandson and namesake—the son of Randolph and his then wife, Pamela Digby, many years later a U.S. ambassador in Paris as Mrs. Averell Harriman—Eleanor was struck by the extraordinary resemblance between infant and old man. When she mentioned it to her host, Churchill replied that his grandson did not look like him; he (Churchill) "just looked like all babies."

Eleanor found Mrs. Churchill attractive, youthful, and charming, but given her husband's notion that women should keep in the background, Eleanor wrote in her autobiography, "One feels that she has had to assume a role because of being in public life and that the role is now part of her, but one wonders what she is like underneath." Clementine worked diligently to support relief efforts for Russia and China, but unlike Eleanor, was "very careful not to voice any opinions publicly or to associate with any political organizations."

Winston Churchill did recognize Eleanor's usefulness in raising the troops' morale and encouraging British women's war efforts. "I thought you would like to know that Mrs. Roosevelt's visit here is a great success," he cabled the president. "Mrs. Roosevelt has been winning golden opinions here from all for her kindness and her unfailing interest in everything we are doing. . . . Mrs. Roosevelt proceeds indefatigably . . . I only wish you were here yourself." He entreated the First Lady to reduce her schedule and put in some days of rest, but to no avail. Indeed, the British had been won over by her boundless energy and her sincere, inexhaustible interest in learning everything about their homefront. Women, struggling with severe clothing rations, loved that she did not wear elegant or trendy fashions; some noted that when she arrived in England, her coat and hat even looked made-over. As Eleanor traveled through Oxford, Cambridge, Bristol, Birmingham, Manchester, Liverpool, Glasgow, Belfast, and Edinburgh, she received spontaneous ovations; London crowds waited outside the U.S. embassy all day hoping to get a glimpse of her. Refreshingly, she had become a celebrity based on her good character rather than her glamour, more so in England than at home. Legends began to circulate around her—for example, that she had worn through all her pairs of shoes in her walking tours of city ruins and army installations.

She did wear out Mrs. Churchill. On an inspection of clothing distribution centers, the prime minister's wife sat down on a staircase while Eleanor bounded up four flights to chat with more workers.

Reporters wilted as well. After a seven-day tour of the Midlands, Ulster, and Scotland, one British reporter wrote, "Hustle, did you say? She walked me off my feet." Reporters estimated that she walked "fifty miles through factories, clubs and hospitals." They returned "glassy-eyed and sagging at the knees." Cecil Beaton, who photographed Eleanor with the royal family, complained to the queen about Eleanor's "lack of repose." The queen responded, "Oh! But she has such *animation.*"

When her driver got lost bringing Eleanor to visit Elliott's unit at Steeple Morton near Cambridge and telephoned the U.S. embassy for directions, his coded message, "Rover has lost her pup," became a favorite wartime quotation. Arriving to a rousing cheer from the troops on the sullen and wet day, she went down the ranks and spoke to as many men as possible before being whisked inside for a cup of tea. Of Elliott, she wrote to Hick, "He has matured, and will be a good citizen I think."

At the beginning of the war in Europe, FDR had written many of Europe's monarchs asking how he could be helpful. Already, Grand Duchess Charlotte of Luxembourg and her seven children, Queen Wilhelmina of the Netherlands, and the Crown Prince and Crown Princess of Norway had shown up at the White House looking for assistance. FDR, keen to strengthen alliances that could later prove useful to him, had given Eleanor lists of royal figures to meet in England. Royalty exiled from various Nazi-occupied countries sought audiences with her to plead for their causes. She was impressed with King Haakon of Norway and his son Crown Prince Olav, whom she already knew; she listened to the concerns of King George II of Greece, but found a meeting with young King Peter of Yugoslavia tedious. Eleanor paid the formidable Queen Wilhelmina of the Netherlands the honor of calling on her. "She greeted me warmly and allowed me to kiss her," Eleanor reported, "which gave me a sense of intimacy I had never quite expected to have but have never since lost." They spent an hour discussing their visions for a postwar world, beginning a lifelong friendship.

In heavy daylight bombing, the Nazis destroyed parts of Canterbury, sending a message to the Roosevelts only one day after the First Lady had been received by the mayor and toured the already damaged cathedral. Eleanor sent an immediate letter of condolence for the mayor to read to the people of Canterbury. Disturbed by the Lady's enthusiastic worldwide press coverage, Nazi propaganda chief Joseph Goebbels issued an order to German journalists: "The hullabaloo about Eleanor Roosevelt should be left to die down gradually and should not result in Mrs. Roosevelt's journey being popularized or invested with a certain importance."

After Canterbury, Eleanor visited the British Red Cross Society, lunched with the American Correspondents Association, held a press conference with representatives of British women's magazines, and left London for tea at Coppins in Buckinghamshire, where she budgeted one hour to meet the widowed Princess Marina, the president's godson Prince Michael, his sister Princess Alexandra, and his brother, the seven-year-old Duke of Kent. Princess Marina asked Eleanor to bring the president a copy of the final photograph taken of the duke and duchess with FDR's infant godson.

At the end of that that long day, she made an incognito nighttime tour of blacked-out London to see how the GIs entertained themselves. She enhanced her reputation when she paid no attention to an air-raid alarm and continued talking to American soldiers and their girlfriends. Nothing could stop her. A few days earlier she had ignored another air-raid warning while she was in the middle of a speech before several thousand women at a training center. When asked if she was nervous, Eleanor laughed and said she was used to American practice alarms.

FDR had asked Eleanor to visit Queen Mary, to repay her for her hospitality to his mother when she had visited in 1934. The day she met with Mary was a typically hectic round of inspections, culminating with a stop at the American Red Cross Club run by Ted Roosevelt's wife, also named Eleanor. With the U.S. midterm elections imminent, reporters were hoping to get a dramatic headline out of the encounter between the doyennes of the two contentious Roosevelt clans. They were disappointed when the two women sat down to a quiet cup of tea.

Promptly at six-thirty that evening, Eleanor and Tommy arrived at the front door of Badminton, the country home of Queen Mary's niece, the Duchess of Beaufort, where Queen Mary stayed during the war, in Gloucestershire. Queen Mary showed Eleanor to her enormous and chilly bedroom, which was "furnished grandly with Chinese

Chippendale furniture," she said in her autobiography, and pointed out a frosty-looking bathroom. At dinner, Queen Mary looked regal in a black velvet evening gown and ermine jacket, adorned with many ropes of pearls, bracelets, and rings. Exhausted, Eleanor felt ill at ease with the formidable Queen Mother. Getting through dinner ("not a hilarious meal") was an ordeal, but she made "valiant efforts" to keep the conversation going, she said. Tommy "escaped and went to bed." Queen Mary drew Eleanor and the Princess Royal (Princess Mary) back to her drawing room where the queen talked while Eleanor remained standing, strictly adhering to royal protocol, for fifteen minutes until the queen gave her a reprieve and invited her to the sitting room and motioned for her to take a seat. "I found it hard to forget enough and yet remember enough! Conversation must flow but you must not sit down or leave until you are given the high sign."

Queen Mary did not notice Eleanor's discomfort. "Mrs. R and I had an agreeable talk both before and after dinner," the queen wrote in her diary: "She has a wonderful grasp of things in general." The queen wrote her brother Lord Athlone, "I liked her very much. She is very intelligent and her grasp of what our women are doing here is splendid, and she hopes to do much in the USA to wake up the women there to emulate our manifold activities. She is on the go from morning till night and I fear will kill her unfortunate secretary Miss Thompson." Eleanor noted later in her memoirs: "I recognized her thoughtfulness of others and the Spartan demands she makes on herself. Every little detail of what she considers the proper treatment of guests, she carries through. . . . She has always shown her appreciation for any slight act of friendliness from our family."

The intimidating Queen Mary could be surprisingly approachable. Eleanor's favorite story about her recounted how the queen was driving through the countryside and stopped to pick up a hitchhiking American GI. After they chatted for a while, she asked if he knew who she was, and he said, "No, ma'am." She plied him with questions about his home life, his army duty, and his reactions to the British people. When he got out of the car, she could not resist giving him a little shock. "I am Queen Mary," she told him. "Oh, you are!" he replied. "I am from Missouri and you'll have to show me." She gave him a memento to prove he had actually met her. Queen Mary had had little medallions made to give as gifts to those who accepted a lift from her.

Queen Mary got up the next morning to see Eleanor off and pose for photographs with her. Knowing the president was a fellow conservationist who loved the Hyde Park trees, she presented Eleanor with a gift carefully chosen for him, a signed photograph showing her "fully dressed in hat, gloves and veil, sawing a dead limb off a tree" with a young Australian dispatch rider at the other end of the saw. FDR was delighted. As gifts for three of the First Lady's granddaughters, the queen also gave Eleanor books on her famous dollhouse at Windsor Castle.

American-born Viscountess Astor hosted a luncheon for Eleanor with the women members of Parliament, who could share with her the difficulties of leading a public political life, and discuss the issues that women faced working in the war effort. Because it would be politically provocative, Eleanor declined a tempting invitation to watch in the House when they debated matters of women's inequality. On November 3, Eleanor paid a proper visit to Parliament, where she inspected the ruins of the House of Commons, destroyed in an air raid eighteen months earlier. An M.P. told her that he had smashed in one of the great oak doors at Westminster Hall with an ax so he could douse flames from a firebomb. She spoke briefly on her major theme: the mixing of U.S. and British troops could lead to greater understanding and cooperation between the two countries.

## Washington, D.C.

Back at home, Americans were increasingly restive about military setbacks in both Europe and the Far East. The Germans were marching toward Stalingrad, and American marines were dying in great numbers on the island of Guadalcanal. FDR could not encourage them by revealing the secret plans to invade North Africa in the coming weeks. As the 1942 elections approached, Americans were also angry about the deprivations of wartime rationing. Days before the election, they were told that adults over fifteen would be limited to one cup of coffee per day because the ships that brought the coffee from South America had to be used to take soldiers and war materials abroad. FDR knew that this did not bode well for the Democrats' chances in the off-year elections. He watched on November 3 as Republicans made major gains in Congress and won a number of governorships as well. He was unhappy about the results, but he was relieved that the Democrats still maintained slim majorities in both houses of Congress.

FDR could barely contain his impatience with the slow pace of preparations for the first big Allied offensive. On November 8, the president waited nervously for news at the presidential retreat Shangri-La (which President Eisenhower would rename Camp David). His secretary Grace Tully noticed FDR's hand shake as he reached to accept a phone call from the War Department. He listened carefully to the news and then exclaimed, "Thank God! Thank God! That sounds grand." Turning to his guests, he explained that two hundred thousand U.S. troops, under the command of General George S. Patton, had landed in North Africa with lower casualties than expected. The president said famously, "We are fighting back."

## Liverpool

Eleanor was in Liverpool when the BBC broadcast the news of the invasion. There was great cheering along the city's docks and streets. People felt "now we are fighting together," she reported to her readers. One woman told her, "God bless your men, may this be the beginning of the end for old Hitler." The previous night in a broadcast, Eleanor had exhorted British women to give maximum effort toward victory in the war and a lasting peace afterward.

Eleanor took Tommy and her aunt Maude out to Windsor Castle to report to the king on her inspections. The king, who had spent the day visiting American air force troops, joined them in the sitting room. Both the First Lady and the king were suffering from bad colds. As they drove away from Windsor, Aunt Maude told Eleanor, "Darling, I was never so humiliated in my life. Your using those nasty little tissues and wadding them up in your hand while the king used such lovely linen handkerchiefs! What could they have thought!"

## Washington, D.C.

Eleanor was concerned neither for linen handkerchiefs nor for her own safety. However, Churchill and Ambassador Winant worried that the Nazis, furious over the success of her trip, would try to shoot down her return plane flight. They pressed for her to choose a safer means of return, but FDR overruled them and said, "Get her home right now." When Eleanor arrived at Washington's Dulles airport on November 17, she was struck by the fact that the president greeted her personally at the airport: "I think Franklin was glad to see me back," she wrote in her diary. "I think he even read this diary and to my surprise he had also read my columns." Eager to discuss her reports on the troops, the British mobilization, and the women's war efforts, she joined him for a rare White House lunch. She gave him souvenirs of the trip: a tin of Scottish shortbread, a shillelagh, and a Londonderry cane. Roosevelt agreed with her request that the government set up day nurseries in the United States, as had been done so successfully in Britain, to free up women to aid the war effort.

For Franklin and Eleanor, it was a rare moment of intimacy amid a war that so often divided them. They dined alone again that night, and spent a weekend together at Shangri-La, but Eleanor did not linger to savor the renewed closeness between them. Within a week, she was traveling to New York, Philadelphia, and Connecticut. Doris Kearns Goodwin points out that, in her autobiography, Eleanor remembered incorrectly that Franklin held a formal dinner the first night she was back and left her out. In fact, the dinner occurred a week later and Eleanor did not attend it; she had snuck off to dine with Joe Lash. Goodwin suggests her own guilt over avoiding intimacy with Franklin twisted Eleanor's memory of events into a story of her neglect.

In a White House press conference, Eleanor stressed England's single-minded focus on winning the war, how people lived with "a sense of cold, and a sense of blackout," working side by side, regardless of class, and tolerating lowered standards of living. Eleanor doubted that the British class system would persist after the war. She told Americans how, according to wartime rules, fires would not be lit in Buckingham Palace until the first of December. "If we could come to realize that shortening the war depends on what we are *willing* to do ourselves we might put a great deal more into the war effort here . . . if women are willing to do a great deal more . . . which would release men for more essential work, we could shorten the war. This would mean doing away with many things we thought were essential, such as bobby pins, hot water bottles etc," she exhorted the country in the press conference. She said she was inspired by her trip. "I am glad I went because I came back with enormous pride in the ability of human nature to rise above things that usually bother us the most—the little things." She added her own credo: "When you have to face things, you can always do it."

Eleanor was very impressed with the innumerable U.S. soldiers she had made such an effort to meet. "They are perfectly grand boys," she declared, who appreciated everything that was being done for them. "It is a hard climate for them to get used to at first, and they all have colds in the beginning." The younger boys, she thought, were "having the thrill of their lives," while the older ones were missing their homes and families.

The First Lady said she "never worked so hard in my life as I did over there" and gave an example of one of her most demanding days. She breakfasted with some army privates, walked through the entire Londonderry naval establishment, placed a wreath for the U.S. forces on a monument for Armistice Day, toured every floor (all of them concrete and hard on the feet) of the hospital, lunched with army men, flew an hour and a half to Glasgow, joined the Red Cross for dinner, had coffee in the Boys' Canteen, went to the Merchant Marine to make a broadcast, visited and thoroughly inspected a factory, made an 11 P.M. speech to 750 women on the night shift, sang anthems with them, and went to the house of the factory head, where she wrote her "My Day" column before going to bed after midnight. She was amused at the reaction of the British press to her frantic schedule: A "little English press girl" asked if she ever spent the morning in bed. "No, why?" Eleanor asked. "Oh, we did wish you would," said the press girl.

After her departure, the London *Daily Mail* paid Eleanor tribute, saying she had created an image of "of a personality as symbolically American as the Statue of Liberty itself." Chalmers Roberts of the London Office of War Information told his boss that Mrs. Roosevelt had done more than any other American ever had accomplished before, to bring the British people an appreciation of the American spirit. Churchill, with whom Eleanor argued about politics, nonetheless wrote her a parting note telling her, "You certainly have left golden footprints behind you."

## London

As 1942 ended, the Roosevelts and the royal family were in dissimilar frames of mind. Even after a year in which America had brought its full resources to the war and the Allies had finally taken an impressive and successful initiative in defeating Rommel in North Africa, the king was depressed. The queen soothed his moods, made him laugh, and treated him with great tenderness at a time when the strains of war bore down on him heavily. Even as they were heartened by the Allies' first major triumph over the Axis powers, at Christmastime they were also mourning the Duke of Kent. As the New Year began, the king began to organize his own affairs in case he too was killed. As he put it, "ever since George's death, these matters loom large in one's mind as one must be prepared for all eventualities."

One source of the king's despondency arose in part from the desperate British situation on the seas. At a time when Operation Torch in North Africa strained the Allied supply lines, the Germans had been all too successful at sinking supply ships. Churchill was sending urgent requests to FDR for even more ships to keep the supplies of food and materials flowing to Britain. In his final diary entry for the year, the king wrote: "We shall be in a bad way here in mid-1943, & we shall have to reduce our war effort here, which will prolong the war & put more work on the U.S.A. to keep us all going. All this is not pleasant news to hear. Outwardly one has to be optimistic about the future in 1943, but inwardly I am depressed at the present prospect."

## Washington, D.C.

In Washington, the Roosevelts greeted the New Year in a much brighter mood than the royal family did, especially compared to the previous, dark Christmas season, right after Pearl Harbor. Eleanor was not as blue as she had been the past year after her sons had first left for war, but she did still feel burdened by the heavy schedule of formal holiday entertaining. As she organized Christmas parties and did her charity work, she told Joe Lash, "I am always with so many people & always so alone inside." On New Year's Eve, however, FDR gave her cause for cheer with his final toasts of the year. After a dinner with

Harry Hopkins, his wife, the Morgenthaus, and the ever present Crown Princess Märtha—now reunited with her husband, Crown Prince Olav—the president, preoccupied with North Africa, showed the Humphrey Bogart and Ingrid Bergman soon-to-be-classic film *Casablanca.* Then at midnight as champagne was served, he made his traditional first toast to the United States, and his second toast to the United Nations—the organization whose founding was Eleanor's great postwar hope. She was deeply pleased, and touched, as he saluted her after her extraordinary year: "To the person who makes it possible for the President to carry on."

Two months after their wedding, Franklin and Eleanor look very much in love in this playful and informal photo taken in May 1905 at Newburgh, New York.

Following World War I, President and Mrs. Wilson made the first official presidential visit to Buckingham Palace in December 1918. Left to right, Edith Wilson, Queen Mary, President Wilson, King George V, and King George's daughter, Princess Mary.

FDR meets the Prince of Wales for the first time at a naval review in Washington, D.C., in November 1919. As assistant secretary of the navy, FDR (far left) joins navy secretary Josephus Daniels (to the left of the prince) in greeting the Prince of Wales (center).

A formal portrait of the Duke and Duchess of York during their seven-month 1927 world tour in which the duke emerged from the shadow of his charming and celebrated brother, the Prince of Wales.

Sara Delano Roosevelt, dubbed the "queen" by White House staff for her autocratic ways, with her son Franklin at Hyde Park shortly after he won the presidency.

On his arrival at the Hollywood Bowl in Los Angeles on September 24, 1932, during his first presidential campaign, FDR is helped out of his limousine. The press cooperated in hiding his disability from the American public.

Lorena Hickok hated to be photographed; she looks away from the camera during this informal photo with Eleanor Roosevelt and two unidentified companions during a visit to Canada.

During their extended honeymoon in March 1935, the Duke of Kent and his glamorous wife, Marina, Duchess of Kent, meeting FDR for the first time on Vincent Astor's yacht *Nourmahal*. The duchess is in the center with FDR second from left and the duke third from right; the actor David Niven is at the far right.

Archrivals Franklin Roosevelt and Joseph P. Kennedy shake hands at the high point of their complicated relationship. Justice Stanley Reed (center) has just sworn in Kennedy on February 18, 1938, as Roosevelt's ambassador to Great Britain.

On the eve of the king and queen's triumphant tour of Canada and the United States, Ambassador Kennedy and his wife host a dinner for the royal couple at the United States embassy in London.

A dress rehearsal for the visit of the British monarchs: Eleanor, FDR, and Sara Roosevelt host Crown Prince Olav and Crown Princess Märtha of Norway for a weekend at Hyde Park in April 1939. Princess Märtha is seated next to FDR; her husband is between Eleanor and Sara on the front porch at Springwood.

FDR was excited to greet the king and queen on their arrival at Washington's Union Station on June 8, 1939. Having previously encountered two of the king's brothers, FDR's first words to King George were "At last we meet."

"A tempest in a teapot" was how one diplomat referred to the social hysteria over the king and queen's garden party at the British embassy in Washington, D.C., on June 8, 1939. Queen Elizabeth does a walkabout with Mrs. Lindsay at the party.

The king and queen were nervous before their meeting at the Capitol rotunda with members of Congress, many of whom were isolationists. They stood awkwardly underneath a painting of British general Cornwallis's surrender at Yorktown.

FDR carefully stage-managed the Sunday morning worship service at his Episcopal parish church of St. James so that it would resemble an English country church service. FDR is leaning on the arm of his eldest son, James.

The famous hot dog picnic. Guests were seated on the lawn to the side of Top Cottage, which FDR designed.

The royal guests and dignitaries dine on the porch of Top Cottage while local children Muriel Ann Smith and her friend sneak a peek at them.

During the picnic lunch King George has a brief afternoon slump following an exciting late-night political conversation with the president.

Eleanor stands behind the queen and next to the king on the Top Cottage porch.

FDR takes the queen (in front), the king, and his favorite daughter-in-law, Betsey, the wife of James (back seat), on a ride around the estate in his hand-operated car. Sixty years after the picnic, the Queen Mother revealed how frightened she had been during her drives with FDR at Hyde Park.

The Oyster Bay rivals: Teddy Roosevelt's daughter Alice and son Ted Jr. at a Republican National Committee meeting in Philadelphia in February 1940. Alice often made fun of Eleanor, and Ted complained that FDR had usurped his place as Teddy Roosevelt's heir.

The Duke and Duchess of Windsor seated together on a bench in 1940 during his time as governor of the Bahamas.

During the Nazi Blitz in September 1940, the king, the queen, and Winston Churchill examine the bomb damage at Buckingham Palace. A German pilot had nearly killed Their Majesties when he dropped a bomb in the palace quadrangle.

The king and queen offer comfort to Londoners after a bombing raid.

In October 1941, Eleanor offers a polite greeting to the Duchess of Windsor, of whom she disapproved, in her office at the Civilian Defense Headquarters. Eleanor had declined to preside at a White House luncheon for the Windsors earlier that day.

The Duke of Kent (in bathing suit) and his wife, Princess Marina, by the pool at Val-Kill Cottage during his visit to Hyde Park in August 1941. The duke's visit with the Roosevelts was part of the British propaganda campaign to win U.S. war support for Britain.

As she begins her secret mission to England in October 1942, nervous about visiting Buckingham Palace without FDR, Eleanor steps off the train and is greeted by the king and queen.

British enthusiasm for the United States and its First Lady is evident as Eleanor visits the Women's Voluntary Service Nursery at Regent's Park in November 1942.

At the First Quebec wartime planning conference at the Citadel in August 1943, FDR, seated next to his host, the Earl of Athlone; Canadian prime minister Mackenzie King; and Winston Churchill begin planning the invasion of Normandy.

Eleanor is seated with Princess Alice, Countess of Athlone (center), and Clementine Churchill at the Second Quebec Conference in August 1944. Their husbands were discussing the disarmament of Germany and the war in the Pacific.

Winston Churchill, FDR, and Russian premier Stalin on the patio of the Livadia Palace at the Yalta Conference, February 1945. Churchill said later that FDR's face had "a transparency . . . there was a far-away look in his eyes."

Eleanor and her daughter, Anna, and son Elliott (in hat at right) at FDR's funeral at Hyde Park, April 1945.

Charles de Gaulle (third from left) joins Eleanor at FDR's grave.

The king, the queen, and Princess Elizabeth (in her ATS uniform) enter St. Paul's Cathedral in London for a memorial service for Franklin Roosevelt on April 17, 1945.

Winston Churchill joins the royal family in celebrating VE Day in May 1945 from the balcony of Buckingham Palace.

Eleanor Roosevelt, a delegate at the United Nations meetings in London in January 1946. When Harry Truman had appointed her, she was afraid she would not be able to do the job.

On the terrace of Windsor Castle, Eleanor with the king and queen during a weekend visit just prior to the unveiling of FDR's statue in London, April 1948.

Eleanor stands with Queen Elizabeth and Queen Mary (third from left) and the king (second from right) in front of the newly unveiled statue of FDR in Grosvenor Square in London, April 1948.

Memorial statue of Franklin Roosevelt in Grosvenor Square in London.

The famous photo of the three queens in mourning for King George VI. Queen Elizabeth II, Queen Mary (center), and Queen Elizabeth, February 1952.

The Queen Mother leaves Westminster Abbey after the coronation of her daughter, Queen Elizabeth II, in June 1953.

Queen Elizabeth reviews the 7th Regiment at the Commonwealth Ball in the Park Avenue Armory in New York City, October 1954.

Eleanor Roosevelt's granddaughter Nina presents her sister Joan to the Queen Mother at a luncheon at Val-Kill Cottage during the Queen Mother's confidence-building visit to the United States in November 1954.

Eleanor Roosevelt's funeral in Hyde Park on November 10, 1962. From left, President John F. Kennedy, future president Lyndon B. Johnson, and former presidents Harry S. Truman and Dwight D. Eisenhower.

The Queen Mother, indomitable as ever, celebrates her ninety-ninth birthday at Clarence House in August 1999. She died in March 2002.

Harry Johannesen, who bought the famous hot dogs for the 1939 Hyde Park picnic, takes a photo of Prince Andrew during his September 2002 visit to Hyde Park. Harry has just presented Prince Andrew with a photograph he had taken of Andrew's grandparents in 1939.

# 14

# A Perfect Team

## January 1943–July 1944

> OVERLORD is backed by the greatest armada in history. It will
> not fail.
>
> —*Dwight D. Eisenhower to King George VI, May 15, 1944*

## England

After the depressing holiday, Their Majesties were encouraged when
Churchill and Roosevelt met in January at Casablanca to plan the next
steps in the war, a campaign that might move the Allies onto the offensive. In a personal letter Churchill delivered to the president, the king
expressed confidence that their plans would lead to victory against "the
enemies of civilization." He hoped that Mrs. Roosevelt had "returned
to you none the worse for her strenuous visit" last fall, and lamented
that FDR could not "come here for your conversations" and meet
British leaders in Britain, so they could "renew friendships." With
Britain well into its fourth year of war, the king, increasingly exhausted,
hoped he could further solidify Britain's crucial alliance with America,
play a more active role in the war by visiting and encouraging the
troops fighting in Europe and Africa, and buttress Britain at home until
the great day when, with the Allied victory assured, he and the queen
could welcome the Roosevelts to England for a celebration of their victory, which would save democracy.

On January 24, FDR wrote the king from Casablanca, where he

and Churchill had planned an invasion of Sicily: "I wish much that you could have been with us during the past ten days—a truly mighty meeting in its thoroughness and in the true spirit of comradeship between each officer and his 'opposite number.'" Expressing his bond with Churchill in terms that might equally apply to Their Majesties, he wrote: "As for Mr. Churchill and myself I need not tell you that we make a perfectly matched team in harness and out—and incidentally we had lots of fun together as we always do." Eleanor, he said, was "thrilled" by her British trip and he was grateful to Their Majesties "for all you did for her."

The royal family felt under siege that winter—indeed, they did throughout the war. Both Windsor Castle and Buckingham Palace were bleak, frightening places, more military installations than homes. At both residences, chandeliers were removed, the furniture was covered with sheets, and all the paintings stored. The contents of Buckingham Palace's Picture Gallery were sent to a storage facility at an abandoned slate quarry in Wales, and Princess Margaret put her own drawings into the elaborate gilt frames where portraits of her ancestors had been in the galleries at Windsor Castle. By the end of the war, Buckingham Palace would be overrun with rats, which terrified the queen. With the royal family a prime enemy target—the king and queen knew of the German plan to capture them and hold them as hostages—Windsor Castle, their primary wartime residence, served again as the fortress it had been early in its history. The castle was surrounded by slit trenches, barbed wire, and squadrons of guards. Princess Margaret later said she had been told Hitler had planned to use Windsor Castle as his headquarters after England had been conquered, which certainly made the royal couple and their children feel even more in the bull's-eye. According to one of the Queen Mother's biographers, Ann Morrow, as bizarre as it sounds, intelligence officers from the War Office had briefed them about the possibility of an airborne invasion; the skies over Windsor would be filled with German parachutists disguised as nuns in black habits. They would land, pull out machine guns from under their fake black habits, and riddle the castle with bullets. Surprisingly, the queen was once caught breaching security during a visit to Glamis Castle. Her informal father, ignoring wartime caution, wanted her visit to be properly celebrated. One night, local police were appalled to find the Queen of England seated at an extravagant banquet in the well-lit grand dining hall of the castle, which might easily be hit by Nazi bombers. The lights were quickly dimmed.

The Germans bombed Windsor regularly. During night bombing, the princesses would pick up their packed suitcases and gas masks and walk through the dark to a shelter in the castle dungeon. During the day they contributed to the war effort by performing the same tasks as teenage girls across Britain: growing vegetables, collecting tinfoil, rolling bandages, and knitting socks for the troops. To relieve the tedium, they would hold lunches, teas, and small dances to entertain their guards. Princess Margaret talked to the author Hugo Vickers about "having been brought up by the Grenadier Guards at Windsor during the war."

Amid the bombs and the tension of siege, the king and queen tried to maintain elements of normality. Possessed of similar values, they worked around their differing passions. They both loved gardening, political discussions, and their children, but while he enjoyed practical jokes and slapstick comedy, she preferred reading poetry, keeping up with the book world, and augmenting the royal art collection. She commissioned paintings from John Piper and Edward Seago. The king did not pretend to know much about art. When he saw John Piper's watercolors of Windsor with his trademark atmospheric skies, he commiserated with Piper about the poor weather conditions he had to paint. The queen was determined that the war would not interfere with her efforts to rear culturally and intellectually sophisticated daughters. At one poetry reading, however, when Edith Sitwell, the grande dame of British poetry, began reciting her "Anne Boleyn's Song" in her own peculiar cadences, the princesses had a hard time keeping a straight face. By the time T. S. Eliot, "a rather lugubrious man in a suit," read "The Waste Land," as the queen later told author A. N. Wilson, "we didn't understand a word and first the girls got the giggles, then I did."

## Malta

For the king, being stuck at Windsor Castle or Buckingham Palace doing paperwork was a worse existence than being a prisoner of war. The queen understood he was a man of action. "He feels so much not being more in the fighting line," the queen told Queen Mary. Despite her fears for his safety, in June 1943 he flew to Gibraltar, Tunisia, and Malta to visit British, U.S., and dominion troops. Before his departure, the king appointed his wife as a counselor of state, allowing her to carry out many of his duties, including an investiture. His travel worried her. She wrote Queen Mary:

> I have had an anxious few hours . . . I heard that the plane had been heard near Gibraltar. . . . Then after an hour & a half I heard that there was a thick fog at Gib. & that they were going on to Africa. Then complete silence till a few minutes ago, when a message came that they have landed in Africa, & taken off again. Of course I imagined every sort of horror, & walked up and down my room staring at the telephone.

Despite a lack of sleep, when the king arrived in Algiers on June 12 he was "buoyant and friendly with General Ike," according to General Eisenhower's driver and intimate Kay Summersby. As he did with Churchill, the king relished talking war strategy with the U.S. general. After a lively dinner one night, the king took Eisenhower aside and presented him with the Knight Grand Cross of the Order of the Bath, to honor his leadership of the Allied armies.

The centerpiece of the king's trip was an extremely hazardous and secret visit to Malta, which was only sixty miles from the Axis airfields on Sicily and surrounded by Italian submarines. The Maltese had nearly starved while enduring daily Axis bombardment from June 1941 until September 1942, and they had played a crucial role in the Allied victory in North Africa by cutting off the enemy supply lines. Suffering from dysentery and nausea, the thin, sunburned king stood in his crisp naval uniform and waved from the bridge of his cruiser as it sailed into the Grand Harbour of Valetta on the morning of June 20. The island's quarter of a million people gave him a tumultuous welcome, many of them cheering wildly from rooftops by the harbor as church bells pealed, which "brought a lump to my throat, knowing what they had suffered from . . . months of constant bombing," the king wrote his mother. Normally fastidious in maintaining his dress, the king was so transported by his twelve-hour visit that he did not seem to mind that his white uniform had turned red from the scarlet geraniums the

Maltese people had tossed at him at his car. The king gave the island's people and its military garrison his personal medal, the George Cross, for their valor.

The visit served to drive home a signal Allied military accomplishment: the Axis powers no longer controlled the Mediterranean. Within several months, British and U.S. troops would be landing on the Italian mainland. The king arrived home from his grueling two-week trip exhausted and very thin but triumphant. He had offered the heartening, fighting-front leadership he had striven to provide. The king and queen then visited Allied bomber bases in the English countryside, where fighters were starting to take the air war to Germany through perilous night skies. To thank them for their service in Britain, the queen also inspected members of the U.S. ambulance service, parading before her at Buckingham Palace on the third anniversary of their founding. Amid deprivation and danger, the king and queen had actively become symbols of the British effort to turn the tide of battle.

## Quebec

In August 1943, Franklin Roosevelt went to the first of two conferences in Quebec hosted by the Athlones and dedicated to war planning. Before he left, he shared a rare day of leisure with Eleanor, who was about to leave for six weeks touring military bases in the South Pacific. Eleanor, well aware that she was entering a war zone, left instructions for disposing of her jewelry in case she did not return.

When the Athlones arrived at the Citadel, the spectacular fortress that sits on heights overlooking the St. Lawrence River, they were appalled that the U.S. detectives, stationed on every landing, were wearing short-sleeve shirts in the searing heat. Lord Athlone, a stickler for correct dress, added a perfectly turned-out Canadian Mountie on each floor. The head American detective informed the Athlones that a U.S. president was assassinated like clockwork every forty-five years (he was inaccurate about this) and that, this being that year, the kind of intense security the president detested would be necessary. Just before Roosevelt arrived, several of the detectives threw themselves on the drawing room sofa, tossing their legs over the arms, and lit up cigars. Princess Alice was furious, and even more livid when told it was too much of a security risk for her to go out on the front terrace to greet her friend the U.S. president. Fortunately, Winston Churchill led her briskly out onto the terrace to welcome Roosevelt.

The war leaders were "delightful guests when we were just en famille, and we enjoyed many thrilling conversations, off the record, as they say," Princess Alice wrote in her memoirs. The Athlones listened as Churchill, still haunted by Dunkirk, reluctantly agreed with Roosevelt on a cross-channel attack on the European mainland in May 1944. Before the conference, the king had lobbied Churchill, urging that the major attack be made from the south through Italy. His advice was not heeded, but an invasion of Italy was scheduled the September following the northern assault. In a matter of increasing strategic importance among the Allies, FDR also agreed to offer Britain information about the atom bomb the United States was developing, and veto power over its ultimate use.

Because such a large proportion of the Allied troops would be American, the Allied nations appointed General Dwight D. Eisenhower as the Supreme Allied Commander of the invasion, but balanced the scale by naming the king's cousin, Lord Louis Mountbatten, as the head of the South East Asian command. Lord Mountbatten, a vain, charming, and ambitious man, had developed his own relationship with FDR; they had hit it off the previous summer during a long dinner discussing Allied strategy at the White House. Churchill had earlier deputized Mountbatten to convince FDR that a cross-channel invasion of Europe in late 1942 or 1943 was premature; he succeeded.

Before Eleanor left for her twenty-thousand-mile trip to Australia, New Zealand, and the Pacific islands, she devoted her August 13 "My Day" column to defending the right of the Jewish people to "grow and improve" without the kind of persecution and annihilation they had suffered under the Nazis. In response to reports that the Nazis had massacred two million Jews at the Treblinka death camps in Poland, she warned of the cost of allowing "great wrongs to occur without exerting ourselves to correct them." Rabbi Stephen Wise, the preeminent spokesman for American Zionism and a friend of the Roosevelts, said in his memoirs about FDR that "no one was more genuinely free from religious prejudice and racial bigotry." Both Eleanor and FDR were vigorously opposed to anti-Semitism and the Nazi creed of superior races. FDR believed that defeating the Nazis was the best way to help the Jews. Starting in late 1942 through public statements and pledges to Jewish leaders, he made clear that the Nazis would be held responsible for every crime against the Jewish people. However, historians continue to debate whether FDR could have taken more effective action to assist the Jewish population of Europe, such as bombing the death camps.

## The South Pacific

Eleanor's trip to the South Pacific was an agonizing exercise in empathy. Like Queen Elizabeth comforting Londoners during the Blitz, she confronted the American suffering firsthand, visiting the troops and seeing as many wounded and dying servicemen as she possibly could, well aware that she represented every American mother who had a son in uniform—and as a mother, felt their anxiety firsthand. When her four sons had left to join the war effort, she experienced the departure as "a sort of precursor of what it would be like if your children were killed. Life had to go on and you had to do what was required of you, but something inside of you quietly died." At the beginning of August 1943, she learned that Franklin Jr.'s destroyer had been bombed off the coast of Sicily. The ship had fought off the bombers, but Eleanor told her readers, "I know the way it feels when someone calls you up and says in what you know is an intentionally casual tone, 'Franklin Jr. is all right.'" When she telephoned her daughter-in-law to give her the news that the ship had been bombed and was indeed safe, there was silence until Franklin Jr.'s wife said, "Please start all over again. I did not hear what you said—the first words gave me heart failure." Eleanor's son James Roosevelt was a marine in the South Pacific, and many of his buddies had fought the fiercest battle of the war at Guadalcanal. Seeing horribly wounded South Pacific soldiers awakened the deadening pain she had felt when her sons left. The danger they all faced came freshly alive.

In a fruitless effort to forestall the condemnation she had received for wasting taxpayers' money and resources by going to England, Eleanor traveled alone on this trip, wearing a uniform as a special delegate of the Red Cross, having left her secretary and traveling companion Tommy Thompson at home. It was a mistake. She faced one of the most depressing experiences of her life without support—lonely, anxious, unmoored. She wrote Hick about her tour, "I can't judge at all whether it will accomplish what FDR hoped for or not." Only one thought consoled her during her grim days: that she might be able to see Joe Lash on Guadalcanal. On the U.S. base at Noumea she met Admiral William Halsey, the celebrated Pacific theater naval commander who had stymied the Japanese at Guadalcanal, and presented him with a letter from FDR requesting she be allowed to visit the island. Halsey claimed he did not have enough planes to spare an escort for her. Desperate to see Joe, she convinced Halsey to suspend his decision until she had done inspections in New Zealand and Australia.

She cabled her husband: "I wish I had not come on this trip. I think the trouble I give far outweighs the momentary interest it may give the boys to see me." For security reasons, troops were told only that a woman was coming to see them. Surely the men would expect a Hollywood starlet or a Betty Grable sex symbol, she thought, not a dowdy and dour president's wife. At each stop, she delivered the same message from FDR, telling the men that he looked each day in his map room to see where they were located, and what they were doing, and that he was profoundly grateful for their superb efforts. In spite of her depression and misgivings, she was acclaimed by the soldiers for her energy and concern. "She took New Zealand by storm," wrote one former newspaperman who had been assigned to cover her by the Air Transport Command. "She did a magnificent job saying the right thing at the right time and doing 101 little things that endeared her to the people." Halsey reported, "When I say that she inspected those hospitals, I don't mean that she shook hands with the chief medical officer, glanced into a sun parlor, and left. I mean that she went into every ward, stopped at every bed, and spoke to every patient: What was his name? How did he feel? Was there anything he needed? Could she take a message home for him?" Some reports suggested that her maternal kisses on the hospital wards had kept grievously wounded men from dying.

Admiral Halsey gave her permission to go to Guadalcanal. While there she received a note telling her that Joe Lash was waiting outside her tent. She rushed into his arms without bothering to conceal her excitement. "When the war is over I hope I never have to be long away from you . . . the whole trip now seems to me worthwhile," she wrote him the next morning—a sentiment that would later incite guilt in her, because she cared for him more than anyone else she knew.

After Eleanor left, Admiral Halsey admitted, "She alone had

accomplished more good than any other person, or any group of civilians, who had passed through my area." FDR cabled frequently with news of uniformly positive press at home. Believing that her husband was pleased with her performance helped her to endure the trip. At home FDR lunched with Crown Princess Märtha and Empress Zita of Austria-Hungry. The empress suggested Eleanor would be exhausted upon her return, but FDR joked, "No, but she will tire everybody else." When Eleanor phoned him from San Francisco, he teased her. "Did you have fun, darling?" he asked, sounding jealous, "as if she had been on a pleasure jaunt which he had been big-hearted enough to fix up for her," as her son-in-law John Boettiger said. Completely exhausted, she overreacted to his teasing, feeling unappreciated and rejected.

## Washington, D.C.

Back at the White House, Eleanor was initially heartened when FDR showed more interest in her trip than she expected, but over the next month she slipped into a worrisome depression. Doris Kearns Goodwin points out how different was her exposure to men's grievous war wounds, their broken spirits, and the rows of crosses in cemeteries than the upbeat experience she had touring war production facilities and army camps in the United States. Lonely and far from home, Eleanor had undergone the kind of life-shattering experience—like FDR's polio—that caused her to revaluate her entire life.

Eager to meet Stalin and frustrated that she had not yet been invited to any wartime conference, she had begged to accompany FDR to the Teheran Conference of the Allies in mid-November. He was taking two sons and his son-in-law. When Anna asked to sail with him on the *Potomac* to the conference, FDR claimed that under navy rules, women were not allowed on board ship. Anna was infuriated by her father's peremptory stance. When they heard that Churchill had brought his daughter Sarah, they were livid. In Teheran, it took FDR several days to find a way to overcome Stalin's mistrust so he could solidify the alliance among the three countries. His ingenuous solution was to tease Churchill vigorously about his British quirks and habits. Eventually Stalin laughed and picked on Churchill, who tolerated the abuse for the sake of the alliance. Stalin then helped FDR overcome Churchill's reluctance to agree to the cross-channel invasion,

Operation Overlord.

The night FDR returned to Washington, he summoned several old friends for dinner, to serve as a buffer against his angry wife and daughter. It became "a complete fiasco," Anna reported. FDR wanted to linger leisurely over drinks and tell the story of the conference at his own pace; Eleanor, anxious and still smarting from her rejection, rushed him through cocktails and pestered him for details of the trip. Exasperated by her hectoring, and hoping to appease her, he began telling indiscreet anecdotes about Churchill and Stalin. Anna chided him that his comments would jeopardize the war effort if they were leaked from the room. After the guests left, Eleanor followed FDR to his room and pressed in vain for more details about how the conference had gone. Only at breakfast the next morning did Anna begin to dispel the tension by sharing with her father mindless gossip about her brothers' latest romantic adventures.

This incident marked a further distancing in the Roosevelts' marriage. FDR, whose health was declining rapidly, avoided Eleanor and anyone else who placed additional strain on him. To protect herself from his rebuffs, Eleanor herself kept apart from him. As always, she masked her depression by working. After a brief family gathering at Hyde Park over Christmas, FDR returned to hold a White House news conference asking that his administration no longer be called the "New Deal." Using an allegory about the United States as a sick patient, he revealed that he would like to be known henceforth as "Dr. Win the War" rather than "Dr. New Deal." Eleanor could not have been happy about the official shift from the New Deal focus, which had drawn her close to her husband in the 1930s. In her own press conference she stressed the ongoing need for the New Deal goals of social justice and improving the lives of the underprivileged.

In the spring of 1944, Anna Roosevelt took over as her father's new surrogate wife, presiding at cocktail hour and doing anything she could to reduce his stress. Although she would later regret it, Eleanor approved of her daughter's role, but only after Anna agreed not to usurp her mother's place as hostess when Eleanor was in residence at the White House, as FDR's other companions had. Anna and her father adored each other. Like him, she was a great storyteller, throwing her head back and laughing with sheer joy at gossip and risqué jokes. Not only her father's buddy but his guardian, Anna soon noticed that her father's hand shook convulsively and that when they went to the movies, his mouth hung open. He complained of constant fatigue, headaches, and lack of sleep. Alarmed, she consulted her mother. Blinded by her impatience with illness and largely ignorant of her husband's symptoms due to her frequent absences from the White House, Eleanor dismissed Anna's concerns. The president's physician, Dr. Ross McIntire, neither an internist nor a heart specialist, claimed he was merely recovering slowly from influenza and bronchitis. Anna insisted on having him undergo a thorough checkup at the hospital.

Dr. Howard Bruenn, a cardiologist at Bethesda Naval Hospital, was alarmed. The president suffered from congestive heart failure, hardening of the arteries, hypertension, and failure of the left ventricle of the heart, he said. He might die at any time. After Dr. McIntire, rigid and ignorant, balked at Dr. Bruenn's recommendations, McIntire called a conference of physicians to agree on a plan to reduce the president's workload and support his heart with digitalis. Remarkably, FDR had no interest in knowing what the doctors found; he took his new pills without asking what they were. The public was told he had been suffering from bronchitis. The president took an extended rest at financier Bernard Baruch's isolated hideaway in South Carolina, where he rehabilitated himself with visits with the newly widowed Lucy Mercer Rutherfurd.

Meanwhile Eleanor and Tommy Thompson made a three-week, thirteen-hundred-mile morale-building tour of bases in the Caribbean and South America, where the enlisted men chafed at feeling left out of the war. Before her trip, she gathered from families the names of soldiers and sailors whom they wanted her to meet. Soldiers, ordered to show up at a central place without explanation, were thrilled to find the First Lady greeting them with messages from their loved ones. When she returned to the White House, Eleanor wrote hundreds of return letters from the troops to their families. Between the time of her South Pacific trip and her husband's death, Eleanor worked at a frenetic pace, traveling, writing, and giving speeches for liberal causes. She avoided the White House and intimacy with her husband as much as possible and seemed to be avoiding dark underlying feelings stirred up by the suffering she had seen in war and by her husband's increasing frailty.

# London

Princess Elizabeth was beginning to take a larger role as a royal exemplar of wartime youth. Her sister Margaret often behaved badly—and usually got away with her antics by making everyone laugh—but Elizabeth was a serious young woman, aware of her eventual role as monarch, and conscientious and thoughtful like her grandmother Queen Mary. Lady Airlie noted another similarity between them: "The carriage of the head was unequaled, and there was about her that indescribable something which Queen Victoria had." When Elizabeth turned eighteen in April 1944, there were no fancy parties, but the king named her a counselor of state. At sixteen, Elizabeth had registered with the wartime youth service organization and begged her father to let her work in the war effort, but he resisted. "Everyone serves except me," she complained. Like any teenager, she chafed at her father's protectiveness. Just before her nineteenth birthday, Elizabeth was allowed to join the Auxiliary Territorial Service. Wearing a workmanlike khaki tunic and skirt, she learned how to operate and repair motorized vehicles, read maps, and drive in convoys. Elizabeth became so obsessed with her duties that the queen was heard to say, "Last night we had sparking plugs all through dinner." Preparing for a royal visit to her unit, Elizabeth wrote her governess, "Now I realize what must happen when Papa and Mama go anywhere. That's something I will never forget."

As D day approached, the king wanted desperately to extend his wartime leadership role by accompanying the Allied assault force as it landed on the beaches of Normandy. He wanted to watch the bombardment of Normandy from one of the cruisers taking part in the action and then tour the beaches. Churchill wanted the same privilege. As the two men jockeyed for a place in the invasion, the king realized they were both being impulsive. He wrote to Churchill:

> I don't think I need emphasize what it would mean to me personally, and to the whole Allied cause, if . . . a chance bomb . . . should remove you from the scene. . . . We should both, I know, love to be there, but . . . I would ask you to reconsider your plan. . . . The anxiety of these coming days would be very greatly increased for me if I thought that, in addition to

everything else, there was risk, however remote, of my losing your help and guidance.

At first, Churchill stubbornly refused to budge in his determination to go along with the troops, but he finally relented grudgingly after the king carefully wrote him a personal appeal. After the invasion occurred, Churchill would have the small victory of visiting Normandy four days ahead of the king.

D day had to be postponed for twenty-four hours due to rainy, overcast, and windy weather. General Dwight Eisenhower was well aware how awful the waiting would be for the two million anxious men. The news of the delay was phoned into the king at Windsor. "This added to my anxieties," he wrote, "as I knew that the men were going on board the ships at the time & that their quarters were very cramped."

The king was also disappointed that Roosevelt was not able come to England to join him and Churchill to monitor the invasion, as they had planned. The deterioration in Roosevelt's health that spring was the main deterrent to the trip, but the king well knew that Roosevelt had felt that buttressing an already strong alliance was less important than conferring with U.S. generals or meeting with Stalin.

## Hyde Park and Washington, D.C.

Eleanor had had difficulty sleeping for weeks before D day. "I feel as if a sword were hanging over my head," she wrote to a reporter friend, "dreading its fall and knowing it must fall to end the war." Eleanor, who had read so many anguished letters from mothers of soldiers, could not stop thinking about the deaths and injuries that would occur on D day. Franklin spent the suspenseful weekend before the invasion without her, preparing a prayer he would deliver to the nation.

At dawn on Tuesday, June 6, Eisenhower told his troops, "You are about to embark on the great crusade, toward which we have striven these many months. . . . The tide has turned! . . . We will accept nothing less than full victory." Many of the men, who leaped off their boats into the dangerous, bullet-ridden waters, had thrown up their breakfast after a night without sleep. In the first day alone there were 6,600 casualties, but amid heavy shelling, most of the troops survived to scramble up onto the beaches and the hills in the hedge and bush country of Normandy and drive the Germans back.

Eleanor was still up at 3 A.M. when General Marshall called to give the president encouraging news about the invasion. She roused her husband, who sat up in bed and got on the telephone. She felt nothing, she said later. "All excitement is drained away." As the news of the invasion spread early, church bells and factory whistles sounded across the country. Stores closed. People gathered in the streets to express excitement and fear; they went to their churches and synagogues to pray. The next day, the *New York Times* captured the moment: "We have come to the hour for which we were born." The evening of June 6, both leaders spoke to their nations in religious terms. The king called on his people to take part in "a world-wide vigil of prayer," and the president delivered a simple prayer for "our sons" and for the nation.

After the enormous strain of preparing the invasion and rallying the nation, FDR was depressed and exhausted. He husbanded his energies and sought comfort with female friends. The state of his health would have a profound effect on others, and arguably the nation; it would worry the king and queen and Churchill as well as FDR's daughter—but not Eleanor. In this state, he put Anna in a dreadful bind, asking her to invite Lucy Mercer Rutherfurd to the White House while her mother was away. While Anna had previously sided with her mother against her father's relationship with Lucy, she was now so worried about her father's failing strength that she risked harming her mother all over again. "It was a terrible decision to have to make in a hurry," Anna later said. On July 7, Lucy slipped in the back door of the White House for the first of a dozen rendezvouses she would have with the president over the next year.

## London

With enormous anxiety, Their Majesties waited during the crucial days after the invasion while Britain's fate was being decided in Normandy. A week after the Allied landing, the king was given permission to go ashore on a beach taken by the Canadians and visit General Montgomery's headquarters, where he decorated some of the officers and their men.

Only ten days after D day, the British faced a new terror. 1 began launching their "secret weapon," pilotless V-1 b......, un England. Carrying more than twelve thousand pounds of explosives, they made a distinctive *chug* sound, and then there was a terrible silence until they exploded. The bombs fell so constantly, it was hard for anyone to sleep or to rest. The British public, already exhausted by nearly five years of war, was profoundly unnerved. Over five hundred people were killed in the first week of bombing alone, including sixty in the Guard's Chapel by Buckingham Palace. What palace windows remained from previous bombings were blown out by the blasts and had to be replaced with squares of talc. "There is something very inhuman about death-dealing missiles being launched in such an indiscriminate manner," the queen wrote to Queen Mary.

As they had during the Blitz, the king and queen again visited the sites of destruction. No matter how grim the scene was, the queen always dressed up in one of Hartnell's pale outfits. One bomb blast survivor described how intimately the queen dealt with the survivors: "The Queen went round putting her arm round people covered in blood and grime and consoled them." The queen made sure that bomb victims were provided with couture outfits and furniture from the palace storerooms. After one tragic visit to the East End, the queen sent sixty suites of furniture along with rugs and linens from the palace basement to families who had lost all their possessions. The historian John Grigg in the London *Times* summed up the power of her visits: "Queen Elizabeth was, in her very different way, a match for Churchill in the popular imagination. Her warm response to crowds and her sympathetic, cozy way of talking to individuals made her visits to blitzed streets and towns so memorable that they have passed into legend."

## Italy

Allied soldiers fighting in Italy were being overshadowed by the battle over Normandy, and the king spent eleven days among them in the summer of 1944 to bolster morale. A couple of nights he stayed in convoys from which he could tour battlefields and watch actual fighting. Covered in dust, he rode through the hilly countryside holding official inspections of troops, but also dining and drinking with the men as if he were a fellow officer. In his memoirs, General Eisenhower said of the king, "He liked the simple life of a soldier and was perfectly at home with all of us." Knowing how much the king appreciated the smooth fabric of American uniforms, Eisenhower sent him a length of the American cloth to Buckingham Palace. The king, indeed, found comfort on the field, like the officer he would have been had he not been from the royal family.

# 15

# Death before Victory

I like to be where things are growing.
—*Franklin Roosevelt to his wife, Eleanor, in late March 1945*

Roosevelt had had three strokes during his term in office, claimed a physician-author of a national magazine article published as the 1944 presidential elections approached. Although that rumor was untrue, FDR's health had visibly crumbled, and he would have to fight to convince the American public that he had the vitality to finish off the war. Over Eleanor's objections, he decided to remove from the ticket the vice president, Henry Wallace, a terrible campaigner who was too liberal for conservative Democrats, replacing him with a solid but unspectacular Missouri senator, Harry Truman.

In July, after the contentious convention had finally endorsed Truman, FDR traveled to the Pacific to consult with General Douglas MacArthur about the strategy for defeating Japan. Aboard ship, the president received word by radiogram that Missy LeHand had suffered a cerebral embolism and died. Eleanor attended her funeral on his behalf. Franklin kept his sadness to himself, but suffered an attack of angina a week later while he was giving a speech to navy yard workers in the state of Washington. Sweating heavily, he gripped the edge of the lectern and spoke his way through fifteen minutes of pain.

As the election campaign escalated, Republican partisans circulated a story claiming that when FDR visited the Aleutian Islands, taxpayers had to pay for a destroyer to retrieve his dog Fala, who had been left behind. FDR used the Fala story to his benefit at a Teamsters Union dinner in Washington, declaring, "Well, of course, I don't resent these attacks . . . but Fala does resent them. You know Fala is Scotch, and being a Scottie, as soon as he learned that the Republican fiction writers in Congress had concocted a story" that he was left behind and that the destroyer sent back to find him had cost "two or three or eight or twenty million dollars—his Scotch soul was furious. He has not been the same dog since." Fala's indignation—and his master's brilliant use of humor to highlight the absurdity of the Republican attacks against him and the Democrats, heard and laughed at by a radio audience across the country—created strong momentum in FDR's campaign against Republican nominee New York governor Thomas Dewey.

## Quebec

In September, the Athlones hosted the Second Quebec Conference at the Citadel, and this time FDR brought Eleanor along. While the men debated the disarmament of Germany and coordination of their efforts in the Pacific, Princess Alice entertained Eleanor and Clementine Churchill with picnics and hikes. With Allied forces entering Belgium and Holland and the conference itself going well, there was a "gay almost hilarious atmosphere," Clementine wrote to her family. But then she was "staggered and reluctant," she wrote her daughter, when she was hounded into joining Mrs. Roosevelt for a broadcast to the Canadian people. Eleanor was calm and professional, while Clementine found the experience "mortifying and frightful." Eleanor enjoyed Churchill's teasing about their political differences, including their long-debated conflict over the virtues of Franco's Spain. In her column, she used the incident to show how one could vehemently disagree with others and remain friends.

In late September, when the Quebec Conference was over, Churchill went to Hyde Park with FDR. At the same time, the Duke of Windsor was in Hot Springs, Virginia, where the duchess was recuperating from surgery to remove an ulcerous growth in her stomach. Churchill telegraphed the duke to invite him to Hyde Park. When the duke greeted the president, he was shocked at his condition: "He had grown very thin since our last meeting and the skin of his face had taken on a strange transparency. I must have made an involuntary gesture of surprise which the president was quick to notice. 'Ah,' he exclaimed, 'you find me thinner. Well, the doctors wanted me to lose some weight and I feel all the better for that.'" During luncheon the duke reported that the president "sat in silence, a frail, almost feeble figure." When he insisted privately to Churchill that the president looked "like a very sick man," Winston insisted, "Oh no, it is only that he is tired, very tired."

Eleanor turned sixty on October 11, 1944, but felt she "really entered old age" when days later she was told she was too old to provide her regular blood donation. As the presidential campaign climaxed, the president and First Lady campaigned with youthful zeal in New York City, drenched to the skin as they rode in an open car through miles of streets in a terrible rainstorm. Despite Eleanor's worries, FDR was exhilarated and strengthened by contact with the crowds. At Hyde Park, the president learned that he had won an unprecedented fourth election with almost 54 percent of the vote.

## London

In November Churchill severely tested his bond with the king and queen when he suggested the royal family officially receive Wallis in London and consider naming the duke as governor of Madras. Worn out and with spirits sagging, Their Majesties could not countenance another challenge from their archrivals. Queen Mary and the queen would never meet Wallis or formally receive her. When the king rejected the idea of posting his brother to Madras, Churchill proposed the duke take a job as the governor of Ceylon. The prime minister backed off only when the king's private secretary bluntly told him he was risking the king's health by pursuing this inessential question. When the queen was told that the marriage had been good for the former king, the evidence being that he no longer had bags under his eyes, she replied, "Who has bags under his eyes now?"

With victory in sight, the king and queen were weary of assaults, both metaphorical and literal. During a visit to antiaircraft batteries to see what was being done to counteract the deadly V-1 bombs, the guns began firing. Their Majesties managed to act unfazed despite earsplitting noise and falling shells. Return fire from the British forces failed to explode the bombs in midair, which spared Their Majesties the danger of the falling debris of V-1 rockets. Hitler soon launched even more deadly V-2 ballistic missiles, which arrived at great speed and with no warning sound, causing devastating damage in and around London. One evening Their Majesties invited a young equerry and lady-in-waiting for dinner. As they ate, an enormous explosion rocked the palace. A nearby pub was destroyed, killing one hundred people.

In November the queen's father, the eighty-nine-year-old Earl of Strathmore, died, further depressing her spirits. She had now lost both her parents and four of her siblings. The day after Christmas, the queen wrote U.S. ambassador John Winant, "In some ways, this last year has been, for us, the most worrying of all these terrible years of war, but I have great faith that good is stronger than evil." Watching Princess Elizabeth as the male lead and Princess Margaret as the leading lady in the Christmas pantomime "Old Mother Red Riding Boots" provided the only antidote to the grim year's end.

## Washington, D.C.

Franklin D. Roosevelt's historic fourth inaugural, on a bitterly cold January 20, 1945, was simple and brief. Like the king and queen, both Eleanor and Franklin were depleted by the demands of the war, but also by the strains in their marriage. James Roosevelt was given military leave so that he could attend his father at the inauguration, bracing the pale and gaunt president on his arm as he took the oath of office at the South Portico of the White House. His hands trembled as, in a weak voice, he gave a five-minute speech to a small crowd gathered in the freshly fallen snow. With the nation's soldiers, resources, and attentions overseas, there were no parades or fancy balls.

Perhaps sensing that he did not have much time left, FDR insisted that all thirteen of his grandchildren come to Washington for the ceremony. Eleanor had to give up her own bedroom and sleep in the maid's quarters. "I was not too comfortable, nor, I fear too sweet about it," she admitted. Mrs. Nesbitt's culinary offerings reached a nadir when she served two thousand guests a sparse inaugural luncheon consisting of chicken salad and unbuttered rolls. Most of the chicken had spoiled the night before, which made the salad mainly celery.

## Yalta

Several days later, Eleanor's feelings were hurt once again when FDR turned down her request to accompany him and Anna to a war conference among the Big Three—the United States, the Soviet Union, and Britain—at Yalta, a resort on the Black Sea. As sick as he was, FDR had to travel there because Stalin refused to leave his home country. Joined by Churchill, they met in the Livadia Palace, which had only one bathroom and had to be sprayed to suppress the bedbugs and lice.

At this point Germany was surrounded by the Soviets in the East and Allied forces in the West. U.S. forces had recaptured Manila, but conquering Japan itself remained a formidable task. Roosevelt, Churchill, and Stalin had to make decisions about the future of the defeated enemy, Eastern Europe, and Asia. FDR made pragmatic compromises about the boundaries of Poland, the partition of Germany and Berlin, and the integration of parts of China into the Soviet Union, partly to ensure the Soviets' commitment to help defeat Japan after the European war was won. To this day, a debate rages about whether FDR, in his weakened and distractible state, gave away too much of Eastern Europe, particularly Poland, to the Communists, or whether—with the Soviets already advancing from the east toward Berlin—he simply made the best deal he could.

Churchill would later say that at Yalta, "I noticed that the President was ailing. His captivating smile, his gay, charming manner had not deserted him, but his face had a transparency, an air of purification, and often there was a far-away look in his eyes." When they parted, Churchill "had an indefinable sense of fear that his strength and health were on the ebb."

At Yalta FDR told Churchill he would visit Great Britain that summer, once the European war was concluded, after he attended the first United Nations Conference. His willingness to reciprocate the king and queen's 1939 visit to North America was the fulfillment of the royal couple's longtime ambition. For the king and queen, who had worked so diligently during the war to solidify Anglo-American relations and to deepen their friendship with the Roosevelts, this visit would be a milestone in what they hoped would be a permanently revi-talized and synergistic family friendship and U.S.-British alliance, which would help both countries thrive in the postwar years. On March 12, the king wrote FDR expressing how glad he was that the U.S. president could "make your long promised visit to my Country," assuring him of a warm welcome and offering an invitation to stay at Buckingham Palace. "We are still under daily bombardment at the moment," he said, "but we hope & trust the situation will be better in a few months' time." The king would make sure the president's party was comfortable, and "it would be a real pleasure . . . to continue that friendship which started so happily in Washington & in Hyde Park in 1939. So much has happened to us all since those days."

## Washington, D.C.

On the first of March, the president reported to Congress on the Yalta Conference. For the first time, he was brought down the aisle in his wheelchair. When he asked to be pardoned for speaking while sitting down, explaining that he was exhausted after a fourteen-thousand-mile trip, there was loud applause. Eleanor, still unable to acknowledge how sick her husband was, mistook his failure to stand as a sign that he was finally accepting his invalidism.

In the middle of March, Lucy Mercer Rutherfurd joined FDR for a drive in the Virginia countryside and for several meals at the White House, arranged by Anna. She departed just as Eleanor returned from North Carolina in time to celebrate her fortieth wedding anniversary with her husband. At the same time, Hick finally moved out of the White House, to return to her house on Long Island. She left Eleanor a note thanking her for "your many kindnesses these past four years," and asserting, "After all these years, we could never drift very far apart."

The Roosevelts entertained the Athlones on an official visit to Washington that March, giving them a "full red-carpet, head-of-state-treatment" including a procession from Union Station through the streets of Washington toward the White House. At the state dinner for the governor general and Princess Alice on March 23, in toasting the Athlones, the president gave his final tribute to the king and queen, who by their absence were so much on everyone's minds: "A few years ago, a young couple came to this table. . . . And we found them not only very delightful people, but they gave us the feeling that they were old friends. And tonight . . . I will have to ask his representative—his uncle and his aunt . . . [to do] something that we have in our hearts very much, and that is drink to the health of the King."

Athlone, in toasting the president, called the visit "the climax of the most exciting moment of our lives." He expressed hope that some of the beauty of Washington could be transported to London, when it was rebuilt, and that he could meet the president again in "the tiny little Isle, which is no great distance by air from the United States."

The president knew that his visit to Britain would be the capstone to victory in the European war, and that meeting with the British king would not only be a powerful acknowledgment of the hard-won Allied success in the war but a reiteration of the necessity of Western democracy in the postwar world. He had always taken seriously the relationship between president and king, as an alliance of institutions that transcended the daily vicissitudes of politics and policy; both men were, after all, heads of state. At times his bond with the king trumped even the political alliance he shared with Prime Minister Churchill. Lord Halifax recorded in his diary during the war that when FDR was in a quandary over some question of production in Hong Kong, he told a government official not once but three times, "If Churchill insists on Hong Kong I will have to take it to the king." The historian Sarah Bradford believes that Roosevelt, with his hazy, impressionistic understanding of the British system of government, assumed a Crown colony was exactly that—the personal possession of the sovereign. FDR clearly felt he could go over Churchill's head to deal with the king.

Did Roosevelt actually believe he would be well enough, or live long enough, to travel to Britain once the war was won? Certainly Eleanor would have thought he could make the trip. During their final time together at Hyde Park, she still resisted every signal that the president was in serious trouble. For the first time, he asked her to drive him around in his car, and had her mix the cocktails. She focused, instead, on his excited talk about the future, for, like her, Franklin was also denying the dire state of his health.

The previous Christmas, he had told his son Elliott that he planned to become reacquainted with his wife, "the most extraordinarily interesting woman" he had ever known, by traveling and doing projects together. They would attend the opening session of the United

Nations and then go to London, Holland, and the battlefields in Europe. They would stay in Buckingham Palace, address Parliament, visit Churchill at Chequers, meet with Queen Wilhelmina in Holland, and finish off the trip in Paris. Later they would travel around the world and then spend several years in the Middle East helping to irrigate and reforest desert areas. Eleanor suggested he might like a few years without major responsibilities after his term was over in 1948, but he quickly turned to her and said, "No I like to be where things are growing." As she explained in her "My Day" column shortly after he died, "That sense of the continuing growth and development was keenly present with him. He never liked to dwell on the past, always wanted to move forward."

## Warm Springs, Georgia

On March 29 Eleanor was pleased when FDR took his cousins Laura Delano and Daisy Suckley—whom he saw so often, she called them his "handmaidens"—off to Warm Springs, Georgia, for a two-week rest. On Easter Sunday in Georgia, FDR was so weak that he dropped his glasses and his prayer book during church. However, his appetite and color returned during the next week amid the colorful azaleas of spring. The war news was encouraging on all sides: the Russians were in Berlin, and the Americans had crossed the Rhine; in the Pacific the Allies had landed on Okinawa, which was only three hundred and fifty miles from Japan. Franklin fretted only about how to set limits with Stalin over the Soviet dictator's mistreatment of Poland. On April 5, he met with the president of the Philippines, Sergio Osmena, to discuss the war in the Pacific and the prospects of independence for the Philippines. Afterward, he held a leisurely press conference.

Just before lunch in Warm Springs on April 12, Roosevelt, wearing a naval cape, grew tired of sitting for his portrait with painter Elizabeth Shoumatoff. Working with a shaky hand on a card table in front of him, he wrote a line at the end of the text for his Jefferson Day speech: "The only limit to our realization of tomorrow will be our doubts of today. Let us move forward with a strong and active faith." He made small talk with his cousin Polly Delano—but she soon realized he was not making sense. He told her that he was going to resign from the presidency and head the United Nations. She was confused.

As Mrs. Shoumatoff was painting in the president's red and blue tie on her canvas, FDR raised his shaky left hand to his forehead and moved it back and forth several times. His head fell forward. Daisy Suckley thought he was looking for something and went over to help. "He looked at me, his forehead furrowed with pain, and tried to smile," Daisy remembered. "He put his left hand up to the back of his head and said, 'I have a terrific pain in the back of my head.' And then he collapsed." He was looking straight ahead at a smiling Lucy Rutherfurd when his eyes closed. Mrs. Shoumatoff screamed and ran out of the front door of the house. As aides moved the president to his bed, someone screamed to Lucy that she had better leave fast. She scurried off with the painter.

Roosevelt had suffered a cerebral hemorrhage. His lips and fingernails were turning blue, his pulse was barely perceptible, and he was in a cold sweat. After a struggle of two and a half hours, he stopped breathing. His physicians gave him a shot of adrenaline in the heart. There was no response. The president was dead.

## Washington, D.C.

That afternoon, Eleanor spoke at a benefit for the Thrift Shop at the Sulgrave Club. Afterward, she was listening to pianist Evelyn Tucker play when, in the middle of the piece, Eleanor had what she later called a "quick start" when she was summoned to the phone to talk to press secretary Steve Early. His voice conveying the worst, he told her to come back to the White House immediately. Eleanor listened to the rest of the piece, made her apologies, and left the room to a standing ovation. "I got into the car and sat with clenched hands all the way to the White House," Eleanor wrote in her memoirs. "In my heart I knew what had happened, but one does not actually formulate these terrible thoughts until they are spoken." Steve Early and Dr. McIntire met her in her sitting room and told her her husband had died.

In shock, Eleanor quickly shifted into an efficient mode. She called for Vice President Truman, changed into a black dress, arranged for a plane to fly her to Georgia later that evening, and cabled her four sons, telling them, "He did his job to the end as he would want you to do." At the Capitol, the vice president was talking politics over drinks when House Speaker Sam Rayburn suddenly remembered that Truman had received a call from the White House. When the vice president got on the telephone, Steve Early told him, "Leave the Hill quietly and come to the main entrance of the White House."

At five-thirty, when Truman arrived in her sitting room, Eleanor stepped forward, placing her arm gently on his shoulder, and said, "Harry, the president is dead." Truman was stunned and could not speak. Recovering, he asked how he could help Eleanor. She replied, "Is there anything we can do for you? For you are the one in trouble now." At 7 P.M. that evening, Eleanor watched as the chief justice of the Supreme Court swore Truman in as president in front of the somber members of FDR's cabinet. After kissing Anna good-bye, and acknowledging the stunned White House staff, the former First Lady briskly left the executive mansion.

Eleanor, so vulnerable to feelings of abandonment, swiftly detached herself from her own emotions and placed her focus on others. "Though this was a terrible blow, somehow one had no chance to think of it as a personal sorrow," she wrote later. "It was the sorrow of all those to whom this man who now lay dead, and who happened to be my husband, had been a symbol of strength and fortitude."

In Warm Springs at midnight, Eleanor sat with Roosevelt cousins Laura, Daisy, and Grace Tully and asked them to tell her exactly what had happened. She heard more than she bargained for. Laura, who had always been jealous of Eleanor's success, took revenge by telling her about the presence of Lucy Rutherfurd. After learning that Lucy had been with her husband when he died, Eleanor spent her final minutes alone with her husband of forty years. Through it all, "a deep and unshakeable affection and tenderness existed between them," her son Jimmy would say later.

She soon learned that Anna had helped arrange the meetings with Lucy, but as she explained, "At a time like that, you don't really feel your own feelings. . . . You build a façade for everyone to see and you live separately inside the façade." The following day, while her husband's body was lying in state at the White House, Eleanor confronted Anna. She was so anguished that Anna feared her mother would never forgive her for overstepping her role as her father's hostess and helper.

It took six months for Eleanor to forgive her daughter. After his death, she came slowly and painfully to accept that she could not have been all things to him, that FDR had needed Lucy, and that Anna had done her best to assist her father at a time when he was under deathly strain. Moving through pain to wisdom, and speaking in general terms, she later wrote in her autobiography: "I decided to accept the fact that a man must be what he is, life must be lived as it is, circumstances force your children away from you, and you cannot live at all if you do not learn to adapt to your life as it happens to be. All human beings have failings, all human beings have needs and temptations and stresses."

## London

At about midnight in London, Churchill heard the news. "I felt as if I had been struck a personal blow," he said. "I was overpowered by a sense of deep and irreparable loss." The king, in particular, mourned FDR in a personal and immediate way, as a leader who had helped him emerge into his full potential. "We were very shocked to hear the sad news of the sudden death of President Roosevelt," he wrote in his diary. "He was a very great man & his loss will be felt the World over. He was a staunch friend of this country." Then, speaking of a disappointment at once political and personal, he added, "I had hoped the Roosevelts would have paid us a visit here this summer, but it cannot be."

On April 13 the king wrote to Churchill, "I cannot tell you how sad I am at the sudden death of President Roosevelt. The news came as a great shock to me. I have lost a friend, but to you who have known him for so long and so intimately during this war the sudden loss to yourself personally . . . must be overwhelming." The prime minister was already thinking ahead about how to bolster the British-U.S. alliance and obtain necessary help in rebuilding Britain: he proposed that President Truman make the visit in FDR's stead that summer.

## Washington, D.C.

Back in Warm Springs, a special bier had been built so that Roosevelt's coffin would be visible through a window as the train made its way north eight hundred miles among mourners lining the tracks. Church choirs sang "Rock of Ages" and "Abide with Me" as the train lumbered by. "I lay in my berth all night with the window shade up, looking at the countryside he had loved," Eleanor recalled, "and watching the faces of all the people at the stations, and even at the crossroads, who came to pay their last tribute all through the night." In Washington, as the funeral cortege made its way from Union Station to the White House, there was silence punctuated with sobbing and sounds of the funeral dirge.

"It seemed that everyone in the world was in the East Room for the funeral services except three of my own sons," Eleanor wrote later. Saying good-bye to her husband, she was comforted only by her estranged daughter and her son Elliott, who had been able to fly back with other dignitaries from London. FDR Jr. and John were stuck in the Pacific war zone, but James was able to fly east in time for the burial at Hyde Park. The funeral in the East Room of the White House began with the hymn "Faith of Our Fathers" and ended with Roosevelt's immortal lines, "We have nothing to fear, but fear itself."

## Hyde Park

That evening the funeral train, carrying almost all of the United States government—the Cabinet, the Supreme Court, the leaders of Congress, the new president—and foreign leaders, made an overnight journey to Roosevelt's beloved Hyde Park. In the morning as the bells of St. James Episcopal Church tolled in the background, the president's coffin was placed on a caisson and carried from the riverfront by six horses, draped in black, to the rose garden at Springwood. A hooded horse, with an empty saddle and reversed stirrups, followed behind.

On that brisk and sunny spring day, the West Point band played a final "Hail to the Chief" as the burial service began. West Point cadets in scarlet capes lined the walls of the garden. After the president's pastor, the Reverend George Anthony, commended "the soul of Thy brother departed" to the ground, the cadets marched to the grave, raised their rifles, and fired three volleys. Crouching at Daisy Suckley's feet, the president's dog, Fala, howled and rolled over on the grass. The lingering notes of taps filled the air. Later, Eleanor Roosevelt watched as workmen shoveled soil onto the president's grave. Then, quietly, she walked away.

Neither Churchill nor Their Majesties could attend the president's funeral. Several British cabinet ministers were already abroad at the time of FDR's death, leaving the top levels of the government shorthanded at home, even as the European war was moving into its complex final weeks. On the day Roosevelt died, the Soviet army entered Vienna and the Allied forces had liberated the concentration camps of Buchenwald and Belsen. Foreign Secretary Anthony Eden attended Roosevelt's funeral in Churchill's stead; the king sent Lord Athlone. The British monarch ordered an unprecedented week's court mourning for the U.S. president. He and Elizabeth cabled their condolences to Mrs. Roosevelt: "The Queen and I are deeply grieved and shocked by the news of President Roosevelt's death. In him humanity has lost a great figure and we have lost a true and honored friend. On behalf of all my peoples I send our most heartfelt sympathy to you and the members of your family." A week later Eleanor wrote to thank the king: "It is a comfort to know that your people, who have been united with the people of this country in the great fight for freedom, are mourning the loss of my husband."

Although Eleanor did not respect the Duke of Windsor, she was unfailingly polite in responding to his personal letter of condolence, which included the order of the memorial service that was held in Christ Church Cathedral in Nassau on April 15 and a copy of his broadcast tribute to her husband. The duke called his speech a "humble but no less sincere tribute from this British colony." The president's death was a tragedy of "the first magnitude," and as the result of his "far-sighted foreign policy . . . the United Nations armies are at the gates of Berlin and the ultimate doom of Japan is already sealed." The duke said he had experienced FDR's "one rare gift which I can never forget: that of making whoever he was talking to feel that he, or she, was the one person he wished to converse with at that precise moment." Eleanor thanked him for his kindness and for sending his tribute. Although she acknowledged the duke and duchess's desire to meet with her while they were in the country, it is not clear whether they ever met in the following years.

## London

April 17 was a day of mourning in London. At St. Paul's Cathedral, U.S. Army privates and WACS joined admirals, generals, and other service heads at a memorial service for their fallen leader. Many American civilians—the women dressed mainly in black and the men wearing black suits, ties, and mourning bands—were among more than two thousand mourners who crammed the cathedral. In the crypt below, five hundred more heard the service through loudspeakers. Outside, thousands of mourners stood bareheaded, listening and joining in with the singing of the Twenty-third Psalm and one of the late president's favorite hymns, "Fight the Good Fight."

As the congregation stood, the king, in naval uniform, and the queen, dressed in black, entered the cathedral with Princess Elizabeth, who wore her ATS uniform. They were followed by Queen Wilhelmina and Princess Juliana of Holland, King Haakon and Crown Prince Olav of Norway, King George of Greece, King Peter of Yugoslavia, and the president of Poland. The dean of St. Paul's, the Very Reverend W. R. Matthews, addressed the congregation: "We pray through our cooperation one with another that the great causes for which he labored may be brought to fruition for the lasting benefit of the world."

The king and queen had tears in their eyes, remembering how much their friend had meant to them and how bitterly disappointed they were that he could not, instead, join them in England for a service celebrating all their wartime accomplishments. The congregation began to weep during a prayer committing the late president's soul to God's keeping and throughout the singing of "The Battle Hymn of the Republic." The sobbing became louder as the Royal Marines, high up in the gallery, played taps followed by the resounding notes of reveille. Soldiers, sailors, and airmen stood stiffly at attention as the service ended with the playing of "The Star Spangled Banner" and "God Save the King." M.P. Chips Channon recalled: "*The Star Spangled Banner* was sung like a Negro spiritual, and the words of the Anthem were magnificent." As church bells tolled and guests left the cathedral, Channon looked back and saw "Winston standing bareheaded framed between two columns of the portico and he was sobbing as the shaft of sunlight fell on his face."

Later that day Churchill told the House of Commons that the death of "the greatest champion of freedom who has ever brought comfort and help from the New World to the Old" was "a loss, a bitter loss, to humanity." Roosevelt "had raised the strength, might and glory" of the United States to a "height never attained by any nation in history." The prime minister acknowledged that he had received his last messages from Roosevelt on the day the president died in Warm Springs, Georgia. "Nothing altered his inflexible sense of duty," Churchill eulogized. He came close to breaking down when he told his peers, "He never lost faith in Britain."

Three days after the service, Ambassador John Winant wrote the king to acknowledge, "I know you really cared." He told Their Majesties that the British people's genuine grief at the loss of the president would stand as an enduring bond between the two countries. The president had often spoken with Winant about the memorable royal visit to Hyde Park, and Winant told the king and queen that it was one of the happiest occasions of Roosevelt's life.

# 16

# Starting Over

## April 1945–November 1947

> You must do the thing you think you cannot do.
>
> —*Eleanor Roosevelt*

## New York

In New York several days after FDR's funeral, a newspaperwoman accosted Eleanor on the steps of her Washington Square apartment and asked her to make a statement. Eleanor quietly told her, "The story is over," and hurried on. The story, in fact, was beginning afresh. As an independent player on the world scene, Eleanor would commit her passions and energies to causes old and new. Starting at age sixty-one, she would completely come into her own. She and her royal counterparts in the West's other leading democracy would be challenged anew in a dangerous, unpredictable, and rapidly evolving postwar world.

Surprisingly, after Roosevelt died, Eleanor did not descend into one of her black depressions, even as she mourned one of the most creative and synergetic relationships of all time. During the war years, she had already distanced herself emotionally from her husband, and had begun preparing for an independent life. Tired of running an "elaborate household" and of leading a demanding public existence, she was most immediately concerned with getting out of the White House as soon as possible. She had an almost impersonal feeling about everything that was happening at the time of her husband's death. She was

266

hugely relieved to give up responsibility for presidential receptions and dinners. "It was almost as though I had erected someone a little outside of myself who was the president's wife," she wrote in her autobiography. "I was lost somewhere deep down inside myself." She could now write unfettered by being First Lady, she told her "My Day" readers, promising to fight all forms of injustice, for "in order to be useful we must stand up for things we feel are right." For Eleanor, the need to be helpful and virtuous was very strong; it gave her the impetus to move through her grief and loneliness.

She would first be useful by comforting the country: "Perhaps in his wisdom the Almighty is trying to show us that a leader may chart the way, may point out the road to lasting peace, but that many leaders and many peoples must do the building. It cannot be the work of one man . . . and so, when the time comes for the people to assume the burden more fully, he is given rest." Denying the magnitude of her own loss, she told her readers, "any personal sorrow seems to be lost in the general sadness of humanity," and on April 25 she wrote to President Truman, "it is still difficult to believe that my husband is not off on a trip."

Once settled into an apartment in New York City, Eleanor began the process of transferring ownership of Sara and Franklin's Hyde Park home, where she never had felt entirely comfortable, to the government. It would serve as a presidential library and museum. She would move to her unpretentious cottage at Val-Kill, while also retaining ownership of Top Cottage, where Elliott would live with his family and manage the farm.

## London

As April ended, the European war moved to a rapid and dramatic close. Mussolini, captured by Italian partisans as he tried to escape to Switzerland, was shot and strung up by his heels in Milan. On April 30, Hitler committed suicide in his Berlin bunker. Two days later, Berlin fell to the Russians. On VE Day, May 8, 1945, the king and queen, both very tired, joined Winston Churchill, Princess Elizabeth, and Princess Margaret on the balcony of Buckingham Palace, making eight separate appearances celebrating the end of the war. The crowd yelled, "We want the Queen, We want the King," over and over again each time, until the royal couple reemerged. "The roar that comes up from the people is like thunder," Cecil Beaton wrote.

"Poor darlings, they have not had any fun yet," the king wrote of his two daughters. That day Princess Elizabeth and Princess Margaret were given a rare moment of freedom: the king sent them outside the palace to mingle with the crowds under the supervision of their uncle David Bowes-Lyon. "It was absolutely wonderful," said Princess Margaret. "Everybody was knocking everybody's hats off, so we knocked off a few too." "We have been overwhelmed by the kind things people have said over our part in the war," the king wrote several days later. "We have only tried to do our duty."

## New York

On April 29, Eleanor wrote to her aunt Maude Gray about FDR's death. "I am sad that he could not see the end of his long work which he has carried so magnificently but I am thankful that he had no pain & no long lingering illness in which he would have watched others not doing as he would have done." Later the same day, Eleanor spoke to the nation on a WNBC radio broadcast. A photograph shows her in a black dress, looking gaunt and grief-stricken, as she offered gratitude on behalf of her late husband to American soldiers and citizens, exhorting them to "win through to a permanent peace. That was the main objective that my husband fought for. That is the goal which we must never lose sight of."

At the end of June the United Nations charter was approved at the San Francisco conference Eleanor had planned to attend with Roosevelt. She saluted the ratification in her "My Day" column: "I don't believe that greed and selfishness have gone out of the human race . . . but I want to try for a peaceful world."

## England

If the king could not give President Roosevelt his triumphant tour of Britain, then he was determined to meet President Truman in FDR's stead. The king knew how imperative it would be for his depleted country to keep a strong postwar link with the United States, the world's new superpower, and hoped that a personal bond with Truman, while unlikely to be as emotionally meaningful as his friendship with Roosevelt, would still allow him to play a key role in rebuilding Britain. He invited the new U.S. leader to visit Buckingham Palace after a post-war planning conference in late July at Potsdam, in Germany, with Churchill and Stalin. Truman, who prided himself on his unpretentiousness, wrote his wife, Bess, that he had received the king's letter and was "not much impressed" receiving a letter from a monarch. While at Potsdam, Truman learned that the atom bomb had been successfully tested and was ready to be used against Japan; he decided to return home quickly, without stopping at Buckingham Palace. The king persisted in his invitation until Truman agreed to meet aboard ship off Plymouth, along the English coast.

On August 2, Truman came on board the battle cruiser HMS *Renown* for what he called a "nice and appetizing" lunch with the king. In his diary, Truman noted with displeasure that "there was much formality etc. in getting on and off the British ship." Meeting alone in the king's cabin before lunch, Truman was surprised to find himself enjoying his talk with the British king, who was avid to hear about developments at Potsdam and the progress on the atom bomb. The president told him "he was horrified at the devastation of Berlin by our combined bombing," the king wrote in his diary. "He could see that the Big Powers would have to combine for all time to prevent another war."

The two leaders were joined for lunch by the British ambassador and foreign secretary and by the U.S. secretary of state, James Byrnes, "a great talker," according to the king. In front of the waiters serving lunch, Byrnes discussed the impending, top-secret atomic assault on Japan. Appalled, the king said, "I think Mr. President, that we should discuss this interesting subject over our coffee on the deck," according to diplomat Harold Nicolson. Later that afternoon, the king joined Truman aboard the USS *Augusta*, where he inspected the guard and looked over the crew. When the king, a "very pleasant and surprising person," "took a snort of Haig & Haig" while meeting with the president, he won his affection, as Truman noted in his diary, adding: "I was impressed with the King as a good man."

On August 6, the B-29 Superfortress bomber the *Enola Gay* dropped the atom bomb on Hiroshima. When Japan did not blink, the Allies dropped a second bomb on the seaport town of Nagasaki several days later. Hundreds of thousands of civilians were killed. On August

14, the emperor of Japan overruled his bellicose military commanders and surrendered.

Eleanor did not feel like rejoicing. "The weight of suffering which has engulfed the world for so many years could not so quickly be wiped out," she wrote in her "My Day" column. She worried about the families of soldiers who would experience a renewed sense of loss when their men did not come home as other servicemen did. On VJ Day, Eleanor sent a telegram of congratulations to Their Majesties, who cabled back, thanking her for her "kind telegram," and agreeing with her that "it is indeed sad that your husband was not spared to see the final victory for which he strove with such courage and determination." In London, the king spoke over loudspeakers to an enormous crowd gathered outside the palace. After that, the royal family came on to the balcony to a deafening roar from the crowds below.

Missing from the balcony was Winston Churchill. On July 26, one of the greatest prime minister–monarch relationships in British history ended—at least for the time being—when Churchill's Conservative Party was overwhelmingly rejected in the country's first general election since before the war. At 7 P.M. on July 26, Churchill met with the king to resign. As the king bluntly recorded in his diary, "It was a very sad meeting. I told him I thought the British people were very ungrateful after the way they had been led during the war." Churchill would become leader of the Conservative opposition. Americans were apprehensive when Labour Party leader Clement Attlee, a shy, taciturn, but highly intelligent man, succeeded Churchill. The king sorely missed Churchill's chattiness and ebullience, but he would develop a remarkably successful partnership with Attlee as the new government made radical changes in its social contract and relationship with its colonies.

On August 21, Truman ambushed Britain. Without even reading it, he casually signed a document ending the Lend-Lease program—and thus undermined the devastated British economy and undid much of the web of Anglo-American relations and goodwill meticulously crafted over the previous decade. In the winter of 1945–1946, Britain was nearly bankrupt, suffering severe shortages of food, stringent rationing, and lack of electric power in its dark, bombed-out cities. The country would continue to stagger economically with little help from the Unites States until three years later when Truman signed the Economic Cooperation Act of 1948, known as the Marshall Plan. Pouring billions into Europe in the form of economic and political aid, it restored agricultural and industrial productivity, thus preventing famine and further chaos.

## New York

In December Eleanor was shocked when President Truman, angling to solidify his position as FDR's heir, offered to appoint her as a delegate to the United Nations, which she viewed as her husband's greatest legacy. Her first reaction was, "Oh, no! It would be impossible." She had no experience as a diplomat; there were many who doubted she had the patience for the slow-moving world of diplomacy. Yet because she believed in the importance of placing peace-loving women on international peacekeeping bodies, she sidestepped her own doubts, accepting the advice of friends and family, and took on the position "in fear and trembling." Only one senator, the racist Theodore Bilbo of Mississippi, voted against her confirmation.

On New Year's Eve 1945, Eleanor boarded the ocean liner *Queen Elizabeth* for Great Britain, where she would attend the first working session of the United Nations. She later confided to a colleague's wife how "terribly frightened I was when I got on that ship that night. I came to the ship alone and I was simply terrified. I felt that I was going to do a job that I knew nothing about." As always, she handled her insecurity by plunging into hard work, reading mounds of State Department documents. Some of them were so dull, they sent her to sleep. Aboard the liner, she was persuaded to hold her first press conference since becoming a widow. Off the record, she told reporters, "For the first time in my life I can say what I want. For your information it is wonderful to feel free."

## London

Arriving in London on January 6, 1946, Eleanor sent American candy to the queen and the two princesses. She returned "on this mission with the great hope that my husband's plans for peace may be realized," she wrote the queen. "May we all work together for a better world!" Her letter crossed in the mail with a thoughtful letter of "cordial greeting" from the queen, which Eleanor received the next day. Their

Majesties were looking forward to the opportunity to "renew our friendship." The queen wrote, "So much has happened to this poor tattered world since those days when you visited us at Buckingham Palace & now so many hopes are centered on this great 'getting together,' which starts next week." She signed her letter, "I am, your sincere friend, Elizabeth R."

"Deeply grateful for your kind note," Eleanor replied, suggesting she would have to meet Their Majesties on a Sunday ("I feel fairly sure they will not expect me to attend meetings on Sunday?"). She told the queen that her diplomatic work "will be very exacting I fear, especially for me who lack the background of the San Francisco conference. . . . I feel as I know you do that we must give all we can to make this undertaking a success. My husband hoped so much that this organization might make the world of the future."

When the two women met, they reminisced about their crucial visits to each other's countries, but they focused on their current concerns. The king and queen sounded out Eleanor's opinions on a British memorial for the late president. Politicians were already disagreeing about the setting and form of tribute. Eleanor said she would give the king and queen an inside view of the workings of the UN and share her reactions to being the only American woman in the delegation.

The UN General Assembly held its first session in Central Hall, Westminster, which King George had had renovated for the occasion. During the meeting, Eleanor deliberately took on a softer, more diplomatic persona and "walked on eggs," she said. "I knew that as the only woman on the delegation, I was not welcome." Other UN delegates, aiming to keep her from roiling their deliberations, treated her the way public women of the era were often handled: she was assigned to a lesser committee on humanitarian and cultural matters. Yet by happenstance, one of the most important postwar issues landed before her committee: the right of refugees to decide whether to return to their home countries or live elsewhere. She debated the Russian deputy, Andrei Vishinsky, whom she described as "one of the Russians' great legal minds, a skilled debater, a man with ability to use the weapons of wit and ridicule," and who wanted refugees who resisted returning to homelands that were now run by Communists to be punished and repatriated as traitors. Although she was "badly frightened" and "trembled" at the thought of speaking against the famous Russian who had been Stalin's unrelenting prosecutor at the infamous Moscow purge trials of the 1930s, her passionate argument convinced a majority of delegates to vote for the right of individuals to make their own decisions about where to settle. Eleanor won the grudging praise and acceptance of the normally patronizing male delegates.

## New York

After Eleanor returned to New York in April, she was elected head of the Commission on Human Rights, charged with creating an international bill of rights, which was sorely needed after a world war that caused so many large-scale atrocities. In this job, she would make decisions that deeply gratified her, strengthening the voices of the weak in the corridors of power. A common standard for basic human freedoms would no longer allow nations to mistreat their citizens with impunity.

Truman's appointment of Eleanor to the United Nations was a brilliant move. She was ideally suited to this job; it allowed her to implement her own deepest-held principles with passion and inexhaustible energy, and the moral authority of her years as First Lady served her well. She could further her husband's legacy while fighting for individual rights and world peace, extending his famous "Four Freedoms" (freedom of expression and of worship; freedom from want and from fear) into international criteria. Blending her characteristic determination with a newly found patience, she guided the Declaration of Human Rights through several years of treacherous diplomacy, negotiating with stubborn and difficult Communist spokesmen. It would become perhaps the most enduring part of her legacy as a leader.

In the seven tumultuous years Eleanor served at the United Nations—at the beginning of 1953, the newly elected Republican president Dwight Eisenhower removed her—she was one of the most powerful people in the world. Using her "My Day" column and her UN pulpit, Eleanor pushed successfully for U.S. backing of the partition of Palestine into separate Arab and Jewish states. As the cold war escalated with the Communist blockade of Berlin in 1948 and 1949 and the Korean War of the early 1950s, Eleanor stood against the Truman Doctrine, which provided cash payments to countries to keep them out of the Communist orbit; instead, she advocated that the United States resist communism by working in partnership with the United Nations. After the Soviets detonated their own atom bomb in 1949, she argued forcefully against an arms race she believed would only encourage more wars. She was disgusted when Senator Joseph McCarthy accused the State Department of harboring Communists. She thought that her fellow citizens' fear that "the Reds" would infiltrate and undermine the U.S. government was overblown.

## London

The British were not initially champions of human rights. FDR had envisioned a postwar world consisting of independent states, but Churchill and the British Foreign Office clung to their ingrained notion of imperial power. The official victory parade, celebrating the end of the war both in Europe and Asia, on June 8, 1946, and presided over by the king, turned out to be last great moment of the British Empire, with its gathering of soldiers from the far ends of the empire. By 1947, Britain could not afford the cost of maintaining its colonial holdings. The British government soon departed from Singapore, Malaya, and Hong Kong. Ceylon declared itself a self-governing dominion. In August 1947, the king lost his title of King-Emperor, when India—which Disraeli had presented as the "jewel" of the empire to the king's great-grandmother Queen Victoria some seventy years before—declared independence. The king watched uncomfortably as his self-promoting cousin Louis Mountbatten, the last viceroy of India, presided over India's departure from the empire.

The fragmentation of the British Empire went against all the king's training and sense of duty and tradition. He had been bred as a child of empire, and his identity was deeply involved in the idea of a greater Britain. But the king and queen, who reigned but did not rule over a nation that, after its finest hour, lay on the brink of starvation, had to acknowledge the postwar realities of America's ascendance and Britain's decline as a global power. They sought solace in the new concept of the Commonwealth of Nations, which would replace the formal institution of empire. As "Head of the Commonwealth," the king was distressed when Burma and Ireland departed, but was consoled when India remained. The British monarch and his consort would take on a new role as a vital link among the free association of self-governing nations. Their role as adhesive symbol of British roots and community would perhaps be even more necessary and significant than before.

But as fellow kings and queens lost their thrones across Europe, with nation after nation proclaiming itself a republic, Their Majesties could no longer take for granted that the monarchy would persist in Britain. The huge vote for the Labour Party and the ascendance of Clement Attlee and his socialist policies was part of a popular revolution against the old class structure that had dominated society before the war. In February 1948 the king heard from writer and gardener Vita Sackville-West that she had had to turn over her childhood home, Knole, to the National Trust because she could no longer afford to maintain it. He raised his hands in despair, saying, "Everything is going nowadays. Before long, I shall have to go."

Britain's mood was persistently grim in the postwar years. With the most bitterly cold weather on record and unexpected amounts of snow and ice, the winter of 1947 paralyzed the entire nation: there was no heat for many homes, businesses, and schools. Roads and railways shut down, electricity failed, the death rate soared, unemployment skyrocketed, and severe food shortages ravaged the country. According to the historian Robert Rhodes James, "The north-east wind was to howl" for the whole month of February.

## South Africa

Against this backdrop of misery, the king, the queen, and the two princesses set sail that same month on the HMS *Vanguard* for South Africa, embarking on a twelve-week imperial tour intended to deepen the bond between the Crown and its troubled dominion. South Africa had long been a deeply divided land, where the white-minority Nationalist Party was agitating for the policy of apartheid, which would separate blacks and whites in just about every aspect of national and economic life. The king would thank the South African people for their part in the war, counter the movement for republicanism among the Dutch-descended Afrikaner population, and, in theory, get some rest. In fact, he lost seventeen pounds while fretting about Britain's worsening winter and enduring an exhausting tour in the harsh summer sun of southern Africa.

The royal family crisscrossed South Africa in an easily identifiable, one-third-mile-long, gold and ivory caravan called *The White Train*, encountering every kind of reaction from hostility to wild enthusiasm. Historian Theo Aronson observed that "at times the heat and the worries irritated the King almost beyond endurance and he would have one of his 'gnashes.'" Normally a considerate man, when provoked the king would lose all control and spew forth a string of expletives. Furious about the Nationalist hostility to Prime Minister Jan Smuts, he was also incensed that the dominion's politicians had ordered him not to speak to black Africans when he decorated them. The queen would rub his arm to soothe him when he "gnashed" in public.

The queen herself never seemed to put a foot wrong. When one of their Boer hosts told her he could never forgive the British for annexing his country, she famously said, "We feel much the same in Scotland." Her composure cracked only once in an unbearably hot, dusty village outside Johannesburg. A Zulu man suddenly sprinted after the royal car, clutching something in one hand, and grabbing hold of the car so tightly with his other that his knuckles went bloodless. The queen raised her parasol and delivered several hard blows on the assailant before a policeman knocked him out. She continued waving cheerfully as if nothing had happened. The "assailant" turned out to be a loyal subject crying "My King, My King" and clutching a ten-shilling note in his hand, that he wanted to give to Princess Elizabeth as a twenty-first birthday present. The king and queen were mortified.

On April 21, 1947, Princess Elizabeth marked her birthday by making a broadcast to the people of the Commonwealth from South Africa, making a "solemn act of dedication," she declared, "before you all that my whole life, whether it be long or short, shall be devoted to your service and the service of our great Imperial Commonwealth to which we all belong." Having come of age at the time of the postwar creation of the Commonwealth, she was able to accept the new British order even more readily than her father, while sharing his belief in the Crown's power as a unifying force in the international community.

The king and queen also intended that the South Africa trip give Princess Elizabeth time to reconsider her secret engagement to Prince Philip of Greece, related to Russian czars and Danish kings and a great-great grandson of Queen Victoria. The king, in particular, worried that his daughter, who had led a sheltered life further constrained by the limitations of war, was too young to marry the first man for whom she had strong feelings. Elizabeth held tenaciously to her commitment to Philip, and the king finally gave in. In July, two months after their return, the king and queen announced their daughter's engagement. She was to wed Lieutenant Philip Mountbatten, who had shed his title and Greek nationality and changed his name to Mountbatten—the surname of his honored uncle Louis Mountbatten—in order to become a British citizen.

## London

On November 20, 1947, the gray austerity of postwar Britain lifted and the splendor of prewar pomp and pageantry returned when Princess Elizabeth married Prince Philip at Westminster Abbey in a ceremony Churchill called a "flash of colour on the hard road we have to travel." Crowds cheered the magnificent Irish State Coach as Elizabeth rode to her wedding. That morning the king bestowed on Prince Philip the Dukedom of Edinburgh and the status of His Royal Highness, thus giving him the title and nomenclature befitting a man marrying the heir to the throne.

The king was deeply attached to his elder daughter, who so resembled him in her shyness and her sense of duty. After her wedding, having led her to the altar, he told her, "When I handed your hand to the Archbishop I felt I had lost something very precious." The king also felt his domestic security was threatened by the marriage. He was truly happy and relaxed only when he was with his wife and daughters. He wrote Elizabeth, "Our family, us four, the 'Royal Family' must remain together with additions of course at suitable moments!! I have watched you grow up all these years under the skillful direction of Mummy, who as you know is the most marvelous person in the World in my eyes." The queen, with her happy childhood, had a much easier time adjusting to change. "What a wonderful day it has been," she said after the wedding; "they grow up and leave us and we must make the best of it."

# 17

# Walking with Death

## April 1948–February 1952

He was a grand man. Worth a pair of his brother Ed.
—*Harry Truman writing in his diary on the death of King George VI*

## London

After President Roosevelt died, British politicians spent several years deciding how to honor him. At first Prime Minister Attlee's government planned to commemorate Franklin Roosevelt's life and work with a memorial tablet in Westminster Abbey, but the lord chancellor, Lord Jowitt, investigated the abbey and reported it was "hopelessly congested with memorials, most of which have no artistic merit and many of which commemorate persons of no national importance." The government decided to erect a public statue instead. But in what pose? Winston Churchill wrote an early memorandum, "I am sure the statue ought to be seated. It is in the seated position that Roosevelt fought his way through party politics of the United States for more than a decade and it was thus that he played his great part in world history." Both the head of the Anglo-American benevolent group the Pilgrims, Sir Campbell Stuart, who had raised the money for the monument, and the sculptor Sir William Reid Dick wanted the statue to depict FDR standing, facing into the wind. They prevailed over Churchill. Churchill and Attlee joined the Pilgrims in a radio fund-raising appeal, which even in a straitened Britain met with overwhelming support.

After Eleanor agreed to officially unveil the statue, situated in London's Grosvenor Square near the U.S. embassy, the king invited her to spend the weekend at Windsor Castle so they could talk over "all that has happened in the world since we last met." Eleanor again responded with a jittery lack of confidence, writing later that "in some ways I rather dreaded the formality of a visit to a castle inhabited by a reigning monarch." The former First Lady focused her anxiety on her clothes, comparing herself unfavorably to Queen Elizabeth, who "always had such a wonderful wardrobe and always looked as if she had just a moment before been in the hands of a skillful maid and hair-dresser, as, indeed, she usually had been." Remembering how embarrassed she was when the palace maids saw her meager wardrobe during her 1942 visit, Eleanor was relieved that her status as a widow restricted her attire. As she said, "A black dress is a black dress."

When she arrived at Windsor on April 3, 1948, "The King and Queen were kindness itself," as she wrote in her autobiography. At the highly formal meals, held in the big dining room with a kilted Highland piper marching around the table playing bagpipes, Eleanor was impressed with Queen Elizabeth's ability to create a relaxed, homey atmosphere in such an historic setting. She was surprised that the king usually sported a tweed jacket and slacks like a Hyde Park country squire. When Princess Margaret and some friends were listening to phonograph records, Eleanor was amused when the king entered the room and said, "Meg, the music is too loud. Will you please turn it down?"

One evening, Eleanor played The Game, a form of charades led by Queen Elizabeth. At times, the queen puzzled over words and sought help from a glum Winston Churchill, who chomped on his cigar and disdainfully boycotted the game. At one point Churchill abruptly turned to Eleanor and asked, "You don't really approve of me, do you, Mrs. Roosevelt?" She gave a polite response, which has been lost to history.

Queen Mary came to Windsor to spend time with Eleanor, and led her and the royal family on a tour of the galleries. Like Sara Roosevelt at her own home, Queen Mary knew the location of every painting and objet d'art. As they stood before a striking portrait of one royal ancestor, the bemused king asked Princess Margaret to stand beneath the portrait on a stool. There was a stunning resemblance.

This visit marked the true beginning of a friendship between the former First Lady and the future Queen Elizabeth II. Touring the castle library, Eleanor was fascinated by the account the eleven-year-old Princess Elizabeth had written at the time of her own parents' 1937 coronation. In her autobiography Eleanor described Elizabeth as "very serious-minded" and wrote, "What struck me at the time was that this young princess was so interested in social problems and how they were being handled." After a dinner at which Eleanor spoke, Princess Elizabeth asked her, "I understand you have been to see some of the homes where we are trying to rehabilitate young woman offenders against the law. I have not yet been to see them but could you give me your opinion?" Eleanor told her she was impressed by how young woman prisoners were working under guidance to rehabilitate some of Britain's historic houses and gardens, rebuilding their own lives in the process.

The unveiling of FDR's statue occurred at 11 A.M. on the blue-skied spring morning of April 12, 1948—the third anniversary of the president's death. The tall plane trees in the square were not yet exhibiting their spring leaves, but the square was filled with colorful flower beds and newly planted small trees in full bloom. Arriving through an Anglo-American guard of honor, Eleanor, dressed in a black coat over a black and white patterned dress, made her way through the crowd of guests and onlookers to the royal dais. The royal family turned out in force. Joining Their Majesties, the two princesses, and the Duke of Edinburgh were Queen Mary, the Duke and Duchess of Gloucester, the Duchess of Kent and her three children (including FDR's two-and-a-half-year-old godson Prince Michael), Princess Alice, and the Earl of Athlone.

The king gave a heartfelt address in which he expressed "deep sorrow" that he and the queen and the British people did not have the opportunity to "show . . . their admiration [and] affection" for the late president, who had died before he could make a postwar trip—so eagerly awaited by Their Majesties—to Britain. "It is fitting that Mr. Roosevelt's statue should look over this square, which was the nerve center of the prodigious American war effort in Britain and in Europe . . . it will stand as a permanent reminder of our comradeship with the American people in the dark days of the war," he said.

After the king and Mrs. Roosevelt climbed the steps of the

monument, marines presented arms and Eleanor pulled a cord. The big Union Jacks covering the monument dropped away, and the statue of FDR emerged, standing twelve feet high in green-gray bronze, with one hand gripping a cane, his cape flowing back from his shoulders. "It gave the impression of a young, vigorous man and I think that is the impression my husband would have liked to leave with the British people," Eleanor later wrote. The king raised his hand in salute while the band played "The Star Spangled Banner."

Eleanor found the ceremony "so simple and dignified in keeping with the occasion," she wrote the king. He replied, saying "how much the Queen & I admired your quiet & calm bearing at a moment when your heart must have been so full of thoughts & memories." Eleanor was consoled, as she wrote in her memoirs, by thinking how "just as Moses was shown the promised land and could not enter, I imagine that there are many men . . . who are never allowed to have on this earth the recognition they might well have enjoyed. One can only hope that, if they labored with the love of God in their hearts, they will have a more perfect satisfaction than we can ever experience here."

As reported in the London *Times*, Eleanor wanted her husband remembered as "Valiant for Friendship," the kind of friendship that "is great enough to break down misunderstandings and differences . . . to build world friendship." On future visits to the statue, Eleanor would note that "there are always people there and I have rarely seen the statue without at least one small home-made bouquet resting on the marble base." A small tablet had also been placed inside Westminster Abbey. It honored Roosevelt as "A Faithful Friend of Freedom and of Britain."

## Zurich

After the ceremony Eleanor flew to Zurich for a rendezvous with the physician David Gurewitsch, a man who had emerged to take an important place in her life. She found an entire delegation of Swiss officials waiting to meet her. Deftly, she greeted them all and then slipped away quickly with David for two quiet days at a hotel. FDR would have been pleased, she told David, that the statue represented him standing.

David Gurewitsch had met Eleanor in 1944 when he was treating Joe Lash's wife Trude. After the president died, David became Eleanor's official physician. Their friendship had blossomed the previous

November, when they had flown together to Switzerland where David, who had contracted tuberculosis, would undergo a year of treatment in the Alps, and Eleanor would work in Geneva with the UN General Assembly, spearheading a successful effort to partition Palestine into Arab and Jewish states. On that flight (much like the train trip she had taken with Hick during the 1932 campaign) they had exchanged their life stories and had sensed the start of a profound connection. At the time, David's marriage was failing and Eleanor had been a widow for nearly three years.

On the surface they seemed an unlikely pair. David, a debonair and handsome ladies' man of Russian-Jewish background, was eighteen years younger than the former First Lady. While Eleanor came from a famous American aristocratic family, David was born to immigrant parents, and spent time in Switzerland and Palestine before coming to the United States in the 1930s. Yet, as his widow Edna Gurewitsch acknowledged in her memoir *Kindred Souls,* David and Eleanor were both shy, lonely adults who persistently felt like outsiders but sought to take care of others. They also shared a passion for history and politics. Although they recognized they would not be lovers, they found in each other the stability and intellectual companionability both craved. After they parted that November, Eleanor wrote him from Brussels: "The people I love mean more to me than all the public things . . . I only do the public things because I really love all people and I only love all people because there are a few close people whom I love dearly. . . . There are not so many of them and you are now one of them."

That same year, 1947, Eleanor narrowly escaped embarrassing damage to her personal and political reputation during the divorce proceedings of her former bodyguard and intimate friend, Earl Miller. During the early 1930s Eleanor had forged a close bond with the handsome bodyguard, who took her horseback riding, introduced her to outdoor sports, and squired her around town. When Miller's wife suggested her husband had had sexual relations with Mrs. Roosevelt, Miller arranged an out-of-court settlement so that the records were sealed.

## London

During the celebrations of the king and queen's silver wedding anniversary in April 1948, the king hid from the public the fact that he had been suffering from cramps in both legs. By that fall, he was numb in both feet, in pain, and had difficulty sleeping at night. The king's physicians diagnosed arteriosclerosis, blocking the blood flow to his legs and feet. They feared they might have to amputate his leg. He was ordered to curtail his official activities and rest—an extremely difficult task for the chronically anxious and activist king.

On July 11, Eleanor wrote to the queen to express her concern and to recall their 1939 visit: "I was so glad to see in a photograph which appeared in our newspapers the other day that the King was able to be with you at a formal function. I hope that means that he is very much better. I have thought of you very often in your anxiety for him and hope that he is improving steadily." When British United Nations members visited her at Hyde Park, she told them about the king and queen's departure from Hyde Park in 1939 "at sun down and the way the people lined the tracks and sang 'Auld Lang Syne.' That has always stayed in my mind as the most moving moment of your visit to this country." Hearing that Princess Margaret might visit the United States that fall, she offered to entertain her.

On July 21, the queen wrote back, saying, "I am glad to be able to tell you that he is *really* better and with care should be well in a year or so. It is always a slow business with a leg and the great thing is not to get overtired during convalescence—You can imagine how difficult it is to achieve with the world in its present state & worries & troubles piling up." She added, "I fear that the story that Margaret is going to the United States this autumn is not true, alas! I do hope that someday she will be able to visit America, as I am sure that she will love it as much as we did those far off days of 1939." She invited Eleanor for another visit where "I am sure that you will find that people are recovering very quickly from the effects of that long and agonizing war—One feels that the anguish & worry reveals itself long after, & last year was bad, & now one feels a definite revival of spirit & serenity."

In early July, in the delicate royal household wording of that era, it was announced that Princess Elizabeth would not be undertaking any more engagements for the rest of the year. Eleanor took a motherly interest in the welfare of the pregnant princess, cabling her congratulations on the impending birth and sending her flowers as the due date neared. The day before the birth, Elizabeth thanked Eleanor for "the kind thought which prompted you to send me those lovely flowers."

The queen shuttled between her ill husband and her expectant daughter in different wings of the palace. On November 12, the doctors had diagnosed severe arteriosclerosis and were worried that they might have to amputate his leg if gangrene set in. The king had sworn the queen to secrecy about his condition; he did not want to worry Elizabeth and complicate her delivery. On the evening of November 14, while the king rested in one wing of the palace and the Duke of Edinburgh played squash, Princess Elizabeth gave birth to Prince Charles Philip Arthur George, the second-in-line to the throne. Prince Charles would form a devoted filial bond with his grandmother—a degree of closeness he would not share with his own mother.

## New York

As the presidential campaign of 1948 began, Eleanor was not eager to endorse Harry Truman. Alarmed that Truman was moving away from the liberal ideals she cherished as her husband's legacy, she gave no hint of her intentions. In March she had charged him with losing control of the State Department and letting the United Nations down, and offered her resignation. Knowing her departure meant political disaster, he insisted that the world needed her leadership and that he could not accept losing her. Eleanor's three oldest sons attempted to replace Truman on the Democratic ticket with General Eisenhower. The rising Democratic politician Hubert Humphrey reported that Eleanor made several calls to Eisenhower expressing support for his candidacy.

Truman won the nomination and attempted to build on the Roosevelts' legacy and rhetoric by offering Americans a "Fair Deal" and broadening the number of citizens who received housing and other forms of assistance. A Washington columnist published rumors that Eleanor preferred Dewey. At the eleventh hour, Eleanor gave a radio broadcast supporting Truman. The president, she said, had "shown courage" and she still believed "in the Democratic Party and its leadership." Thanks in part to her endorsement, Truman pulled out a famous late-night, come-from-behind victory over the Republican candidate, New York governor Thomas Dewey.

After the final draft of the Universal Declaration of Human Rights was ratified in 1949, the former First Lady stepped further into the public arena, with radio shows, a television talk show, and publication of *This I Remember*, the memoir of her White House years. Still feeling guilty over her abstracted treatment of her children while they were growing up, she compensated by creating career opportunities for them. For Anna, in financial trouble after divorcing her second husband, John Boettiger, who later killed himself, Eleanor created the *The Eleanor and Anna Show*, broadcast at its peak on over two hundred radio stations, and gave her daughter all the income from it. When the show failed, Eleanor enlisted Elliott to broker a deal for a television talk show in which Mrs. Roosevelt chatted with important guests on controversial topics. Again, all her earnings went to Anna. After that television show failed, she did a WNBC radio program with Elliott as the commercial announcer. Elliott arranged for *McCall's* magazine to buy the serial rights to *This I Remember* for one hundred and fifty thousand dollars and to offer her a new monthly column at three thousand dollars a month. When her memoir was critically praised and sold well, she had the financial resources she needed to stabilize her children's livelihoods.

## London

The Duke of Windsor needed money as well. To maintain a lifestyle that included the duchess's fifty-thousand-dollar annual clothing budget, in 1950 he had written a series of articles for *Life* magazine about his youth before World War I. The king said nothing publicly, but pointedly did not invite his brother to Princess Elizabeth's wedding. The duke also discussed with the king a plan to live in the United States and work on behalf of Anglo-American relations. When the British government opposed his plans, the duke and duchess remained in France. They did not want to move to America as private citizens and pay taxes there.

In March 1949, despite months of enforced rest, the king needed another operation. Physicians performed a right lumbar sympathectomy, cutting the nerve at the base of the spine, which would allow maximum blood flow to his legs. He was still recovering from the surgery that autumn when he was horrified to learn the duke was publishing his memoirs, *A King's Story*. The king would not look kindly on the Duke of Windsor for writing his version of the abdication crisis and refocusing attention on that painful and damaging time. That

December, nearly twelve years to the day since he had abdicated, the duke once again beseeched his brother to give the duchess royal status. After a final rebuff from the king, the two men never spoke again.

Over the next two years, as Britain continued to suffer from the grim realities of a depleted economy (meat and sugar rations were cut), and the Korean War began, the king's health would continue its slow decline, exacerbated by his unrelenting sense of duty. In the winter of 1951 Eleanor sent the king and queen two newly published books of Franklin's personal letters, which included several of the king's wartime missives. When Eleanor returned to England to speak on international issues, she was so busy that all she could do was send her friends a box of chocolates. On May 23, the queen wrote to Eleanor: "I was so sad not to see you when you were here on a literally flying visit, but you were so busy, and we were away from London, but we saw you on television, & very much admired the wonderful way you coped with the occasional rather awkward questions! You really were splendid, and I am sure that those sort of talks do a great deal of good, especially when they are on a high plane, such as your appearance. I hope we shall meet again before too long."

Concerned about the king's physical weakness that spring, his physicians ordered more tests, which showed that the fifty-five-year-old monarch had a small inflammation of the left lung. He was ordered to take a prolonged summer rest. At Balmoral, the king wrote a friend, "I am getting stronger every day." But then physicians discovered that he had lung cancer. As was customary in that era, they did not reveal their diagnosis to their patient, telling him only that a blockage necessitated removing one lung. The king hated the idea of another operation. "If it is going to help me get well again I don't mind but the very idea of the surgeon's knife again is hell," he wrote a friend. Only the queen knew about his cancer. During his recovery from the surgery, he was cheered by two major events: the return of Churchill as prime minister and the laudatory reports of his daughter's trip to the United States.

On October 27, Winston Churchill, in power again after a general election evicted Clement Attlee's Labour Party, met with the king in his study at Buckingham Palace. The king was too ill to greet Churchill at the top of the stairs leading to his study, as was his custom. Churchill, with his hand trembling and his speech slurred from a recent stroke,

had to move close to hear the king's strained voice. Each m;
meeting fearing for the other's life. Churchill would outlive tl
more than a decade.

# Washington, D.C.

When Eleanor heard that Elizabeth and Philip would be coming to the
United States that fall, she invited them to Hyde Park: "If you are
long enough in New York City and cared to dine with me quietly at
my apartment in the Park Sheraton Hotel and go to the theater, I
think you would enjoy seeing 'The King and I.' I can arrange to get
seats and ask anyone whom you would like to have me invited."
Uncharacteristically, the princess did not reply. Frustrated, Eleanor
wrote a second time, requesting a response. Finally on September 14,
the princess wrote to apologize for "appearing so rude" in not answering her letter, which somehow had been mislaid: "I am afraid we are
unable to pay a visit to New York . . . I fear you will have already left for
Paris. It is very disappointing for we should have been very happy to
come and see you. Perhaps it will be possible for us to pay a less formal
visit to the United States some time, and manage to see New York and
see a show there—it sounds such fun!"

On October 7, Princess Elizabeth and the Duke of Edinburgh left
for a thirty-five-day imperial tour of Canadian provinces and a quick
visit to Washington, D.C. Canadians took the royal couple to heart.
Eleanor was on a ship bound for the General Assembly meetings in
Paris when Their Majesties arrived in the United States. Disappointed,
she left them "some little trifles of American craftsmanship." The
British ambassador gave the princess a bowl made in Pennsylvania and
two handwoven ties for her husband.

Grateful to Elizabeth for entertaining his daughter Margaret at
Buckingham Palace, President Truman took the unusual step of meeting the royal couple at the Washington airport, and addressed
Elizabeth affectionately as "my dear." Elizabeth presented Truman
with gifts from her parents for the newly restored White House: a late
seventeenth-century English overmantel glass and an eighteenth-
century pair of gilded bronze and blue spar candelabra. The royal couple stayed in Blair House. Truman took them upstairs to meet his
nearly deaf, bedridden mother. The president yelled in her ear, "I've

brought Princess Elizabeth to see you." Knowing that Churchill had just returned to power, the elderly woman told her, "I am so glad your father has been re-elected." The young couple and the Trumans were amused. While in Washington, the princess, calling her mother every day to check on the progress of the king, was heartened to hear that he could now sit up, his progress a sobering indication of how ill he remained.

Truman introduced the young princess to the American people, saying, "When I was a little boy, I read about a fairy-tale princess—and here she is." At a gala reception for the cabinet, members of Congress, the Supreme Court, and the press at the British embassy, the princess and her husband shook sixteen hundred hands. After they left Washington, Truman wrote to the king in his homespun manner, "We've just had a visit from a lovely young lady and her personable husband. They went to the hearts of all the citizens of the United States. . . . As one father to another we can be very proud of our daughters. You have the better of me—because you have two!"

## London and Sandringham

Ever since GIs had flooded England during the war, the British had been fascinated with the United States and its most recent reaction to royalty. They flocked to movie theaters to see the newsreels of Elizabeth's visit. Sir Oliver Franks, the British ambassador to Washington, reported to the king that the royal family was "the embodiment of all they [the Americans] so much admire in Britain." He added, "Given the opportunity the American people delight to show there is a real and abiding bond between themselves and the British people." This was particularly heartening news for a king who had always considered one of his major roles to be representing the best of Britain to the United States. That his daughter could solidify the bridge he had labored to build with America gave him enormous joy at a time when he was prone to gloom. At the end of 1951, the king was depressed. He summed up his last demoralizing year in his diary: "The incessant worries and crises through which we have to live have got me down something proper."

Just before Christmas, the king thanked Truman for entertaining his daughter. "Much has happened to the world since we met in

Plymouth Sound in 1945," he wrote. "I am glad that you are going to renew your relations with Mr. Churchill shortly. He is a wise man and understands the problems of this troubled world. I have always felt that our two countries cannot progress one without the other, & feel that this meeting will unite us even more closely."

The king's last Christmas was a happy time. He enjoyed playing with Prince Charles and his sister, Princess Anne, who had been born in August 1950. For once, he did not have to make a nerve-wracking Christmas Day broadcast live to the nation. He had prerecorded the speech to reduce the strain on his hoarse voice. He told his people that "I trust you yourselves realize how greatly your prayers and good wishes have helped . . . me in my recovery."

On January 29, 1952, the king consulted with his physicians, who seemed to be satisfied with his progress. The following night the family celebrated with an evening at the Drury Lane Theatre to see *South Pacific*. The next day, with his physician's permission, the king stood bareheaded in cold weather on the tarmac of London airport, waving good-bye to his daughter and son-in-law as they left to represent him on a trip to Australia and New Zealand, which he was not well enough to make.

On February 5, the king went out shooting in perfect winter weather—sunny, dry, and cold. In six hours he bagged nine hares. While he was hunting, the queen and Princess Margaret went to lunch with the artist Edward Seago at his riverside home in Ludham. They returned late with pictures they had commissioned Seago to make of Sandringham. As the queen wrote Seago, "as I always did, I rushed straight to the King's room . . . I found him so well, so gay . . . and . . . we went straight to the hall where they [the pictures] had been set out. . . . We had such a truly gay dinner with the King, like his old self, and more picture looking after dinner."

For half an hour before bedtime, Princess Margaret played the piano for her father. The king and queen then listened to the ten o'clock BBC News for word of Elizabeth and Philip, who had made a stop in Africa. Reassured, they retired for the night. At eleven o'clock a footman took a cup of cocoa to the king, who was in bed reading about his favorite subjects—guns and dogs. At midnight, a watchman saw him fiddling with a recently repaired latch on his bedroom window.

At seven-thirty the next morning, James Macdonald, the king's valet, entered bearing a cup of tea and pulled the curtain on the royal bed, but the king did not move. He had died during the night from a coronary thrombosis. The queen was drinking her morning tea when her equerry gave her the news. "I must go to him," she said immediately. After she had kissed his forehead and sat with him awhile, she requested that a constant vigil should be kept by the open door to the king's room.

One of the king's private secretaries went immediately to Downing Street, where Churchill was lying in bed, papers strewn all around, a cigar in his mouth, and told him, "I've got bad news, Prime Minister, the King died last night. I know nothing else." After a stunned pause, Churchill said, "Bad news, the worst." He threw away the pages of a speech he had been preparing about foreign affairs, saying, "How unimportant these matters are." Later, when he tried to get back to the day's work and read through his speech, he broke down. A few weeks later Churchill suffered a small arterial spasm.

At Marlborough House, Lady Cynthia Colville broke the news to the king's mother. As she entered her room, Queen Mary asked, "Is it the King?" Told that her son had died, Queen Mary murmured, "What a shock." She would live only thirteen months more, dying before her favorite granddaughter, Elizabeth, was crowned queen.

The new monarch, Elizabeth II, seemed to be one of the last to know that she had become queen. At the moment her father's body was discovered, Elizabeth was watching herds of rhinoceroses and elephants from the balcony of Treetops, a hut in a giant fig tree, overlooking a water hole in a nature preserve in Kenya. Prince Philip's equerry, Michael Parker, beckoned the prince to step outside the lodge so he could tell him. Parker remembered that "he looked as if you'd dropped half the world on him." Prince Philip took his new queen out to the garden where they "walked slowly up and down the lawn while he talked and talked and talked to her."

In London the BBC announced the news at 10:45 A.M. and went silent for the rest of the day. Drivers stopped their cars, wept, and stood at attention to honor the late king. Stunned crowds filled the rainy streets and people stood in long, orderly lines waiting to buy the newspapers. Church bells rang fifty-six times, once for each year of the king's life. The next day Churchill told the British people, "During these last months the King walked with death, as if death were a companion, an acquaintance, whom he recognized and did not fear . . . we all saw him approach his journey's end." Churchill's famously poetic tribute was only partially true. The king did not dwell on the possibility of death. In truth, it was the queen who had walked alone over his last months with the sure knowledge of the king's approaching death.

In the United States, where His Majesty's crucial contribution to the Anglo-American alliance was still remembered vividly, there was an extraordinary outpouring of respect and commemoration. As they had done only once before on the death of Queen Victoria, the House of Representatives adopted a resolution of sympathy and adjourned for the day. The Massachusetts Senate passed a resolution calling the king the "beloved Monarch . . . who laboured to the point of exhaustion in showing . . . the proper discharge of royal duties." The *Los Angeles Times* editorialized that the dead king would be remembered as "George the Good." General Eisenhower wrote to the king's widow that he was "a model of character and deportment for those in high places. Our respect for him as an inspirational force was equaled by our affection for him as a gentle human being."

The evening of the day he died, the queen came downstairs to play with Prince Charles and Princess Anne. "I've got to start sometime and it might as well be now," she said, trying to resume some semblance of normality. Later she accompanied her husband's body across the park to the small church of St. Mary Magdalene, where the people of Sandringham would pay their respects. She wrote a friend, "One cannot yet believe that it has all happened, one feels rather dazed."

The king's body was brought to London to lie in state in Westminster Hall. As they awaited his body, the three queens—Mary, Elizabeth, and Elizabeth II—were photographed together, dressed in black, in an unforgettable portrait of grief. Through three days of rain, sleet, and snow, three hundred thousand people stood in lines stretching four miles. The Duke of Windsor returned to England and marched with the Duke of Edinburgh, the Duke of Gloucester, and the young Duke of Kent behind the gun carriage bearing the king's body to the burial service at St. George's Chapel in Windsor. Big Ben chimed fifty-six times to the sound of muffled drums, as five kings, three queens, twelve princes, three princesses, four duchesses, and three presidents headed the somber procession of mourners. "My only wish now," the widowed queen told the nation, "is that I may be allowed to continue the work that we sought to do together. I want you to know how your concern for me has upheld me in my sorrow, and how proud you have made me by your wonderful tribute to my dear husband, a great and noble king."

Eleanor was stunned and sad when she heard the news in Paris, just as the sixth United Nations General Assembly ended and David Gurewitsch arrived to join her. She would have loved to attend her friend the king's funeral, but she was scheduled to visit refugee camps in the Mideast and study the plight of the displaced Arabs. She wrote Anna from the Hotel de Crillon on February 7 that the king's death "was a shock." With her distinctive perspective as the widow of a great leader, she wrote to comfort Queen Elizabeth, but her letter has disappeared. The widowed queen replied to Eleanor, "It is impossible to believe that the King is no longer with us. He was so full of plans and ideas for the future, & zest for life, & it is hard to think of life without him."

# 18

# First Ladies of the World

## FEBRUARY 1952–NOVEMBER 1954

> She is completely and utterly indomitable, absolutely unstoppable.
> —*Prince Charles speaking about the Queen Mother*

Following the king's death, Eleanor and Elizabeth had more in common than ever before. As "First Ladies," they had had been married to men whose leadership had possessed great symbolic value in the most tumultuous era in memory. George VI had come to represent the civilization and courage of Britain, while FDR personified America's confident vision and advocacy for the disadvantaged. Both men had cast long shadows from which their widows would struggle to emerge. Seeking their own place while honoring and expanding their husbands' visions, they would be watched by the world. Interestingly, they both gravitated beyond their own nations, where their husbands' legacies were so strong, traveling abroad to work for international understanding and cooperation. During the 1950s and 1960s, the former first ladies became First Ladies of the world, exemplars of the fully realized woman who can reinvent her life and expand her role innovatively and productively.

Eleanor and Elizabeth were two of the most energetic people of the twentieth century, and their vigor alone propelled them through the worst ordeals. Near the end of her life, as Elizabeth was recovering from a hip operation, her grandson Charles praised her in words that characterized both Eleanor and Elizabeth: "She is completely and utterly indomitable, absolutely unstoppable." At the time, BBC correspondent Jennie Bond quoted one of the Queen Mother's staff as saying that once when she was asked if she was tired, she replied, "I have been tired for the last thirty years." However, the Queen Mother's page, Billy Tallon, told the author that "she was never an old woman. When she entered a room, she was always the youngest person in it." In later years, Eleanor would shake off being hit by a taxi, limping her way straight to a speaking engagement, while Elizabeth, after she tripped in front of Westminster Abbey, would smile and wave her shoe at the crowds. Possessed of extraordinary stamina and a stoical philosophy, both women were impatient with illness. Historian Kenneth Rose says that there were three things Elizabeth did not like confronting—misfortune, illness, and death, all of which she faced continuously during the war.

## London

Like Eleanor in 1945, Elizabeth had lost not only her husband and her home, but most of her power as well. Eleanor had been in the White House for twelve years, while Elizabeth had lived in Buckingham Palace for fourteen. Eleanor, having already established her identity as a writer and liberal crusader, and having grown somewhat detached from her husband, was able to let go of her former life quickly. Elizabeth had a much tougher time. Enveloped in "black clouds of unhappiness and misery," as she put it, she remained in the palace for fifteen months after the king died, moving out only a month before the coronation. The crown jewels and the royal residences all reverted to her daughter. She had the perplexing task of watching the new queen take on all of her prerogatives at a time when she was awash in grief and, by the fact of her widowhood, removed from the public role that challenged and defined her.

However, she did immediately establish a new, untraditional identity for herself. On Valentine's Day, only a week after the king died, the widowed queen announced she henceforth would be known as Queen Elizabeth The Queen Mother. There would be no gloomy "dowager queen" appellation for her. Her new title would differentiate her from her daughter the queen but also bespeak its own authority. Yet she took the title long before she was willing and able to make it meaningful. First she had to pass through a bewildering period of emptiness, physically painful depression, and psychic disorientation. Years after her husband's death, when the Queen Mother was asked if being a widow got any better, she replied, "It doesn't get any better, but you get better at it."

It was commonly thought of the royal couple that Elizabeth was the stronger personality and that the king had been entirely dependent on her. In fact, they had been so intertwined that they had functioned as an interactive identity. Bertie had shared even the most secret political news with his wife. "The King always told me everything first. I do so miss that," she told a friend. They were not only confidants but playmates. After one long and tiring official function, according to Lady Donaldson, "someone opened a door on to a corridor and caught sight of the King and Queen, hand in hand, skipping gaily down it together." On May 3, 1952, Elizabeth wrote author Osbert Sitwell, "He was so young to die and was becoming so wise in kingship. He was so kind too, and had a sort of natural nobility of thought & life, which sometimes made me ashamed of my narrower & more feminine point of view." She told Sitwell that sorrow "is a very strange experience—it really changes one's whole life, whether for better or worse I don't know yet."

Her lady-in-waiting, Ruth Fermoy, explained the Queen Mother's distinctive predicament after the king's death: "Loneliness is the hardest thing to bear, not having by you the one person to whom you can say anything and everything. This was probably worse for her because, as Queen, she had many friends, but not many intimates—the reserve she had learned as queen made her lonelier than others would otherwise have been." Nearly eight years into her widowhood, the Queen Mother could still write her friend Lady Waverly saying how glad she was that Christmastime ("Such a time of memories") had passed. A friend recalled for the biographer Sarah Bradford the depth of the Queen Mother's grief. "She was absolutely heartbroken, for a few months I thought she wasn't going to pull herself together." She took months to answer her friends' condolence letters. Osbert Sitwell's sister Edith sent her a poetry anthology, *A Book of Flowers*, in which George Herbert's lines particularly heartened her: "Who would have thought my shrivel'd heart/could have recovered greenness?/ It was gone quite underground." The Queen Mother wrote Edith, "I thought how small and selfish is sorrow. But it bangs one about until one is quite senseless."

Just after her husband died, Elizabeth endured the ordeal of a meeting with the Duke of Windsor, toward whom she felt intense bitterness; in her view, the duke's abdication was the cause of her husband's early death, forcing on him the depleting duties of kingship. For weeks after the funeral, she referred to the duchess as the "woman who killed my husband." The duke was under strict instructions from his wife ("I am sure you can win her over with a more friendly attitude") to rekindle his relationship with "Cookie," as they derisively called the Queen Mother, so as to enhance their chances of returning to England and royal favor. "Cookie was sugar," the duke told his wife after their meeting. "She listened without comment & closed on the note that it was nice to be able to talk about Bertie with someone who had known him so well." He mistook her manners for her meaning.

## Scotland

The Queen Mother retreated to Scotland in June to mourn with her friends the Vyners, at their house on the bleak coast of Caithness, the northernmost coast of Scotland. One day they took her on a tour of the neighborhood and spotted a derelict castle. "I was driving along and from the high road saw this old castle; when I heard it was going to be pulled down, I thought it must be saved," she later said. Hoping that "the peace and tranquility of the open countryside with the rugged glory of a magnificent coastline" would soothe her, she paid twenty-six thousand pounds for it. She refurbished the castle herself. It was her version of Eleanor's Val-Kill, a place where she could begin living an independent life. With its legends and its ghostly atmosphere, the renamed Castle of Mey may have reminded the Queen Mother of her childhood home of Glamis. She would visit every year for six weeks.

Worried that the Queen Mother would remain a recluse, Churchill surprised her with a visit to Birkhall, urging her to take on a public role; the country and the new queen needed her, and her late husband would want her to have a significant purpose. Churchill would arrange for her to have a healthy allowance and live in splendor in Clarence House, which would be redecorated to her specifications. To soften her resistance, Churchill went ahead and refurbished Clarence House, moving the fireplace from her bedroom in Buckingham Palace to her new quarters. "I was going to throw in Big Ben," he joked. Impressed at the vigor of his appeal and able to imagine a revitalized public role for herself, she promised she would emerge once more.

Unlike Queen Victoria, who did not carry out public engagements for years after Prince Albert's death, or Queen Mary, who kept to herself at first, the new Queen Mother waited only three months before her first public outing. As colonel-in-chief of the First Battalion of the Black Watch (the Royal Highland Regiment), the Queen Mother flew to Fife, Scotland, to inspect her men and see them off to join Allied forces in the Korean War. Dressed in black, relieved only by a pearl necklace and a diamond regimental brooch, she told them they were "so dear to my heart and to many of my family."

## Washington, D.C.

In March 1952, President Truman announced that he would not run for a third term. The year before, congressional Republicans had pushed through a constitutional amendment to ensure that no future president could serve more than two terms. Truman, as sitting president, was exempt, but he was deeply unpopular and sensed that the country was ready for a change after twenty years of Democratic administrations. Some of the New Deal faithful proposed Eleanor as the Democratic presidential candidate, but she had no interest. In 1976 her son James would declare, "I've always wondered whether, if mother had run, she might not have won as the presidential candidate."

Indeed, Eleanor would have been a powerful, if polarizing, nominee. Since 1948, when the Gallup poll first posed the question, Eleanor had been voted the most admired woman in the world, a status she maintained throughout the 1950s. The country did not yet appear ready for a woman president, and it is unlikely she could have matched the drawing power of the eventual Republican candidate, the celebrated Dwight D. Eisenhower. In January 1952 she had written to Joe Lash about Eisenhower, "He will win but as a hero he will be tarnished & it will get worse and worse. We need our heroes & we need him here & I doubt we need him more as President."

Eleanor championed Illinois governor Adlai Stevenson. Addressing the Democratic Convention, she extolled Stevenson for his integrity, his intellect, and his knowledge of foreign affairs. She felt Stevenson was the one candidate who could deal effectively with Stalin and the Communist threat. Although her sons Elliott and John joined the Oyster Bay clan in supporting Eisenhower, she felt he lacked integrity, having failed to stand up to the anticommunist demagoguery of Senator Joe McCarthy. Despite her willingness to campaign for Stevenson, she was inexplicably left on the sidelines like Bill Clinton in 2000. Eisenhower won by a landslide.

## Eleanor Abroad

In May 1949 at the Women's National Press Club, President Truman presented Eleanor with an award and dubbed her "the First Lady of the World" for her advocacy of international understanding and justice. Her international reputation grew when she went to Pakistan and India to observe the nascent democracies in action. With a down-to-earth and empathetic address, she won over the icy Indian Parliament, easing anti-American sentiments. In India she went to see the moonlit Taj Mahal, the one site her father, Elliott Roosevelt, had said he wanted to share with her. While she generally retained her equanimity under the sometimes intractable demands of foreign diplomacy, she experienced one notable incident of angry despair in India. When David Gurewitsch refused to attend yet another diplomatic banquet with her, Eleanor—already overwhelmed by the Indian government's pressures and hurt by what she saw as David's rejection of her—wrote out telegrams to Indian prime minister Jawaharlal Nehru and Secretary of State Dean Acheson, threatening to cancel her trip. Ultimately she recovered and carried on with her program—as she always did.

In Japan the next year, Eleanor, who had tangled with Sara Roosevelt for more than thirty years, noted how Japanese mothers-in-law dominated their son's wives and fostered the subservient position of women. The attention Japanese politicians paid to Eleanor helped improve the status of the country's women. Americans watched rapt as she toured Hiroshima and met burn victims. Gingerly but firmly she made the connection between the bombing of Pearl Harbor and the devastation at Hiroshima. There was no better place for her to stress the importance of the United Nations and its mission to end war.

# London

Over Christmas 1952, the increasingly frail Queen Mary spent most of her time in her room at Sandringham, venturing forth only in the afternoons. Mary, a national institution "like St. Paul's Cathedral," in the phrase of diarist Chips Channon, was struggling to live long enough to see Elizabeth crowned in June. She recovered enough strength by February to drive through the streets of London and see the preparations for the coronation, but she would not linger long enough for the actual ceremony. On the afternoon of March 24, the Queen Mother called at Clarence House to say good-bye to her mother-in-law. She died later that evening. "The world will be the poorer," Channon wrote.

Unlike Eleanor, who was full of unresolved feelings and went numb upon the death of Sara Roosevelt, the Queen Mother genuinely mourned her mother-in-law, who had been a great support to her. Rather than attempt to control the younger woman, as Sara had Eleanor, Queen Mary had led Elizabeth by example. Remembering FDR's fondness for Queen Mary and her generous if formal hospitality, Eleanor cabled the Queen Mother. "All sympathy in this hour of sadness," she wrote. Two days later the Queen Mother cabled back: "So grateful for your kind message of sympathy."

# New York

Several deaths in the early 1950s severed Eleanor's links with her childhood, leaving her again feeling orphaned and vulnerable. In 1950, her cousin Susie, in whose house Eleanor had been married, died. In 1952 she lost her aunt and faithful correspondent, Maude Gray. On the eighth anniversary of FDR's death, April 12, 1953, Eleanor's longtime companion, secretary, and gatekeeper, Tommy—Malvina Thompson—died from a brain hemorrhage. Eleanor felt widowed all over again. She later wrote that Tommy "not only made my life easier, but gave me a reason for living." The loss was so keen that she vowed never again to form such a close working relationship.

Eleanor relied more and more on her intimate friendship with David Gurewitsch, who served as both ideal son and surrogate husband. In 1955, on his fifty-fifth birthday, she wrote him, "I love you as

I love and have never loved anyone else." In a February 1956 letter, she sought greater intimacy: "I'd love to hear you call me by my first name but you can't. Perhaps it is my age! I do love you and you are always in my thoughts and if that bothers you I could hide it. I'm good at that." In 1958, when David sent her a telegram announcing his engagement to art dealer Edna Perkel, whom Eleanor had known for several years and entertained, Mrs. Roosevelt's face turned ashen, according to her secretary Maureen Corr. Surmounting her emotions, Eleanor held the wedding in her own living room and wrote poems for the newlyweds. On that day, Edna wrote later, Eleanor's "manner was cordial but restrained, different from before—kind, not warm." Shortly afterward, Eleanor invited Edna to lunch, a grim and self-conscious affair that ended when Eleanor made an atypically hostile remark: "Don't worry, David will give you *everything* you want." Eventually reassured that she would not lose David's companionship, Eleanor bought and shared a town house, with separate apartments for Eleanor and for the couple, in Manhattan. In this radical arrangement, Eleanor was careful to give them their privacy, but creative and flexible enough to meet her own needs for intimacy at a lonely time in her life.

## London

The Queen Mother created her own unconventional family at Clarence House, where she surrounded herself with a loyal circle of long-serving ladies-in-waiting and equerries. For many years, her stalwart private secretary, Sir Martin Gilliat, was her main support and traveling companion, while her loyal page, Billy Tallon, created a stimulating atmosphere. Both men invited many fun, interesting, and artistic people (like the playwright Noël Coward, the choreographer Sir Frederick Ashton, the poets Sir John Betjeman and Ted Hughes, and the writers Kenneth Rose and Lord David Cecil), people from the horse racing world, and the bishop of New York (Horace Donegan) into her life. In 1960 rumors that she would marry Sir Arthur Penn, her seventy-four-year-old treasurer, were quickly quashed as "complete and absolute nonsense."

The story of the alliance of the royals and the Roosevelts is full of barely missed connections and instances of public duties trumping occasions where they could meet as friends. Theodore Roosevelt had planned to meet his pen pal, Edward VII, but the king died while the former president was on his way to England. FDR had a cerebral hemorrhage just before he was to make a state visit to England. The Duke of Kent was killed in an airplane crash just after naming FDR godfather to his son. In the postwar years, Eleanor would often have to turn down royal invitations because of her work commitments. The new queen invited Eleanor to her coronation, but Eleanor had to decline: "Months ago I promised to do a five week stint in Japan trying to explain what democracy means from the Western point of view. I will probably fail but, nevertheless I must try and fulfill my obligation."

She would be in London that summer and hoped "that you will allow me to pay my respects, but I do not wish to add to your burdens. I know your time must be all too short to fulfill the many obligations which crowd your days. I shall think of you on Coronation Day and wish you God's blessing . . . I know that all you can do for the good of your own nation and the world, you will do in these years to come." Eleanor was briefly in London that August, but the royal family was ensconced at Balmoral on their annual summer holiday.

Coronation day, June 2, 1953, was unseasonably cold and rainy. As the two-hour procession headed to Westminster Abbey, the most colorful coach carried the tall and massive Queen Salote of Tonga, dressed in striking red, sitting next to and dwarfing "a frail little man in white," the Sultan of Kelantan. As playwright Noël Coward watched them pass by, his guest asked, "Who can he be?" "Her lunch," Coward replied. The coronation would be the first to be televised, but its most sacred moments—the anointing and taking of communion—would not be broadcast live. In 1953 there was not yet live cross-Atlantic television transmission, but approximately one hundred million North American viewers watched delayed broadcasts and saw the pale and composed queen and her mother perform their assigned roles of sovereign and witness at the ceremony.

Queen Elizabeth became only the second British queen mother (following Queen Mary) to attend her successor's coronation. Anne Edwards of the *Daily Express* described the dramatic moment of her entry into the abbey: "In she came, glittering from top to toe, diamonds everywhere, a two-foot hem of solid gold on her open dress—the Queen Mother playing a second lead as beautifully as she had played the first. On she came up the aisle with a bow here . . . a bow there . . . no hesitation . . . no nervous nods of her head." Elizabeth watched as her young daughter, wearing a diamond diadem and a crimson velvet robe, entered the abbey, prayed, and was disencumbered of her outer garments, wearing a simple white dress for the solemn act of coronation.

The four-year-old Prince Charles, in a white satin suit, his hair shining with brilliantine, sat between his grandmother and his Aunt Margaret. As the Queen Mother watched the ceremony, she answered the prince's whispered questions, pulled him back from leaning too far over the railing, and retrieved him after he searched on the floor for candies fallen from her handbag. Her face alight, she watched her daughter repeat the statements of religious commitment she had made sixteen years earlier at her own coronation. Cecil Beaton, who took the coronation photographs, was struck by the "enormous presence and radiance of the petite Queen Mother." At the same time he also noted, "Yet in the Queen Widow's expression we read sadness combined with pride."

When the supreme moment arrived for the monarch's crowning, the Queen Mother brought her hand to her forehead for a brief moment of emotion. Commentators noted that the Queen Mother seemed to have surmounted her mixed feelings—an amalgam of wistfulness for all that she had lost and of hopes for Britain's future. Britons, remembering the extraordinary progress during the reigns of its two most prominent previous queens, Victoria and Queen Elizabeth I, expected the new reign to usher in political ascendance and economic prosperity. The press grandly dubbed the event the beginning of the New Elizabethan Age.

Within minutes of Queen Elizabeth II's crowning, her younger sister made a gesture that would touch off a two-year furor and conflict between love and duty, open the wounds of Edward's VIII's abdication, cause damage to her sister's young reign, and lead to fissures in the tight-knit "family firm"—as George VI used to call the royal family. Cameras caught Margaret flirtatiously and tenderly brushing the lint off the uniform of the vulnerably charming and handsome comptroller of her mother's household, RAF group captain Peter Townsend. Townsend had been a decorated hero of the Battle of Britain and a favorite equerry of the late king. He was also divorced.

It is debatable whether Princess Margaret's tender gesture was merely the spontaneous act of a woman in love or an unconscious attempt to upstage her sister at her supreme moment. Regardless, American newspapers noted her gesture; some even carried pictures of Margaret brushing off Townsend's uniform alongside those of the queen being crowned. The British press kept silent, but only for twelve days. After claiming that rumors Margaret was in love with a divorced man could not possibly be true, the British press began an onslaught of attacks on the twenty-two-year-old princess, saying she was being irresponsible and unmindful of her position.

When Townsend told the queen's private secretary, Sir Alan Lascelles, that he was indeed in love with the princess, Lascelles was appalled. "You must be either mad or bad," he said, and recommended to the queen that Townsend take a distant foreign posting. Instead, the queen, hoping that the furor and the romance would die down, gently removed him from Clarence House, where he had regular contact with the princess, and posted him to her staff at the palace. It is unclear whether the Queen Mother was furious with Margaret for creating such a controversy at the beginning of her sister's reign or deeply in denial, but she remained frostily silent. In the royal family's terminology, Margaret's mother was "ostriching"—avoiding direct confrontation on a difficult subject. A friend of the Queen Mother explained that she "was completely unapproachable and remote. She refused to believe it at all or discuss it with anyone so Princess Margaret could never consult her about it."

At times of crisis, the Queen Mother had previously counted on the guidance of her husband; now, for the first time, she faced a national and family predicament without him. She knew that her late husband would have been tormented, as she was—wanting her daughter to be happy in love and marriage, yet keenly aware of the role of the sovereign as head of the Church of England, which prohibited divorce, and the need to uphold the dignity and reputation of a monarchy still traumatized by Edward VIII's abdication over the very same issue just sixteen years before. One member of the royal household reported that Queen Elizabeth burst into tears while discussing the dilemma—the only time he had ever seen her cry.

Along with the king, the queen had indulged their younger daughter as an *enfant terrible*, unwittingly encouraging a sense of entitlement in Margaret, who was as sexy, talented, and rebellious as a wayward film star, but also restricted by her life and without a major role or public purpose, like many younger siblings of monarchs throughout history. Like her uncle the Duke of Windsor years before, Margaret frequented all the latest London clubs and was the darling of café society. As loyal as she professed to be to the family firm, and whatever her motive, Margaret had tarnished the golden reputation of her newly sovereign sister, whom Winston Churchill had called a "young, gleaming champion."

As he had in 1936, Churchill, for sentimental reasons, initially misjudged the effect the affair would have on the monarchy, claiming that the course of love "must always be allowed to run smooth." Clementine Churchill told her husband, "If you are going to begin the abdication all over again, I'm going to leave [you]." At the height of the uproar, when the newspapers brought interest in the crisis to a fever pitch, Churchill suffered a major stroke affecting his speech and gait. Haunted by the abdication crisis, he and the queen, as head of the Church, quickly decided that the British monarchy needed to support duty over love. Townsend would be exiled to Brussels as an air attaché to the British embassy. Margaret would delay her decision about marriage for two years until she turned twenty-five—old enough to marry without the queen's assent, according to the Royal Marriages Act.

## Southern Rhodesia and London

At the end of June, in the middle of the crisis, the Queen Mother began her new life as a royal ambassador—in the company of her reluctant daughter. The Queen Mother took Margaret on a sixteen-day tour of Southern Rhodesia to celebrate the centenary of the birth of the British tycoon and imperialist Cecil Rhodes. Traveling fifteen hundred miles by car and train, they were greeted by signs saying "Greeting great White Queen and great White Princess." Halfway through the trip, Margaret heard that Townsend would be sent out of England before she returned. She collapsed. Her absence from public events was explained away as due to "Bulawago flu," but it is more likely that, realizing she might never be able to be with the man she loved, she dissolved into fury and tears. Biographer Theo Aronson quotes Lady Hambleden, lady-in-waiting to the Queen Mother, as witnessing the scene: "It was *not* very pleasant."

Even after she turned twenty-five, Parliament had to give approval to a marriage, lest Margaret be required to give up her right of succession and her royal income. When the Townsend controversy had begun, politicians privately had decided she would never be allowed to marry a divorced man and keep her royal prerogatives, but they did not tell her that during the two years she waited for Townsend's return. The Queen Mother may have worked subtly behind the scenes, as was her style, to derail her daughter's chances of making a marriage to Townsend, which would tarnish the crown her husband had worked so hard to brighten for his elder daughter. Townsend returned to Britain in mid-October 1955. The next week at an unveiling of a statue of the late king in Carlton Gardens, the Queen Mother stood beside the queen, who made their joint position clear. "Much was asked of my father in personal sacrifice," the queen declared, "and to the end he never faltered in his duty to his people." Princess Margaret got the message.

A few days later Margaret capitulated. She was too proud of her heritage and too accustomed to wealth and privilege to live happily in a cottage with a husband on a retired air force pilot's salary. She ended the intense speculation by announcing her intention to end her relationship with Townsend: "Mindful of the Church's teaching that Christian marriage is indissoluble, and conscious of my duty to the Commonwealth, I have resolved to put these considerations before all others." It would be another generation before the Queen Mother would accommodate herself to divorce in the royal family, and even then, the trauma of royal divorce would shake the roots of the monarchy.

# 19

# Valiant for Friendship

## February 1954–August 1967

Back of tranquility lies always conquered unhappiness.
—*Eleanor's favorite quote from* A Countryman's Year

Hearing in February 1954 that the Queen Mother would visit the United States in the fall, Eleanor wrote her, saying, "I know of course that you will be the guest of President and Mrs. Eisenhower but I wonder if you would care at some point in your visit to have a very quiet few days in the country. I have only a cottage there now since the government has the big house, but I would love to have you . . . here. I would, of course, be more than glad to arrange a party in New York also if you wanted to go to the theater or do anything of that kind." Receiving no reply, she wrote again in May, passing on a request that the Queen Mother attend a big ball at the Waldorf-Astoria to benefit the therapeutic music programs offered in veterans' hospitals. As FDR had in 1939, she offered a visit to Hyde Park as a respite from a demanding tour: "I am sure from what I hear that every moment of your stay is being planned but perhaps you will want to steal away for a couple nights and if you do, I could promise you rest and seclusion. I would be happy to see you again."

By August, frustrated by a lack of response, she wrote to the British ambassador saying her two letters had not been answered and reiterating her offer. Finally on September 1, the Queen Mother's private secretary wrote to tell her "how enormously the Queen Mother is looking forward to seeing you sometime during her visit." He told her that her friend would be "most distressed to hear of this apparent discourtesy," but that he could not find any trace of her letters. "Her Majesty realizes how exceptionally busy you are," he told her.

Just as Britain had memorialized Franklin Roosevelt six years previously, Americans were now honoring the late king. Former U.S. ambassador to Britain Lewis Douglas, backed by President and Mrs. Eisenhower, raised $433,481 to pay for American technical training of students from the Commonwealth. Invited to return to the United States, the Queen Mother first replied, "Who is going to be interested in the middle-aged widow of a King?" The initial invitation came at the end of her first year of mourning, when she was still having difficulty imagining a role beyond that of queen consort. She was unsure what she could offer Americans, who had such indelible memories of the king, and was reluctant to return alone to a country where she had had such a momentous experience with her husband. In the end, she would use the trip to further define a new role as royal ambassador. Americans would do for her what FDR had done for her late husband: bolster her confidence with timely respect and appreciation.

## New York

Sailing to New York on her namesake liner *Queen Elizabeth*, she was greeted by the applause of her fellow passengers every time she appeared outside her cabin. Her ship's delayed arrival merited first-page coverage in the *New York Times*, and she was greeted with an editorial proclaiming, "Of all the many reasons for welcoming Queen Elizabeth the Queen Mother, the pleasantest is that she is so nice." The *Times* noted that though Americans had long ago given up allegiance to the Crown, "one would be an abnormal human being not to think of a queen with something akin to awe," and noted that her ability to withstand intense scrutiny over three decades was a testament to a remarkable character. Remembering Elizabeth's kindness when, as a lonely widow, she had first arrived in London, Eleanor sent the Queen Mother flowers upon her arrival in New York. Her lady-in-waiting Olivia Mulholland wrote to say that the flowers were "another proof of the friendship which Queen Elizabeth values so highly."

A New York taxi driver who caught sight of the Queen Mother

arriving to see the Broadway musical *The Pajama Game* gave her his tribute: "If she wasn't a Queen there is many a man who'd like to marry her." He added, "She'd be a pleasing handful at playtime." Crowds gave her another form of accolade: she was nearly mobbed by cheering, horn-honking fans, who almost swept over police barricades in their attempt to touch her as she left the Empire State Building.

In New York, she unveiled a painting of her husband, toured forty-four rooms at the Metropolitan Museum of Art and the Cloisters museum, spoke with Vice President Richard Nixon and Senator Joe McCarthy at the British embassy, visited a children's center, and chatted amiably with Eleanor's Russian rival, Andrei Vishinsky, at the United Nations. At the Commonwealth Ball at the Park Avenue Armory, she entered with great pomp through a guard of honor. As a regimental band played "Colonel Bogey," she took her place in the royal box. Showing her common touch, she requested that the band play "Hey There (you with the stars in your eyes)" and "Hernando's Hideaway."

On her 1939 trip to New York City, traveling as a reigning monarch in a motorcade, Elizabeth had only glimpsed Fifth Avenue. This time she wanted to roam through art galleries, department stores, and tourist attractions. Unfortunately, "hunting the Queen Mum" became a New York pastime. At Saks, the manager took her up and down in the elevator in a vain attempt to outwit the crowds appearing at every floor. Eventually the Queen Mother took refuge in a boutique where samples of merchandise were brought to her for her inspection. Saying, "I'm afraid I am buying too much," she picked up jeweled cashmere sweaters for her two daughters, a magnetic bottle opener for Prince Philip, and a game of Scrabble for herself. At FAO Schwartz she chose "very American" toys, including a tea set and chocolate drink mixer for Princess Anne, and a steam shovel for Prince Charles.

As part of Columbia University's bicentennial celebrations—in 1754 King George II had signed the charter inaugurating the college— before eight thousand people at the Cathedral of St. John the Divine, she received the honorary degree of Doctor of Law. In a ceremony that confirmed her new role, she was honored with forty-eight others, among them Adlai Stevenson, UN secretary-general Dag Hammarskjöld, the chief justice of the United States, Earl Warren, and Chancellor Konrad Adenauer of West Germany. When she stepped forward, the last to be honored, to have the blue-lined purple hood draped over her shoulders, the crowd rose to give her an ovation sur-passing the others. Columbia cited her as "a noble queen, whose quiet and constant courage in time of great stress sustained a nation and inspired a world."

The Queen Mother made her return visit to Hyde Park on Tuesday, November 2, a miserably rainy Election Day. She met Eleanor at the FDR Library and went to lay a wreath on the president's grave. At a Val-Kill Cottage luncheon, Eleanor served her an American Thanksgiving dinner with roast turkey, candied sweet potatoes, and all the trimmings. That day, Franklin D. Roosevelt Jr. would lose his bid to become attorney general of New York, failing once again to achieve the kind of office his father had. Eleanor's youngest son John, the only Republican among the Hyde Park Roosevelts, brought not only his wife and three children with him but a whiff of political controversy. Elizabeth's 1939 Top Cottage luncheon companion, former secretary of the Treasury Henry Morgenthau Jr., his wife, and David Gurewitsch were among the other guests.

Eleanor's granddaughter Nina Gibson, who grew up in Val-Kill and often met her grandmother's guests, remembers how casual Eleanor was about these visits and how she would be amused when guests made "a big deal" out of the event—most notably Nikita Khrushchev, who showed up in a caravan of limousines with an entourage of Secret Service agents. As she put it, her grandmother "never primed us that somebody important was coming and we had to be dressed up. You were in bare feet and suddenly there was the Queen of Greece." Her brother Haven, who was fourteen at the time, has only vague recollec-tions of the Queen Mother's time at Val-Kill; he has much stronger memories of the visit of Haile Selassie, emperor of Ethiopia. However, he did recall the Queen Mother as "a heavy set woman dressed in frilly stuff and a large hat—just not my grandmother's style at all." Nina was twelve when the Queen Mother visited. "This time we had to clean up," she said. "There was a casual significance to this visit. The Queen Mother came as somebody very important, but as a friend." When the Queen Mother arrived for lunch, Nina felt shy. She covered over her feelings by trying to make her two-year-old sister Joan "behave herself," and by presenting her to the Queen Mother. "Very sweet and grand-motherly," according to Nina, the Queen Mother "held her hand out to Joan and drew her closer. She brushed her hair way back the way a grandmother would." At the luncheon, she focused on getting to know Eleanor's grandchildren.

Eleanor and Elizabeth were at their most relaxed with each other. No longer queen and First Lady, they were both grandmothers who looked after their extended families and traveled on ambassadorial missions for their countries. Gone were the traumas of nursing their nations through a grueling war and their worn-out husbands through deteriorating health. It seems unfortunate that this cozy visit would be their last extended time together. Due to their busy schedules in future years, they would—as was the royal–Roosevelt predilection—just miss each other.

Photographers took shots of the Queen Mother saying good-bye to Eleanor. After they had taken several photos, Eleanor asked them, "Have you had enough?" "They never seem to have enough," the Queen Mother quipped. After a visit to the Victoria Home for the Aged British Men and Women in Ossining, she capped off a typically full day by returning to New York City to dine with Lewis Douglas and his wife and daughter Sharman at their Park Avenue apartment. Sharman, who had become a close friend of Princess Margaret, had done much to acquaint the royal family with American styles and habits.

The Queen Mother spent the next day at the Waldorf-Astoria. At a luncheon for five hundred, hosted by Mayor and Mrs. Robert Wagner, she was described, to enthusiastic applause, as "one of the most beloved visitors ever to come to our shores." That evening, dressed in a pale gold satin ball gown embroidered in sequins and jewels, a diamond tiara and a ruby and diamond necklace, and the brilliant blue ribbon of the Order of the Garter, the Queen Mother wowed the crowd at the banquet honoring her late husband. As the *World-Telegram* proclaimed, "The royal lady with the peaches-and-cream complexion and twinkling orbs not only drew a record crowd of 2,800 smart-setters to the Waldorf-Astoria Ballroom; she sent them away humming 'God Save The Queen' like a first-night audience whistling the top tunes of the hit show."

Ten thousand individuals had given just short of one-half million dollars (several million in today's currency) to commemorate George VI's contributions to Anglo-American relations. Moved by the obvious admiration for her husband, Queen Elizabeth thanked Americans, saying that understanding between the two countries "is much too precious to be taken for granted. For misunderstandings are like weeds: neglect to tend your garden and they spring up everywhere . . . understanding, by contrast, needs constant fostering."

## Washington, D.C.

After flying to Washington on President Eisenhower's plane, the Queen Mother went straight to the White House. Her Washington visit echoed her previous state visit in many respects. She attended another gold-plated dinner in the State Dining Room, followed by the obligatory musicale, and reprised her visit to Arlington National Cemetery and the Tomb of the Unknown Soldier. This time, though, she was surrounded by Republican Roosevelts. Alice Roosevelt Longworth, Eleanor's old nemesis, greeted her at the White House. It would have been fascinating to overhear that conversation between the acidic and gossipy Alice, who called herself "Washington's only perambulatory monument," and the sweet but steely former queen. Eleanor's son John, who had helped elect President Eisenhower, was also on hand for the White House dinner. Eleanor was not invited. Eisenhower, who had never liked Eleanor's style, had dismissed her from her post at the United Nations with only a perfunctory letter of thanks, and had banned her from the White House because he believed false rumors that she had defamed his wife Mamie.

Elizabeth and Eleanor were not the first U.S. First Lady and British queen to be united in grief. At the Library of Congress, the Queen Mother saw on display a letter Queen Victoria had written in 1865 to Mary Todd Lincoln after the assassination of President Lincoln. Writing in strangely capitalized words and underlining for effect, the queen, who had been widowed four years previously, wrote to Mrs. Lincoln to express "my deep & heartfelt sympathy with you under the circumstances of your present dreadful misfortune." She continued: "No one can better appreciate than I can, who am myself utterly brokenhearted by the loss of my own beloved Husband, who was the Light of My Life—my Star, my All—what your sufferings must be." Some fifty years before Queen Elizabeth's 1939 triumph in the United States, Queen Victoria had won America's affections. After Britain meddled in the American Civil War, relations between the two countries had been tense until the latter part of Queen Victoria's reign, when U.S. respect for her character and appreciation for her strong interest in American life—she sent several of her best paintings to the 1876 centenary of American independence—helped warm up Anglo-American relations, which would then deteriorate in the 1930s, only to be ameliorated again by Queen Elizabeth and King George VI.

The Queen Mother was particularly interested in anything related to her American ancestor, George Washington. On a visit to the United States Naval Academy in Annapolis, she toured the State House, where Washington resigned as commander in chief of the Continental Army in 1783, and examined a painting of a British ship aflame—Maryland's equivalent of the Boston Tea Party. In Richmond she stood before the Houdon statue of George Washington, the only statue of him done from life. Celebrating Veterans Day in a Williamsburg parish church, she asked to sit in George Washington's pew.

Returning to the capital on November 9, the day before she left the United States, the Queen Mother reprised her famous 1939 British embassy garden party with a reception at the embassy for two thousand members of Congress and government. After being presented to Her Majesty, the guests had refreshments in a tent on the lawn. As she was leaving, Senator Joseph McCarthy arrived. So that the Queen Mother would not appear to be rude to a prominent senator, hasty arrangements were made for the Queen Mother to meet America's foremost demagogue, who would be censured by the Senate for his behavior just weeks later.

## Abroad

In the period following their last meeting in 1954, the two First Ladies of the World traveled extensively. The Queen Mother served as a unifying link among the disparate peoples of the British Commonwealth. In the next thirty years she visited Canada nine times, Southern Rhodesia four times (where she had accepted a post as the chancellor of Southern Rhodesia), and Northern Rhodesia, Australia, New Zealand, Fiji, and Uganda twice each, as well as Kenya, the Caribbean islands, Germany, Italy, France, and Turkey. At home she served as the chancellor of the University of London.

While the Queen Mother had a passively symbolic influence as a world figure, Eleanor maintained a direct and political role, debating world leaders and delivering her own speeches. At seventy, showing no signs of slowing down, she stopped in Japan a second time on her way to Bali, Jakarta, Thailand, and Cambodia. Among her many travels to Europe with her grandchildren or with David Gurewitsch and his wife, she toured Israel, visited the Soviet Union twice, and met in Yugoslavia with Marshal Josip Tito, who took her on a nerve-wracking speedboat ride.

New York publisher Dorothy Schiff sent Eleanor to Russia to report on the communist way of life. With David Gurewitsch at her side, she tape-recorded a hard-hitting interview with Russian leader Nikita Khrushchev at his vacation villa on the outskirts of Yalta. Sitting on his front porch, she pressed him for two and a half hours about why the Soviet Union had broken the Yalta agreements, confronted him directly about the treatment of Soviet Jews, and debated who was responsible for the cold war, the arms race, and the escalation of tensions in the Middle East. At times Khrushchev became red-faced with anger, but he never conceded a point. As she was leaving, he asked, "Can I tell our papers that we have had a friendly conversation?" They could call it friendly, she replied, but they must add that they differed.

It is hard to imagine the Queen Mother engaging in this kind of tough debate. Eleanor and Elizabeth had radically different styles of handling conflict; Eleanor's firm and direct style was more traditionally masculine, while Elizabeth's approach was stereotypically feminine. Even though she expressed strong conservative opinions in private, Elizabeth was more likely to work quietly behind the scenes than to force an issue publicly. Elizabeth was steely underneath her rosy exterior, while Eleanor often seemed aggressive on the surface, but only to cover the softest of hearts.

## London

In 1957, Nina Roosevelt accompanied her grandmother to Europe and went to Buckingham Palace for tea with the queen. They missed the Queen Mother, who was in Scotland. The day before, nine-year-old Prince Charles's tonsils and adenoids had been removed. Impressed that the queen entertained her the day after her son's surgery, Eleanor mentioned it in her daily column: "I went into the Queen's study and found her just as calm and composed as if she did not have a very unhappy little boy on her mind. I asked if he felt well enough yet to demand ice cream and she said he had already had two portions, making me feel that he probably was on the mend."

Eleanor saw herself in the young queen. "I have the greatest respect for this young woman who must combine the responsibilities of a Queen with the requirements and emotional stresses of a young mother," she wrote. "I think, too, the British people are fortunate in having the royal family to hold them together."

Nina was struck by the warmth and friendliness of the occasion. "It was just my grandmother, the Queen and me—just three ladies," she recalled. "We had a wonderful time." The queen knew how to make a teenage girl feel special: Her Majesty discovered that Nina loved honey and arranged for the butler to bring her an additional portion. Nina remembers that while sitting together on airplane flights, she and her grandmother would talk about the king and queen. Eleanor always wanted to make sure that Nina understood "how much she appreciated the Queen and Queen Mother as people," not just as public figures.

Eleanor told the queen that her daughter Anna had suggested that she should begin to cut back her schedule. Even at seventy-three, this was extremely difficult for her to do, Eleanor admitted. The queen smiled. "I've got this mother and she is racing all about and I think I should be worrying about her, but you can't stop her," Nina recalled her saying. It was Eleanor's turn to grin.

Age was, however, taking its toll on Eleanor's legendary stamina and alertness. The next year, flying to Kansas City for a day trip, she realized she had no idea why she had agreed to go. Puzzled, she sat politely at dinner until, to her great relief, one of her hosts said how happy the group was that she could come to their first FDR dinner. When she turned seventy-five, she said, "One of the big advantages of being this age is that one can take life calmly and look at things while saying, 'This too will pass.'" Reflecting the triumphant example of her own life, Eleanor often quoted a line from the book *A Countryman's Year*: "Back of tranquility lies always conquered unhappiness." Increasingly wise, she turned her energies to encouraging younger people: "I think perhaps one of the things to be desired in old age is the power to acquire new interests and to meet whatever situation comes with a gallantry which makes people feel that you are conferring a privilege on them when you share a little of your life with them." She could have been speaking for the Queen Mother as well.

For both widows, their grandchildren became a focal point. Elizabeth doted on Prince Charles, the son she never had, while Eleanor kept track of twenty-seven grandchildren (including five who were adopted). On February 19, 1960, Queen Elizabeth became the first reigning British monarch in over one hundred years to give birth to a child, her third, Prince Andrew. The next day Eleanor wrote the Queen Mother, saying she could not "refrain from sending you a line of congratulation on the birth of your new grandson." She added, "Being a grandmother is a particularly delightful role, I think, since one has primarily the pleasure and none of the responsibility of the children!" But while Elizabeth could find refuge in the security of family, even as she worried about her less predictable younger daughter Margaret, Eleanor spent her widowhood figuring out ways to help her children thrive financially, politically, and emotionally.

## New York

Eleanor was closest to her daughter Anna, who continued to have money problems until she entered into a stable marriage with physician James Halstead in 1952. Eleanor's sons encountered difficulties in their careers until middle age. James ran as the Democratic candidate for governor of California in 1950, but lost when President Truman failed to endorse him. He did go on to serve six terms in the U.S. House of Representatives. FDR Jr. failed in his two attempts to follow his father and become governor of New York, but was later named John Kennedy's undersecretary of commerce. Elliott moved to Florida and ultimately published mystery stories, which featured his mother Eleanor as an amateur detective. Only the youngest son, John, found an easy path outside their father's arena, as a businessman and banker.

In September 1961 the Queen Mother's brother and inseparable childhood playmate David died. Remembering the painful loss of her brother Hall, Eleanor sent her "deep sympathy" to Elizabeth. "It seems so young to have been taken, and I know it means a great sorrow for you and the rest of the family," she wrote.

Eleanor's enduring antipathy for Joseph Kennedy became a factor in the 1960 presidential election. She could not forgive his defeatist attitudes and his admiration for the Nazi war machine as Britain fought for its survival. Suspecting that Joe Kennedy was trying to buy the presidential election for his son, Massachusetts senator John F. Kennedy, she feared that as president he would take orders from his father. Senator Kennedy had failed to gain her respect when he did not take a strong stand against Senator Joe McCarthy's Communist witch hunt in the early 1950s. She supported her old liberal standard-bearer Adlai Stevenson, who was not an announced candidate. Watching the Republican Convention on television, she was irked by the clamorous applause her son John received while placing Richard Nixon's name in nomination. "Look at them. How they love to have a Roosevelt introduce a Republican candidate," she snapped.

After Kennedy won the Democratic nomination on the first ballot at the Los Angeles convention, he phoned Eleanor, who was already at the airport, rushing home early. She declined to meet him. Kennedy knew how crucial it would be to win her support, and he courted her until she finally agreed to meet him in August at Val-Kill. To his friend William Walton, Kennedy likened the encounter to the meeting of Napoleon and Czar Alexander in 1807 when Napoleon had used all his powers of persuasion to talk the czar into an agreement, the Treaty of Tilsit, which allowed Napoleon to be the dominant power in Europe. Their summit was nearly canceled when Eleanor's granddaughter Sally (John's daughter) was killed in a fall from her horse. Eleanor insisted they carry on with their meeting, and met Kennedy after staying up almost all night with her son and daughter-in-law.

The former First Lady doubted Kennedy's humility, openness to new ideas, and sincere desire to help people have better lives—all qualities she had in abundance. But he won her over. That fall she campaigned actively for him and against Richard Nixon, whom she loathed. By Election Day, when Kennedy was elected by the narrowest of margins, she was convinced he possessed the three crucial characteristics of a superb president: confidence, an optimistic disposition, and a trust in God. However, at Kennedy's cold and snowy inauguration day, perhaps still angry about the new president's failure to name Stevenson secretary of state, and unwilling to sit with Joe Kennedy, she declined his invitation to watch the inaugural parade from the presidential box.

The royal family appeared to support Richard Nixon during the

1960 campaign. Influenced by her mother's antipathy to Joe Kennedy, and swayed by her great fondness for the late king's wartime friend, President Eisenhower, the queen gave indirect but strong approval to Eisenhower's vice president. On a visit to New York City to open a British exhibition, Prince Philip announced that "the Queen was particularly delighted that our dear friend President Eisenhower agreed to join her as patron for this exhibition." After touring the exhibits with Vice President Nixon, he made a special point of being photographed with him.

## London

In June 1961, the Kennedys stopped in London after a triumphant visit to France, about which the president famously declared, "I am the man who accompanied Jacqueline Kennedy to Paris." Massive crowds in London paid homage to the new First Lady's glamour. Although theirs was not an official visit, the queen bowed to the advice of the prime minister and buried the hatchet with the Kennedys: she entertained them at a dinner party for fifty in Buckingham Palace. Kennedy would be the first U.S. president to dine at the palace since Woodrow Wilson in 1919. There were, however, tense discussions beforehand about whether the queen would allow Mrs. Kennedy's sister and brother-in-law Prince and Princess Radziwill, both previously divorced, to attend the dinner. The queen finally relented. The Kennedys had asked the queen to include Princess Margaret and Princess Marina, Duchess of Kent, whom the president remembered from his father's embassy days, to the dinner party. Mrs. Kennedy joked, "The Queen had her revenge. No Margaret, no Marina, no one except every Commonwealth minister of agriculture they could find." The queen did give the young First Lady advice on how to protect herself from the rigors of official travel, and then took her to the picture gallery to look at a Van Dyck painting of a horse, which she knew the horse-loving and cultured Mrs. Kennedy would appreciate.

## New York

During the previous year, secretary Maureen Corr had noticed that Eleanor would fall asleep during working sessions and that her legendary energy had begun to fade. David Gurewitsch ordered medical tests, which showed that Eleanor suffered from anemia. Treated with steroids, her system weakened and became susceptible to infections; she had to be hospitalized in mid-1962. She developed a rare form of tuberculosis, which she had been exposed to years earlier. Her illness waxed and waned as infections, fevers, and pains came and then disappeared.

A week after she turned seventy-seven, on October 18, 1962, Eleanor insisted on leaving the hospital and returning home to her apartment. Her friend Trude Lash wrote an account of her last weeks:

> There was only anger, helpless anger at the doctors and nurses and the world who tried to keep her alive. . . . She was not afraid of death at all. She welcomed it. She was so weary and infinitely exhausted, it seemed as though she had to suffer every human indignity, every weakness, every failure that she had resisted and conquered so daringly during her whole life. . . . I had never see anyone die this way and it seemed to me like a crucifixion.

Eleanor implored David Gurewitsch not to make heroic efforts to keep her alive. Sitting on the edge of her bed, David whispered in her ear, "We can cure you!" She told him, "David I want to die."[33] And so she did, early in the evening of November 7.

Queen Elizabeth wrote to Eleanor's oldest son, California representative James Roosevelt, "The British people held her in deep respect and affection and mourn her passing. My husband and I and my family greatly valued her friendship and send you and your family our sincere sympathy."

On an overcast and rainy November day, former presidents Truman and Eisenhower, President John F. Kennedy, Vice President Lyndon Johnson, and UN secretary-general U Thant waited while Eleanor's friends, family, and household staff took precedence in the funeral procession into Hyde Park's St. James Episcopal Church. David Gurewitsch, his wife, Edna, and Joe and Trude Lash were among the first mourners, the two men banding together with their wives, even though they had often competed for standing as her closer "adopted son."

At the burial in Hyde Park, many of the twentieth century's most famous men smiled briefly when the sun suddenly broke through the clouds as the ceremony began. Afterward, David Gurewitsch approached Eisenhower and asked, "How could it happen that you did not make use of this lady? We had no better ambassador."[35] The former president walked away without answering. Truman witnessed the incident and told David, "I made use of her. I told her she was First Lady of the World."

In November 1964, Truman wrote to the chairman of the Nobel Prize Committee, recommending they circumvent their rules and award the Peace Prize posthumously to Eleanor. "If she didn't earn it, then no one has," he declared. "It's an award for peace in the world. I hope you'll make it." Eleanor would have been very pleased to know that the 1965 Peace Prize was awarded to the United Nations Children's Fund. Although the committee declined to give her the Nobel Prize she deserved, historians have given her a finer distinction. They agree that she was, in words she had used about her husband, "valiant for friendship," a concept she broadened to include the world.

## Campobello, Maine

Franklin Roosevelt Jr.'s twenty-three-year-old son, Christopher, woke up on the morning of July 13, 1967, at Campobello to nerve-wracking news. Although he had never seen his grandfather's summer cottage at Campobello, he was expected to give a speech welcoming the Queen Mother to the site, and then serve as her guide that day. A heavy fog shrouded Passamaquoddy Bay and the surrounding areas; his father, who had planned to be the official guide, and his uncles, expected to arrive by plane, would not be able to get to Campobello. As the eldest male Roosevelt in attendance, he would oversee the first visit of a member of the British royal family to the Roosevelts in thirteen years, and do it without help from his experienced and better-informed older relations. This was a daunting task for a young man, who later described himself (in a letter written to the Queen Mother's private secretary just days before she died) as "slightly wet behind the ears."

The Queen Mother had last visited Eleanor Roosevelt at Hyde Park in 1954. Now she had been invited by a joint U.S.-Canadian commission to help open a park commemorating her friend Franklin D. Roosevelt. Sailing into the foggy bay on the royal yacht *Britannia*, she had stopped at Campobello on her way to a tour of Canada and was received at the new visitors' center by the governor of Maine, Senators Edmund Muskie and Margaret Chase Smith, as well as the prime minister of New Brunswick and other members of the commission, which had overseen the park's development. Christopher remembered that he managed "with some trepidation to get through my welcoming remarks." The Queen Mother, opening the reception center, said, "In 1939, that beautiful summer overshadowed by the thought of war, the King and I spent a brief and happy time with President and Mrs. Roosevelt at Hyde Park. . . . For each of us memories are personal things, of places and people, of strength and weakness of joy and sorrow. There are few human beings whose service to mankind has been so noble that a whole world—a world indeed of strangers remembers them in a personal sense. Such a man was Franklin Roosevelt."

The Queen Mother went on to speak of the symbolic importance of a park developed by two countries, and, in comments prepared for her, used that day's fog as a metaphor for international misunderstandings: "Here in this corner of the North American Continent there has been established this joint domain—a symbol of the firm and enduring friendship of our nations. We live again in times of strife and passion, and people perhaps tend to forget the simple truth, that we are all brothers one of another, here to serve the world, but not to master it. If we can see through the fog of our differences to that truth, then we may indeed make a better world."

After the Queen Mother spoke, she unveiled a plaque commemorating the opening of the park, the laying of the cornerstone, and the fact of her visit. Two hundred guests, including many local residents of Campobello—including fishermen, schoolteachers, carpenters, and the postmistress—would join the Queen Mother for tea after she visited the cottage. But first, Christopher would have to surmount his embarrassment at being an unprepared tour guide. He nervously took the Queen Mother's arm and directed her toward the cottage. He then "fell on his sword," as he put it later, leaning over and telling her, "I have never been to the cottage before" and "I would hardly be an adequate guide."

"Christopher," the Queen Mother assured him, "isn't that wonderful: we will be discovering this cottage together for the first time." With just the right words, she had put him at ease.

The Queen Mother would live for another thirty-five years after her visit to Campobello. She would survive Eleanor Roosevelt by forty years, Franklin Roosevelt by fifty-seven, and her husband, King George VI, by half a century. When she died, she was the last surviving leader of the generation that saw the Allies through World War II, and the last living spouse of a pair of couples whose friendship helped solidify the friendship of the United States and Britain after the familial breach of the American Revolution.

# Epilogue

# The Lessons of History

## Dutchess County

Toby Roosevelt—Mrs. Franklin D. Roosevelt Jr.—was surprised by a call from the FDR Library one day in May 1997. The British counsel-general's office wanted her to come to Hyde Park on short notice to give Prince Andrew a tour of Springwood and the FDR Library. Prince Andrew, the Duke of York, is the queen's second son and a decorated helicopter pilot, who served with distinction during the 1981 Falklands War. He was working in the diplomacy section of the naval staff at the British Ministry of Defence.

The prince wanted to see the place his grandparents had visited in 1939. It would be the first time since the Queen Mother had Thanksgiving luncheon with Eleanor Roosevelt at Val-Kill Cottage in 1954 that a member of the British royal family would return to the site of the famous picnic that had reinvigorated the ties between Britain and the United States.

On May 19, the thirty-seven-year-old prince arrived in a motor-cade with aides and officials from the British counsel-general's office. Escorting him through Springwood, Toby was struck by his youth and ease of manner. She showed him FDR's screened-in porch—which FDR called "the buggery" because there were flies everywhere. Taking him to a second-floor fire escape that afforded the best view of the Hudson River, she explained that they had recently cut down trees to restore the vista as it had been in the 1930s. Five years later, when

Prince Andrew returned to Hyde Park, he remembered that view and told Toby he had been inspired to cut down overgrown trees at Royal Lodge, the country estate he had inherited from his grandmother.

The prince promised Toby that he would return one day to help raise money for the presidential library. He later told the FDR Library he would make his second visit to Hyde Park only after being assured that his grandmother and grandfather's 1939 visit would be treated as a world historical event that advanced the relationship between the two countries.

## Hyde Park

Prince Andrew returned to Hyde Park on September 24, 2002, for a benefit gala called "An Evening on the Hudson" to raise funds for new furniture at Top Cottage and for a temporary-exhibit gallery in the Roosevelt Library. Arriving at the FDR home and library in a helicopter, he emerged as the Poughkeepsie Boys Choir sang the British and U.S. national anthems, and was greeted by Sara Olsen, the superintendent of the Roosevelt National Historic Park; Chris Breiseth, the president of the Eleanor and Franklin Roosevelt Institute; and Cynthia Koch, the director of the FDR Library. The prince mingled with the public at a tent set up on the front lawn of the library, playfully telling a group of schoolchildren that they should be home doing their homework. But as was true for his grandparents at this same site and throughout their public careers, there was in him what Koch called "always close to the surface a privacy that needed to be maintained."

Eighty-nine-year-old Harry Johannesen, whose mother had been the Roosevelts' cook and who provided the hot dogs for the 1939 picnic, presented Prince Andrew with a photograph he had taken of his grandparents at that event. When the prince realized Harry was using the same camera with which he had photographed the king and queen in 1939, he asked to have his picture taken with it. After a whispered "hot dog conversation," as the prince called it, he posed while Johannesen took his picture and called out laughingly to the crowd, "This is going to be one hell of an historic picture." The encounter with the prince "kind of spirited me up a bit," Johannesen said.

Koch escorted the prince to the rose garden where Eleanor and Franklin are buried. Standing with Prince Andrew in front of the

Roosevelts' graves, Cynthia was reminded of the recent funeral and burial of the prince's grandmother. Queen Elizabeth, the Queen Mother, had died the previous March at the age of 101, almost seventy-nine years after she had married Prince Albert, the Duke of York, and embarked on a public career that lasted more than three-quarters of a century, during which she was witness to, and participated in, dramatic changes in the shape of the world and the role of the royal family. During the war, Hitler was reported to have paid Queen Elizabeth the ultimate tribute: he had called her "the most dangerous woman in Europe." The Queen Mother's final resting place was within St. George's Chapel in Windsor in a vault beside her husband in the small King George VI Memorial Chapel, which had been dedicated in the presence of the Queen Mother after the late king's body had been moved there in 1969. In March 2002, when Lord Chamberlain broke his wand over his knees and placed it over her coffin in a traditional ceremony, it symbolized not only the completion of his job, but also the end of the work of these four great wartime leaders.

Inside the FDR Library, as the prince toured a special exhibit of letters, photographs, and film footage of his grandparents' historic visit, he was both relaxed and reverent. He showed great curiosity about some of the items on display—he was fascinated to hear that the presidential yacht, on which his grandparents had ridden, had been sold to a private individual—and curious to know who stood beside FDR in a photograph of the royal couple standing with the Roosevelts outside St. James Church (it was the president's son James). He pored over a list of the newspapers provided to the king and queen during their 1939 visit. When he signed the guest book for the second time, he was told that former president Bill Clinton was a three-time signer. The prince replied that he would have to come back and sign a third time, then. Many of the guests noted that he seemed "very jolly," in the words of Harry Johannesen, but also to have depth and maturity.

The prince was the guest of honor at a benefit dinner for 235 guests, set up in a big white tent on the lawn overlooking the Hudson at sunset. After opening remarks by William vanden Heuvel, cochair of the Franklin and Eleanor Roosevelt Institute, and historian Arthur Schlesinger Jr., the two men unveiled a commemorative plaque, arranged by this author in conjunction with the Queen Mother's private secretary Sir Alistair Aird, displaying the Queen Mother's recollections of her visit to Hyde Park and the historic hot dog picnic. This plaque has since been placed at Top Cottage in her memory.

Then Prince Andrew addressed guests, who included former New York governor Hugh Carey, former New Jersey governor Tom Kean, the arts activist and actress Kitty Carlisle Hart, and the evening's organizers, Toby Roosevelt and Vera Fairbanks. Vera's husband, Douglas Fairbanks Jr., had helped arrange the 1939 visit. Speaking a year after September 11 and calling the fund-raising event "particularly important in the year my grandmother died and symbolic to come again at this uncertain time," the Duke of York saluted the singular relationship between the royal family and the Roosevelts. He said he admired the statesmanship of Franklin Roosevelt, who engineered the 1939 visit of the king and queen "through a great deal of subterfuge and underhanded planning."

The prince reminded the guests that the visit "changed the tone of . . . relations . . . served as a prelude to the close Anglo-American relationship of World War II . . . and lay the psychological foundation for more immediate results like the Lend Lease program." The king and queen's trip to the United States "helped to draw a line under a difficult time," he said. He told the guests that before her death, he had spoken to his Granny, who, at the end of her long life, still remembered the views of the Hudson from Hyde Park. When she and the king had left Hyde Park, there "was not a dry eye in Dutchess County that night," he said. The prince added that "we are living in times of stress and difficulty, but we must always remember the lessons of history. History to a nation is as memory is to a person."

As the prince was speaking, he was temporarily drowned out by the loud, whirring sound of a helicopter. Soon it was directly overhead. He pointed to it as "the sound of modern freedom," and added, "What really is funny is that I used to drive those things. Inside they're quite quiet." As soon as he finished speaking, he rushed off to the helicopter waiting behind some trees several hundred yards from the tent. After lifting off, its whirling red and white lights were visible for a brief time before it disappeared, heading south along the Hudson.

During his visit, the prince followed in the tradition of his late grandparents and their friends, the Roosevelts, blending charm and duty to further foster British-American relations at a perilous time, when the alliance between the two countries was more necessary than it had been in many years. Their story gives fresh vigor to the concept of duty, which is too often perceived today as an obsolete virtue. In their vibrant, extended, intimate, and difficult journey of friendship, all four of them met Eleanor's criteria for the purpose of life: "the full development of whatever we have in us."

It was a friendship that helped save democracy.

# Notes

In writing *The Roosevelts and the Royals*, I have drawn upon many excellent biographies of the British royal family and the Roosevelts. I am particularly indebted to Sarah Bradford for her superb *Reluctant King*, which was extremely helpful in covering every aspect of King George VI's life, including his relationship with the United States and the Roosevelts, and to Doris Kearns Goodwin for her masterful *No Ordinary Time*, which was crucial to understanding Eleanor and Franklin's relationship and their role during World War II. John Wheeler-Bennett's official biography of King George VI was a key reference on the royal family and on their relationship with the Roosevelts. Theo Aronson's *Royal Family at War* gave a detailed and fascinating portrait of King George VI and Queen Elizabeth's role during the war. Blanche Wiesen Cook's extraordinary two-volume biography of Eleanor Roosevelt and Linda Donn's beautifully written *The Roosevelt Cousins* made it possible for me to offer a thorough picture of Eleanor and Franklin's early years and their marriage. Joseph Lash's many books on Eleanor Roosevelt, most particularly his *Eleanor and Franklin*, were indispensable. Kati Marton's impressive portrait of the Roosevelt marriage in *Hidden Power* was fresh and penetrating. Edna Gurewitsch's *Kindred Souls* brought Eleanor to life in her later years. Anthony Holden's *The Queen Mother: A 90th Birthday Tribute* offered lively details and important quotations. I have relied on Fred Leventhal's article "Essential Democracy" in *Singular Continuities* for covering the buildup to the royal visit and its aftermath in chapters six and eight. Nicholas Cull's *Selling War* helped me portray the British propaganda campaign in chapter eleven.

## Abbreviations Used in Source Notes

### Books

| | |
|---|---|
| BWC | Blanche Wiesen Cook, *Eleanor Roosevelt, Vol. 1 and Vol. 2* |
| BTT | Geoffrey Ward, *Before the Trumpet* |
| CC | Geoffrey Ward, *Closest Companion* |
| EF | Joseph Lash, *Eleanor and Franklin* |
| EOG | David Duff, *Elizabeth of Glamis* |
| EWY | Rodger Streitmatter, *Empty without You* |
| HP | Kati Marton, *Hidden Power* |
| LE | Joseph Lash, *Love, Eleanor* |
| MD | Eleanor Roosevelt, *My Day: The Best of Eleanor Roosevelt's Acclaimed Newspaper Columns, 1936–1962* |
| NOT | Doris Kearns Goodwin, *No Ordinary Time* |
| QE | Anthony Holden, *The Queen Mother* |

RC       Linda Donn, *The Roosevelt Cousins*
RFAW     Theo Aronson, *Royal Family at War*
RK       Sarah Bradford, *The Reluctant King*
SW       Susan Williams, *The People's King: The True Story of the Abdication*
TQM      Elizabeth Longford, *The Queen Mother*
WB       John Wheeler-Bennett, *King George VI*

### Articles

ED       Fred Leventhal, "Essential Democracy" in *Singular Continuities*
GCG      Philip Catelon, "Greetin' Cousin George" in *American Heritage*

### Newspapers

NYT      *New York Times*
WP       *Washington Post*
LT       London *Times*

### People

ER       Eleanor Roosevelt
FDR      Franklin Delano Roosevelt
QE       Queen Elizabeth
KG       King George VI

### Libraries

FDRL     Franklin Roosevelt Library
RA       Royal Archives, Windsor Castle
PRO      Public Record Office, England

## Prologue: A Picnic Savored around the World

2   *"sink her . . . wait for consequences."* WB, p. 391.

3   *"How do you eat . . . all gone."* Arthur Schlesinger speech, Vertical File, George VI, Anniversary of Royal Picnic, 1989.
    *"overhand delivery . . . with gusto."* NYT, June 12, 1939.
    *"Sir, may we smoke?"* CC, p. 132.
    *"King Eats Hot Dog, Asks for More."* NYT, June 13, 1939.
    *"kindness and courtesy . . . American gentlefolk."* Interview with the Queen Mother on the author's behalf, by Sir Alastair Aird, Dec. 2001.

## Chapter 1: Eleanor and Franklin

5   *"You could not find . . . Father."* HP, p. 49.

6   *"a Delano, not a Roosevelt at all."* EF, p. 113.
    *"Her mouth and teeth seem to have no future."* Collier and Horowitz, *The Roosevelts: An American Saga*, p. 20.
    *"I shall never be able to hold him . . . too attractive."* Ibid.
    *"the ugly duckling may turn into a swan."* Ibid.
    *"very much in love with Eleanor when he married her."* RC, p. 102.
    *"E is an angel."* HP, p. 48.

7   *"had a deep and abiding interest . . . and everyone."* RC, p. 104.
    *"No other success in life . . . true woman."* BWC, vol. 1, p. 164.
    *"Darling Franklin . . . house is."* Ibid., p. 160.

8  *"you would invite to the dance, but not the dinner."* Ibid., p. 165.
   *"all the honors and pleasures . . . by its restrictions."* Brough, *Princess Alice,* p. 142.
9  *"tulle veils . . . tipped with silver."* NYT, Mar. 18, 1905.
   *"had more claim to good looks than any of the Roosevelts."* BWC, vol. 1, p. 164.
10 *"Well, Franklin . . . in the family."* Collier and Horowitz, *The Roosevelts: An American Saga,* p. 23.
   *"Father always wanted to be the bride . . . at every funeral."* BWC, vol. 1, p. 167.
   *"Baby went to his first party yesterday . . . hold him."* Ward, *Before the Trumpet,* p. 113.
   *"Oh, for freedom."* RC, p. 32.
   *"We never tried to influence him . . . shape his life."* Angelo, *First Mothers,* p. 7.
11 *"I always felt entirely out of things . . . sadly wrong."* Ward, *Before the Trumpet,* p. 180.
   *"the greatest disappointment of my life."* Ibid., p. 236.
12 *"the spontaneous joy or mirth of youth."* NOT, p. 91.
   *"You have no looks . . . have manners."* HP, p. 48.
   *"I was always disgracing my mother."* BWC, vol. 1, p. 70.
13 *"I learned to stare down each of my fears . . . on to the next."* ER, *You Learn by Living,* p. 25.
   *"I think I must have a good deal of my uncle . . . enjoy a good fight."* ER, *This Is My Story,* p. 428.
   *"the greatest knack . . . the women in New York."* Alsop, *FDR: A Centenary Remembrance,* p. 40.
   *"perfect quality of her soul . . . full of sympathy."* BWC, vol. 1, p. 110.
14 *"Of what was inside him . . . Father talked to no one."* HP, p. 71.
   *"an ordeal to be borne."* Angelo, *First Mothers,* p. 23.
   *"never had any interest in dolls . . . or feeding a baby."* ER, *This Is My Story,* p. 142.
   *"I was your real mother . . . bore you."* BWC, vol. 1, p. 179.
   *"would appear, day or night."* Ibid, p. 183.
   *"I'll have to ask my mother."* Ibid, p. 184.
15 *"I can still remember . . . name to an age."* William Turner Levy, *The Extraordinary Mrs. R,* p. 103.
   *"The kings have been fairly scrambling . . . conversation."* RC, p. 123.
16 *"He was fascinated by kings . . . royalty."* Elliott Roosevelt, *A Rendezvous with Destiny,* p. 148.
   *"a charming man, came to see me . . . satisfactory."* Rose, *King George V,* p. 345.
   *"delightfully easy."* Ward, *Before the Trumpet,* p. 392.
17 *"That ain't the half of it . . . Von Hindenberg."* Ibid.
   *"nice smile . . . . a German gentleman."* Davis, *FDR: The Beckoning of Destiny,* pp. 519–510.

## Chapter 2: Bertie and Elizabeth

18 *"Bertie has more guts . . . sons combined."* Airlie, *Thatched with Gold,* p. 202.
19 *"Now that you are five . . . made me much happier."* WB, p. 18.
20 *"My principle contribution . . . steel into him."* Ibid., p. 131.
   *"I was hunted . . . all the time."* Ibid., p. 64.
   *"rough channel crossing."* Ibid., p. 17.
21 *"I was sitting . . . didn't try the experience again."* Ibid., pp. 95–96.
   *"When I was on top . . . every possible way to the enemy."* Ibid., p. 97.

"*In the back of a taxi? How quaint!*" Seward, *The Last Great Edwardian Lady*, p. 10.
"*fun, kindness, and a marvelous sense of security.*" RK, p. 99.
22 "*knitting . . . in the lining of sleeping bags.*" Morrow, *Without Equal*, p. 16.
"*You would see . . . spaniel Peter at her side.*" Grania Forbes, *My Darling Buffy*, p. 77.
"*in a big house . . . head is tied up in a cloth.*" Ibid., p. 88.
23 "*a perfect brick . . . a veritable heroine.*" Ibid., pp. 82–84.
"*very exciting.*" RK, p. 76.
24 "*Who is that bug . . . Where is his crown?*" Edith Wilson, *My Memoir*, p. 196.
"*Excuse me . . . Put it there!*" Ibid.
25 "*gay and witty companion.*" Bloch, *The Secret File of the Duke of Windsor*, p. 173.
"*got in with the milkman.*" Rose, *King George V*, p. 345.
"*drowned the sound of brass . . . cheer him frenziedly.*" Donaldson, *Edward VIII*, p. 87.
26 "*I know that you have behaved . . . in any way tarnish it.*" WB, p. 140.

## Chapter 3: A Radical Partnership

27 "*He might have been happier . . . other people.*" ER, *This I Remember*, p. 279.
28 "*It is probably the sense of being really needed . . . greatest bond.*" LE, p. 74.
29 "*I can either be President . . . attend to Alice.*" RC, p. 77.
"*Franklin deserved a good time . . . married to Eleanor.*" Alsop, *FDR: A Centenary of Remembrance*, p. 216.
"*The bottom dropped out . . . for the first time.*" NOT, p. 19.
"*Unless you can swear . . . I know it does now.*" LE, p. 41.
"*Why me? I am plain . . . 'happiness' really meant.*" FF, p. 13.
30 "*viewed his family dispassionately . . . incapable of emotion.*" LE, p. 70.
"*After that father and mother . . . his embrace.*" Ibid., p. 72.
"*All of my self-confidence is gone . . . on edge.*" Ibid., p. 73.
"*gave him the strength and courage . . . persistence.*" BWC, vol. 1, p. 313.
32 "*I did not want my husband . . . life of my own.*" BWC, vol. 1, p. 458.
33 "*I remember . . . lips.*" BWC, p. 479.
34 "*I've never known a man who gave one . . . to solve.*" Marton, *Hidden Power*, p. 70.
35 "*It was just a great big house . . . be in.*" Ibid., p. 66.
36 "*I ache to hold you close.*" LE, p. 137.
"*With her queenly bearing . . . white hair.*" Angelo, *First Mothers*, p. 33.
"*anyone was her social equal . . . sure about that.*" Ibid., p. 35.
37 "*amused by some of the strange ways . . . letters a day.*" Elliott Roosevelt, *FDR: His Personal Letters 1928–1945*, vol. 3, pt. 1, pp. 370–371.
"*I gave the King your message . . . as you do.*" Ward, *A First-Class Temperament*, p. 782.
"*I'm afraid I wasn't born to be a high life lady.*" LE, p. 47.
"*Mama . . . love it.*" EWY, p. 117.

## Chapter 4: The Happy Yorks

38 "*She drew him out . . . lean on him.*" QE, p. 54.
"*Who was that lovely girl . . . Introduce me to her.*" Seward, *The Last Great Edwardian Lady*, p. 43.
39 "*radiant vitality . . . irresistible.*" QE, p. 26.
40 "*heavy with atmosphere . . . lugubrious.*" Rhodes James, *Chips: The Diaries of Sir Henry Channon*, p. 397.

"*You will be a lucky fellow if she accepts you.*" WB, p. 150.

"*I like him so much . . . made or marred by his wife.*" QE, p. 29.

41 "*more than ever convinced . . . love affairs.*" RK, p. 102.

"*deeply in love . . . as the King's daughter-in-law.*" Airlie, *Thatched with Gold,* p. 202.

"*It is delightful here . . . the more I like her.*" WB, p. 148.

"*The Queen had let her feelings . . . away for awhile.*" Seward, *The Last Great Edwardian Lady,* p. 52.

"*exile to Siberia.*" Ibid., p. 53.

42 "*I must say I dread . . . and always have.*" Duff, *Mother of the Queen,* p. 50.

"*You are not late, my dear . . . two minutes too early.*" QE, p. 48.

"*The better I know . . . fell in love with her here.*" WB, p. 151.

"*really worried . . . torn.*" TQM, p. 23.

"*It's the third time . . . the last.*" RK, p. 106.

43 "*At the bottom of the garden . . . a big oak.*" EOG, p. 18.

"*If you are going to keep it up . . . say yes now.*" Seward, p. 56.

"*My dream has at last been realized.*" Bradford, *Elizabeth R.,* p. 24.

"*There is not a man in England . . . in gloom.*" QE, p. 31.

"*Now look at me . . . have to ask twice?*" Christina Banks and Sue Leonard (Eds.), *Queen Elizabeth, The Queen Mother,* p. 29.

44 "*You have received from Him . . . it will be noble.*" WB, p. 153.

"*It was my duty . . . afterwards.*" QE, p. 30.

"*a princely marriage . . . rivets mankind.*" WB, p. 132.

45 "*we have come to regard . . . head of morality.*" Ibid.

"*Only those . . . different from others.*" RK, p. 29.

"*I do hope . . . than I usually am.*" WB, p. 208.

"*Bertie got through his speech . . . long pauses.*" Ibid.

46 "*The disillusionment . . . in the body.*" Ibid., p. 212.

"*a slim, quiet man . . . set the sign.*" Ibid., p. 213.

"*The baby was so sweet . . . broke me up.*" Hugh Massingbred, *The Daily Telegraph Book of the Queen Mother: Woman of the Century,* p. 31.

47 "*almost everywhere . . . do his job better.*" QE, p. 50.

"*she shines . . . like sunlight.*" WB, p. 219.

"*I've done with it for good and all.*" Ibid.

"*whole continent . . . in love with her.*" Editors Christina Banks and Sue Leonard, *Queen Elizabeth, The Queen Mother,* p. 40.

48 "*Every hour . . . real trouble.*" Christopher Warwick, *King George VI & Queen Elizabeth,* p. 68.

"*the Foreman.*" Aronson, *The Royal Family,* p. 97.

## Chapter 5: Rocking the World

50 "*That boy will ruin himself within twelve months.*" Aronson, *The Royal Family,* p. 97.

51 "*intimate friends.*" EWY, p. 122.

"*going to have a stroke . . . all purple.*" Lorena Hickok, *Eleanor Roosevelt: Reluctant First Lady,* p. 166.

52 "*Franklin said I would never . . . expected of me.*" EWY, p. 143.

53 "*achieve territorial revision.*" BWC, vol. 2, p. 263.

"*My calm has returned . . . that way.*" Ibid., p. 259.

"*I know I've got to stick . . . how I feel.*" Ibid.

"*lively, refreshing spirit.*" EOG, p. 150.

"*You make family life such fun.*" Ibid.

"*tended to be withdrawn . . . life I relished.*" The Duke of Windsor, *A King's Story*, p. 258.

54 "*I pray to God . . . and the throne.*" RK, p. 151.

55 "*Unlike his own children . . . funny too!*" TQM, p. 29.

"*No, one can't be sorry . . . beyond the barrier.*" BWC, vol. 2, p. 341.

"*Christ! What's going to happen next . . . of the new reign.*" RK, p. 155.

56 "*I left with the distinct impression . . . American interest.*" QM, p. 69.

"*these tartans must go.*" RK, p. 172.

"*I came to dine with the King.*" Ibid.

57 "*For me the question is . . . worthy of her.*" The Duke of Windsor, *A King's Story*, p. 334.

"*Because she is an adventuress!*" Ibid., p. 220.

"*economic royalists . . . rendezvous with destiny.*" BWC, vol. 2, p. 370.

58 "*for the good of the country . . . I have been leading.*" EWY, p. 187.

"*a skin as tough as a rhinoceros hide.*" BWC, vol. 2, p. 372.

"*Gee! I wish I could even be excited . . . I hate myself.*" EWY, p. 188.

"*Alice is good at that sort of thing.*" EF, p. 377.

"*We didn't elect her . . . horning in for?*" Ibid., p. 445.

59 "*No man who has brought himself . . . mollycoddle philosophy.*" Ibid., p. 446.

"*Never before in all our history . . . met their master.*" Ibid., p. 449.

"*Loads and loads of love . . . Devotedly F.*" BWC, vol. 2, p. 398.

"*I confess that the arrangements . . . live thro' it.*" EWY, pp. 201–202.

"*Darling, if he wanted to be King . . . fight for him.*" BWC, vol. 2, p. 389.

60 "*Bertie was so taken aback . . . innermost feelings.*" RK, p. 186.

"*Oh, he said, that's a dreadful thing . . . least of all.*" Ibid., p. 180.

"*like the proverbial sheep . . . . slaughter.*" WB, pp. 283–284.

"*surprised and horrified.*" Ibid, p. 284.

"*No, I will come and see you at once.*" Ibid., p. 285.

61 "*The awful and ghastly suspense . . . that he would go.*" RK, p. 108.

"*Isn't he wonderful? . . . soul of the party.*" Ibid., p. 196.

"*broke down and sobbed like a child.*" WB, p. 286.

"*the one person it did not touch.*" RK, p. 196.

"*dreadful . . . never-to-be forgotten.*" WB, p. 287.

"*He has one matchless blessing . . . wife and children.*" Zeigler, *King Edward VIII*, p. 331.

"*We were so very unhappy . . . lost the common touch.*" SW, p. 255.

"*You did not seem . . . a lesser sacrifice.*" RK, p. 179.

"*the King's wife runs the King . . . runs his wife.*" Ibid., p. 246.

62 "*Don't be weak . . . on the throne.*" Ibid., p. 240.

"*crumble under the shock . . . of the Abdication.*" WB, p. 300.

63 "*Do I or do I not propose . . . diplomatic protocol.*" LE, p. 243.

"*never any one person's happiness . . . of people.*" BWC, vol. 2, p. 260.

"*Well, and so . . . his love too!*" Ibid., p. 403.

"*Poor little King . . . very bad times.*" Ibid.

"*I can hardly now believe . . . many good friends.*" Howarth, *George VI*, p. 66.

64 *"Dickie, this is absolutely terrible . . . I know about."* WB, pp. 293–294.
*"there is no finer training for a King."* Ibid., p. 294.
*"time will be allowed me . . . what has happened."* Ibid., p. 300.
*"With my wife and helpmeet . . . lies before me."* Ibid., p. 288.
*"For a few terrible seconds . . . the words out."* RK, p. 216.
*"When his people listen to him . . . to him who speaks."* WB, p. 310.
65 *"The actual ceremony . . . were losing theirs."* RK, p. 213.
*"sinking feeling inside."* Ibid.
*"nearly put the hilt of my sword . . . in my belt."* WB, p. 313.
*"When this great moment . . . words of the Oath."* RK, pp. 213–214.
*"I was brought up . . . nearly fell down."* WB, p. 313.
66 *"Some One Else was with him."* RK, p. 212.
*"gained greatly in presence . . . of the inner man."* Ibid., p. 217.
*"I cannot find words . . . that I should choose."* Howarth, *George VI*, p. 67.
67 *"very nearly killed poor Queen Mary . . . nearly collapsed."* RK, p. 276.
*"was pleased to declare . . . the title."* Ibid., p. 244.
*"Now we must protect WE."* Ibid., p. 241.
68 *"There is a lovely story going about . . . the Middle Ages!"* Ibid., p. 128.
*"like the medieval monarch . . . suspicion."* Ibid., p. 254.
*"It is as if . . . haunted by him."* TQM, p. 68.
*"unmitigated horror."* Howarth, *George VI*, p. 75.

## Chapter 6: Joining Forces

70 *"We may not like pomp and ceremony . . . about royalty."* MD, June 7, 1939, Speech and Article File, ER papers, FDRL.
*"The nearest I ever got . . . back again."* Rose, *King George V*, p. 344.
71 *77 percent of respondents . . . or war materials.* Gallup polls, Mar. and Apr. 1939.
72 *"I hold that East and West . . . that move America."* ED, p. 163.
*"I have had . . . the great privilege . . . the Queen."* RA PS/GVI/PS 03400/003/01/001. President Roosevelt to King George VI, Sept. 17, 1938.
*"The Prince Gets In With the Milkman."* Rose, *King George V*, p. 345.
74 *"appealed to Roosevelt's weakness . . . counterparts."* Beschloss, *Kennedy & Roosevelt*, p. 153.
74-75 *"Would you mind taking your pants down . . . most bowlegged . . . Joe."* Collier and Horowitz, *The Kennedys: An American Dream*, p. 80.
75 *"a great joke, the greatest joke in the world."* Smith (Ed.), *Hostage to Fortune*, p. 223.
*"America's nine-child envoy."* Beschloss, *Kennedy & Roosevelt*, p. 159.
76 *"one of the most fabulous, fascinating events . . . East Boston."* Rose Kennedy, *Times to Remember*, p. 221.
*"What the American people fear . . . same way myself."* Goodwin, *The Fitzgeralds and the Kennedys: An American Saga*, p. 526.
*"But if we had the United States . . . dictators."* Ibid.
*"Fired by an idea . . . photographs."* Ibid., p. 526.
*"You could charm them . . . me."* Ibid., p. 526.
77 *"I only know three Americans . . . know more."* Beschloss, *Kennedy & Roosevelt*, p. 187.
Chamberlain and . . . Kennedy seemed an unlikely pair. Goodwin, *The Fitzgeralds and the Kennedys*, p. 528.
*"I pressed it with the persistence of a horse-leech."* WB, p. 372.

78 *"I need not assure you . . . United States."* RA PS/GVI/PS 03400/003/01/001. President Roosevelt to King George VI, Sept. 17, 1938.

*"It occurs to me . . . relaxation."* Ibid.

79 *"There would probably be great pressure . . . play with them!"* Ibid.

*"Believing that we all might soon . . . deep bond."* ER, *This I Remember,* pp. 183–184.

80 *"peace with honor . . . unmitigated defeat."* Davis, *The Kennedys: Dynasty and Disasters, 1848–1983,* p. 80.

81 *"came as a pleasant relief . . . preservation of peace."* RA PS/GVI/PS 03400/003/01/004. King George VI to President Roosevelt, Oct. 8, 1938.

*"deeply touched . . . a dummy . . . glorified errand boy."* Beschloss, *Kennedy & Roosevelt,* p. 188.

*"all the disagreeable traits of rich men . . . their virtues."* Davis, *The Kennedys: Dynasty and Disasters, 1848–1983,* p. 7.

*"At a time when we should be sending the best . . . United States."* Ibid.

82 *The visit of the king and queen placed fifth.* Gallup poll, Dec. 1939.

83 *"The democratic hope . . . of the intellectuals."* Arthur Schlesinger speech, Vertical File, George VI, Anniversary of Royal Picnic, 1989.

*"He wanted to make contacts . . . conflict came."* ER, *This I Remember,* p. 183.

84 *"We drove them around . . . they left."* LE, p. 265.

*"Lord it must be awful to be royalty . . . so many?"* Ibid.

*"to the American people . . . most excellent effect."* Letter FDR to KG, Nov. 2, 1938, PSF: Diplomatic Correspondence: Great Britain: King and Queen, FDRL.

*"I am one of the few English people . . . stay there."* PRO FO 371/22799/232. Lady Reading to Halifax, February 16, 1939.

*"New York ought to be made secondary to Washington . . . to New York."* ED, p. 168.

85 *"I think that Lindsay should not call Washington . . . at Hyde Park."* Ibid., p. 177.

*"not in the least bit insistent on it."* Ibid.

*"rather vulgarized . . . reigning monarchs."* Ibid, p. 167.

*"narrow crowded streets."* RA PS/GVI/PS 03400/003/01/015. President Roosevelt to George VI, November 2, 1938.

*"whatever you wish except an honorary degree . . . not speak."* Benjamin Rhodes, "The British Royal Visit of 1939 and the Psychological Approach to the United States," p. 203.

*Roosevelt was reluctant to dine at the embassy.* ED, p. 171.

86 *"cast him aside . . . like an old boot."* WB, p. 375.

87 *"We may not like pomp . . . looked up to."* MD, p. 102.

88 *"I hadn't the faintest idea . . . operetta."* James Roosevelt, *Affectionately FDR,* p. 321.

*"Dear Pa: It's a little larger . . . beds are no longer . . . uproariously."* Ibid., p. 320.

89 *"beef and mashed potatoes."* Ben Robertson, "King George Strives To Please," *Saturday Evening Post,* Feb. 4, 1939, pp. 65–69.

*"will be the difference between success . . . does not help Elizabeth."* Josef Israels II, "Selling George VI to the U.S.," *Scribner's* magazine, Feb. 1939, pp. 16–21.

## Chapter 7: A Genius for Publicity

91 *"There must be no more . . . could not be done."* WB, p. 393.

*"Norwegians . . . One is over."* LE, p. 265.

*"had left the door open an inch."* NOT, p. 150.

92  *"They are nice . . . how bored they must be."* LE, p. 265.
"*worked like a dog over the picnic.*" Ibid.
"*a day tomorrow . . . are over.*" Ibid.
"*are all nice . . . liking them.*" Ibid.

93  "*a little weep.*" Smith (Ed.), *Hostage to Fortune*, p. 333.
"*I hate leaving here . . . it is.*" WB, p. 376.
"*to wave, not to cry.*" EOG, p. 206.

94  "*For three & a half . . . the same date!*" WB, pp. 377–388.
"*brotherly love . . . not at fever heat.*" Morgan, *FDR*, p. 510.

95  "*Bertie had behaved . . . little woman.*" PSF, Bullitt, FDRL.
"*Last Sunday . . . rest nowadays!*" WB, p. 378.
"*Reception to King . . . Quebec Rites.*" NYT, May–June 1939.

96  "*royal torture.*" *Life* magazine, May 1939.
"*Canadian crowds . . . sadly.*" *Time* magazine, May 29, 1939.

97  "*lingering, fatherly patting.*" Ibid.
"*anticipation too great . . . side by side.*" Ibid.

98  "*she has a perfect genius . . . marvelous.*" WB, p. 380.
"*It is just that life . . . evolved.*" Aronson, *The Royal Family*, p. 148.

99  "*Cecile departed . . . buttons.*" *Time* magazine, May 29, 1939.

100  *By one estimate, . . . between the two world wars.* Gallup poll, January 1937.

101  *57 percent of the American people . . . to allow the sale of munitions to Britain and France.* Gallup poll, April 1939.

103  "*I'm from Boston . . . tea, wasn't it?*" RK, p. 290.
"*What a wonderful mixture . . . humor.*" Ibid., p. 289.
"*Words cannot begin . . . particular.*" Buchan Papers, Tweedsmuir to Baldwin, June 19, 1939.

104  "*in the character of a student.*" Brooke-Shepard, *Uncle of Europe*, p. 32.
"*Come back . . . President.*" Ibid., p. 34.
"*a short . . . rippling muscles.*" Philip Magnus, *King Edward the Seventh*, p. 36.
*the King . . . happiest around war veterans.* WP, June 8, 1939.

106  "*I may someday be . . . unfortunately they arrived too late . . . failure . . . United States.*" Letters to the Roosevelts, FDR, PPOF, OF 48-a, Great Britain: Visit of the King and Queen, 1938–1942, FDRL.

107  "*The little Queen . . . frightened boy.*" Memorandum, Ambassador Bullitt to FDR, May 9, 1939, PSF, Diplomatic Correspondence: France: Bullitt, William C., Jan.–June 1939, FDRL.
"*I've been housekeeping . . . visit.*" LE, p. 267.
"*Gee I will be glad . . . here and gone.*" Ibid.

## Chapter 8: Conquering Washington

108  "*The British sovereigns . . . have expected.*" RK, pp. 298–299.
"*the most opulent royal caravan.*" WP, June 7, 1939.

109  *attempt on the life of the Duchess of Kent.* NYT, June 6, 1939.
"*simply thrilling.*" WP, June 5, 1939.

110  *a majority of Americans . . . to come live in the United States.* Gallup poll, June 1937.
"*caused more heartburns . . . in this country.*" *Life* magazine, May 1939.

*"some are taken and some are not."* GCG, p. 11.

111 *"royal visitors ever have . . . burden than a joy."* MD, vol. 2, p. 121.
*thirty-four page research document.* Vade Mecum 1939, RK, p. 296.

112 *"subtly strengthen."* WP, June 8, 1939.
*"safeguard against tyranny."* NYT, June 8, 1939.
*"is notice . . . see eye to eye."* The Washington Star, June 8, 1939.

113 *"young, fit and earnest."* RK, p. 292.
*"perfect Queen . . . it was regal."* Time magazine, June 19, 1939.
*"perhaps the most important . . . of modern times."* EOG, p. 219.
*"Well, at last I greet you . . . to see you."* WP, June 9, 1939.
*"It is, indeed, a pleasure . . . to be here."* Ibid.
*"Roosevelt was almost suffocating . . . suit of armor."* GCG, p. 9.

114 *"In the course of a long life . . . the White House."* WB, p. 383.
*"She had the most gracious manner . . . them personally."* ER, *The Autobiography of Eleanor Roosevelt*, p. 188.
*"That's the Queen . . . mows 'em down."* NYT, June 9, 1939.
*"Hiya, King . . . a great queen picker."* WB, p. 384.
*The queen's seat had a special spring installed.* This I Remember, p. 191.

115 *"they are such a charming and united family."* WB, p. 390.
*"I saw in the paper . . . their grievances."* ER, *The Autobiography of Eleanor Roosevelt*, p. 202.

116 *"You see . . . I stopped the rain for you . . . turn off the heat?"* Vera Bloom, "Royal Close-ups" in *Katharine Graham's Washington*, p. 411.
*"whimsical, homespun."* GCG, p. 11.
*"Finder's Keepers."* Time magazine, June 19, 1939.
*"a lot of uninteresting . . . people."* GCG, p. 11.

117 *"I am the queen's maid . . . big shot, hey?"* ER, *The Autobiography of Eleanor Roosevelt*, p. 203.
*"an almost life-sized . . . not very good."* Ibid., p. 191.
*"If that man ever again utters . . . throat."* Ibid.
*"plain foods plainly prepared."* Whitcomb and Whitcomb, *Real Life at the White House*, p. 305.

117-118 *"the worst I have ever eaten . . . justice to the automat."* Ibid., p. 304.

118 *The queen had never been in a hotter place.* Smith (Ed.), *Hostage to Fortune*, p. 350.
*"looked like pigmies."* Ickes, *The Secret Diaries of Harold L. Ickes*, vol. 2, p. 650.
*terrapin.* Smith (Ed.), *Hostage to Fortune*, p. 302.
*"Why I believe that you have a more democratic . . . hangs on."* Ickes, *The Secret Diaries of Harold L. Ickes*, vol. 2, p. 646.

119 *"as if in a semi-embrace . . . visiting Elk."* Ibid.
*"I am persuaded . . . the one against the other."* WP, June 9, 1939.
*"If we have had our moments of anxiety . . . world of peace."* Ibid.
*"nothing, but 'nerve-wracking noises'"* Vera Bloom, "Royal Close-ups" in *Katharine Graham's Washington*, p. 411.
*"nearly swooned away . . . flushed and slightly swollen with sunburn."* Davis, *Into the Storm*, p. 448.

120 *"one of our greatest singers."* GCG, p. 108.

*"a type one would expect to hear . . . performance."* EF, p. 580.

*"dozed off . . . raised the roof."* GCG, p. 108.

121 *"an insult to the British . . . entertainment."* ED, p. 174.

*"Negro spirituals . . . divine."* LE, p. 167.

*"He is very nice . . . quiet conversation."* Ibid.

*"they are very, very delightful people."* *Time* magazine, June 19, 1939.

121-122 *"These sovereigns . . . liberty."* MD, June 10, 1939, Speech and Article File, ER Papers, FDRL.

122 *"the Queen reminds me of Queen Victoria!"* LE, p. 267.

*"I was fascinated by the Queen . . . all the time."* ER, *This I Remember*, p. 191.

*"The heat is oppressive . . . reading wedged in."* LE, p. 267.

*"a keen sense . . . it is interesting to find . . . desperation."* MD, June 9, 1939, Speech and Article File, ER Papers, FRDL.

123 *"present for King George."* WP, June 10, 1939.

*"get used to these fancy affairs."* Ibid.

*"British propaganda to entangle us with them."* Ibid.

*"The British are coming!"* GCG, p. 6.

*"Cousin George . . . debt as cancelled."* GCG, p. 108.

"Vôtre Majesties." Ibid.

124 *"It is just that her loveliness . . . of a mun."* WP, June 10, 1939.

*"one of the loveliest places . . . ever seen."* EOG, p. 221.

125 *"If they expect me to go . . . will go."* RK, p. 293.

126 *"Oh, Daddy, I have seen the Fairy Queen."* ER, *The Autobiography of Eleanor Roosevelt*, p. 195.

*"Three cheers . . . the Queen."* Vera Bloom, "Royal Close-ups" in *Katharine Graham's Washington*, p. 407.

126-127 *"brittle sophistication . . . femininity."* Ibid., p. 410.

127 *"group after group . . . The King.'"* Ibid., p. 414.

*"climax of climaxes."* Ibid., p. 407.

*"This day is also over . . . in training."* LE, p. 268.

## Chapter 9: Hot Dog Diplomacy

128 *"Oh, dear . . . be imperiled."* EF, pp. 579–580.

*"Oh my God! How I hate . . . scream."* RFAW, p. 99.

130 *"When do we eat?"* GCG, p. 109.

131 *"King and Queen did not fall for Grover."* LE, p. 268.

132 *"My responsibility in Hyde Park . . . their own fireside."* MD, June 7, 1939, Speech and Article File, ER Papers, FDRL.

*"coming away for a quiet weekend . . . old Ford."* EOG, p. 223.

132-133 *"they came of . . . Edith Wharton."* WB, p. 385.

133 *"Now Franklin . . . cocktails?"* Ibid., p. 387.

*"My husband . . . in readiness."* ER, *This I Remember*, p. 206.

133-134 *"Granny, naturally . . . royalty visited."* Elliott Roosevelt, *A Rendezvous with Destiny*, p. 149.

134 *"Kings are never late . . . time."* GCG, p. 110.

135 *"My mother does not approve . . . prefer a cocktail."* WB, p. 387.

*"I cannot be a party . . . Monarchy."* RK, p. 295.

136 *"I hope none of my dishes . . . broken."* WB, p. 387.

  *"Sir, may we smoke?"* CC, p. 132.

  *"hurtled into space . . . second base."* GCG, p. 110.

  *"That's number 2 . . . next?"* CC, p. 132.

  *"If my butler had been used . . . happened."* EF, p. 581.

  *"The King and Queen sat here."* Levy, *The Extraordinary Mrs. R.,* p. 168.

137 *"He is so easy to get to know . . . a talker."* WB, p. 388.

  *"Young man, it's time for you to go to bed."* WB, p. 389.

  *"Why don't my Ministers . . . tonight?"* Ibid.

  *"I feel exactly as though . . . wise advice."* Ibid.

138 *"We talked of the firm . . . they will want more later."* Ibid., pp. 391–392.

  *"At last we have heard you tell a funny story!"* Smith (Ed.), *Hostage to Fortune,* p. 343.

139 *"he walked with great difficulty . . . aisle."* CC, p. 130.

  *"the service is* exactly *the same . . . how natural?"* WB, p. 389.

140 *"The nations represented . . . every Sunday."* Elliott Roosevelt (Ed.), *FDR: His Personal Letters, 1928–1945,* vol. 3, pt. 2, p. 380.

141 *"President Roosevelt drove us . . . to the picnic."* Black, *Franklin Delano Roosevelt: Champion of Freedom,* p. 524.

  *"There is a hill . . . go to it."* CC, p. 18.

  *"our hill."* Ibid., p. 35.

  the *"start of a voyage."* Ibid., p. 34.

142 *"both hands must be on the wheel."* Ibid., p. 66.

  *"experienced in gardening . . . qualifications in mind."* CC, p. 61.

  *"this begging trip . . . Queen."* Letters to Mrs. Roosevelt, FDR, Papers as President, Official File 48-a, Miscellaneous: Visit of the King and Queen, 1938–1942, FDRL.

  *"Must you feed . . . a lady."* Ibid.

142-143 *"great sorrow . . . Christian nation."* Ibid.

143 *"outstanding distributors . . . served to Their Majesties."* Ibid.

  *"they are the best."* Author interview with Harry Johannesen.

144 *"It's all so silly."* NYT, June 12, 1989.

  *"standing around . . . in the press."* Ibid.

145 *"boring . . . not very good."* EF, p. 581.

  *"would know better."* CC, p. 61.

  *"about in a little brown gingham dress . . . family party."* EF, p. 581.

  *"a thing with vestigial remnants . . . Edward VII."* James Roosevelt, *My Parents,* p. 322.

  *"The wails of anguish . . . heart-rending."* Ibid.

146 *"if you are a Queen, you cannot risk . . . disheveled."* *The Autobiography of Eleanor Roosevelt,* p. 207.

  *"the beauty of its woods . . . Hudson River."* Vertical File, George VI, Anniversary of Royal Picnic, 1989, FDRL.

  *"Mr. President . . . may we smoke?"* CC, p. 132.

146-147 *"lovely . . . sustaining . . . The picnic was* great *fun . . . Hot-Dogs!"* Letter QE to ER, June 11, 1940, FDRL, PSF, Diplomatic Correspondence, Great Britain, King and Queen, July 1939–1942.

147 *"the people who were gathered . . . heavy heart."* *The Autobiography of Eleanor Roosevelt,* p. 207.

*"vibrant tenor voice . . . in the world."* Davis, *Into the Storm*, p. 449.

*"FDR was satisfied & all went well . . . friends."* LE, p. 269.

*"a gift for friendship."* WP, June 10, 1939.

148 *"They themselves were nice . . . in time!"* LE, p. 268.

*"He says the king . . . can't be true."* CC, p. 131.

*"on the other hand . . . a fine person."* Ibid.

*"living so like English people . . . country house."* WB, p. 390.

*"our time in America was an idyllic experience."* Letter, Queen Mother greetings to participants, Vertical File, George VI, Anniversary of Royal Picnic, 1989, FDRL.

*"true American gentlefolk."* Interview with Queen Mother on author's behalf by Sir Alastair Aird.

*"a source of strength and comfort . . . after our visit."* Letter, Queen Mother greetings to participants, Vertical File, George VI, Anniversary of Royal Picnic, 1989, FDRL.

*"he had never met a person . . . enjoyed more."* WB, p. 390.

149 *"I cannot allow you . . . American people."* NYT, June 12, 1939.

*"heartfelt thanks . . . memories of kindly feeling . . . treasure."* Ibid.

*Everyone unanimous in their praise . . . to cooperate."* Smith (Ed.), *Hostage to Fortune*, pp. 341–342.

150 *"The American people . . . nation again."* Leventhal, *Anglo-American Attitudes*, p. 219.

*"was to overcome Yankee republican ambivalence . . . domestic responsibilities."* ED, p. 174.

*"a beginning of the coming . . . after the war."* Meacham, *Franklin and Winston*, p. 152.

*"nothing fraught with so great significance . . . race."* In Arthur Schlesinger speech, Vertical File, George VI, Anniversary of Royal Picnic, 1989, FDRL.

151 *"Americans today feel closer . . . strengthened."* Lindsay to Halifax, June 20, 1939, FO 414/276/A4443.

*"although I doubt that there will be any relaxation . . . foreign affairs."* Ickes, *The Secret Diaries of Harold L. Ickes*, vol. 11, p. 650.

*"might give Hitler and Mussolini food for thought."* LE, p. 269.

## Chapter 10: "Our Hearts Are Near Breaking"

152 *"When we think . . . pride and joy are uppermost."* Letter, QE to ER, June 11, 1940, PSF, Diplomatic Correspondence, Great Britain, K&Q, 1939–1942, FDRL.

*"a potent force . . . among mankind . . . liberty and justice."* WB, pp. 393–394.

153 *"received a spiritual shock."* EF, p. 584.

154 *"It is all so senseless . . . danger."* EWY, pp. 217–218.

*"We are called . . . we shall prevail."* David Duff, *George & Elizabeth*, p. 168.

*"It is the end . . . of everything."* Michael Beschloss, *Kennedy & Roosevelt*, p. 190.

*"friendly . . . not very pleasant interview."* RK, p. 434.

155 *"I said to the man . . . safer than a known way."* David Duff, *George & Elizabeth*, p. 172.

*"the vast majority of the people . . . so hard to be."* QM, pp. 101–103.

*"a bad day . . . except me."* Ibid., p. 104.

156 *"The U.S. is not coming in . . . make them."* WB, p. 436.

*"a serious dearth . . . and misery."* Ibid., p. 507.

*"Last June seems years distant . . . effect on this country."* Letter, FDR to KG, May 1, 1940, PSF, Diplomatic Correspondence, Great Britain K&Q, 1939–1942, FDRL.

*"warm sympathy . . . must be yours."* Letter, ER to QE, May 1, 1940, PSF, Diplomatic Correspondence, Great Britain K&Q, 1939–1942, FDRL.

156-157 *"Sometimes one's heart . . . a far better world."* Letter, QE to ER, June 11, 1940, PSF, Diplomatic Correspondence, Great Britain K&Q, 1939–1942, FDRL.

157 *"there is only one person . . . Winston as P.M."* WB, p. 446.

158 *"We will extend to the opponents . . . full speed ahead."* NOT, p. 68.

159 *"the St. Helena of 1940."* RK, p. 436.
    *"the delightful days . . . to a successful conclusion."* David Duff, *George & Elizabeth*, p. 177.
    *"The King was told everything . . . as well."* RFAW, p. 104.

160 *"the president's girlfriend."* NOT, p. 153.
    *"There was always a Martha . . . for every breath."* Ibid., p. 154.

161 *"old fashioned muddle . . . fell . . . under his spell . . . such a matriarch."* Princess Alice, *For My Grandchildren*, p. 254.
    *"I shall not go down like the others . . . all the good in the world."* TQM, p. 107.
    *"They will not leave me . . . the King will never leave."* Ibid.

162 *"German paratroopers . . . right now."* QM, p. 106.
    *"If the poor people . . . best clothes."* RFAW, p. 49.
    *"Ain't she just bloody lovely."* QM, p. 107.
    *"We all feel a warmth . . . recharged."* RFAW, p. 51.
    *"Many an aching heart . . . gracious smile."* QM, p. 107.

163 *"We heard an aircraft . . . not to become 'dugout-minded.'"* WB, p. 469.
    *"I am glad we have been bombed . . . in the face."* Ibid., p. 470.

164 *"I think it is odd . . . occasion soon."* Collection of the author.
    *"I am a tired and weary man."* EF, p. 618.
    *"This is no ordinary time . . . country as a whole."* EWY, p. 230.

165 *"Always be on time . . . as you're not needed."* EF, p. 612.
    *"Ah, Joe . . . hear your voice . . . I'm dying to talk to you."* Michael Beschloss, *Kennedy & Roosevelt*, p. 215.

167 *"After all, I have a great stake . . . hostages to fortune."* Edward Renehan Jr., *The Kennedys at War*, p. 173.
    *"Democracy is all finished . . . here."* Ibid., p. 175.
    *"Then you drive him around . . . dreadful four hours of my life."* Ibid.

## Chapter 11: The Propaganda Campaign

167 *"Despite the constant & murderous . . . to win through."* WB, pp. 516–517.

167-168 *"in the way of acceleration . . . we can spare."* WB, p. 517.
    "After what they did to me . . . a lone woman!" RFAW, p. 39.

168 *"I think we are fated . . . open his mouth."* Michael Bloch, *The Secret File of the Duke of Windsor*, p. 181.

169 *"He never missed a chance . . . our former monarch."* Ibid., p. 183.
    *"Your father . . . deep conviction."* Bloch, *The Duke of Windsor's War*, p. 174.
    *"most dignified and no harm . . . that I am aware."* Higham, *The Duchess of Windsor: The Secret Life*, p. 317.

170 *"At times like these . . . between 1 and 3 A.M."* EF, p. 634.
    *"had more respect . . . 'little Windsor.'"* Conrad Black, *Franklin Delano Roosevelt: Champion of Freedom*, p. 744.
    *excelled at hiding his real feelings.* Author interview with Curtis Roosevelt.
    *"very robust on war . . . in the Bahamas."* Ziegler, *King Edward VIII*, p. 461.

*"crumbling lighthouse . . . fleets to harbor."* NOT, p. 212.

170-171 *"The one thing that counted . . . the British people."* RK, p. 441.

171 *"If ever two people realized . . . these two."* RFAW, p. 78.

*"Put your confidence in us . . . finish the job."* NOT, p. 213.

*"No man can tame a tiger . . . arsenal of democracy."* Ibid., p. 195.

*"After so many years of anxiety . . . betterment of the world."* David Duff, *George & Elizabeth*, p. 180.

172-173 *"led public opinion . . . remarkable spirit . . . write back to me in a personal way."* Letter, KG to FDR, June 3, 1941, PSF, Diplomatic Correspondence, GB folder, FDRL.

173 *"Oh, so he's got it . . . never had any acknowledgement yet."* RK, p. 337.

*"was really incapable of personal friendship with anyone."* NOT, p. 306.

*"Each imagines he is indispensable . . . fulfill a purpose of his."* Ibid., p. 204.

174 *"how glad I am . . . in pursuit of our common goal."* WB, p. 527.

*"I wish you could have been with us . . . I hope you will see a movie of it."* David Duff, *George & Elizabeth*, p. 180.

*"Here in Britain our women are working . . . we fight in a great cause."* LT, Aug. 11, 1941.

*"really perfect in every way."* WB, p. 530.

175 *"charming . . . endless conversations . . . what you had told me."* RA/GVI/PRIV/ 01/08/14. Letter, Duke of Kent to King George VI, Aug. 30, 1941.

*"most unnerving performance . . . will tell you when I see you."* Ibid.

*"an endless day . . . I went to Baltimore . . . what it was all about."* Ibid.

175-176 *"The gratitude of the British people . . . in your country."* Christopher Warwick, *George and Marina*, pp. 121–122.

176 *"I think what impresses me . . . constant flow of aid from this country."* Ibid.

*"one and only . . . peace of mind."* NOT, p. 271.

177 *"shut himself off from the world . . . present post."* Ibid., p. 272.

*"I think Franklin will forget . . . only pleasant things."* EF, p. 642.

*"a very vital person . . . jealousy . . . where her own were concerned."* MD, September 7, 1941, Speech and Article File, ER Papers, FDRL.

*"It is dreadful . . . feel no deep affection or sense of loss."* EF, p. 643.

*"Mother went to father . . . and father knew that."* James Roosevelt, *My Parents*, p. 113.

*"most sincere sympathy in your great sorrow."* Telegram, Duke of Kent to FDR, Sept. 7, 1941, PPF, 7710, FDRL.

*"heartfelt sympathy . . . remarkable mother."* Telegram, Earl of Athlone to FDR, Sept. 7, 1941, PPF, 7710, FDRL.

178 *"Father struggled to her side . . . could not break."* James Roosevelt, *My Parents*, p. 113.

*"If I feel depressed, I go to work . . . for depression."* Purcell and Purcell, *Critical Lives: Eleanor Roosevelt*, p. 185.

*"shoot on sight . . . the rattlesnakes of the Atlantic."* NOT, p. 278.

179 *"Public opinion is distinctly better . . . than is the Congress."* WB, p. 531.

*"I am a bit worried over the Japanese situation . . . force his hand."* Ibid.

179-180 *"more serene . . . long time . . . steadying to know that the die was cast."* NOT, p. 289.

180 *"We know what we have to face . . . ready to face it."* EF, p. 643.

*"a bomb shell arrived . . . news."* WB, p. 532.

*"We are all in the same boat now."* NOT, p. 290.

*"My thoughts and prayers . . . common enemy."* WB, p. 533.

*"It had not occurred to him . . . press conference."* MD, Dec. 22, 1941, Speech and Article File, ER Papers, FDRL.

181  *"Mother would just fume . . . Churchill would sit there."* NOT, p. 303.

*"I cannot help reflecting . . . a lesson . . . the world will never forget?"* NYT, Dec. 27, 1941.

## Chapter 12: Hitting Close to Home

182  *"From Berlin . . . to the Marines."* NOT, p. 321.

182-183  *"Perhaps it is good for us . . . days go by."* MD, Feb. 16, 1942, Speech and Article File, ER Papers, FDRL.

183  *"Shipping is our one great obstacle . . . to be with us."* Letter, KG to FDR, Mar. 11, 1942, PSF, GB folder, FDRL.

184  *"A little of my heart . . . Joe."* NOT, p. 337.

*"I could have kissed the telegram . . . from you."* Ibid., p. 338.

184–185  *"talked and talked . . . comparable renown."* Bloch, *The Duke of Windsor's War,* p. 266.

185  *"We should be especially pleased . . . Independence Day."* Warwick, *George and Marina,* p. 123.

*"I am much thrilled . . . going is good."* Ibid.

*"Tell the King . . . godfather myself."* Ibid.

*"most personable . . . Allied operations."* NOT, p. 349.

186  *"We were all left in silence . . . had been killed."* RK, p. 345.

*"immediately sensed catastrophe . . . It's George, isn't it?"* Warwick, *George and Marina,* p. 128.

187  *"was so stunned . . . could not believe it."* Pope, *Queen Mary,* p. 608.

*"It really is a tragedy . . . miss him terribly."* Howarth, *George VI,* p. 141.

*"I have attended very many . . . breaking down."* Ibid.

*"Active Service."* RFAW, p. 93.

*"We had such a good time . . . affection for him."* WB, p. 547.

188  *"united as never before . . . practices."* NOT, pp. 372–373.

*"I think he was really asking . . . all aspects."* EF, p. 658.

189  *"my entire time . . . over there."* EF, p. 658.

*"I confide . . . hit it off beautifully."* NOT, p. 379.

## Chapter 13: Eleanor in England

190  *"Mrs. Roosevelt has done more . . . these islands."* LE, p. 668.

*"Mrs. Roosevelt Breaks . . . Traditions."* NYT, Oct. 25, 1942.

190–191  *"I can never get used . . . the part."* EOG, p. 181.

191  *"I quaked over this visit."* Asbell, *Mother and Daughter,* p. 151.

*"I had been worried . . . not worry."* ER, *This I Remember,* p. 239.

*"I hope you left . . . in good health."* LT, Oct. 24, 1942.

*"I wish much . . . official reports."* WB, p. 550.

*"We welcome you . . . greatest pleasure."* LT, Oct. 24, 1942.

192  *"I have never seen . . . one moment."* NOT, p. 380.

*"Buckingham Palace . . . electric heater."* WB, p. 550.

*"as though I had dropped off . . . homelike environment."* MD, p. 71.

192-193  *"quite serious . . . questions."* EF, p. 660.

193 *"She is about the same age . . . not so pretty."* Asbell, *Mother and Daughter*, p. 151.
*"doing an extraordinarily . . . to duty."* ER, *Autobiography*, p. 240.
*"like two boys playing soldier."* Stafford, *Roosevelt and Churchill*, p. 127.
*"Churchill wasn't very fond . . . at heart."* NOT, p. 312.
*"Sometimes I think . . . three times."* RK, p. 349.

194 *"He looks well . . . I fear."* Asbell, *Mother and Daughter*, p. 151.
*"You come to everything . . . badly needed."* LT, Oct. 25, 1942.

195 *"He died that England might live."* LT, Oct. 25, 1942.
*"That she should . . . arranged for her."* WB, p. 551.
*"Hi, Eleanor . . . Mrs. Roosevelt."* NYT, Oct. 26, 1942.

196 *"Saw a lot of boys . . . quite ordinary!"* EF, p. 662.
*"I don't want you to lose . . . change now."* Ibid., p. 664.

197 *"just looked like all babies."* ER, *This I Remember*, p. 242.
*"One feels that she . . . political organizations."* EF, p. 664.
*"I thought you would like to know . . . success."* Ibid., p. 665.
*"Mrs. Roosevelt has been winning . . . here yourself."* Churchill and Roosevelt Correspondence, vol. 1, p. 655.

198 *"Hustle, did you say . . . at the knees."* EF, p. 661.
*"lack of repose . . . animation."* Vickers, *Cecil Beaton: The Authorized Biography*, p. 268.
*"He has matured . . . I think."* NOT, p. 383.
*"She greeted me warmly . . . never since lost."* EF, p. 665.

199 *"The hullabaloo . . . importance."* NOT, p. 382.

200 *"furnished grandly . . . given the high sign."* EF, p. 666.
*"Mrs. R and I . . . Miss Thompson."* RFAW, p. 150.
*"I recognized her thoughtfulness . . . our family."* ER, *This I Remember*, p. 270.
*"I am Queen Mary . . . show me."* Ibid., pp. 270–271.

201 *"fully dressed . . . off a tree."* EF, p. 666.

202 *"Thank God! . . . We are fighting back."* Miller, *The Roosevelt Chronicles*, p. 490.
*"now we are fighting . . . for old Hitler."* MD, Nov. 9, 1942; Speech and Article File, ER Papers, FDRL.
*"Darling, I was never so humiliated . . . have thought!"* ER, *This I Remember*, p. 276.

203 *"I think Franklin . . . columns."* EF, p. 668.

204 *"a sense of cold . . . we did wish you would."* RA, PS/GVI/PS 06093.
*"of a personality . . . Statue of Liberty itself."* EF, p. 659.
*"You certainly have left . . . behind you."* Ibid., p. 668.

205 *"ever since George's death . . . eventualities."* WB, p. 558.
*"We shall be in a bad way . . . present prospect."* WB, p. 557.
*"I am always with so many people . . . alone inside."* LE, p. 418.

206 *"To the person who makes it . . . carry on."* Roseman, *Working with Roosevelt*, p. 364.

## Chapter 14: A Perfect Team

235 *"OVERLORD is backed . . . will not fail."* RK, p. 358.
*"the enemies of civilization . . . renew friendships."* WB, pp. 558–559.

236 *"I wish much . . . all you did for her."* WB, p. 559.
Hitler had planned to use Windsor Castle. RFAW, p. 119.

237 *"having been brought . . . the war."* Author conversation with Hugo Vickers.

*"a rather lugubrious man . . . giggles, then I did."* RFAW, p. 119..

237-238  *"He feels so much not being more in the fighting line."* Ibid., p. 129.

238  *"I have had a few anxious hours . . . telephone."* WB, p. 568.

*"buoyant and friendly with General Ike."* RK, p. 353.

*"brought a lump . . . constant bombing."* RK, p. 356.

240  *"delightful guests when we were . . . as they say."* Princess Alice, *For My Grandchildren*, p. 267.

*"grow and improve . . . correct them."* MD, pp. 82–83.

*"no one was more genuinely free . . . bigotry."* Wise, *The Challenging Years: The Autobiography of Stephen Wise*, p. 232.

241  *"a sort of precursor . . . quietly died."* Purcell, *Critical Lives: Eleanor Roosevelt*, p. 205.

*"I know the way it feels . . . heart failure."* MD, p. 81.

242  *"I can't judge . . . or not."* NOT, p. 462.

*"I wish I had not come . . . to see me."* Lash, *World of Love*, p. 60.

*"She took New Zealand by storm."* NOT, p. 463.

*"She did a magnificent job . . . home for him?"* EF, p. 685.

*"When the war is over . . . worthwhile."* Lash, *World of Love*, p. 71.

243  *"She alone had accomplished more . . . my area."* EF, p. 691.

*"No, but she will tire everybody else . . . fix up for her."* NOT, p. 466.

244  *"a complete fiasco."* NOT, p. 479.

246  *"The carriage of the head . . . Queen Victoria had."* Bradford, *Elizabeth*, p. 98.

*"Everyone serves except me."* TQM, p. 115.

*"Last night we had sparking plugs . . . never forget."* EOG, p. 190.

246–247  *"I don't think I need to emphasize . . . help and guidance."* RK, p. 359.

247  *"This added to my anxieties . . . very cramped."* WB, p. 607.

*"I feel as if a sword . . . end the war."* NOT, p. 506.

*"You are about to embark . . . full victory."* Ibid., p. 509.

248  *"All excitement is drained away."* MD, p. 91.

*"We have come to the hour . . . were born."* NOT, p. 510.

*"It was a terrible decision . . . in a hurry."* Ibid., p. 517.

249  "There is something very inhuman . . . manner." WB, p. 610.

*"The Queen went round . . . consoled them."* Morrow, *Without Equal*, p. 112.

*"Queen Elizabeth was . . . into legend."* Hamilton, *The Times. The Queen Mother*, p. 87.

250  "He liked the simple life . . . all of us." RK, p. 364.

## Chapter 15: Death before Victory

251  *"I like to be where things are growing."* NOT, p. 597.

252  *"Well, of course, I don't resent . . . same dog since."* NOT, p. 548.

*"gay, almost hilarious atmosphere . . . mortifying and frightful."* Soames, *Clementine Churchill*, p. 472.

253  *"He had grown very thin . . . very tired."* Bloch, *The Duke of Windsor's War*, p. 343.

*"really entered old age."* ER, *This I Remember*, p. 336.

*"Who has bags under his eyes now?"* Aronson, *Royal Family: Years of Transition*, p. 157.

254  *"In some ways, this last year . . . stronger than evil."* Letter, QE to John Winant, Dec. 26, 1944, Royal Family, H.M. The King, John Winant Papers, FDRL.

*"I was not too comfortable . . . about it."* NOT, p. 571.

255 *"I noticed that the President . . . on the ebb."* NYT, Apr. 18, 1945.

256 *"make your long promised . . . those days."* WB, p. 619.

   *"for your many kindnesses . . . far apart."* Faber, *The Life of Lorena Hickok*, p. 300.

   *"full red-carpet, head-of-state treatment."* RFAW, p. 184.

257 *"A few years ago . . . from the United States."* Toast to the Earl of Athlone and Princess Alice, Mar. 23, 1945, FDR, Master Speech File, FDRL.

   *"If Churchill insists . . . king."* RK, p. 375.

   *"the most extraordinarily interesting woman."* NOT, p. 568.

258 *"The only limit to our realization . . . faith."* Miller, *The Roosevelt Chronicles*, p. 509.

259 *"He looked at me . . . collapsed."* NOT, p. 602.

   *"quick start."* Ibid., p. 603.

   *"I got into the car . . . spoken."* ER, *This I Remember*, p. 276.

   *"He did his job . . . to do."* NYT, April 13, 1945.

260 *"Leave the Hill quietly . . . White House."* Bishop, *FDR's Last Year*, p. 546.

   *"Harry, the President is dead . . . trouble now."* Ibid., p. 547.

   *"Though this was a terrible blow . . . fortitude."* ER, *This I Remember*, p. 276.

   *Laura . . . had been jealous . . . took revenge.* NOT, p. 611.

   *"a deep and unshakeable . . . between them."* James Roosevelt, *Affectionately FDR*, p. 313.

   *"At a time like that . . . façade."* NOT, pp. 611–612.

261 *"I decided to accept the fact . . . stresses."* EF, p. 722.

   *"I felt as if I had been struck . . . loss."* Churchill, *The Second World War*, vol. VI, p. 412.

   *"We were very shocked . . . it cannot be."* WB, p. 620.

   *"I cannot tell you how sad . . . overwhelming."* Howarth, *George VI*, p. 175.

261–262 *"I lay in my berth . . . the night."* EF, p. 723.

262 *"It seemed that everyone . . . own sons."* ER, *This I Remember*, p. 277.

263 *"The Queen and I are deeply grieved . . . your family."* Cable, KG and QE to ER, Apr. 13, 1945, ER papers, Special Condolence Correspondence, FDRL.

   *"It is a comfort . . . my husband."* Letter, ER to KG, Apr. 20, 1945, Special Condolence Correspondence, ER papers, FDRL.

   *"humble but no less sincere . . . at that precise moment."* Letter and copy of speech, Duke of Windsor to ER, May 21, 1945, Special Condolence Correspondence, ER papers, FDRL.

264 *We pray through our cooperation . . . of the world."* NYT, Apr. 18, 1945.

   *"The Star Spangled Banner . . . fell on his face."* Edwards, *Royal Sisters*, pp. 142–143.

264–265 *"the greatest champion of freedom . . . never lost faith in Britain."* NYT, Apr. 13, 1945.

265 *"I know you really cared."* Letter, John Winant to KG, Apr. 20, 1945, Royal Family, H.M. The King, John Winant Papers, FDRL.

## Chapter 16: Starting Over

266 *"You must do the thing you think you cannot do."* ER, *You Learn by Living*, p. 30.

   *"The story is over."* Lash, *Eleanor Alone*, p. 15.

266–267 *"It was almost as though . . . myself."* Neal (Ed.), *Eleanor and Harry*, p. 21.

267 *"in order to be useful . . . right."* Ibid., p. 18.

   *"Perhaps in his wisdom . . . given rest."* MD, p. 99.

   *"any personal sorrow . . . humanity."* Ibid.

*"it is still difficult to believe . . . trip."* Neal (Ed.), *Eleanor and Harry*, p. 24.
*"The roar . . . is like thunder."* Edwards, *Royal Sisters*, p. 143.

268  *"Poor darlings . . . yet."* WB, p. 626.
*"It was absolutely wonderful . . . a few too."* Duff, *George & Elizabeth*, p. 194.
*"We have been overwhelmed . . . duty."* WB, p. 606.
*"I am sad . . . would have done."* NOT, p. 619.
*"win through . . . lose sight of."* NYT, May 9, 1945.
*"I don't believe that greed . . . peaceful world."* Glendon, *A World Made New*, p. 19.

269  *"not much impressed."* Truman, *Dear Bess: Letters from Harry Truman to Bess*, p. 517.
*"nice and appetizing . . . off the British ship."* McCullough, *Truman*, p. 453.
*"he was horrified . . . prevent another war."* WB, p. 644.
*"I think Mr. President . . . on the deck."* RK, p. 379.
*"very pleasant and . . . good man."* Ibid.

270  *"The weight of suffering . . . wiped out."* MD, p. 104.
"kind telegram . . . courage and determination." Telegram, Aug. 21, 1945, KG and QE to ER, General Correspondence, '45–52, King George VI, ER papers, FDRL.
*"It was a very sad meeting . . . during the war."* James, *A Spirit Undaunted*, p. 274.

271  *"Oh, no . . . fear and trembling."* ER, *The Autobiography of Eleanor Roosevelt*, p. 299.
*"terribly frightened . . . knew nothing about."* Glendon, *A World Made New*, p. 25.
*"For the first time . . . feel free."* Lash, *The Years Alone*, p. 38.
*"on this mission . . . better world!"* Letter, ER to QE, Jan. 6, 1946, RA QEQM/PRIV. Eleanor Roosevelt to Queen Elizabeth, Jan. 6, 1946.

271–272  *"cordial greeting . . . poor tattered world . . . Elizabeth R."* Letter, QE to ER, Jan. 6, 1946, General Correspondence, '45–52, The Queen Mother, ER papers, FDRL.

272  *"Deeply grateful . . . make the world of the future."* RA, QEQM/PRIV. Letter, ER to QE, Jan. 7, 1946.
*"walked on eggs . . . not welcome."* Purcell and Purcell, *Critical Lives: Eleanor Roosevelt*, p. 224.
*"one of the Russians' . . . badly frightened . . . trembled."* ER, *On My Own*, p. 51.

275  *"Everything is going . . . I shall have to go."* James, *A Spirit Undaunted*, p. 313.
*"The north-east wind was to howl."* Ibid., p. 293.

275–276  *"At times the heat and the worries . . . 'gnashes.'"* Edwards, *Royal Sisters*, p. 172.

276  *"We feel much the same in Scotland."* QM, p. 124.
*"solemn act . . . to which we all belong."* WB, p. 692.

277  *"flash of colour . . . we have to travel."* RK, p. 423.
*"When I handed your hand . . . very precious."* TQM, p. 110.
*"Our family . . . in my eyes."* Ibid., p. 111.
*"What a wonderful day . . . make the best of it."* Ibid., p. 112.

## Chapter 17: Walking with Death

278  *"He was a grand man . . . brother Ed."* RK, p. 461.
*"hopelessly congested . . . no national importance."* Howarth, *George VI*, p. 219.
*"I am sure the statue . . . in world history."* Ibid., p. 219.

279  *"all that has happened . . . since we last met."* Letter, KG to ER, Oct. 17, 1947, General Correspondence, '45–52, King George VI, ER papers, FDRL.
*"in some ways I rather dreaded . . . monarch."* ER, *On My Own*, p.32.

*"always had such a wonderful . . . is a black dress."* Ibid., p. 31.

*"The King and Queen were kindness itself . . . turn it down?"* Ibid., p. 32.

*"You don't really approve of me . . . Mrs. Roosevelt?"* Ibid., p. 297.

280 *"very serious-minded . . . What struck me . . . your opinion?"* Ibid., p. 33.

*"deep sorrow . . . dark days of the war."* LT, Apr. 13, 1948.

281 *"It gave the impression . . . with the British people."* ER, *On My Own*, p. 37.

*"so simple and dignified . . . occasion."* Letter, ER to KG, Apr. 14, 1948, General Correspondence, '45–52, King George VI, ER papers, FDRL.

*"how much the Queen & I admired . . . memories."* Letter, KG to ER, Apr. 14, 1948, General Correspondence, '45–52, George VI, ER papers, FDRL.

*"just as Moses . . . can ever experience here."* ER, *On My Own*, p. 37.

*"Valiant for Friendship . . . world friendship."* LT, Apr. 13, 1948.

*"there are always people . . . marble base."* Ibid.

282 *"The people I love mean more . . . one of them."* Gurewitsch, *Kindred Souls*, p. 27.

283 *"I was so glad to see . . . visit to this country."* Letter, ER to QE, July 11, 1949, General Correspondence, '45–52, Elizabeth, The Queen Mother, ER papers, FDRL.

*"I am glad to be able to tell you . . . revival of spirit & serenity."* Letter, QE to ER, July 21, 1949, General Correspondence, '45–52, Elizabeth, The Queen Mother, ER papers, FDRL.

*"the kind thought . . . those lovely flowers."* Letter, Princess Elizabeth to ER, Nov. 13, 1948, General Correspondence, '45–52, Elizabeth II, ER papers, FDRL.

284 *"shown courage . . . leadership."* Lash, *The Years Alone*, p. 153.

286 *"I was so sad . . . before too long."* Letter, QE to ER, May 23, 1951, General Correspondence, '45–52, Elizabeth, The Queen Mother, ER papers, FDRL.

*"I am getting stronger every day."* WB, p. 787.

*"If it is going to help . . . is hell."* Ibid., p. 788.

287 *"If you are long enough . . . me invited."* Letter, ER to Princess Elizabeth and Prince Philip, Aug. 5, 1951, General Correspondence, '45–52, Elizabeth II, ER papers, FDRL.

*"appearing so rude . . . such fun!"* Letter, Princess Elizabeth to ER, Sep. 14, 1951, General Correspondence, '45-52, Elizabeth II, ER papers, FDRL.

*"some little trifles . . . craftsmanship."* Letter, ER to Princess Elizabeth, Oct. 16, 1951, General Correspondence, '45–52, Elizabeth II, ER papers, FDRL.

287–288 *"I've brought Princess Elizabeth . . . re-elected."* Bradford, *Elizabeth*, p. 163.

288 *"When I was a little boy . . . here she is."* Edwards, *Royal Sisters*, p. 248.

*"We've just had a visit . . . you have two!"* RK, p. 457.

*"the embodiment of all . . . the British people."* WB, p. 800.

*"The incessant worries . . . down something proper."* QM, p. 126.

288–289 *"Much has happened . . . even more closely."* WB, p. 799.

289 *"I trust you yourselves realize . . . my recovery."* WB, p. 802.

*"as I always did . . . after dinner."* TQM, p. 121.

290 *"I must go to him."* Warwick, *King George VI & Queen Elizabeth*, p. 133.

*"I've got bad news . . . these matters are."* RK, p. 459.

*"Is it the King . . . a shock."* Ibid., p. 460.

*"he looked . . . the world on him."* Lacey, *Monarch*, p. 170.

*"During these last months . . . journey's end."* RK, p. 449.

291 *"beloved Monarch . . . duties . . . George the Good."* Ibid., pp. 460–461.

*"a model of character . . . human being."* Howarth, *George VI*, p. 258.

*"I've got to start sometime . . . now."* Duff, *George & Elizabeth*, p. 223.

*"One cannot yet believe . . . dazed."* TQM, p. 121.

291–292 *"My only wish now . . . noble king."* TQM, p. 119.

292 *"was a shock."* Asbell, *Mother and Daughter*, p. 289.

*"It is impossible . . . think of life without him."* Letter, QE to ER, February, 28, 1952, General Correspondence, '45–52, Elizabeth, The Queen Mother, ER papers, FDRL.

## Chapter 18: First Ladies of the World

293 *"She is completely . . . unstoppable."* Edwards and Rae, *The Queen Mother: Her First 100 Years*, p. 113.

294 *"I have been tired . . . thirty years."* Jenny Bond, Overseas League Lecture, 2001.

*"she was never an old woman . . . youngest person in it."* Author conversation with Billy Tallon.

*There were three things Queen Elizabeth did not like confronting.* Author interview with Kenneth Rose.

*"black clouds of unhappiness and misery."* Morrow, *Without Equal*, p. 147.

295 *"It doesn't get any better . . . better at it."* Edwards and Rae, *The Queen Mother: Her First 100 Years*, p. 84.

*"The King always told me everything . . . miss that."* Morrow, *Without Equal*, p. 144.

*"someone opened a door . . . down it together."* Warwick, *King George VI & Queen Elizabeth*, p. 142.

*"He was so young to die . . . don't know yet."* Bradford, *Elizabeth*, p. 168.

*"Loneliness is the hardest thing to bear . . . would otherwise have been."* Seward. *The Last Great Edwardian Lady*, p. 215.

*"Such a time of memories."* Author's collection.

*"She was absolutely heartbroken . . . herself together."* Bradford, *Elizabeth*, p. 169.

295–296 *"Who would have thought . . . senseless."* Mortimer, *Queen Elizabeth*, p. 240.

296 *"woman who killed my husband."* Edwards and Rae, *The Queen Mother: Her First 100 Years*, p. 84.

*"I am sure you can win her . . . friendly attitude."* Michael Bloch, *The Secret File of the Duke of Windsor*, p. 261.

*"Cookie was sugar . . . him so well."* Ibid., pp. 264–265.

*"I was driving along . . . coastline."* Seward, *The Last Great Edwardian Lady*, p. 249.

297 *"I was going to throw in Big Ben."* Morrow, *Without Equal*, p. 147.

*"so dear to my heart . . . my family."* Warwick, *King George VI & Queen Elizabeth*, p. 143.

*"I've always wondered . . . presidential candidate."* Neal (Ed.), *Eleanor and Harry*, p. 207.

*"He will win . . . as President."* Ibid., p. 208.

299 *"like St. Paul's Cathedral . . . will be the poorer."* Rhodes, *Chips: The Diaries of Sir Henry Channon*, p. 473.

*"All sympathy in this hour of sadness."* Cable, ER to QE, March 25, 1953, General Correspondence, Elizabeth, The Queen Mother, ER papers, FDRL.

*"So grateful for your kind . . . sympathy."* Cable, QE to ER, March 27, 1953, General Correspondence, Elizabeth, The Queen Mother, ER papers, FDRL.

*"not only made my life easier . . . for living."* Purcell and Purcell, *Critical Lives: Eleanor Roosevelt*, p. 238.

299–300 "I love you as . . . I have never loved anyone else." Gurewitsch, *Kindred Souls*, p. 78.

300 *"I'd love to hear you call . . . good at that."* Ibid., p. 91.

*"manner was cordial . . . not warm."* Ibid., p. 128.

*"Don't worry, David will give . . . you want."* Ibid., p. 130.

*"complete and absolute nonsense."* EOG, p. 336.

301 *"Months ago I promised . . . to come."* Letter, ER to Queen Elizabeth II, May 16, 1953, folder Elizabeth II, Queen of England and Queen Mother, 1953–1956; General Correspondence 1953–1956, ER Papers, FDRL.

*"a frail little man in white . . . Her lunch."* Edwards, *Royal Sisters*, p. 282.

301–302 *"In she came . . . of her head."* Ibid., pp. 280–281.

302 *"enormous presence and radiance . . . with pride."* TQM, p. 126.

303 *"You must be either mad or bad."* Morrow, *Without Equal*, p. 169.

*"was completely unapproachable . . . about it."* Bradford, *Elizabeth*, p. 205.

304 *"young, gleaming champion."* Aronson, *Royal Family: Years of Transition*, p. 189.

*"must always be . . . I'm going to leave."* TQM, p. 130.

*"It was not very pleasant."* Aronson, *Princess Margaret*, p. 133.

305 *"Much was asked of my father . . . to his people."* Edwards, *Royal Sisters*, p. 335.

*"Mindful of the Church's teaching . . . all others."* TQM, p. 131.

## Chapter 19: Valiant for Friendship

306 *"Back of tranquility . . . unhappiness."* Feldman, *Lucy*, p. 195.

*"I know of course . . . of that kind."* Letter, ER to QE, Feb. 23, 1954, folder Elizabeth II, Queen of England and Queen Mother, 1953–1956; General Correspondence 1953–1956, ER papers, FDRL.

*"I am sure from what I hear . . . again."* Letter, ER to QE, May 27, 1954, folder Elizabeth II, Queen of England and Queen Mother, 1953–1956; General Correspondence 1953–1956, ER Papers, FDRL.

*"how enormously . . . exceptionally busy you are."* Letter from the Queen Mother's private secretary to ER, Sept. 1, 1954, folder Elizabeth II, Queen of England and Queen Mother, 1953–1956; General Correspondence 1953–1956, ER Papers, FDRL.

307 *"Who is going to be interested . . . of a King?"* QE, p. 130.

*"Of all the many reasons . . . awe."* NYT, Oct. 26, 1954.

*"another proof . . . highly."* Letter, Lady in Waiting Olivia Mulholland to ER, Oct. 29, 1954, folder Elizabeth II, Queen of England and Queen Mother, 1953–1956; General Correspondence 1953–1956, ER Papers, FDRL.

308 *"If she wasn't a Queen . . . playtime."* Penelope Mortimer, *Queen Elizabeth*, p. 256.

*"I'm afraid I am buying too much."* Morrow, *Without Equal*, p. 164.

309 *"noble queen . . . world."* NYT, Nov. 1, 1954.

*"a big deal . . . Greece."* Author interview with Nina Gibson.

*"a heavy set woman . . . style at all."* Author interview with Haven Roosevelt.

309–310 *"This time we had to clean up . . . way a grandmother would."* Author interview with Nina Gibson.

310 *"Have you had enough . . . have enough."* NYT, Nov. 3, 1954.

*"one of the most beloved visitors . . . shores."* NYT, Nov. 4, 1954.

"*The royal lady . . . hit show.*" EOG, p. 326.

310–311   "*is much too precious . . . fostering.*" NYT, Nov. 4, 1954.

311   "*Washington's only perambulatory monument.*" Brough, *Princess Alice: A Biography of Alice Roosevelt Longworth,* p. 260.

"*my deep & heartfelt sympathy . . . sufferings must be.*" NYT, Nov. 7, 1954.

"*Can I tell our papers . . . conversation?*" Lash, *Eleanor Alone,* p. 271.

"*I went into the Queen's study . . . on the mend.*" MD, p. 246.

"*I have the greatest respect . . . them together.*" Ibid.

"*It was just my grandmother . . . as people.*" Author interview with Nina Gibson.

"*I've got this mother . . . stop her.*" Ibid.

"*One of the big advantages . . . will pass.*" Lash, *A Friend's Memoir,* p. 362.

314–315   "*I think perhaps one of the things . . . your life with them.*" Ibid., p. 366.

315   "*refrain from sending you a line . . . of the children!*" Letter, ER to QE, Feb. 20, 1960, folder Elizabeth II, Queen of England and Queen Mother, 1956–1962; General Correspondence 1953–1956, ER Papers, FDRL.

"*It seems so young to have been taken . . . rest of the family.*" Letter, ER to QE, Sept., 1961, folder Elizabeth II, Queen of England and Queen Mother, 1956–1962; General Correspondence 1953–1956, ER Papers, FDRL.

316   "*Look at them . . . Republican candidate.*" Gurewitsch, *Kindred Souls,* p. 150.

317   "*the Queen was particularly delighted . . . exhibition.*" Kitty Kelley, *The Royals,* p. 189.

"*The Queen . . . they could find.*" Bradford, *America's Queen,* p. 200.

318   "*There was only anger . . . like a crucifixion.*" Gurewitsch, *Kindred Souls,* pp. 367–368.

"*We can cure you . . . I want to die.*" Ibid., p. 285.

"*The British people held her . . . our sincere sympathy.*" WP, Nov. 9, 1962.

319   "*How could it happen . . . this lady ambassador.*" Neal (Ed.), *Eleanor and Harry,* p. 271.

"*I made use of her . . . First Lady of the World.*" Ibid.

"*If she didn't earn it . . . hope you'll make it.*" Ibid., p. 277.

319–320   "*slightly wet behind the ears . . . welcoming remarks.*" Letter from Christopher Roosevelt to Sir Alistair Aird, copy to author, March 14, 2001.

320   "*In 1939, that beautiful summer . . . make a better world.*" Materials from Campobello Visitors Center.

"*fell on his sword . . . together for the first time.*" Author interview with Christopher Roosevelt.

## Epilogue: The Lessons of History

322–323   *Prince Andrew's 1997 visit.* Author interview with Tobie Roosevelt.

323   "*hot dog conversation . . . spirited me up a bit.*" NYT, June 13, 1989.

324   "*the most dangerous woman in Europe.*" *Wall Street Journal,* April 2, 2002.

325   "*particularly important in the year . . . quite quiet.*" Author notes during "Evening on the Hudson," September 24, 2002.

# Bibliography

## Articles

Arnstein, Walter. "Queen Victoria and the United States" *in Anglo-American Attitudes: From Revolution to Partnership*, pp. 91–106.

Catelon, Philip. "Greetin' Cousin George" in *American Heritage*, Dec. 1967, pp. 6–11 and 108–111.

Israels II, Josef. "Selling George VI to the U.S." in *Scribner's Magazine*, 195, Feb. 1939, pp. 16–21.

Leventhal, Fred. "Essential Democracy: The 1939 Royal Visit to the United States" in *Singular Continuities: Tradition, Nostalgia, and Identity in Modern British Culture*, pp. 163–177.

Leventhal, Fred. "Public Face and Public Space: The Projection of Britain in America Before the Second World War" in *Anglo-American Attitudes: From Revolution to Partnership*, pp. 212–226.

Rhodes, Benjamin. "The British Royal Visit of 1939 and the 'Psychological Approach' to the United States" in *Diplomatic History*, Spring 1978, pp. 197–211.

Robertson, Ben. "King George Strives to Please" in *Saturday Evening Post*, 211, Feb. 4, 1939, pp. 5–7 and 66–69.

Swift, Will. "Resolute Relations" in *Majesty*, Vol. 22, No. 9, Sep. 2001, pp. 22–27.

## Books

Alsop, Joseph. *FDR: A Centenary Remembrance*. New York: Viking Press, 1982.

Angelo, Bonnie. *First Mothers: The Women Who Shaped Presidents*. New York: HarperCollins, 2001.

Aronson, Theo. *Grandmama of Europe: The Crowned Descendants of Queen Victoria*. Indianapolis/New York: The Bobbs-Merrill Company, 1973.

——. *Princess Margaret*. Great Britain: Michael O'Mara Books, 1997.

——. *The Royal Family at War*. London: John Murray, 1993.

——. *Royal Family: Years of Transition*. London: John Murray Publishers, 1983.

——. *Royal Subjects*. London: Pan Books, 2001.

Asbell, Bernard. *Mother and Daughter: The Letters of Eleanor Roosevelt and Anna Roosevelt*. New York: Putnam Publishing Group, 1982.

Banks, Christina, and Sue Leonard, eds. *Queen Elizabeth, The Queen Mother*. London: Dorling Kindersley, 2000.

Behlmer, George K., and Fred M. Leventhal, eds. *Singular Continuities: Tradition, Nostalgia, and Identity in Modern British Culture*. Stanford: Stanford University Press, 2000.

Beschloss, Michael. *Kennedy & Roosevelt: The Uneasy Alliance*. New York: Norton, 1980.

———. *The Conquerors: Roosevelt, Truman and the Destruction of Hitler's Germany*. New York: Simon & Schuster, 2002.

Bishop, Jim. *FDR's Last Year: April 1944–April 1945*. New York: William Morrow, 1974.

Black, Conrad. *Franklin Delano Roosevelt: Champion of Freedom*. New York: Public Affairs, 2003.

Bloch, Michael. *The Duke of Windsor's War: From Europe to the Bahamas, 1939–1945*. New York: Coward-McCann, Inc., 1983.

———. *The Secret File of the Duke of Windsor: The Private Papers 1937–1972*. New York: Harper & Row, 1988.

———. *Wallis & Edward Letters: 1931–1937*. New York: Summit Books, 1986.

Bradford, Sarah. *America's Queen: The Life of Jacqueline Kennedy Onassis*. New York: Penguin Books, 2000.

———. *Elizabeth*. New York: Riverhead Books, 1996.

———. *The Reluctant King: The Life & Reign of George VI 1895–1952*. New York: St. Martin's Press, 1989.

Brooke-Shepard, Gordon. *Uncle of Europe: The Social and Diplomatic Life of Edward VII*. New York: Harcourt Brace Jovanovich, 1976.

Brough, James. *Princess Alice: A Biography of Alice Roosevelt Longworth*. Boston: Little, Brown, 1975.

Burns, James MacGregor. *Roosevelt: The Lion and the Fox*. New York: Harcourt Brace, 1956.

———. *Roosevelt: The Soldier of Freedom*. New York: Harcourt Brace Jovanovich, 1970.

Burns, James MacGregor, and Susan Dunn. *The Three Roosevelts: Patrician Leaders Who Transformed America*. New York: Grove Press, 2001.

Cain, Richard. *Eleanor Roosevelt's Valkill*. Charleston, SC: Arcadia, 2002.

Caroli, Betty Boyd. *Inside the White House*. New York: Canopy Books, 1992.

Churchill, Winston. *The Second World War*, vol. VI. London: Cassell & Co., 1964.

Collier, Peter, and David Horowitz. *The Kennedys*. New York: Summit Books, 1984.

———. *The Roosevelts: An American Saga*. New York: Simon & Schuster, 1994.

Cook, Blanche Wiesen. *Eleanor Roosevelt, Vol. I 1884–1933*. New York: Penguin, 1992.

———. *Eleanor Roosevelt: The Defining Years 1933–1938*. New York: Penguin, 1999.

Cull, Nicholas John. *Selling War*. New York: Oxford University Press, 1995.

Davis, John. *The Kennedys: Dynasty and Disasters 1848–1983*. New York: McGraw-Hill, 1984.

Davis, Kenneth S. *FDR: The Beckoning of Destiny, 1882–1928*. New York: Putnam, 1971.

———. *FDR: Into the Storm, 1937–1940*. New York: Random House, 1993.

Donaldson, F. *Edward VIII*. Philadelphia, J. B. Lippincott Company, 1974.

Donn, Linda. *The Roosevelt Cousins: Growing Up Together, 1882–1924*. New York: Alfred A. Knopf, 2001.

Duff, David. *Elizabeth of Glamis*. London: Frederick Muller, 1973.

———. *George & Elizabeth: A Royal Marriage*. London: Collins, 1983.

———. *Mother of the Queen*. London: Frederick Muller, 1965.

Edwards, Anne. *Royal Sisters*. New York: Jove, 1991.

Edwards, Arthur and Charles Rae. *The Queen Mother: Her First 100 Years*. London: HarperCollins, 2000.

Faber, Doris. *The Life of Lorena Hickok: E.R.'s Friend.* New York: Morrow, 1980.

Feldman, Ellen. *Lucy: A Novel.* New York: W. W. Norton, 2003.

Fields, Alonzo. *My 21 Years in the White House.* New York: Coward-McCann, 1961.

Forbes, Grania. *My Darling Buffy: The Early Life of the Queen Mother.* Great Britain: Headline Book Publishing, 1999.

Gilbert, Martin. *Winston S. Churchill. Vol. VI, Finest Hour 1939–1941.* Boston: Houghton Mifflin. 1983.

Glendon, Mary Ann. *A World Made New: Eleanor Roosevelt and the Universal Declaration of Human Rights.* New York: Random House, 2001.

Goodwin, Doris Kearns. *The Fitzgeralds and the Kennedys: An American Saga.* New York: Simon & Schuster, 1987.

———. *No Ordinary Time: Franklin & Eleanor Roosevelt: The Home Front in World War II.* New York: Simon & Schuster, 1994.

Gould, Lewis. *The Modern American Presidency.* University Press of Kansas, 2003.

Graham, Katharine. *Katharine Graham's Washington.* New York: Alfred A. Knopf, 2002.

Gurewitsch, Edna P. *Kindred Souls: The Friendship of Eleanor Roosevelt and David Gurewitsch.* New York: St. Martin's Press, 2002.

Hamilton, Alan. *The Times. The Queen Mother.* London: Times Books, 1999.

Hickok, Lorena. *Eleanor Roosevelt: Reluctant First Lady.* New York: Dodd, Mead, 1980.

Higham, Charles. *The Duchess of Windsor.* New York: McGraw-Hill, 1988.

———. *Wallis: Secret Lives of the Duchess of Windsor.* London: Sidgwick & Jackson, 1988.

Hillman, William. *Mr. President.* New York: Farrar, Straus & Young, 1952.

Holden, Anthony. *The Queen Mother: A 90th Birthday Tribute.* London: Little, Brown & Co., 1990.

Howarth, Patrick. *George VI.* London: Hutchinson, 1987.

Ickes, Harold L. *The Secret Diaries of Harold L. Ickes. Vol. III, The Lowering Clouds, 1939–1941.* New York: Simon & Schuster, 1954.

Judd, Denis. *The Life and Times of George V.* London: George Weidenfeld and Nicolson Limited, 1973.

Kelley, Kitty. *The Royals.* New York: Warner Books, 1997.

Kennedy, Joseph. Edited by Amanda Smith. *Hostage to Fortune: The Letters of Joseph P. Kennedy.* New York: Viking, 2001.

Kennedy, Rose. *Times to Remember.* New York: Doubleday & Co., 1974.

Kimball, Warren F., ed. *Churchill and Roosevelt: The Complete Correspondence*, vol. 1. Princeton University Press, 1984.

Lacey, Robert. *Queen Mother.* New York: Little, Brown and Co., 1987.

———. *Monarch.* New York: Simon & Schuster, 2002.

Lanctot, Gustave. *The Royal Tour of King George VI and Queen Elizabeth in Canada and the United States of America, 1939.* Toronto, E.P. Taylor Found, 1939.

Lash, Joseph P. *Eleanor and Franklin: The Story of Their Relationship.* New York: Norton, 1971.

———. *Eleanor Roosevelt: A Friend's Memoir.* Garden City, NY: Doubleday, 1964.

———. *Eleanor: The Years Alone.* New York: Norton, 1972.

———. *Love, Eleanor: Eleanor Roosevelt and Her Friends.* New York: Doubleday, 1982.

———. *A World of Love: Eleanor Roosevelt and Her Friends 1943–1962.* New York: Doubleday, 1984.

Leamer, Laurence. *The Kennedy Men: 1901–1963.* New York: William Morrow, 2001.

Leventhal, Fred M., and Roland Quinault. eds. *Anglo-American Attitudes: From Revolution to Partnership.* Aldershot: Ashgate Publishing, 2000.

Levy, William Turner, and Cynthia Eagle Russett. *The Extraordinary Mrs. R: A Friend Remembers Eleanor Roosevelt.* New York: John Wiley & Sons, 1999.

Longford, Elizabeth. *The Queen Mother: A Biography.* London: Weidenfeld and Nicolson, 1981.

Lowenheim, Francis. *Roosevelt and Churchill: Their Secret Wartime Correspondence.* New York: Dutton, 1975.

Magnus, Philip. *King Edward the Seventh.* New York: E. P. Dutton & Co., 1964.

Marton, Kati. *Hidden Power.* New York: Pantheon Books, 2001.

Massingbred, Hugh. *The Daily Telegraph Book of the Queen Mother: Woman of the Century.* London: Macmillan, 1999.

McCullough, David. *Truman.* New York: Simon & Schuster, 1993.

Meacham, Jon. *Franklin and Winston: An Intimate Portrait of an Epic Friendship.* New York: Random House, 2003.

Miller, Nathan. *The Roosevelt Chronicles.* Garden City, NY: Doubleday, 1979.

Morgan, Ted. *FDR: A Biography.* New York: Simon & Schuster, 1985.

Morris, Edmund. *The Rise of Theodore Roosevelt.* New York: Coward, McCann & Geoghegan, 1979.

Morrow, Ann. *Without Equal: H.M. Queen Elizabeth, The Queen Mother.* U.K.: The House of Strauss, 2000.

Mortimer, Penelope. *Queen Elizabeth: A Portrait of the Queen Mother.* New York: St. Martin's Press, 1986.

Mulvaney, Jay. *Diana & Jackie: Maidens, Mothers, Myths.* New York: St. Martin's Press 2002.

Pope-Hennessy, James. *Queen Mary, 1867–1953.* New York: Alfred A. Knopf, 1960.

Purcell, Sarah J., and Purcell, L. Edward. *Critical Lives: Eleanor Roosevelt.* Indianapolis: Alpha Books, 2002.

Renehan, Edward Jr. *The Kennedys at War.* New York: Doubleday, 2002.

Rhodes James, Robert. *A Spirit Undaunted: The Political Role of George VI.* Great Britain: Abacus, 1999.

———. *Chips: The Diaries of Sir Henry Channon.* London: Weidenfeld and Nicolson, 1967.

Roosevelt, Eleanor. *The Autobiography of Eleanor Roosevelt.* New York: Da Capo Press, 1997.

———. *It Seems to Me.* New York: Norton & Co., 1954.

———. *My Days.* New York: Dodge Publishing Company, 1938.

———. *My Day: The Best of Eleanor Roosevelt's Acclaimed Newspaper Columns 1936–1962.* Edited by David Emblidge. New York: Da Capo Press, 2001.

———. *On My Own.* New York: Curtis Publishing Co., 1958.

———. *This I Remember.* New York: Harper & Brothers, 1949.

———. *This Is My Story.* New York: Harper, 1937.

———. *Tomorrow Is Now.* New York: Harper, 1963.

———. *You Learn by Living.* New York: Harper and Bros., 1960.

Roosevelt, Eleanor, and Harry S. Truman. *Eleanor and Harry: The Correspondence of Eleanor Roosevelt and Harry S. Truman.* New York: Scribner, 2002.

Roosevelt, Elliott. *As He Saw It.* New York: Duell, Sloane & Pearce, 1946.

———. *A Rendezvous with Destiny: The Roosevelts of the White House.* New York: Putnam, 1975.

Roosevelt, Elliott, and James Brough. *An Untold Story: The Roosevelts of Hyde Park.* New York: Putnam, 1973.

Roosevelt, Elliott, ed. *FDR: His Personal Letters. Vol I, The Early Years.* New York: Duell, Sloane & Pearce, 1947.

Roosevelt, James, with Bill Libby. *My Parents: A Differing View.* Chicago: Playboy Press, 1976.

Roosevelt, James, and Sidney Schalett. *Affectionately FDR: A Son's Story of a Lonely Man.* New York: Harcourt Brace, 1959.

Rose, Kenneth. *King George V.* New York: Alfred A. Knopf, 1984.

Roseman, Samuel. *Working with Roosevelt.* New York: Harper & Brothers, 1952.

Schlesinger, Arthur M., Jr. *The Age of Roosevelt.* Boston: Houghton Mifflin. *Vol. I, The Crisis of the Old Order, 1919–1933,* 1957. *Vol. II, The Coming of The New Deal,* 1958. *Vol. III, The Politics of Upheaval,* 1960.

Seward, Ingrid. *The Last Great Edwardian Lady.* London: Century Publishing Co., 1999.

Soames, Mary. *Clementine Churchill: The Biography of a Marriage.* Boston: Houghton Mifflin, 1979.

Stafford, David. *Roosevelt & Churchill: Men of Secrets.* Great Britain: Little, Brown & Company, 1999.

Streitmatter, Rodger, ed. *Empty Without You: The Intimate Letters of Eleanor Roosevelt and Lorena Hickok.* New York: The Free Press, 1990.

Talbot, Godfrey. *The Country Life Book of Queen Elizabeth the Queen Mother.* London: Country Life Books, 1978.

Teague, Michael. *Mrs. L: Conversations with Alice Roosevelt Longworth.* Garden City, NY: Doubleday, 1981.

Vickers, Hugo. *Cecil Beaton: The Authorized Biography.* London: George Weidenfeld & Nicolson Limited, 1985.

Ward, Geoffrey C. *A First-Class Temperament: The Emergence of Franklin Roosevelt.* New York: Harper & Row, 1989.

———. *Before the Trumpet: Young Franklin Roosevelt, 1882–1905.* New York: Perennial Library, 1986.

———. *Closest Companion: The Unknown Story of the Intimate Friendship Between Franklin Roosevelt and Margaret Suckley.* New York: Houghton Mifflin, 1995.

Warwick, Christopher. *George and Marina: The Duke and Duchess of Kent.* London: Weidenfeld and Nicolson, 1988.

———. *King George VI & Queen Elizabeth.* London: Sidgwick & Jackson, 1985.

———. *Princess Margaret.* New York: St. Martin's Press, 1983.

West, J. B., with Mary Lynn Katz. *Upstairs at the White House: My Life with the First Ladies.* New York: Coward, McCann & Geoghegan, 1973.

Wheeler-Bennett, John W. *King George VI: His Life and Reign.* London: MacMillan & Co., Ltd., 1958.

Whitcomb, John, and Whitcomb, Claire. *Real Life at the White House.* New York: Routledge, 2000.

Williams, Susan. *The People's King: The True Story of the Abdication.* London: Palgrave Macmillan, 2003.

Wise, Stephen. *The Challenging Years: The Autobiography of Stephen Wise.* New York: G.P. Putnam's Sons, 1949.

Ziegler, Philip. *King Edward VIII: The Official Biography.* London: William Collins Sons & Co., Ltd., 1990.

# Photo Credits

# Index